TI MSP432 ARM Programming for Embedded Systems

Using C Language

Muhammad Ali Mazidi

Sepehr Naimi

Shujen Chen

Misagh Salmanzadeh

ARM, Cortex, Keil, and uVision are registered trade mark of ARM Limited.

To contact authors, use the following email addresses:

mazidibooks@gmail.com

Sepehr.Naimi@gmail.com

Visit our website at

http://www.MicroDigitalEd.com

ISBN-13: 978-0997925913

ISBN-10: 0997925914

"Regard man as a mine rich in gems of inestimable value. Education can, alone, cause it to reveal its treasures, and enable mankind to benefit therefrom."

Baha'u'llah

Dedication

To the faculty, staff, and students of BIHE university for their dedication and steadfastness.

Table of Contents

Preface

Since early 2000, hundreds of companies have licensed the ARM CPU and the number of licensee is growing very rapidly. While the Licensee must follow the ARM CPU architecture and instructions set, they are free to implement the peripherals such as I/O port, ADC, Timer, DAC, SPI, I2C and UART as they please. In other words, while one can write an Assembly language program for ARM chip and it will run on any ARM chip, a program written for I/O ports of an ARM chip for company A will not run on an ARM chip from company B. This is due to the fact that special function registers and their physical address locations to access the I/O ports are not standardized and every licensee implements it differently. We have dedicated the first volume in this series to the assembly language programming and architecture of ARM since the assembly language is standard and runs on any ARM chip regardless of who makes them. Our ARM assembly book is called "ARM Assembly Language Programming and Architecture, Second edition." and is available from Amazon in both Kindle and printed formats.

For the peripheral programming of the ARM, we had no choice but to dedicate a separate volume to each vendor. This volume covers the peripheral programming of the TI (Texas Instruments) ARM MSP432 chip. Throughout the book, we use C language to access the special functions registers and program the TI ARM MSP432 peripherals. We have provided an assembly language programs for I/O ports in chapter 2 for those who want to experiment with assembly language in accessing the I/O ports and their special function registers. The assembly language programs also help to see the contrast between the C and Assembly versions of the same program in ARM.

Two approaches in programming the ARM chips

When you program an ARM chip, you have two choices:

1) Use the functions written by the vendor to access the peripherals. The vast majority of the vendors/ companies making the ARM chip provide a proprietary device library of functions allowing access to their peripherals. These device library functions are copyrighted and cannot be used with another vendor's ARM chip. For students and developers, the problem with this approach is you have no control over the functions and it is very hard to customize them for your project.
2) The second approach is to access the peripheral's special function registers directly using C language and create your own custom library since you have total control over each function. Much of these functions can be modified and used with another vendor if you decide to change the ARM chip vendor. In this book, we have taken the second approach since our primary goal is to teach how to program the peripherals of an ARM chip. We know this approach is difficult and tedious, but the rewards are great.

Compilers and IDE Tools

For programming the AM chip, you can use any of the widely available compilers from Keil (www.keil.com), IAR (www.IAR.COM) or any other one. Some vendors also provide their own compiler IDE for their ARM chip. TI provides Code Composer Studio™ (CCStudio) free of charge. For this book, we have used the Keil ARM compiler IDE to write and test the programs. They do work with other compilers including the TI CCStudio.

TI ARM Trainer

The TI has many inexpensive trainers for the ARM MSP432 series. Among them are TI MSP432P401R Launchpad development kit. Although we used the TI MSP432 Launchpad to test the programs, the programs can run on other TI kits as long as they are based on MSP432 ARM microcontroller series.

Chapter Summary

In Chapter 1, we examine the C language data types for 32-bit systems. We also explore the new ISO C99 data types since they are widely used in IDE compilers for the embedded systems.

Chapter 2 examines the simple I/O port programming and shows sample programs on how to access the special function registers associated with the general purpose I/O (GPIO) ports.

Chapter 3 shows the interfacing of the ARM chip with the real-world devices such as LCD and keypad. It provides sample programs for above devices.

In Chapter 4, the interfacing and programming of serial UART ports are examined.

Chapter 5 is dedicated to the timers in ARM. It also shows how to use timers as an event counter.

The Interrupt programming of the ARM is discussed in Chapter 6.

Chapter 7 examines the ADC concepts and shows how to program them with the ARM chip. It also examines the sensor interfacing and signal conditioning.

Chapter 8 shows DAC interfacing with ARM with sample programs.

The I2C bus protocol and interfacing of an I2C based RTC is discussed in Chapter 9.

Chapter 10 explores the relay and stepper motor interfacing with ARM.

The DC motor and PWM are examined in Chapter 11.

The Graphics LCD concepts and programming are discussed in Chapter 12.

Appendix A provides an introduction to IC chip technology and IC interfacing along with the system design issues and failure analysis using MTBF. This is available on our web site www.MicroDigitalED.com

Online support for this book

All the programs in this book are available on our web site:

http://www.microdigitaled.com/ARM/MSP432_books.htm

Many of the interfacing programs such as LCD can be tested using the TI ARM MSP432 Launchpad evaluation connected to an LCD on a breadboard. However, many courses use a system approach to the course by using an ARM trainer. For this reason, we have modified the programs for the EduBase board using TI ARM MSP432 Launchpad. See the following for the sample programs:

http://www.microdigitaled.com/ARM/MSP432_books.htm

Where to buy TI ARM MSP432 Launchpad Evaluation kit?

See the link below for TI MSP432 ARM Launchpad evaluation kit and MSP432 datasheet.

http://www.ti.com/tool/MSP-EXP432P401R#1

Where to buy EduBase board?

See the link below for purchasing the EduBase board:

http://www.microdigitaled.com/ARM/MSP432_books.htm

End of the chapter problems

Please contact the authors if you use this book for a university course:

mazidibooks@gmail.com

Chapter 1: C for Embedded Systems

In reading this book we assume you already have some understanding of how to program in C language. In this chapter, we will examine some important concepts widely used in embedded system design that you may not be familiar with due to the fact that many generic C programming books do not cover them. In section 1.1, we examine the C data types for 32-bit systems. The bit-wise operators are covered in section 1.2.

Section 1.1: C Data types for Embedded Systems

In general C programming textbooks, we see *char*, *short*, *int*, *long*, *float*, and *double* data types. We need to examine the size of C data types in the light of 32-bit processors such as ARM. The C standards do not specify the size of data types. The compiler designers are free to decide the size for each data type. The *float* and *double* data types are standardized by the IEEE754 and covered in Volume 1 of this book series and are often followed by all the compilers. The sizes of char and short are often set at 1 byte and 2 bytes. The size of int is often depending on the data size of the CPU but rarely go below 16 or above 32. The sizes of long and long long are implemented the same way everywhere.

If you think this is confusing, there are three methods that may help you to find out the exact sizes of the data types.

1. Read the manuals of the compiler. Because the data sizes are not standardized, the compile user's manuals usually specify them.

2. Use pseudo function sizeof(). C compilers supports a pseudo function sizeof(), which returns the size of the parameter in the number of byte(s). The parameter may be a data type or a variable. For example, sizeof(int) returns the number of bytes in an int variable.

3. Use C99 data types. Realized the confusion of lack of standard for data size, the C standard committee developed a new set of well-defined data type with standard sizes. We will cover them later in this chapter.

For now, we will discuss the data types defined by Keil MDK-ARM first.

char

The *char* data type is a byte size data whose bits are designated as D7-D0. It can be *signed* or *unsigned*. In the signed format the D7 bit is used for the + or - sign and takes values between -128 to +127. In the *unsigned char* we have values between 0x00 to 0xFF in hex or 0 to 255 in decimal since there is no sign and the entire 8 bits are used for the magnitude. (See Chapter 5 of Volume 1.)

short int

The *short int* (or usually referring as *short*) data type is a 2-byte size data whose bits are designated as D15-D0. It can be *signed* or *unsigned*. In the signed format, the D15 bit is used for the + or - sign and takes values between -32,768 to +32,767. In the *unsigned short int* we have values between

0x0000 to 0xFFFF in hex or 0 to 65,535 in decimal since there is no sign and the entire 16 bits are used for the magnitude. See Chapter 5 of Volume 1 (the ARM assembly book).

A 32-bit processor such as the ARM architecture with 32-bit data bus reads the memory with a minimum of 32 bits on the 4-byte boundary (address ending in 0, 4, 8, and C in hex). If a short int variable is allocated straddling the 4-byte boundary, access to that variable is called an *unaligned access*. Not all the ARM processors support unaligned access. Those devices (including the MSP432 used in the MSP432 LaunchPad) supporting unaligned access pay a performance penalty by having to read/write the memory twice to gain access to one variable (see Example 1-1). Unaligned access can be avoided by either padding the variables with unused bytes (Keil) or rearranging the sequence of the variables (CCS) in allocation. The compilers usually generate aligned variable allocation.

Example 1-1

Show how memory is assigned to the following variables in aligned and unaligned allocation. Begin from memory location 0x20000000.

unsigned char a;
unsigned short int b;
unsigned short int c;

Solution:

Unaligned allocation of variable c

a	b	b	c
20000000	20000001	20000002	20000003
c			
20000004	20000005	20000006	20000007

Aligned allocation of variables by padding one byte between variable a and b

a		b	b
20000000	20000001	20000002	20000003
c	c		
20000004	20000005		

Aligned allocation of variables by rearranging the variable sequence

b	b	c	c
20000000	20000001	20000002	20000003
a			
20000004	20000005	20000006	20000007

int

The *int* data type usually represents for the native data size of the processor. For example, it is a 2-byte size data for a 16-bit processor and a 4-byte size data for a 32-bit processor. This may cause confusion and portability issue. The C99 standard addressed the issue by creating a new set of integer variable types that will be discussed later. For now, we will stick to the conventional data types.

The *int* data type of the ARM processors is 4-byte size and identical to *long int* data type described below.

long int

The long int (or *long*) data type is a 4-byte size data whose bits are designated as D31-D0. It can be signed or unsigned. In the signed format the D31 bit is used for the + or - sign and takes values between -2^{31} to $+2^{31}-1$. In the unsigned long we have values between 0x00000000 to 0xFFFFFFFF in hex. See Chapter 5 of Volume 1. In the 32-bit microcontroller when we declare a long variable, the compiler sets aside 4 bytes of storage in SRAM. But it also makes sure they are aligned, meaning it places the data in locations with addresses ending with 0, 4, 8 and C in hex. This avoids unaligned data access performance penalty covered in Volume 1. The unsigned long is widely used in ARM for defining addresses since ARM address size is 32-bit long.

Example 1-2

Show how memory is assigned to the following variables in aligned and unaligned allocation. Begin from memory location 0x20000000.

unsigned char a;
unsigned short int b;
unsigned short int c;
unsigned int d;

Solution:

Unaligned allocation of variable c

a	b	b	c
20000000	20000001	20000002	20000003
c	**d**	**d**	**d**
20000004	20000005	20000006	20000007
d			
20000008	20000009	2000000A	2000000B

Aligned allocation of variables by padding byte(s) between variable a and b

a		b	b
20000000	20000001	20000002	20000003
c	**c**		
20000004	20000005	20000006	20000007
d	**d**	**d**	**d**
20000008	20000009	2000000A	2000000B

Aligned allocation of variables by rearranging the variable sequence

d	d	d	d
20000000	20000001	20000002	20000003
b	**b**	**c**	**c**
20000004	20000005	20000006	20000007
a			
20000008	20000009	2000000A	2000000B

long long

The *long long* data type is an 8-byte size data whose bits are designated as D63-D0. It can be signed or unsigned. In the signed format the D63 bit is used for the + or - sign and takes values between -2^{63} to $+2^{63}-1$. In the *unsigned long long* we have values between 0x0000000000000000 to 0xFFFFFFFFFFFFFFFF in hex. In the 32-bit microcontroller, when we declare a long long variable, the compiler sets aside 8 bytes of storage in SRAM and it makes sure they are aligned, meaning it places the data in locations with addresses ending with 0 and 8. This avoids unaligned data access performance penalty.

Why should I care about which data type to use?

There are three major reasons why a programmer should care about data type, performance, overflow, and coercion.

Performance

It must be noted that while in the 8-bit microcontrollers we need to use the proper data type for the variables to improve the performance, this is less of problem in 32-bit CPUs such as ARM. For example, for the number of days working in a month (or number of hours in a day) we use unsigned char since it is less than 255. Using unsigned char in 8-bit microcontroller is important since it saves RAM space, memory access time, and computation clock cycles. If we use int instead, the compiler allocates 2 bytes in RAM and that is a waste of RAM resource. The CPU will have to access the additional byte and perform additional arithmetic instructions with it even if the byte contains zero and has no effect on the result. This is a problem that we should avoid since an 8-bit microcontroller usually has few RAM bytes with slower clock speed for bus and CPU. In the case of 32-bit systems such as ARM, 1, 2, or 4 bytes of data will result in the same memory access time and computation time. Most of the 32-bit systems also have more generous amount of RAM to alleviate the concern of memory usage and allow padding for aligned access.

Data type	Size	Range
char	1 byte	-128 to 127
unsigned char	1 byte	0 to 255
short int	2 bytes	-32,768 to 32,767
unsigned short int	2 bytes	0 to 65,535
int	4 bytes	-2,147,483,648 to 2,147,483,647
unsigned int	4 bytes	0 to 4,294,967,295
long	4 bytes	-2,147,483,648 to 2,147,483,647
unsigned long	4 bytes	0 to 4,294,967,295
long long	8 bytes	-9,223,372,036,854,775,808 to 9,223,372,036,854,775,807
unsigned long long	8 bytes	0 to 18,446,744,073,709,551,615

Table 1-1: ANSI C (ISO C89) integer data types and their ranges

Notes

1. By default variables are considered as *signed* unless the *unsigned* keyword is used. As a result, *signed long* is the same as *long*; the *long long* is the same as *signed long long*, and so on with the exception of *char*. Whether *char* is signed or unsigned by default varies from compiler to compiler. In some compilers, including Keil, there is an option to choose if the char variable should be considered as *signed char* or *unsigned char* by default. (To choose this in Keil, go to *Project* menu and select *Options*. Then, in the *C/C++* tab, check or uncheck the choice *Plain char is signed*, as you desire.) It is a good practice to write out the *signed* keyword explicitly, when you want to define a variable as *signed char*.

2. In some compilers (including Keil and IAR) the *int* type is considered as long int while in some other compilers (including AVR and PIC compilers) it is considered as *short int*. In other words, the *int* type is commonly defined so that the processor can handle it easily. As we will see next, we can use int16_t and int32_t instead of short and long in order to prevent any kind of ambiguity and make the code portable between different processors and compilers.

Overflow

Unlike assembly language programming, high level program languages do not provide indications when an overflow occurs and the program just fails silently. For example, if you use a short int to hold the number of seconds of a day, 9 hours 6 minutes and 7 seconds into the day, the second count will overflow from 32,767 to -32,768. Even if your program handles negative second count, the time will jump back to the day before.

With 32-bit int in a 32-bit ARM processor, overflow is a much less frequent problem because a 32-bit int will hold a number up to 2,147,483,647 but it does not eliminate the potential of the problem. One of the critical overflow problem waiting to happen is the Unix Millennium Bug. Unix keeps track of time using a 32-bit int for the number of seconds since January 1st 1970. This variable is going to overflow comes January 19, 2038. Because of the popularity of Unix, not only Unix systems are extensively used, many other systems use the same or similar format to keep track of time. So far, there is no universal solution to mitigate this problem yet.

Coercion

In C language, the data types of the operands must be identical for binary operations (the operator with two operands such as A + B). If you write a statement with different operand data types for a binary operation, the compiler will convert the smaller data type to the bigger data type. If it is an assignment operator (A = B), the right hand side operand is converted to the left hand side data type before the assignment. These implicit data type conversion is called *coercion*. The compiler may or may not give you warning when coercion occurs.

In two conditions, coercion may result in undesirable result. If the variable is signed and the data sized is increased, the new bits are filled with the sign bit (most significant bit) of the original value. For example, if an 8-bit number 0b10010010 is coerced into a 16-bit signed number, the result will be

0b1111111110010010. This may work just fine in most cases, but there are few occasions that will became an issue.

The other problem is when you assign a larger data type to a smaller data type variable, the higher order bits will be truncated. For example, in the statement "A = B;" if A is 8-bit and B is 16-bit, the upper 8 bits of B is discarded before the assignment.

There is not a simple solution for the data type size issues. As a programmer, you have to be cognizant about them all the time.

Data types in ISO C99 standard

While every C programmer has used ANSI C (ISO C89) data types, many C programmers are not familiar with the ISO C99 standard. In C standards, the sizes of integer data types were not defined and are up to the compilers to decide.

In ISO C99 standard, a set of data types were defined with number of bits and sign clearly defined in the data type names. See Table 1-2. The C99 standard is used extensively by embedded system programmer for RTOS (real time operating system) and system design. It is also supported by most of C compilers. Notice the range is the same as ANSI C standard except it uses explicitly descriptive syntax.

These integer data types are defined in a header file called *stdint.h*. You need to include this header file in order to use these data types.

Data type	Size	Range
int8_t	1 byte	-128 to 127
uint8_t	1 byte	0 to 255
int16_t	2 bytes	-32,768 to 32,767
uint16_t	2 bytes	0 to 65,535
int32_t	4 bytes	-2,147,483,648 to 2,147,483,647
uint32_t	4 bytes	0 to 4,294,967,295
int64_t	8 bytes	-9,223,372,036,854,775,808 to 9,223,372,036,854,775,807
uint64_t	8 bytes	0 to 18,446,744,073,709,551,615

Table 1-2: ISO C99 integer data types and their ranges

Review Questions

1. In an 8-bit system we use (char, unsigned char) for the number of months in a year.
2. For a system with 16-bit address, bus we use (int, unsigned int) for address definition.
3. For an ARM system the address is _____bit wide and we use _____data type for it.
4. True or false. In C programming of ARM, compiler makes sure data are aligned.

Section 1.2: Bit-wise Operations in C

One of the most important and powerful features of the C language is its ability to perform bit manipulations. Because many books on C do not cover this important topic, it is appropriate to discuss it in this section. This section describes the action of bit-wise logic operators and provides some examples of how they are used.

Bit-wise operators in C

While every C programmer is familiar with the logical operators AND (&&), OR (||), and NOT (!), many C programmers are less familiar with the bitwise operators AND (&), OR (|), EX-OR (^), invert (~), right shift (>>), and left shift (<<). These bit-wise operators are widely used in software engineering for embedded systems and control; consequently, their understanding and mastery are critical in microprocessor-based system design and interfacing. See Table 1-3.

A	B	AND (A & B)	OR (A | B)	EX-OR (A ^ B)	Invert ~B
0	0	0	0	0	1
0	1	0	1	1	0
1	0	0	1	1	1
1	1	1	1	0	0

Table 1-3: Bit-wise Logic Operators for C

The following shows some examples using the C bit-wise operators:

```
0x35 & 0x0F results in 0x05      /* ANDing */
0x04 | 0x68 results in 0x6C      /* ORing:  */
0x54 ^ 0x78 results in 0x2C      /* XORing */
~0x55 results in 0xAA            /* Inverting 0x55 */
```

Examples 1-3 and 1-4 show how the bit-wise operators are used in C. Run the following programs on your simulator and examine the results.

Example 1-3

Run the following program on your simulator and examine the results.

```c
int main(void) {
    volatile unsigned char temp;   /* declare volatile otherwise the optimizer will remove it. */
    temp = 0x35 & 0x0F;     /* ANDing    : 0x35 & 0x0F = 0x05 */
    temp = 0x04 | 0x68;     /* ORing     : 0x04 | 0x68 = 0x6C */
    temp = 0x54 ^ 0x78;     /* XORing    : 0x54 ^ 0x78 = 0x2C */
    temp = ~0x55;           /* Inverting : ~0x55 = 0xAA */
    while (1);
    return 0;

}
```

Setting and Clearing (masking) bits

As discussed in Volume 1 of the series, OR can be used to set a bit or bits, and AND can be used to clear a bit or bits. If you examine Table 1-3 closely, you will see that:

- Anything ORed with a 1 results in a 1; anything ORed with a 0 results in no change.

- Anything ANDed with a 1 results in no change; anything ANDed with a 0 results in a zero.

- Anything EX-ORed with a 1 results in the complement; anything EX-ORed with a 0 results in no change.

See Example 1-4.

Example 1-4

The following program toggles only bit 4 of var1 repetitively without disturbing the rest of the bits.

```
int main(void)
{
   unsigned char var1;
   while(1)
   {
      var1 = var1 | 0x10;      /* Set bit 4 (5th bit) of var1 */
      var1 = var1 & 0xEF;      /* Clear bit 4 (5th bit) of var1 */
   }
}
```

Notice that we can also toggle the bit using EX-OR as shown below:

```
var1 = var1 ^ 0x10;
```

Testing bit with bit-wise operators in C

In many cases of system programming and hardware interfacing, it is necessary to test a given bit to see if it is high or low. For example, many devices send a high signal to signify that they are ready for an action or to indicate that they have data available. How can the bit (or bits) be tested? In such cases the unused bits are masked and then the remaining data is tested. See Example 1-5.

Example 1-5

Write a C program to monitor bit 5 of var1. If it is HIGH, change value of var2 to 0x55; otherwise, change value of var2 to 0xAA.

Solution:

```
...
   while(1)
   {
      if (var1 & 0x20)      /* check bit 5 (6th bit) of var1 */
         var2 = 0x55;       /* this statement is executed if bit 5 is a 1 */
      else
         var2 = 0xAA;       /* this statement is executed if bit 5 is a 0 */
   }
...
```

Bit-wise shift operation in C

There are two bit-wise shift operators in C. See Table 1-4.

Operation	Symbol	Format of Shift Operation
Shift Right	>>	data >> number of bit-positions to be shifted right
Shift Left	<<	data << number of bit-positions to be shifted left

Table 1-4: Bit-wise Shift Operators for C

The following shows some examples of shift operators in C:

1. 0b00010000 >> 3   /* it equals 00000010. Shifting right 3 times */
2. 0b00010000 << 3   /* it equals 10000000. Shifting left 3 times */
3. 1 << 3   /* it equals 00001000. Shifting left 3 times */

Compound Operators

In C language, whenever the left-hand-side of the assignment operator (=) and the first operand on the right-hand-side are identical we can avoid repeating the operand by using the compound operators. As shown in Table 1-5, in compound operators, one of the operands is written just on the left-hand-side of the equal sign.

Instruction	Its equivalent using compound operators
a = a + 6;	a += 6;
a = a − 23;	a −= 23;
y = y * z;	y *= z;
z = z / 25;	z /= 25;
w = w	0x20;	w |= 0x20;
v = v & mask;	v &= mask;
m = m ^ togBits;	m ^= togBits;

Table 1-5: Some Compound Operator Examples

Review Questions

1. What is result of 0x2F & 0x27?
2. What is result of 0x2F | 0x27?
3. What is result of 0x2F ^ 0x27?
4. What is result of 0x2F >> 3?
5. What is result of 0x27 << 4?
6. In Example 1-5 what is stored in var2 if the value of var1 is 0x03?

Bit-wise operations using compound operators

The majority of hardware access level code involves setting a bit or bits in a register, clearing a bit or bits in a register, toggling a bit or bits in a register, and monitoring the status bits. For the first three cases, the operations read the content of the register, modify a bit of bits then write it back to the same register. The compound operators are very suitable for these operations.

To set bit(s) in a register,

register |= MASK;

where MASK is a number that has '1' at the bit(s) to be set.

register |= 0x08;

The number 0x08 has a '1' at bit 3, therefore the statement sets bit 3 of the register.

register |= 0x42;

The number 0x42 has a '1' at bit 6 and bit 1, therefore the statement sets bit 6 and bit 1 of the register.

To clear bit(s) in a register,

register &= ~MASK;

where MASK is a number that has '1' at the bit(s) to be cleared.

register &= ~0x20;

The number 0x20 has a '1' at bit 5, therefore the statement clears bit 5 of the register.

register &= ~0x12;

The number 0x12 has a '1' at bit 4 and bit 1, therefore the statement clears bit 4 and bit 1 of the register. Notice the mask for clearing the bits is the same as the mask for setting the bits, where the bits to be modified are '1' and the rest of the bits are '0' except that in clearing the bits, the mask is complemented in the statements.

To toggle bit(s) in a register,

register ^= MASK;

The examples are similar to setting bits so we will skip them here.

Using shift operator to generate mask

With the statements above, one challenge may be to generate the mask with the correct bit(s) set to 1 depending on how proficient you are with converting binary numbers to hexadecimal. Some compilers allow you to write a literal binary number in the format of 0b00000000 but since it is not in the C standards, many compilers do not accept this notation.

One way to ease the generation of the mask is to use the left shift operator. To generate a mask with bit n set to 1, use the expression:

1 << n

If more bits are to be set in the mask, they can be "or" together. To generate a mask with bit n and bit m set to 1, use the expression:

(1 << n) | (1 << m)

Now to set bit 3 of the register, we can rewrite the statement

register |= 0x08;

as

register |= 1 << 3;

And to set bit 6 and bit 1 of the register, we can rewrite the statement

register |= 0x42;

as

register |= (1 << 6) | (1 << 1);

The same goes for clearing bit 5 of the register, we can use the statement

register &= ~(1 << 5);

And to clear bit 4 and bit 1 of the register

register &= ~((1 << 4) | (1 << 1));

Notice that regardless of setting or clearing bits, the mask always has 1s at the bit locations for the bits to be modified and when multiple bits are used in the mask, they are always ORed together. We will leave the toggling of the bits for the readers.

Setting the value in a multi-bit field

Some of the bits in a register form a field with meaningful values. For example, if register bits 30-28 determine the divisor value to divide the clock and we would like to set the divisor to 5. One way of doing so is to set or clear the bits one by one.

```
register |= 1 << 30;
register &= ~(1 << 29);
register |= 1 << 28;
```

Although this method will achieve the desired result, the divisor value 5 is not apparent from reading the code. An alternative way is to clear the field first then set the value.

```
register &= ~(7 << 28);
register |= 5 << 28;
```

The first statement clears bit 30-28 and the second statement set the value 5 in the field. With this method, the divisor 5 is visible in the second statement.

These two statements may be combined into a single statement:

```
register = (register & ~(7 << 28)) | (5 << 28);
```

Reading of the articles by Michael Barr on embedded.com is strongly recommended:

http://www.embedded.com/user/Michael.Barr

Answer to Review Questions

Section 1.1: C Data types for Embedded Systems

1. unsigned char
2. unsigned int
3. 32 – unsigned long (or uint32_t)
4. True

Section 1.2: Bitwise Operations in C

1. 0x27
2. 0x2F
3. 0x08
4. 0x05
5. 0x70
6. 0xAA

Chapter 2: MSP432 ARM I/O Programming

In microcontroller, we use the general purpose input output (GPIO) pins to interface with LED, switch (SW), LCD, keypad, and so on. This chapter covers the programming of GPIO using LEDs, switches, and seven segment LEDs as examples. This is a very important chapter since the vast majority of embedded products have some kinds of I/O. More importantly, this chapter sets the stage for understanding of peripheral I/O addresses and how they are accessed and used in ARM processors. Because some of the core materials, covered in this chapter, are commonly used in subsequent chapters, we urge you to study this chapter thoroughly before moving on to other chapters. Section 2.1 examines the memory and I/O map of the MSP432 ARM chip. Section 2.2 shows how to access the special function registers associated with the GPIO of MSP432 ARM. In Section 2.2, we also use simple LEDs and switches to show the programming of GPIO. Section 2.3 examines the 7-segment LED connection to ARM and how to program it. In Section 2.4, we examine the MSP432 I/O programming in Assembly language. The 16-bit I/O port option of MSP432 is discussed in Section 2.5.

Section 2.1: MSP432 Microcontroller and LaunchPad

The MSP432 LaunchPad is a low-cost development platform for MSP432 MCUs built on ARM® Cortex™-M4 processor. The TI (Texas Instruments) MSP432 LaunchPad board uses the MSP432P401R, a 100-pin microcontroller chip. The MSP432P401R chip has 256K bytes (256KB) of on-chip Flash memory for code, 64KB of on-chip SRAM for data, and a large number of on-chip peripherals, as shown in Figures 2-1 and 2-2.

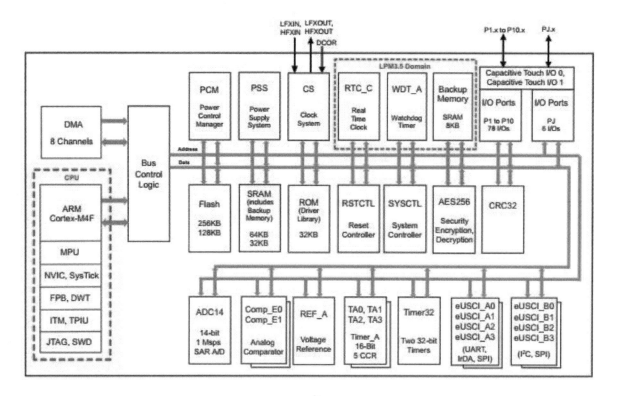

Figure 2-1: TI MSP432P401R Microcontroller High-Level Block Diagram

24

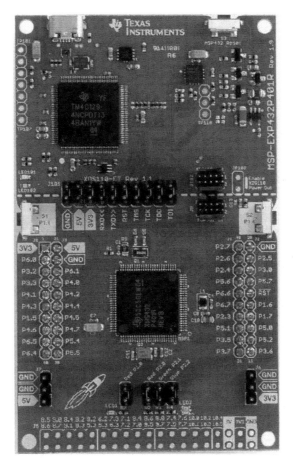

Figure 2-2: TI MSP432 Launchpad board

As we stated in Volume 1, the ARM has 4GB (Giga bytes) of memory space. It also uses memory mapped I/O meaning the I/O peripheral ports are mapped into the 4GB memory space. See Table 2-1 and Figure 2-3 for memory map of MSP432P401R chip.

	Allocated size	Allocated address
Flash	256KB	0x00000000 to 0x0003FFFF
SRAM	64KB	0x20000000 to 0x2000FFFF
I/O	All the peripherals	0x40000000 to 0x4001FFFF

Table 2-1: Memory Map in MSP432401P401R

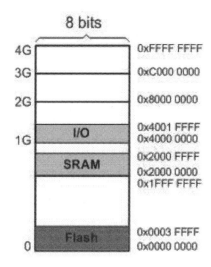

Figure 2-3: Memory Map

Regarding Figure 2-3, the following points must be noted:

1) 256KB of Flash memory is used for program code. It starts at address 0x00000000 and goes to 0x0003FFFF. One can also store in Flash constant (fixed) data such as look-up table if needed. The Flash memory is organized in 4-KB block. Each block can be independently erased and written to. The 256KB Flash can be viewed as two independent, identical banks of up to 128KB each, allowing simultaneous read/execute from one bank while the other bank is undergoing program/erase operation. It supports up to 20,000 write/erase cycles.

2) The 64KB SRAM is for variables, scratch pad, and stack. It starts at address 0x20000000 and goes to 0x2000FFFF.

3) The peripherals such as I/Os, Timers, and ADCs are mapped to addresses starting at 0x40000000. In MSP432P401R the upper limit is 0x4001FFFF since 128KB of memory space is assigned to peripherals. The upper limit address can vary among the family members of ARM chips depending on the number of peripherals the chip supports.

TI's naming convention for MSP432

TI MSP432 part numbers have the following format:

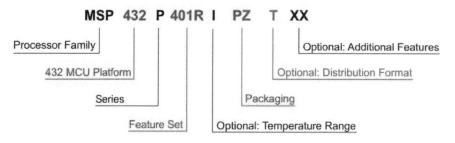

Figure 2-4: TI MSP432 Part Number Format

Table 2-2 lists the possible values for each field in the part number (not all combinations are valid):

Processor Family	MSP = Mixed Signal Processor XMS = Experimental Silicon			
432 MCU Platform	TI's 32-bit Low-Power Microcontroller Platform			
Series	P = Performance and Low-Power Series			
Feature Set	First Digit 4 = Flash based devices up to 48 MHz	Second Digit 0 = General Purpose	Third Digit 1 = ADC14	Fourth Digit R = 256KB of Flash 64KB of SRAM M = 128KB of Flash 32KB of SRAM
Optional: Temperature Range	S = 0°C to 50 °C I = 40 °C to 85 °C T = -40 °C to 105 °C			
Packaging	PZ = LQFP			

Table 2-2: Fields Values Description

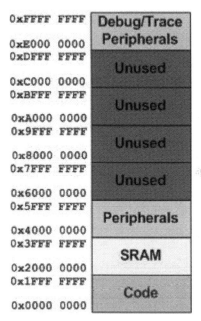

Memory Zones in MSP432

The MSP432 microcontroller divides the 4GB memory space into 8 zones with 512MB for each. The 8x512MB gives us the 4GB ARM memory space. The lowest three zones are Flash, SRAM, and Peripheral I/O. See Figure 2-5. Although a zone has 512MB of space, not all of it is used by a given chip. For example, only 128KB of the 512MB space of peripheral zone are used by the MSP432P401R chip. In Peripheral zone, address aliases are used for a portion of peripherals to allow individual bit-access. This is called *bit-banding* and is discussed in Volume 1 of this book series. The SRAM zone also uses bit-banding for a portion of SRAM memory. See MSP432 datasheet for further discussion of memory zones.

Figure 2-5: Memory zones in MS432

History and Features of MSP432

For many years, TI used the venerable 8051 microcontroller for their mixed signal processors. In mixed signal processor you have both high performance analog devices and microcontrollers on a single chip. Due to the need for low power chip and 8051 limitations, TI came up with MSP430 chip. MSP stands for Mixed Signal Processor. The MSP430 is a 16-bit RISC CPU designed and marketed exclusively by TI for their customers. In 2009, TI purchased the Luminary Micro Inc. which was a leading ARM chip producer. Since then TI has become a major force in ARM-based semiconductor chips. In 2015, TI introduced an ARM-based device to the MSP430 Family and called it MSP432. In the case of MSP432, the CPU of MSP430 was replaced with an ARM Cortex-M4 core and kept all the peripherals. In Figure 2-6, the MSP432 Families and their features are shown.

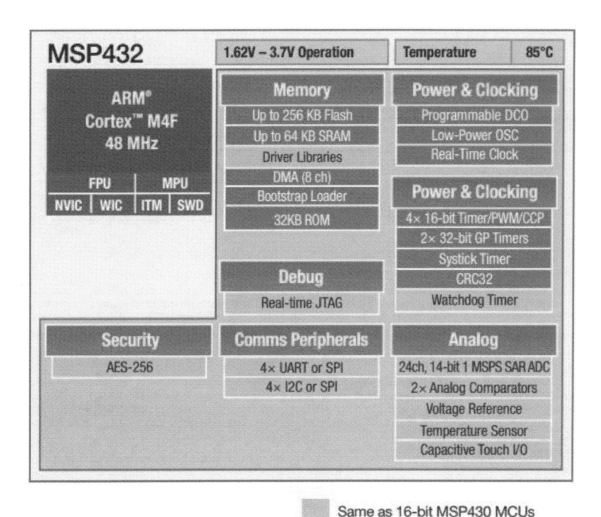

Figure 2-6: MSP432 MCU Portfolio

Review Questions

1. MSP432P401R has _____KB of on-chip Flash memory.
2. MSP432P401R has _____KB of on-chip SRAM memory.
3. MSP432P401R Flash memory is used mainly for _____ (program code, data).
4. MSP432P401R SRAM memory is used for _____ (program code, data).
5. Give the address space assigned to the Flash memory of MSP432P401R.
6. Give the meaning of R inMSP432P401R.

Section 2.2: GPIO (General Purpose I/O) Programming and Interfacing

While memory holds code and data for the CPU to process, the I/O ports are used by the CPU to access input and output devices. In the microcontroller, we have two types of I/O. They are:

a. **General Purpose I/O (GPIO):** The GPIO ports are used for interfacing devices such as LEDs, switches, LCD, keypad, and so on.

b. **Special purpose I/O:** These I/O ports have designated function such as ADC (Analog-to-Digital), Timer, UART (universal asynchronous receiver transmitter), and so on.

We have dedicated many chapters to these special purpose I/O ports. In this chapter, we examine the GPIO and its interfacing to LEDs, switches, and 7-segment LEDs and show how to access it using C programs.

GPIO

The general purpose I/O ports in MSP432 are designated as port P1 to P10. The general purpose I/O ports in MSP432 are also referred as the Simple I/O or Digital I/O ports. In addition, we also have PJ. While P1 to P10 can be used for GPIO, port J has special function such as external crystal oscillator and JTAG connections. The base address of I/O port is 0x40004C00, as shown in Table 6-1 of MSP432 datasheet. The MSP432 reference manual gives the offset address of each port and the registers associated with it. We add the offset address to base address to get the exact physical location of a given I/O port. The following shows the offset address assigned to each GPIO port of P1 to P10:

- GPIO P1   : 0x40004C00 + 0 (even addresses)
- GPIO P2   : 0x40004C00 + 1 (odd addresses)
- GPIO P3   : 0x40004C00 + 20(even addresses)
- GPIO P4   : 0x40004C00 + 21(odd addresses)
- GPIO P5   : 0x40004C00 + 40(even addresses)
- GPIO P6   : 0x40004C00 + 41(odd addresses)
- GPIO P7   : 0x40004C00 + 60(even addresses)
- GPIO P8   : 0x40004C00 + 61(odd addresses)
- GPIO P9   : 0x40004C00 + 80(even addresses)
- GPIO P10   : 0x40004C00 + 81(odd addresses)

I/O Pins in MSP432 LaunchPad board

In MSP432 ARM chip, I/O ports are named with numbers P1, P2, P3, and so on. The pins are designated as P1.0-P1.7, P2.0-P2.7, P3.0-P3.7, and so on. See Figure 2-7. The MSP432P401R 100-pin chip used in the MSP432 LaunchPad has Ports P0, P1, P2, P3, P4, P5, P6, P7, P8, P9, P10 and PJ. P10 and PJ have only 6 pins (P10.0 to P10.5 and PJ.0 to PJ.5) while all other ports have 8 pins (8-bit). It must be noted that although the default is 8-bit (Px.0-Px.7), we can combine two 8-bit ports to come up with 16-bit port, as shown in Section 2.6 of this chapter.

Notice from Figure 2-7, for port 10 only P10.0-P10.5 pins are implemented and for port J only PJ.0-PJ.5 pins are implemented. This is for a 100-pin package. For packages with fewer pins, more port pins are not implemented.

The ARM chips have two buses: *APB (Advanced Peripheral Bus)* and *AHB (Advanced High-Performance Bus)*. The AHB bus is faster than APB. The AHB allows one clock cycle access to the peripherals. The APB is slower and its access time has a minimum of 2 clock cycles. MSP432 uses the AHB buses. For APB, AHB, and single cycle access-time see Chapter 6 of "ARM Assembly Language Programming and Architecture" By Mazidi and Naimi book in this series.

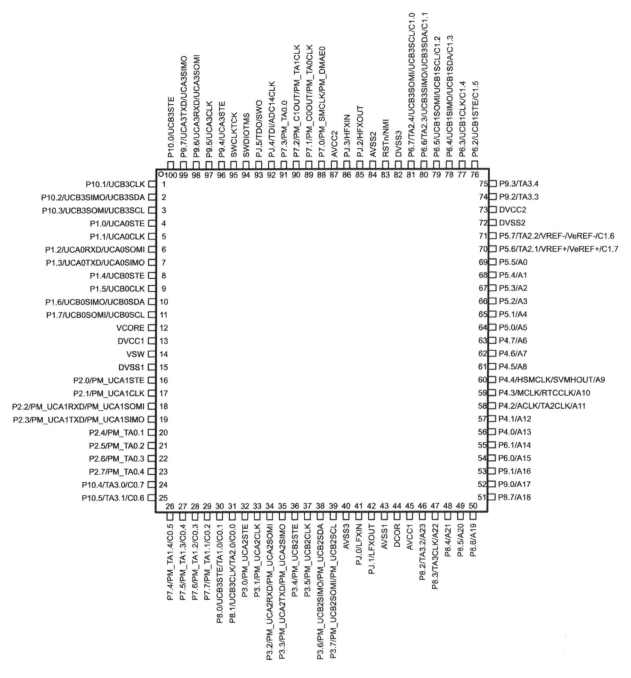

Figure 2-7: MSP432P401R 100-pin Package Pin-out

Direction and Data Registers

Generally, every microcontroller has minimum of three registers associated with each of GPIO port. They are *Data IN*, *Data Out*, and *Direction*. The Direction register is used to make the pin either input or output. After the Direction register is properly configured, then we use the Data registers to actually write to the pin (PxOUT) or read data from the pin (PxIN). It is the PxDIR register (when configured as output) that allows the information written to the PxOUT register to be driven to the pins of the device. See Figure 2-8.

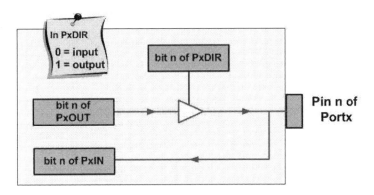

Figure 2-8: The Data and Direction Registers and a Simplified View of an I/O pin

Direction Register in MSP432 ARM

In the case of MSP432 ARM chip, each of the Direction register bit needs to be a 0 to configure the port pin as input and a 1 as output. This is shown below.

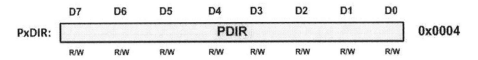

Figure 2-9: PxDIR (Port x Direction Register, x=0, 1, 2, 3, 4 ... 10)

For example, by writing 0x03 (0b00000011 in binary) into the P1DIR register, pins 0 and 1 of P1 become outputs while the other pins become inputs.

See Example 2-1 and Table 2-3.

Example 2-1

In a given MSP432 circuit, the P2.0, P2.1, and P2.2 are connected to LEDs. Find the value for P2DIR for P2.0, P2.1, and P2.2 pins to be configured as output. Give the physical address of P2DIR registers.

Solution:

P2DIR=0b00000111=0x07.
The physical address of 0x40004C00 + 1 (odd addresses) is assigned to P2 and PxDIR has address 0x0004. So, the physical address location for P2DIR is 0x40004C00 + 1 + 0x0004 = 0x40004C05.

Port Data Output Register (PxOUT) in MSP432ARM

To send data to pins, we write it to PxOUT register after the pin is configured as an output in the PxDIR register. This is shown below.

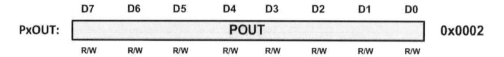

Figure 2-10: PxOut (Portx Output Register)

Port Data Input Register (PxIN) in MSP432 ARM

To bring into CPU data from a pin, we read it from PxIN register after the pin is configured as an input in the PxDIR register. This is shown below.

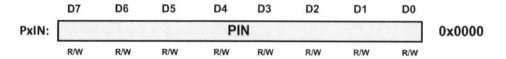

Figure 2-11: PxIN (Portx Input Register)

Table 2-3 shows some of the registers associated with PORT1.

Address	Name	Description	Type	Reset Value
0x40004C00	P1IN	Port1 Input Register	R	0b00000000
0x40004C02	P1OUT	Port1 Output Register	R/W	0b00000000
0x40004C04	P1DIR	Port1 Direction Register	R/W	0b00000000
0x40004C06	P1REN	Port1 Resistor Enable Register	R/W	0b00000000
0x40004C08	P1DS	Port1 Drive Strength Register	R/W	0b00000000
0x40004C0A	P1SEL0	Port1 Select 0 Register	R/W	0b00000000
0x40004C0C	P1SEL1	Port1 Select 1 Register	R/W	0b00000000

Table 2-3: Some commonly Used Registers of PORT1

It must be noted that we have these registers for all the ports 1 to 10 in the MSP432 ARM. See Table 2-4 to Table 2-6Table 2-6.

Address	Name	Description	Type	Reset Value
0x40004C01	P2IN	Port2 Input Register	R	0b00000000
0x40004C03	P2OUT	Port2 Output Register	R/W	0b00000000
0x40004C05	P2DIR	Port2 Direction Register	R/W	0b00000000
0x40004C07	P2REN	Port2 Resistor Enable Register	R/W	0b00000000
0x40004C09	P2DS	Port2 Drive Strength Register	R/W	0b00000000
0x40004C0B	P2SEL0	Port2 Select 0 Register	R/W	0b00000000
0x40004C0D	P2SEL1	Port2 Select 1 Register	R/W	0b00000000

Table 2-4: Some commonly Used Registers of PORT2

Address	Name	Description	Type	Reset Value
0x40004C20	P3IN	Port3 Input Register	R	0b00000000
0x40004C22	P3OUT	Port3 Output Register	R/W	0b00000000
0x40004C24	P3DIR	Port3 Direction Register	R/W	0b00000000
0x40004C26	P3REN	Port3 Resistor Enable Register	R/W	0b00000000
0x40004C28	P3DS	Port3 Drive Strength Register	R/W	0b00000000
0x40004C2A	P3SEL0	Port3 Select 0 Register	R/W	0b00000000
0x40004C2C	P3SEL1	Port3 Select 1 Register	R/W	0b00000000

Table 2-5: Some commonly Used Registers for PORT3

Address	Name	Description	Type	Reset Value
0x40004C21	P4IN	Port4 Input Register	R	0b00000000
0x40004C23	P4OUT	Port4 Output Register	R/W	0b00000000
0x40004C25	P4DIR	Port4 Direction Register	R/W	0b00000000
0x40004C27	P4REN	Port4 Resistor Enable Register	R/W	0b00000000
0x40004C29	P4DS	Port4 Drive Strength Register	R/W	0b00000000
0x40004C2B	P4SEL0	Port4 Select 0 Register	R/W	0b00000000
0x40004C2D	P4SEL1	Port4 Select 1 Register	R/W	0b00000000

Table 2-6: Some commonly Used Registers of PORT4

Port Pull-up or Pull-down Resistor Enable Register (PxREN) in MSP432 ARM

To bring into CPU data from a pin, we read it from PxIN register after the pin is configured as an input in the PxDIR register. When a pin is configured as an input pin, you may enable the built-in pull-up or pull-down resistor attached to that pin. To enable the pull resistor, you need to set the corresponding bit in the PxREN register of that port. See Figure 2-12 and Figure 2-13.

Figure 2-12: PxREN (Portx Pull-up or Pull-down Resistor Enable Register)

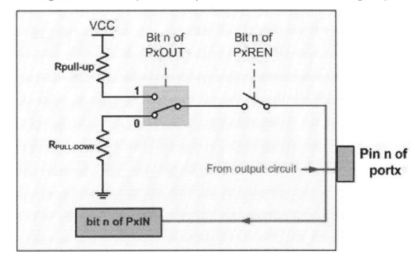

Figure 2-13: PxREN (Portx Pull-up or Pull-down Resistor Enable Register)

When the pull resistor is enabled for an input pin, whether the pull-up or pull-down resistor is attached is determined by the corresponding bit in the PxOUT register of that port. Pull-up or pull-down resistor is only used when the pin is configured as an input pin and therefore the content of PxOUT register has no output function. See Example 2-2.

Example 2-2

Find the value for P2DIR, P2OUT, and P2REN to configure the P2 pins as inputs. Pull down P2.0 and pull up P2.1.

Solution:

P2DIR=0b00000000=0x00
P2REN=0b00000011= 0x03
P2OUT=0b00000010= 0x02

Alternate pin functions and the simple GPIO

Each pin of the MSP432 ARM chip can be used for one of several functions including GPIO. The function associated with a pin is chosen by programming PxSEL1 and PxSEL0 function selection registers.

Using a single pin for multiple functions is called *pin multiplexing* and is commonly used by today's microcontrollers. For example, a given pin can be used as simple digital I/O (GPIO), analog input, or I2C pin. In the absence of pin multiplexing, a microcontroller will need many more pins to support all of its on-chip features.

The PxSEL1 and PxSEL0 (Portx Selection 1 and 0 function selection) registers allow us to program a pin to be used for a given alternate function. Upon reset, ports 1 to 10 are configured for simple I/O. At any given situation, to use a pin as simple digital I/O, we must choose PxSEL1:PxSEL0=00 option. See Figures 2-14 and 2-15 and Example 2-3.

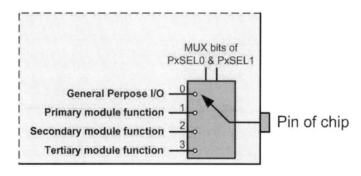

Figure 2-14: Alternative functions of a pin are selected by a multiplexer with bits in PxSEL0 and PxSEL1

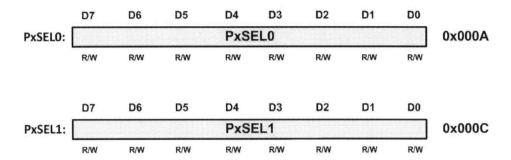

Figure 2-15: PxSEL1:PxSEL0 Registers are used to select alternate pin functions

PxSEL1.y	PxSEL0.y	Meaning
0	0	Alternative 0 (Default) Simple I/O
0	1	Alternative 1 (UART, SPI, I2C, …)
1	0	Alternative 2 (Timers, …)
1	1	Alternative 3 (ADC, Comparator, …)

Table 2-7: PxSEL1:PxSEL0 Registers

Example 2-3

Show how to enable the simple digital I/O feature of for P2.0, P2.1, and P2.2 pins.

Solution:

As shown in Table 2-7, we need to clear bits 2, 1, and 0 in both P2SEL1 and P2SEL0 registers.

Upon power-on reset, the default selection is Simple I/O (PxSEL1:PXSEL0=00) for all pins. For option PxSEL1:PXSEL0=01, the pins may have alternate functions of UART, SPI, and I2C, timers, and so on. For option 2, some of the alternate functions are associated with timers. The analog functions ADC and comparators use alternate function 3. The possible alternate functions are pin dependent and you can see the details in Table 2-8. We will examine all these alternate functions in the future chapters since this chapter is dedicated to simple I/O.

Pin Name	SEL = 00	SEL = 01	SEL = 10	SEL = 11
P1.0	Simple I/O	UCA0STE	-	-
P1.1	Simple I/O	UCA0CLK	-	-
P1.2	Simple I/O	UCA0RXD/UCA0SOMI	-	-
P1.3	Simple I/O	UCA0TXD/UCA0SIMO	-	-
P1.4	Simple I/O	UCB0STE	-	-
P1.5	Simple I/O	UCB0CLK	-	-
P1.6	Simple I/O	UCB0SIMO/UCB0SDA	-	-
P1.7	Simple I/O	UCB0SOMI/UCB0SCL	-	-
P2.0	Simple I/O	PM_UCA1STE	-	-
P2.1	Simple I/O	PM_UCA1CLK	-	-

P2.2	Simple I/O	PM_UCA1RXD/ PM_UCA1SOMI	-	-
P2.3	Simple I/O	PM_UCA1TXD/ PM_UCA1SIMO	-	-
P2.4	Simple I/O	PM_TA0.1	-	-
P2.5	Simple I/O	PM_TA0.2	-	-
P2.6	Simple I/O	PM_TA0.3	-	-
P2.7	Simple I/O	PM_TA0.4	-	-
P3.0	Simple I/O	PM_UCA2STE	-	-
P3.1	Simple I/O	PM_UCA2CLK	-	-
P3.2	Simple I/O	PM_UCA2RXD/ PM_UCA2SOMI	-	-
P3.3	Simple I/O	PM_UCA2TXD/ PM_UCA2SIMO	-	-
P3.4	Simple I/O	PM_UCB2STE	-	-
P3.5	Simple I/O	PM_UCB2CLK	-	-
P3.6	Simple I/O	PM_UCB2SIMO/ PM_UCB2SDA	-	-
P3.7	Simple I/O	PM_UCB2SOMI/ PM_UCB2SCL	-	-
P4.0	Simple I/O	-	-	A13
P4.1	Simple I/O	-	-	A12
P4.2	Simple I/O	ACLK	TA2CLK	A11
P4.3	Simple I/O	MCLK	RTCCLK	A10
P4.4	Simple I/O	HSMCLK	SVMHOUT	A9
P4.5	Simple I/O	-	-	A8
P4.6	Simple I/O	-	-	A7
P4.7	Simple I/O	-	-	A6
P5.0	Simple I/O	-	-	A5
P5.1	Simple I/O	-	-	A4
P5.2	Simple I/O	-	-	A3
P5.3	Simple I/O	-	-	A2
P5.4	Simple I/O	-	-	A1
P5.5	Simple I/O	-	-	A0
P5.6	Simple I/O	TA2.1	-	VREF+/VeREF+/C1.7
P5.7	Simple I/O	TA2.2	-	VREF-/VeREF-/C1.6
P6.0	Simple I/O	-	-	A15
P6.1	Simple I/O	-	-	A14
P6.2	Simple I/O	UCB1STE	-	C1.5
P6.3	Simple I/O	UCB1CLK	-	C1.4
P6.4	Simple I/O	UCB1SIMO/ UCB1SDA	-	C1.3
P6.5	Simple I/O	UCB1SOMI/ UCB1SCL	-	C1.2

P6.6	Simple I/O	TA2.3	UCB3SIMO/ UCB3SDA	C1.1
P6.7	Simple I/O	TA2.4	UCB3SOMI/ UCB3SCL	C1.0
P7.0	Simple I/O	PM_SMCLK/ PM_DMAE0	-	-
P7.1	Simple I/O	PM_C0OUT/ PM_TA0CLK	-	-
P7.2	Simple I/O	PM_C1OUT/ PM_TA1CLK	-	-
P7.3	Simple I/O	PM_TA0.0	-	-
P7.4	Simple I/O	PM_TA1.4	-	C0.5
P7.5	Simple I/O	PM_TA1.3	-	C0.4
P7.6	Simple I/O	PM_TA1.2	-	C0.3
P7.7	Simple I/O	PM_TA1.1	-	C0.2
P8.0		UCB3STE	TA1.0	C0.1
P8.1		UCB3CLK	TA2.0	C0.0
P8.2		TA3.2		C0.0
P8.3		TA3CLK		A22
P8.4				A21
P8.5				A20
P8.6				A19
P8.7				A18
P9.0				A17
P9.1				A16
P9.2		TA3.3		
P9.3		TA3.4		
P9.4		UCA3STE		
P9.5		UCA3CLK		
P9.6		UCA3RXD/ UCA3SOMI		
P9.7		UCA3TXD/ UCA3SIMO		
P10.0		UCB3STE		
P10.1		UCB3CLK		
P10.2		UCB3SIMO/ UCB3SDA		
P10.3		UCB3SOMI/ UCB3SCL		
P10.4		TA3.0		C0.7
P10.5		TA3.1		C0.6

Table 2-8: MSP432 Alternative Pin Functions

PortJ is designed to serve the connections to external crystal oscillators or debug interface and used as such on the LaunchPad. Their alternate function selects are different and not included in this table.

LED connection in MSP432 LaunchPad board

In the MSP432 LaunchPad board, we have a tri-color RGB LED connected to P2.0 (red), P2.1 (green), and P2.2 (blue). The tri-color RGB (red, blue, green) LED is popular in many trainer kits for embedded systems.

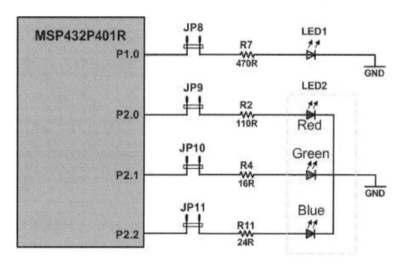

Figure 2-16: LED connection to P2 of MSP432 LaunchPad board

Toggling LEDs in MSP432 LaunchPad board in C

To toggle the green LED of the LaunchPad board, the following steps must be followed.

1) Configure P2.1 (P2SEL1:P2SEL0 Register) to select simple GPIO function for P2.1,
2) set the Direction register bit 1 of P2DIR as output,
3) write HIGH to bit 1 of P2OUT register to turn on the green LED,
4) call a delay function,
5) write LOW to bit 1 of P2OUT register to turn off the green LED,
6) call a delay function,
7) Repeat steps 3 to 7.

Notice, step 1 is optional if MSP432 LaunchPad comes out of Reset since all the ports are configured as simple I/O upon power-on reset. Program 2-1 shows one way to toggle the green LED continuously. Program 2-2 shows how to toggle the red LED on MSP432 LaunchPad.

Program 2-1: Toggling green LED on MSP432 Launch Pad in C

```
/* p2_1.c Toggling green LED in C using header file register definitions.
 * This program toggles green LED for 0.5 second ON and 0.5 second OFF.
 * The green LED is connected to P2.1.
```

38

```
 * The LEDs are high active (a '1' turns ON the LED).
 *
 * Tested with Keil 5.20 and MSP432 Device Family Pack V2.2.0.
 * It might require editing delay timing for other compilers.
 */

#include "msp.h"

void delayMs(int n);

int main(void) {
    P2->SEL1 &= ~2;          /* configure P2.1 as simple I/O */
    P2->SEL0 &= ~2;
    P2->DIR |= 2;            /* P2.1 set as output pin */

    while (1) {
        P2->OUT |= 2;        /* turn on P2.1 green LED */
        delayMs(500);
        P2->OUT &= ~2;       /* turn off P2.1 green LED */
        delayMs(500);
    }
}

/* delay milliseconds when system clock is at 3 MHz */
void delayMs(int n) {
    int i, j;

    for (j = 0; j < n; j++)
        for (i = 250; i > 0; i--);       /* Delay 1 ms */
}
```

All the programs in this book are written using Keil MDK-ARM v5.20 with TI MSP432 Device Family Pack V2.2.0. The programs should compile and run with minor changes using other compilers including TI Code Composer Studio (CCS or CCS Cloud). But because a different compiler is used, the timing of the program will be different. This is evident when a delay loop is used in the program. You can download the step by step tutorials of IDEs together with the source codes of our books from the following website:

http://www.microdigitaled.com/ARM/MSP432_books.htm

According to CMSIS new conventions, the registers are specified as "modulex->register." For example, the Direction register of Port 2 (P2DIR) is written as P2->DIR. Since the registers of the peripheral modules are memory mapped, the registers are defined as memory locations in a header file specific to the device used in the file "msp432p401r.h", which is part of the Device Family Pack of MDK-ARM for MSP432 at with the MSP432 CMSIS Update:

C:\Keil\ARM\Pack\TexasInstruments\MSP432P4xx_DFP\2.0.0\Device\Include

You may use

```
#include "msp432p401r.h"
```

in the program to get the register definitions or you may simply use

```
#include "msp.h"
```

in the program and Keil will find the file msp432p401r.h from the device selection you made when you start the project.

Program 2-2: Toggling red LED on MSP432 LaunchPad

```c
/* p2_2.c Toggling red LED in C using header file register definitions.
 * This program toggles red LED for 0.5 second ON and 0.5 second OFF.
 * The red LED is connected to P2.0.
 * The LEDs are high active (a '1' turns ON the LED).
 *
 * Tested with Keil 5.20 and MSP432 Device Family Pack V2.2.0.
 */

#include "msp.h"

void delayMs(int n);

int main(void) {
    P2->SEL1 &= ~1;          /* configure P2.0 as simple I/O */
    P2->SEL0 &= ~1;
    P2->DIR |= 1;            /* P2.0 set as output pin */

    while (1) {
        P2->OUT |= 1;        /* turn on P2.0 red LED */
        delayMs(500);
        P2->OUT &= ~1;       /* turn off P2.0 red LED */
        delayMs(500);
    }
}

/* delay milliseconds when system clock is at 3 MHz */
void delayMs(int n) {
    int i, j;

    for (j = 0; j < n; j++)
        for (i = 250; i > 0; i--);      /* Delay */
}
```

Program 2-3 shows how to toggle all three LEDs on the MSP432 LaunchPad.

Program 2-3: Toggling all three LEDs on MSP432 LaunchPad board

```c
/* p2_3.c Toggling all three LEDs of the tri-color LEDs.
 * When all three LEDs are on, it appears to be white.
 * The red LED is connected to P2.0.
```

40

```
 * The green LED is connected to P2.1.
 * The blue LED is connected to P2.2.
 * The LEDs are high active (a '1' turns ON the LED).
 *
 * Tested with Keil 5.20 and MSP432 Device Family Pack V2.2.0.
 */

#include "msp.h"

void delayMs(int n);

int main(void) {
    P2->SEL1 &= ~7;          /* configure P2.2-P2.0 as simple I/O */
    P2->SEL0 &= ~7;

    P2->DIR |= 7;            /* P2.2-2.0 set as output */
    P2->OUT |= 7;            /* turn all three LEDs on */

    while (1) {
        P2->OUT ^= 7;        /* toggle P2.2-P2.0 all three LEDs */
        delayMs(500);
    }
}

/* delay milliseconds when system clock is at 3 MHz */
void delayMs(int n) {
    int i, j;

    for (j = 0; j < n; j++)
        for (i = 250; i > 0; i--);        /* Delay */
}
```

Program 2-4 shows how to generate all 8 color combinations of the tri-color LEDs. In this program an incrementing counter is used. The bit 0 of the counter is used to control the red LED. The bit 1 of the counter is used to control the green LED. The bit 2 of the counter is used to control the blue LED. More colors may be generated by using the PWM (pulse width modulation) but that is a subject of a later chapter.

Program 2-4: Cycle through all color combinations of LEDs

```
/* p2_4.c Cycle through all color combinations of the tri-color LEDs.
 * The red LED is connected to P2.0.
 * The green LED is connected to P2.1.
 * The blue LED is connected to P2.2.
 * The LEDs are high active (a '1' turns ON the LED).
 *
 * Tested with Keil 5.20 and MSP432 Device Family Pack V2.2.0.
 */

#include "msp.h"

void delayMs(int n);
```

```
int main(void)
{
    int counter = 0;

    P2->SEL1 &= ~7;            /* configure P2.2-P2.0 as simple I/O */
    P2->SEL0 &= ~7;

    P2->DIR |= 7;              /* P2.2-2.0 set as output */

    while (1) {
        /* turn on/off the tri-color LEDs by the least significant three bits of the
counter */
        P2->OUT = counter & 7;
        delayMs(500);
        counter++;             /* increment counter */
    }
}

/* delay milliseconds when system clock is at 3 MHz */
void delayMs(int n) {
    int i, j;

    for (j = 0; j < n; j++)
        for (i = 250; i > 0; i--);     /* Delay */
}
```

CPU clock frequency and time delay

Most of the modern microcontrollers have at least two types of clock source, the on-chip oscillator and the oscillator connected to external crystal.

The advantage of the external crystal oscillator is the higher precision. The advantage of the on-chip oscillator is that it is always there, so it is usually used as the default clock source upon power-up reset. The clock from the source may be modified by a divider to reduce the clock rate or use a phase lock loop (PLL) circuit to produce a wider range of clock rates.

The MSP432 has two oscillators connected to external crystal, LFXT and HFXT for low frequency crystal and high frequency crystal. The LFXT is designed to use a 32.768 KHz watch crystal. The HFXT can be used with crystals or resonators ranging from 1 MHz to 48 MHz.

The MSP432 has five internal oscillators, among them the Digitally Controlled Oscillator (DCO) is the most flexible clock source that provides a wide range of clock frequencies. It is also used as the power-up default clock source and the default configuration of the startup code in Keil MDK-ARM provides 3 MHz as the DCO output clock frequency. Throughout this book, we will use this default 3 MHz clock for the CPU and peripheral modules.

Measuring time delay in a C program loop

One simple way of creating a time delay is using a **for**-loop in C language. The length of time delay loop for a given system is function of two factors: a) the CPU frequency and b) the compiler. It must be noted that a time delay C loop measured using a given compiler (e.g. Keil) may not give the same result if a different compiler such as TI Code Composer Studio is used. Regardless of clock source to CPU and the C compiler used, always use oscilloscope to measure the length of time delay loop for a given system with a given compiler and compiler option setting.

Connecting switches to MSP432

We can connect an external SW to the board and experiment with the concept of inputting data via a port pin. Depending on how we connect an external SW to a pin, we need to enable the internal pull-up or pull-down resistor for the pin. This must be done in addition to configuring the Direction register as input. See Figure 2-17 for connecting external switches to microcontroller.

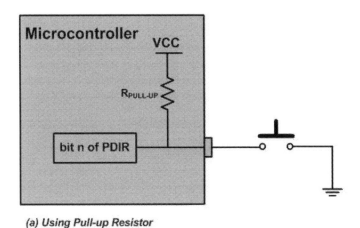

(a) Using Pull-up Resistor

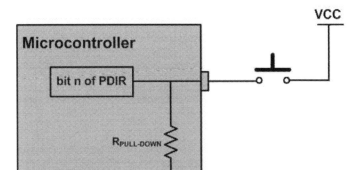

(b) Using Pull-down Resistor

Figure 2-17: Connecting External Switches to the Microcontroller

As described earlier, the bits of PxREN are used to enable the internal pull resistor and the corresponding bit in the PxOUT resistor is used to determine whether pull-up or pull-down resistor is used.

Reading a switch in MSP432 LaunchPad board

The MSP432 LaunchPad board comes with two user programmable push-button switches. They are connected to pins P1.1 and P1.4. See Figure 2-18 and Example 2-4.

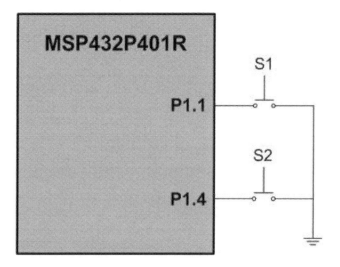

Figure 2-18: MSP432 LaunchPad push-button connections

Example 2-4

Assume P1.1 and P1.4 pins are connected to switches which are grounded when the switch is pressed. Find the contents of the P1DIR, P1REN, and P1OUT registers so that these pins will function as to input pins to sense the switch positions.

Solution:

We need to clear bit 4 and bit 1 inP1DIR to make P1.1 and P1.4 pins as input. And to activate the internal pull resistor, the P1REN register needs to be 0b00010010 and the P1OUT needs to be 0b00010010 to enable the pull-up option.

To read the status of a switch on P1.1 and display it on the LED on P2.0, the following steps must be taken:
1) configure P1.1 as simple I/O in P1SEL1:P1SEL0 registers,
2) make P1.1 input pin in P1DIR register for push-button switch S1,
3) configure P1REN register to enable the pull resistor,
4) configure P1OUT register to select the pull-up resistor,

5) configure P2.0 as simple I/O in P2SEL1:P2SEL0 registers,

6) make P2.0 output pin in P2DIR register for red LED,

7) read switch from P1.1,

8) if P1.1 (switch) is high, set P2.0 (red LED)

9) else clear P2.0 (red LED)

10) Repeat steps 7 to 9.

See Programs 2-5.

Program 2-5: Reading a switch and displaying it on LED

```c
/* p2_5.c Read a switch and write it to the LED.

 * This program reads an external SW connected to P1.1 and writes
 * the value to the red LED on P1.0.
 * When switch is pressed, it connects P1.1 to ground and bit 1 of
 * P1IN reads as '0'. P1.1 pin pull-up is enabled so that it is high
 * when the switch is not pressed and bit 1 of P1IN reads as '1'.
 * The LEDs are high active (a '1' turns ON the LED).
 *
 * Tested with Keil 5.20 and MSP432 Device Family Pack V2.2.0.
 */

#include "msp.h"

int main(void)
{
    P1->SEL1 &= ~2;         /* configure P1.1 as simple I/O */
    P1->SEL0 &= ~2;
    P1->DIR &= ~2;          /* P1.1 set as input */
    P1->REN |= 2;           /* P1.1 pull resistor enabled */
    P1->OUT |= 2;           /* Pull up/down is selected by P1->OUT */

    P2->SEL1 &= ~1;         /* configure P2.0 as simple I/O */
    P2->SEL0 &= ~1;
    P2->DIR |= 1;           /* P2.0 set as output pin */

    while (1)
    {
        if (P1->IN & 2)     /* use switch 1 to control red LED */
            P2->OUT &= ~1;  /* turn off P2.0 red LED when SW is not pressed */
        else
            P2->OUT |= 1;   /* turn on P2.0 red LED when SW is pressed */
    }
}
```

Review Questions

1. MSP432 has _____ GPIO ports.
2. True or false. Every ARM microcontroller must have minimum of 3 memory spaces of Flash (for code), SRAM (for data), and I/O.
3. Each port in MSP432P401Rhas____pins.
4. Give the address location assigned to P2OUT.
5. Give the port pins used in LaunchPad for tri-color LEDs.

Section 2.3: Seven-segment LED interfacing and programming

A popular display is the seven-segment LED. The 7-seg LED can have common anode or common cathode. With common anode, the anodes of the LEDs are connected to the positive supply voltage and the microcontroller drives the individual cathodes LOW for current to flow through the LEDs to light up. In this configuration, the sink current capability of the microcontroller is critical. With common cathode, the cathodes of the LEDs are grounded and microcontroller drives the individual anodes HIGH to light up the LED. In this configuration, the microcontroller pins must provide sufficient source current for each LED segment. In either configuration, if the microcontroller does not have sufficient drive or sink current capacity, we must add a buffer between the 7-seg LED and the microcontroller. The buffer for the 7-seg LED can be an IC chip or transistors.

The seven segments of LED are designated as a, b, c, d, e, f, and g. See Figure 2-19.

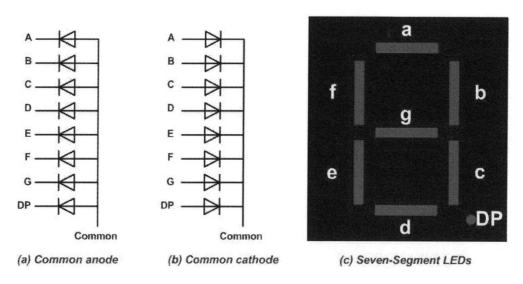

(a) Common anode   (b) Common cathode   (c) Seven-Segment LEDs

Figure 2-19: Seven-Segment LED

An 8-bit port is sufficient to drive all of the segments. In the example below, segment 'a' is assigned to bit D0, segment b is assigned to bit D1, and so on as shown below:

D7	D6	D5	D4	D3	D2	D1	D0
.	g	F	e	d	c	b	a

Table 2-9: Assignments of port pins to each segments of a 7-seg LED

The D7 bit is assigned to decimal point if it exists in the display. One can create the following patterns for numbers 0 through 9 for the common cathode configuration:

Num	D7	D6	D5	D4	D3	D2	D1	D0	Hex value
	.	G	F	e	d	c	b	a	
0	0	0	1	1	1	1	1	1	0x3F
1	0	0	0	0	0	1	1	0	0x06
2	0	1	0	1	1	0	1	1	0x5B
3	0	1	0	0	1	1	1	1	0x4F
4	0	1	1	0	0	1	1	0	0x66
5	0	1	1	0	1	1	0	1	0x6D
6	0	1	1	1	1	1	0	1	0x7D
7	0	0	0	0	0	1	1	1	0x07
8	0	1	1	1	1	1	1	1	0x7F
9	0	1	1	0	1	1	1	1	0x6F

Table 2-10: Segment patterns for the 10 decimal digits for a common cathode 7-seg LED

In Figure 2-20 and Figure 2-21 the connection for 2-digit 7-seg LED and the microcontroller are shown. The Program 2-6 shows the code.

Notice since the same segment for both digit 1 and digit 2 are connected to the same I/O port pin, the common cathode of each digit must be driven separately so that only one digit is on at a time. The two digits are turned on alternatively. For example, if we want to display number 75 on the 7-seg LED, the following steps should be used:

1) Configure Port 4 as output port to drive the segments,
2) Configure Port 5 as output port to select the digits,
3) Clear the P5.0 pin to turn off the ones digit,
4) Write the pattern of numeral 7 from Table 2-10 to Port 4,
5) Set the P5.1 pin HIGH to activate the tens digit,
6) Delay for some time,
7) Clear the P5.1 pin to turn off the tens digit,
8) Write the pattern of numeral 5 from Table 2-10 to Port 4,
9) Set the P5.0 pin HIGH to activate the ones digit,
10) Delay for some time,
11) Repeat from step 3 to 11.

At lower frequency of alternating digits, the display will appear to be flickering. To eliminate the display flickering, each digit should be turned on and off at least 60 times per second. From the example above, the delay for steps 6 and 10 should be 8 milliseconds or less.

1 second / 60 / 2 = 8 millisecond

See Program 2-6.

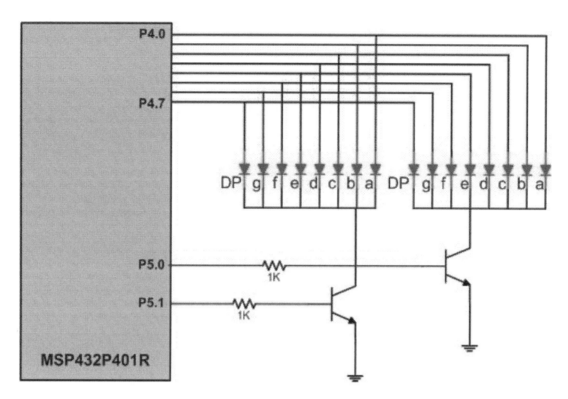

Figure 2-20: Microcontroller Connection to 7-segment LED

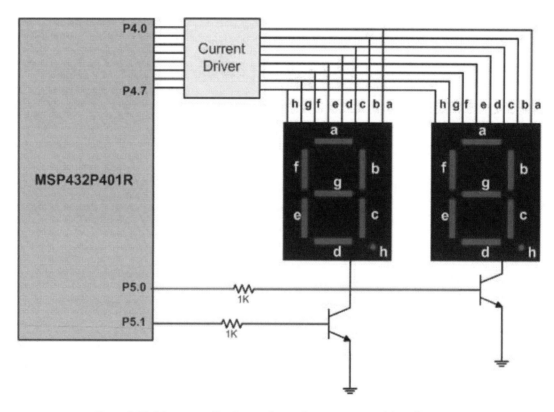

Figure 2-21: Microcontroller Connection to 7-segment LED with Buffer Driver

```c
/* p2_6.c
 *
 * Display number 75 on a 2-digit 7-segment common cathode LED.
 * The segments are driven by Port4.
 * The digit selects are driven by P5.1 and P5.0.
 *
 * Tested with Keil 5.20 and MSP432 Device Family Pack V2.2.0.
 */

#include "msp.h"

void delayMs(int n);

int main(void)
{
    const unsigned char digitPattern[] =
        {0x3F, 0x06, 0x5B, 0x4F, 0x66, 0x6D, 0x7D, 0x07, 0x7F, 0x6F};

    P4->SEL1 &= ~0xFF;       /* configure P4 as simple I/O */
    P4->SEL0 &= ~0xFF;
    P4->DIR  |= 0xFF;        /* P4 set as output */

    P5->SEL1 &= ~3;          /* configure P5.1, P5.0 as simple I/O */
    P5->SEL0 &= ~3;
    P5->DIR  |= 3;           /* P5.1, P5.0 set as output pins */

    while(1){
        P5->OUT &= ~1;                  /* deselect ones digit */
        P4->OUT = digitPattern[7];      /* display tens digit */
        P5->OUT |= 2;                   /* select tens digit */
        delayMs(8);
        P5->OUT &= ~2;                  /* deselect tens digit */
        P4->OUT = digitPattern[5];      /* display ones digit */
        P5->OUT |= 1;                   /* select ones digit */
        delayMs(8);
    }
}

/* delay milliseconds when system clock is at 3 MHz */
void delayMs(int n) {
    int i, j;

    for (j = 0; j < n; j++)
        for (i = 250; i > 0; i--);      /* Delay */
}
```

Notice in Figure 2-21, a single pin is used to select each digit. That means if we want 4 digits we must use a total of 12 pins. That is 8 pins for the segments a through h (decimal point), and 4 pins to select each digit. This might not be feasible in applications in which we have a limited number of microcontroller pins to spare. One solution is to use a decoder for the digit selection. For example, a 74LS138 decoder can be used for up to 8-digit 7-seg LED with three select pins. Another approach is to

49

use a 7-segment LED driver chip such as MAX7221, which only uses four interface pins. An additional advantage of MAX7221 is that the refreshing of the segments is handled by the driver chip itself so the microcontroller does not have to spend time refreshing the display and can concentrate on other tasks. The MAX7221 is an SPI device and the vast majority of microcontrollers come with on-chip SPI serial communication feature, which we will discuss in a separate chapter.

Review Questions

1. In a common cathode 7-seg LED connection, to turn on a segment the microcontroller drives it (high, low).
2. True or false. In connecting the 7-seg LED directly to microcontroller, the refreshing of digits is done by microcontroller itself.
3. What is the disadvantage of letting microcontroller to do the refreshing of 7-seg LEDs?
4. List two advantages of using an IC chip such as MAX7221 chip?
5. In an application, we need 8 digits of 7-seg LED. How many pins of microcontroller will be used if we connect microcontroller to 7-seg directly (similar to Figure 2-20)? How about if we use 3-8 decoder for digit selection?

Section 2.4: I/O Port Programming in Assembly

In the paragraph after Program 2-1, we described how the registers of the peripheral modules are defined in the header file "msp432p401r.h". If we added the line

```
#include "msp432p401r.h"
```

at the beginning of the program, we are able to use all the register definitions in that header file. We have used that for all the programs up to this point.

In Program 2-7, we will define the registers with their memory addresses in the program without using the header file. Notice that the #include line is no longer needed because all the registers used in the program are defined locally.

The purpose of this sample program is to demonstrate how the memory addresses of the peripheral registers are referenced in a C program. Doing so is a tedious task and error prone where there are a large number of registers used by the program. Most often the manufacturer of the microcontroller supplies the header file with the definitions of the registers. You should take advantage of that and use the header file.

Program 2-7: Toggling Red LED in C (using special function registers by their addresses)

```
/* p2_7.c Toggling LED in C references registers by addresses.
 * This program toggles red LED for 0.5 second ON and 0.5 second OFF.
 * The red LED is connected to P1.0.
 * The LEDs are high active (a '1' turns ON the LED).
 *
 * Tested with Keil 5.20 and MSP432 Device Family Pack V2.2.0.
 */
```

```c
#define P1_DIR (*((volatile unsigned char*)0x40004C04))
#define P1_OUT (*((volatile unsigned char*)0x40004C02))

void delayMs(int n);

int main(void) {
    P1_DIR |= 1;                /* P1.0 set as output */

    while (1) {
        P1_OUT |= 1;            /* turn on P1.0 red LED */
      delayMs(500);
        P1_OUT &= ~1;           /* turn off P1.0 red LED */
      delayMs(500);
    }
}

/* delay milliseconds when system clock is at 3 MHz */
void delayMs(int n) {
    int i, j;

    for (j = 0; j < n; j++)
        for (i = 250; i > 0; i--);      /* Delay 1 ms */
}
```

Program 2-8 shows the assembly version of the Program 2-7. The same register addresses used in the program above are used in the assembly code below.

ARM Unified Assembler Language (UAL) is widely accepted by most of the assemblers. The syntax of the instructions in the following program should be recognized by most of the software development tools. But the syntax of the other parts of the program such as directive and comment are not common among all the software development tools. Program 2-8 was written for Keil MDK-ARM and will not work with TI assembler or GNU assembler.

This assembly program is added here for reference only. For details of assembly programming, please refer to the first volume of this book series, "ARM Assembly Language Programming & Architecture".

Program 2-8: Toggling Red LED in Assembly Language

```
; p2_8.s Toggling LED using assembly language
; This program toggles red LED for 0.5 second ON and 0.5 second OFF.
; The red LED is connected to P1.0.
; The LEDs are high active (a '1' turns ON the LED).
;
; Tested with Keil 5.20 and MSP432 Device Family Pack V2.2.0.

; Port 1 Pin Direction Register
P1DIR EQU 0x40004C04
; Port 1 Pin Output Register
P1OUT EQU 0x40004C02
```

```
        THUMB
        AREA    |.text|, CODE, READONLY, ALIGN=2
        EXPORT  __main

__main
        ; make P1.0 an output pin
        LDR     R0, =P1DIR      ; load Dir Reg in R1
        LDRB    R1, [R0]
        ORR     R1, #1          ; set bit 0
        STRB    R1, [R0]        ; store back to Dir Reg

loop
        ; turn off red LED
        LDR     R0, =P1OUT      ; load Output Data Reg in R1
        LDRB    R1, [R0]
        MVN     R2, #1          ; load complement of bit 0 mask
        AND     R1, R2          ; clear bit 0
        STRB    R1, [R0]        ; store back to Output Data Reg

        ; delay for 0.5 second
        MOV     R0, #500
        BL      delayMs

        ; turn on red LED
        LDR     R0, =P1OUT      ; load Output Data Reg in R1
        LDRB    R1, [R0]
        ORR     R1, #1          ; set bit 0
        STRB    R1, [R0]        ; store back to Output Data Reg

        ; delay for 0.5 second
        MOV     R0, #500
        BL      delayMs

        B       loop            ; repeat the loop

; This subroutine performs a delay of n ms (for 3 MHz CPU clock).
; n is the value in R0.
delayMs
        MOVS    R0, R0          ; if n = 0, return
        BNE     L1
        BX      LR
L1      MOV     R1, #250        ; do inner loop 250 times
L2      SUBS    R1, #1          ; inner loop
        BNE     L2
        SUBS    R0, #1          ; do outer loop n times
        BNE     L1
        BX      LR

        ALIGN
        END
```

Review Questions

1. Give the physical port address for P1IN.
2. True or false. In Assembly language programming of I/O ports, we need to know the physical addresses of the ports.
3. Give the physical port address for P1OUT.
4. Give the physical port address for P1DIR.
5. Give the physical port address for P2DIR.

Section 2.5: 16-BIT I/O ports in MSP432

Since the original MSP430 data bus is 16-bit wide, many of the peripheral registers are also 16-bit wide. To maintain compatibility with the original peripherals, the MSP432 ARM gives us the option of configuring the ports as 16-bit. In other words, although the default is 8-bit (Px.7-Px.0), we can combine two 8-bit ports to form a 16-bit port. This explains the reason why we have even and odd addresses for 8-bit ports since by combining two 8-bit ports, we get a 16-bit port with an aligned even address. See Figure 2-22.

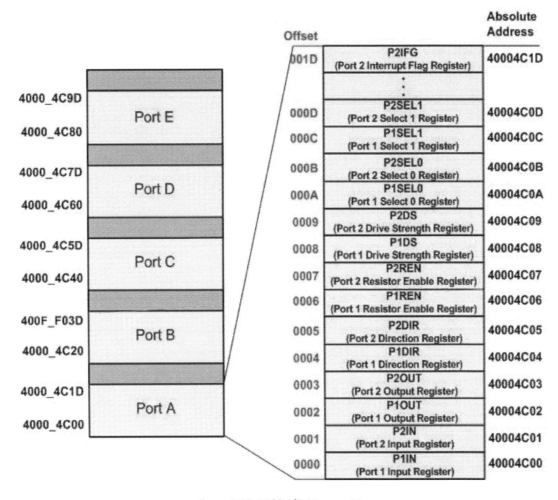

Figure 2-22: 16-bit I/O Memory Map

For example, P1 and P2 are combined together to make a 16-bit port called PA. That means we have five 16-bit ports and they are designated as PA to PE. The base addresses assigned to each of 16-bit ports are as follow:

- GPIO PA (P1:P2)   : 0x4000_4C00
- GPIO PB (P3:P4)   : 0x4000_4C20
- GPIO PC (P5:P6)   : 0x4000_4C40
- GPIO PD (P7:P8)   : 0x4000_4C60
- GPIO PE (P9:P10)   : 0x4000_4C80

Review Questions

1. Ports in MSP430 are (8-bit, 16-bit).
2. True or false. MSP432 ports can be used as 8-bit and 16-bit.
3. What is the base address of PA?
4. How many 16-bit ports do we have in MSP432?
5. True or false. In MSP432, all the 16-bit ports have even base addresses.

Section 2.6: Port Mapping Controller

The selections of alternate functions of the I/O pins in MSP432 are limited. With only two bits in SEL0 and SEL1 registers, there are only three choices in addition to the general purpose I/O. Even that, most of the pins have fewer than three I/O functions available to choose from.

Port Mapping is a feature of the MSP432 devices that allows you a wide selection of alternate functions. Behind each pin of the ports, there is a 1:32 multiplexer to choose one of the 31 alternate I/O functions besides the general purpose I/O. There is a register associated with each pin for the selection of the function. The enumerations of the alternate functions for port mapping are device specific. For MSP432P401x, port mapping controller is available only for P2, P3, and P7. The alternate functions of each pin are specified in Table 6-19 of the MSP432 datasheet. Each pin also has a default power-up function selected. The default function for each pin can be found in Table 6-20 of the MSP4322 reference manual.

To avoid accidental modifications of port mapping, the port mapping controller is locked when powered up. The program needs to unlock the controller before changing the mapping and lock the controller after the mapping.

To use the port mapping controller, the program has to take the following steps:

1) Unlock the port mapping controller by writing the key (0x2D52) to PMAPKEYID register
2) Write the selected function number to the mapping register (PxMAP->PMAP_REGISTERy for Px.y pin)
3) Configure the PxSEL0, PxSEL1, and PxDIR registers to use pin mapping for the pin
4) Lock the selection by writing a 1 to PMAPCTL register
5) Clear the PMAPKEYID register

To see a full example of using pin mapping, check out Program 6-7 in Chapter 6. In that program, Timer_A0.4 output comes out at pin P2.7 by default. The program uses port mapping to connect the output to pin P2.1 so that the timer output is visible at the green LED. The code snippet for port mapping is included below.

Code snippet to map P2.7 (timer TA0.4 output) to P2.1 pin

```
PMAP->KEYID = 0x2D52;      /* unlock PMAP */
P2MAP->PMAP_REGISTER1 = 23;  /* 23, map P2.1 to TA0.4 */
P2->DIR |= 2;              /* set up P2.1 to take TA0.4 output */
P2->SEL0 |= 2;
P2->SEL1 &= ~2;
PMAP->CTL = 1;             /* lock PMAP */
PMAP->KEYID = 0;
```

Review Questions

1. True or false. In MSP432, port mapping is not available for all ports.
2. In MSP432, which ports have port mapping capability?
3. True or false. Upon power on reset, default port mapping is locked.
4. In MSP432, how do we unlock the port mapping feature?
5. True or false. After selecting a new function for a pin using port mapping, we need to lock it.

Answer to Review Questions

Section 2-1

1. 256KB
2. 64KB
3. Program code
4. Data
5. 0x00000000 to 0x0003_FFFF
6. R means 256KB of on-chip Flash while M means 128KB

Section 2-2

1. 10 (P1-P10)
2. True
3. 8
4. 0x40004C03
5. P2.0, P2.1, and P2.2

Section 2-3

1. High
2. True

3. The time and pins of microcontroller is used to scan the 7-segments when it may be used for other purposes.
4. (1) It refreshes the 7-segments, (2) it is connected to the microcontroller using I^2C which uses just 2 pins of the microcontroller.
5. 8 pins for data and 8 pins for selector; 8 pins for data and 3 pins for selector.

Section 2-4

1. 0x4000 4C00
2. True
3. 0x4000 4C02
4. 0x4000 4C04
5. 0x4000 4C05

Section 2-5

1. 16-bit
2. True
3. 0x4000 4C00
4. 5 (PA to PE)
5. True

Section 2-6

1. True
2. P2, P3, and P7
3. True
4. By writing key (0x2D52) to PMAPKEYID register.
5. True

Chapter 3: LCD and Keyboard Interfacing

In this chapter, we show interfacing to two real-world devices: LCD and Keyboard. They are widely used in different embedded systems.

Section 3.1: Interfacing to an LCD

This section describes the operation modes of the LCDs and then shows how to program and interface an LCD to the TI MSP432P401R.

LCD operation

In recent years the LCD is replacing LEDs (seven-segment LEDs or other multi-segment LEDs). This is due to the following reasons:

1. The declining prices of LCDs.
2. The ability to display numbers, characters, and graphics. This is in contrast to LEDs, which are limited to numbers and a few characters. (The new OLED panels are relatively much more expensive except the very small ones. But their prices are dropping. The interface and programming to OLED are similar to graphic LCD.)
3. Incorporation of the refreshing controller into the LCD itself, thereby relieving the CPU of the task of refreshing the LCD.
4. Ease of programming for both characters and graphics.
5. The extremely low power consumption of LCD (when backlight is not used).

In this chapter, we will limit the discussions to the character LCD modules. The graphic LCD modules will be discussed in a later chapter.

LCD module pin descriptions

For many years, the use of Hitachi HD44780 LCD controller dominated the character LCD modules. Even today, most of the character LCD modules still use HD44780 or a variation of it. The HD44780 controller has a 14 pin interface for the microprocessor. We will discuss this 14 pin interface in this section. The function of each pin is given in Table 3-1. Figure 3-1 shows the pin positions for various LCD modules.

Pin	Symbol	I/O	Description
1	VSS	--	Ground
2	VCC	--	+5V power supply
3	VEE	--	Power supply to control contrast
4	RS	I	RS = 0 to select command register, RS = 1 to select data register
5	R/W	I	R/W = 0 for write, R/W = 1 for read
6	E	I	Enable
7	DB0	I/O	The 8-bit data bus
8	DB1	I/O	The 8-bit data bus
9	DB2	I/O	The 8-bit data bus
10	DB3	I/O	The 8-bit data bus
11	DB4	I/O	The 4/8-bit data bus
12	DB5	I/O	The 4/8-bit data bus
13	DB6	I/O	The 4/8-bit data bus
14	DB7	I/O	The 4/8-bit data bus

Table 3-1: Pin Descriptions for LCD

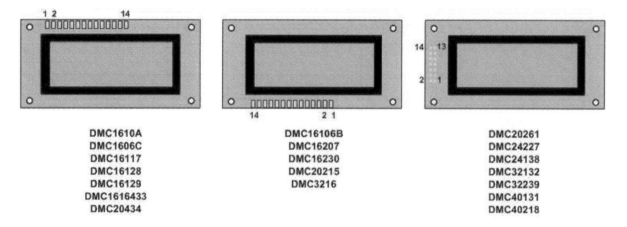

Figure 3-1: Pin Positions for Various LCDs from Optrex

VCC, VSS, and VEE: While VCC and VSS provide +5V power supply and ground, respectively, VEE is used for controlling the LCD contrast.

RS, register select: There are two registers inside the LCD and the RS pin is used for their selection as follows. If RS = 0, the instruction command code register is selected, allowing the user to send a command such as clear display, cursor at home, and so on (or query the busy status bit of the controller). If RS = 1, the data register is selected, allowing the user to send data to be displayed on the LCD (or to retrieve data from the LCD controller).

R/W, read/write: R/W input allows the user to write information into the LCD controller or read information from it. R/W = 1 when reading and R/W = 0 when writing.

E, enable: The enable pin is used by the LCD to latch information presented to its data pins. When data is supplied to data pins, a pulse (Low-to-High-to-Low) must be applied to this pin in order for the LCD to latch in the data present at the data pins. This pulse must be a minimum of 230 ns wide, according to Hitachi datasheet.

D0–D7: The 8-bit data pins are used to send information to the LCD or read the contents of the LCD's internal registers. The LCD controller is capable of operating with 4-bit data and only D4-D7 are used. We will discuss this in more details later.

Code (Hex)	Command to LCD Instruction Register
1	Clear display screen
2	Return cursor home
6	Increment cursor (shift cursor to right)
F	Display on, cursor blinking
80	Force cursor to beginning of 1st line
C0	Force cursor to beginning of 2nd line
38	2 lines and 5x7 character (8-bit data, D0 to D7)
28	2 lines and 5x7 character (4-bit data, D4 to D7)

Table 3-2: Some commonly used LCD Command Codes

To display letters and numbers, we send ASCII codes for the letters A–Z, a–z, numbers 0–9, and the punctuation marks to these pins while making RS = 1.

There are also instruction command codes that can be sent to the LCD in order to clear the display, force the cursor to the home position, or blink the cursor. Table 3-2 lists some commonly used command codes. For detailed command codes, see Table 3-4.

Sending commands to LCDs

To send any of the commands to the LCD, make pins RS = 0, R/W = 0, and send a pulse (L-to-H-to-L) on the E pin to enable the internal latch of the LCD. The connection of an LCD to the microcontroller is shown in Figure 3-2.

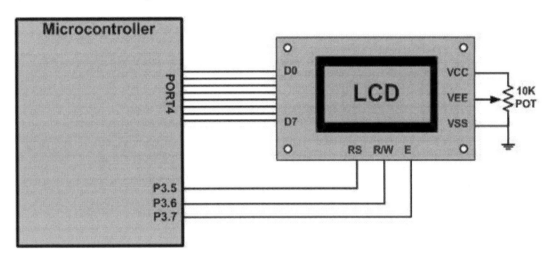

Figure 3-2: LCD Connection to Microcontroller

Notice the following for the connection in Figure 3-2:

1. The LCD's data pins are connected to PORT 4 of the microcontroller.
2. The LCD's RS pin is connected to Pin 5 of PORT 3 of the microcontroller.
3. The LCD's R/W pin is connected to Pin 6 of PORT 3 of the microcontroller.
4. The LCD's E pin is connected to Pin 7 of PORT 3 of the microcontroller.
5. Both Ports 3 and 4 are configured as output ports.

Sending data to the LCD

In order to send data to the LCD to be displayed, we must set pins RS = 1, R/W = 0, and also send a pulse (L-to-H-to-L) to the E pin to enable the internal latch of the LCD.

Because of the extremely low power feature of the LCD controller, it runs much slower than the microcontroller. The first two commands in Table 3-2 take up to 1.64 ms to execute and all the other commands and data take up to 40 us. (At the highest clock speed, MSP432 can execute almost 2,000 instructions in 40 us.) After one command or data is written to the LCD controller, one must wait until the LCD controller is ready before issuing the next command/data, otherwise the second command/data will be ignored. An easy way (not as efficient though) is to delay the microcontroller for the maximal time it may take for the previous command. We will use this method in the following examples. All the examples in this chapter use much more relaxed timing than the original HD44780 datasheet (See Table 3-4) to accommodate the variations of different LCD modules. You may want adjust the delay time for the LCD module you use.

Program 3-1: This program displays a message on the LCD using 8-bit mode and delay.

```
/* p3_1.c: Initialize and display "Hello" on the LCD using 8-bit data mode.
 *
 * Data pins use Port 4; control pins use Port 3.
 * This program does not poll the status of the LCD.
 * It uses delay to wait out the time LCD controller is busy.
 * Timing is more relax than the HD44780 datasheet to accommodate the
 * variations among the LCD modules.
 * You may want to adjust the amount of delay for your LCD controller.
 *
 * Tested with Keil 5.20 and MSP432 Device Family Pack V2.2.0.
 */

#include "msp.h"

#define RS 0x20     /* P3.5 mask */
#define RW 0x40     /* P3.6 mask */
#define EN 0x80     /* P3.7 mask */

void delayMs(int n);
void LCD_command(unsigned char command);
void LCD_data(unsigned char data);
void LCD_init(void);

int main(void)
{
    LCD_init();

    for(;;) {
        LCD_command(1);      /* clear display */
        delayMs(500);
        LCD_command(0x80);   /* set cursor at beginning of first line */
        LCD_data('H');       /* write the word "Hello" */
        LCD_data('e');
        LCD_data('l');
        LCD_data('l');
        LCD_data('o');
        delayMs(500);
    }
}

void LCD_init(void) {
    P3->DIR |= RS | RW | EN; /* make P3 pins output for control */
    P4->DIR = 0xFF;          /* make P4 pins output for data */

    delayMs(30);             /* initialization sequence */
    LCD_command(0x30);
    delayMs(10);
```

```c
    LCD_command(0x30);
    delayMs(1);
    LCD_command(0x30);

    LCD_command(0x38);          /* set 8-bit data, 2-line, 5x7 font */
    LCD_command(0x06);          /* move cursor right after each char */
    LCD_command(0x01);          /* clear screen, move cursor to home */
    LCD_command(0x0F);          /* turn on display, cursor blinking */
}

void LCD_command(unsigned char command)
{
    P3->OUT &= ~(RS | RW);   /* RS = 0, R/W = 0 */
    P4->OUT = command;          /* put command on data bus */
    P3->OUT |= EN;              /* pulse E high */
    delayMs(0);
    P3->OUT &= ~EN;             /* clear E */
    if (command < 4)
        delayMs(4);             /* command 1 and 2 need up to 1.64ms */
    else
        delayMs(1);             /* all others 40 us */
}

void LCD_data(unsigned char data)
{
    P3->OUT |= RS;              /* RS = 1 */
    P3->OUT &= ~RW;             /* R/W = 0 */
    P4->OUT = data;             /* put data on bus */
    P3->OUT |= EN;              /* pulse E */
    delayMs(0);
    P3->OUT &= ~EN;             /* clear E */
    delayMs(1);                 /* wait for controller to do the display */
}

/* delay milliseconds when system clock is at 3 MHz */
void delayMs(int n) {
    int i, j;

    for (j = 0; j < n; j++)
        for (i = 250; i > 0; i--);      /* Delay */
}
```

Checking LCD busy flag

The above programs used a time delay before issuing the next data or command. This allows the LCD a sufficient amount of time to get ready to accept the next data. However, the LCD has a busy flag. We can monitor the busy flag and issue data when it is ready. This will speed up the process. To check the busy flag, we must read the command register (R/W = 1, RS = 0). The busy flag is the D7 bit of that register. Therefore, if R/W = 1, RS = 0. When D7 = 1 (busy flag = 1), the LCD is busy taking care of internal operations and will not accept any new information. When D7 = 0, the LCD is ready to receive new information.

Doing so requires switching the direction of the port connected to the data bus to input mode when polling the status register then switch the port direction back to output mode to send the next command. If the port direction is incorrect, it may damage the microcontroller or the LCD module. The next program example uses polling of the busy bit in the status register.

Program 3-2: This program displays a message on the LCD using 8-bit mode and polling of the status register

```c
/* p3_2.c: Initialize and display "Hello" on the LCD using 8-bit data mode.
 *
 * Data pins use Port 4; control pins use Port 3.
 * Polling of the busy bit of the LCD status register is used for timing.
 *
 * Tested with Keil 5.20 and MSP432 Device Family Pack V2.2.0.
 */

#include "msp.h"

#define RS 0x20      /* P3.5 mask */
#define RW 0x40      /* P3.6 mask */
#define EN 0x80      /* P3.7 mask */

void delayMs(int n);
void LCD_command(unsigned char command);
void LCD_command_noPoll(unsigned char command);
void LCD_data(unsigned char data);
void LCD_init(void);
void LCD_ready(void);

int main(void) {
    LCD_init();

    while(1) {
        LCD_command(1);          /* clear display */
        delayMs(500);
        LCD_command(0x80);       /* set cursor at beginning of first line */
        LCD_data('H');           /* write the word "Hello" */
        LCD_data('e');
        LCD_data('l');
        LCD_data('l');
        LCD_data('o');
        delayMs(500);
    }
}

void LCD_init(void) {
    P3->DIR |= RS | RW | EN;  /* make P3 pins output for control */
    P4->DIR = 0xFF;           /* make P4 pins output for data */

    delayMs(30);             /* initialization sequence */
    LCD_command_noPoll(0x30);    /* LCD does not respond to status poll yet */
    delayMs(5);
    LCD_command_noPoll(0x30);
    delayMs(1);
    LCD_command_noPoll(0x30);    /* busy flag cannot be polled before this command */
```

62

```c
    LCD_command(0x38);          /* set 8-bit data, 2-line, 5x7 font */
    LCD_command(0x06);          /* move cursor right after each char */
    LCD_command(0x01);          /* clear screen, move cursor to home */
    LCD_command(0x0F);          /* turn on display, cursor blinking */
}


/* This function waits until LCD controller is ready to
 * accept a new command/data before returns.
 * It polls the busy bit of the status register of LCD controller.
 * In order to read the status register, the data port of the
 * microcontroller has to change to an input port before reading
 * the LCD. The data port of the microcontroller is return to
 * output port before the end of this function.
 */
void LCD_ready(void) {
    char status;

    /* change to read configuration to poll the status register */
    P4->DIR = 0;                /* Port 4 as input port */
    P3->OUT &= ~RS;             /* RS = 0 for status */
    P3->OUT |= RW;              /* R/W = 1, LCD output */

    do {    /* stay in the loop until it is not busy */
        P3->OUT |= EN;          /* pulse E high */
        delayMs(0);
        status = P4->IN;        /* read status register */
        P3->OUT &= ~EN;         /* clear E */
        delayMs(0);
    } while (status & 0x80);     /* check busy bit */

    /* return to default write configuration */
    P3->OUT &= ~RW;             /* R/W = 0, LCD input */
    P4->DIR = 0xFF;             /* Port 4 as output */
}


/* This function waits for LCD controller ready before issuing
 * the next command.
 */
void LCD_command(unsigned char command) {
    LCD_ready();                /* wait for LCD controller ready */
    P3->OUT &= ~(RS | RW);      /* RS = 0, R/W = 0 */
    P4->OUT = command;          /* put command on data bus */
    P3->OUT |= EN;              /* pulse E high */
    delayMs(0);
    P3->OUT &= ~EN;             /* clear E */
}


/* This function is used at the beginning of the initialization
 * when the busy bit of the status register is not readable.
 */
void LCD_command_noPoll(unsigned char command) {
    P3->OUT &= ~(RS | RW);      /* RS = 0, R/W = 0 */
    P4->OUT = command;          /* put command on data bus */
    P3->OUT |= EN;              /* pulse E high */
    delayMs(0);
    P3->OUT &= ~EN;             /* clear E */
```

```
}

/* This function waits for LCD controller ready before issuing
 * the next data.
 */
void LCD_data(unsigned char data) {
    LCD_ready();                /* wait for LCD controller ready */
    P3->OUT |= RS;              /* RS = 1 */
    P3->OUT &= ~RW;             /* R/W = 0 */
    P4->OUT = data;             /* put data on bus */
    P3->OUT |= EN;              /* pulse E */
    delayMs(0);
    P3->OUT &= ~EN;
}

/* delay milliseconds when system clock is at 3 MHz */
void delayMs(int n) {
    int i, j;

    for (j = 0; j < n; j++)
        for (i = 250; i > 0; i--);      /* Delay */
}
```

LCD 4-bit Option

To save the number of microcontroller pins used by LCD interfacing, we can use the 4-bit data option instead of 8-bit. In the 4-bit data option, we only need to connect D7-D4 to microcontroller. Together with the three control lines, the interface between the microcontroller and the LCD module will fit in a single 8-bit port. See Figure 3-3.

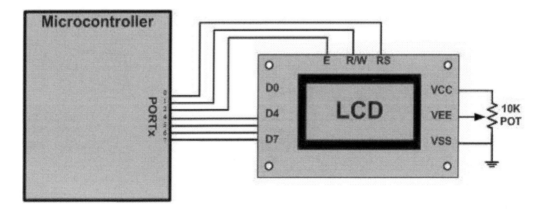

Figure 3-3: LCD Connection for 4-bit Data

With 4-bit data option, the microcontroller needs to issue commands to put the LCD controller in 4-bit mode during initialization. This is done with command 0x20 in Program 3-3. After that, every command or data needs to be broken down to two 4-bit operations, upper nibble first. In Program 3-3, the upper nibble is extracted using **command & 0xF0** and the lower nibble is shifted into place by **command << 4**.

```c
/* p3_3.c: Initialize and display "hello" on the LCD using 4-bit data mode.
 * Data and control pins share Port 4.
 * This program does not poll the status of the LCD.
 * It uses delay to wait out the time LCD controller is busy.
 * Timing is more relax than the HD44780 datasheet to accommodate the
 * variations among the LCD modules.
 * You may want to adjust the amount of delay for your LCD controller.
 *
 * Tested with Keil 5.20 and MSP432 Device Family Pack V2.2.0.
 */
#include "msp.h"

#define RS 1       /* P4.0 mask */
#define RW 2       /* P4.1 mask */
#define EN 4       /* P4.2 mask */

void delayMs(int n);
void LCD_nibble_write(unsigned char data, unsigned char control);
void LCD_command(unsigned char command);
void LCD_data(unsigned char data);
void LCD_init(void);

int main(void) {
    LCD_init();

    for(;;) {
        LCD_command(1);        /* clear display */
        delayMs(500);
        LCD_command(0x80);     /* set cursor at beginning of first line */
        LCD_data('h');         /* write the word "Hello" */
        LCD_data('e');
        LCD_data('l');
        LCD_data('l');
        LCD_data('o');
        delayMs(500);
    }
}

void LCD_init(void) {
    P4->DIR = 0xFF;        /* make P4 pins output for data and controls */
    delayMs(30);                   /* initialization sequence */
    LCD_nibble_write(0x30, 0);
    delayMs(10);
    LCD_nibble_write(0x30, 0);
    delayMs(1);
    LCD_nibble_write(0x30, 0);
    delayMs(1);
    LCD_nibble_write(0x20, 0);  /* use 4-bit data mode */
    delayMs(1);

    LCD_command(0x28);         /* set 4-bit data, 2-line, 5x7 font */
    LCD_command(0x06);         /* move cursor right after each char */
    LCD_command(0x01);         /* clear screen, move cursor to home */
    LCD_command(0x0F);         /* turn on display, cursor blinking */
}
```

```
/* With 4-bit mode, each command or data is sent twice with upper
 * nibble first then lower nibble.
 */
void LCD_nibble_write(unsigned char data, unsigned char control) {
    data &= 0xF0;                /* clear lower nibble for control */
    control &= 0x0F;             /* clear upper nibble for data */
    P4->OUT = data | control;         /* RS = 0, R/W = 0 */
    P4->OUT = data | control | EN;  /* pulse E */
    delayMs(0);
    P4->OUT = data;                   /* clear E */
    P4->OUT = 0;
}


void LCD_command(unsigned char command) {
    LCD_nibble_write(command & 0xF0, 0);     /* upper nibble first */
    LCD_nibble_write(command << 4, 0);       /* then lower nibble */

    if (command < 4)
        delayMs(4);              /* commands 1 and 2 need up to 1.64ms */
    else
        delayMs(1);              /* all others 40 us */
}


void LCD_data(unsigned char data) {
    LCD_nibble_write(data & 0xF0, RS);       /* upper nibble first */
    LCD_nibble_write(data << 4, RS);         /* then lower nibble  */

    delayMs(1);
}

/* delay milliseconds when system clock is at 3 MHz */
void delayMs(int n) {
    int i, j;

    for (j = 0; j < n; j++)
        for (i = 250; i > 0; i--);         /* Delay */
}
```

LCD cursor position

In the LCD, one can move the cursor to any location in the display by issuing an address command. The next character sent will appear at the cursor position. For the two-line LCD, the address command for the first location of line 1 is 0x80, and for line 2 it is 0xC0. The following shows address locations and how they are accessed:

RS	R/W	DB7	DB6	DB5	DB4	DB3	DB2	DB1	DB0
0	0	1	A6	A5	A4	A3	A2	A1	A0

where $A_6A_5A_4A_3A_2A_1A_0$ = 0000000 to 0100111 for line 1 and $A_6A_5A_4A_3A_2A_1A_0$ = 1000000 to 1100111 for line 2. See Table 3-3.

	DB7	DB6	DB5	DB4	DB3	DB2	DB1	DB0
Line 1 (min)	1	0	0	0	0	0	0	0
Line 1 (max)	1	0	1	0	0	1	1	1
Line 2 (min)	1	1	0	0	0	0	0	0
Line 2 (max)	1	1	1	0	0	1	1	1

Table 3-3: LCD Addressing Commands

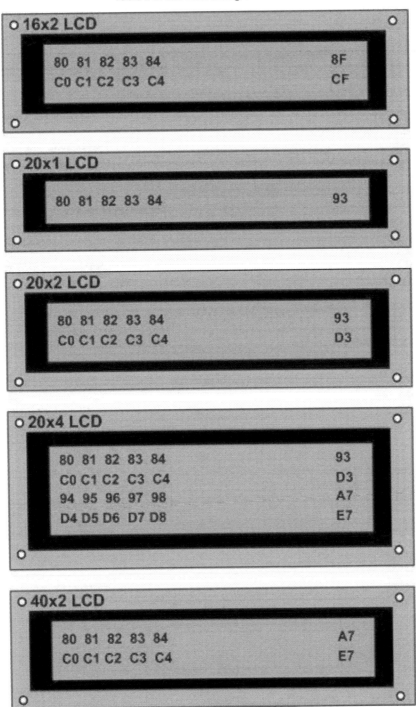

Figure 3-4: Cursor Addresses for Some LCDs

The upper address range can go as high as 0100111 for the 40-character-wide LCD while for the 20-character-wide LCD the address of the visible positions goes up to 010011 (19 decimal = 10011 binary). Notice that the upper range 0100111 (binary) = 39 decimal, which corresponds to locations 0 to 39 for the LCDs of 40 × 2 size. Figure 3-4 shows the addresses of cursor positions for various sizes of LCDs. All the addresses are in hex. Notice the starting addresses for four line LCD are not in sequential order.

As an example of setting the cursor at the fourth location of line 1 we have the following:

`LCD_command(0x83);`

and for the sixth location of the second line we have:

`LCD_command(0xC5);`

Notice that the cursor location addresses are in hex and starting at 0 as the first location.

LCD timing and data sheet

Figures 3-5 and 3-6 show timing diagrams for LCD write and read timing, respectively.

Notice that the write operation happens on the H-to-L transition of the E pin. The microcontroller must have data ready and stable on the data lines before the H-to-L transition of E to satisfy the setup time requirement.

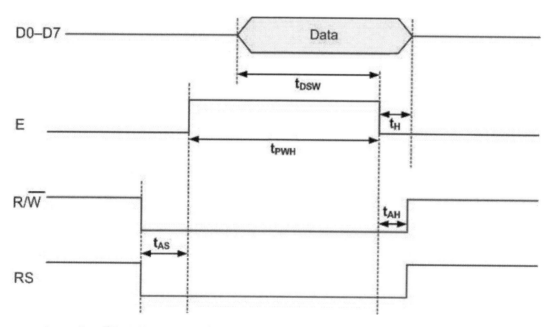

t_{PWH} = Enable pulse width = 230 ns (minimum)
t_{DSW} = Data setup time = 80 ns (minimum)
t_H = Data hold time = 10 ns (minimum)
t_{AS} = Setup time prior to E (going high) for both RS and R/W = 40 ns (minimum)
t_{AH} = Hold time after E has come down for both RS and R/W = 10 ns (minimum)

Figure 3-5: LCD Write Timing

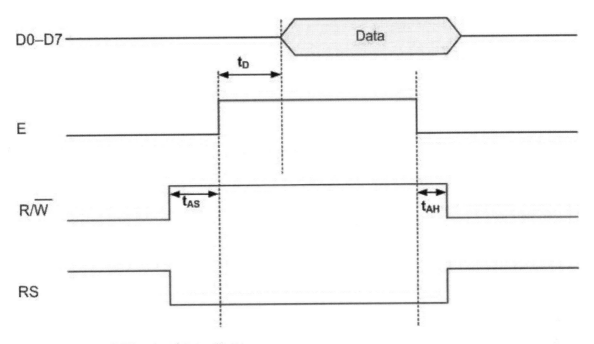

t_D = Data output delay time
t_{AS} = Setup time prior to E (going high) for both RS and R/W = 40 ns (minimum)
t_{AH} = Hold time after E has come down for both RS and R/W = 10 ns (minimum)

Note: Read requires an L-to-H pulse for the E pin.

Figure 3-6: LCD Read Timing

The read operation is activated by the L-to-H pulse of the E pin. After the delay time, the LCD controller will have the data available on the data bus if the R/W line is high. The microcontroller should read the data from the data lines before lowering the E pulse.

Table 3-4 provides a more detailed list of LCD instructions.

Instruction	RS	R/W	DB7	DB6	DB5	DB4	DB3	DB2	DB1	DB0	Description	Execution Time (Max)
Clear display	0	0	0	0	0	0	0	0	0	1	Clears entire display and sets DD RAM address 0 in address counter	1.64 ms
Return Home	0	0	0	0	0	0	0	0	1	-	Sets DD RAM address to 0 as address counter. Also returns display being shifted to original positions. DD RAM contents remain unchanged.	1.64 ms
Entry Mode Set	0	0	0	0	0	0	0	1	I/D	S	Sets cursor move direction and specifies shift of display. These operations are performed during data write and read.	40µs

Instruction											Description	Time
Display On/Off Control	0	0	0	0	0	0	1	D	C	B	Sets On/Off of entire display (D), cursor On/Off (C), and blink of cursor position character (B).	40µs
Cursor or Display shift	0	0	0	0	0	1	S/C	R/L	-	-	Moves cursor and shifts display without changing DD RAM contents.	40µs
Function Set	0	0	0	0	1	DL	N	F	-	-	Sets interface data length (DL), number of display lines (L), and character font (F)	40µs
Set CG RAM Address	0	0	0	1	AGC						Sets CG RAM address. CG RAM data is sent and received after this setting.	40µs
Set DD RAM Address	0	0	1	ADD							Sets DD RAM address. DD RAM data is sent and received after this setting.	40µs
Read Busy Flag & Address	0	1	BF	AC							Reads Busy flag (BF) indicating internal operation is being performed and reads address counter contents.	40µs
Write Data CG or DD RAM	1	0	Write Data								Writes data into DD or CG RAM.	40µs
Read Data CG or DD RAM	1	1	Read Data								Reads data from DD or CG RAM.	40µs

Abbreviations:

DD RAM: Display data RAM

CG RAM: Character generator RAM

AGC: CG RAM address

ADD: DD RAM address, corresponds to cursor address

AC: address counter used for both DD and CG RAM addresses

I/D: 1 = Increment, 0: Decrement

S =1: Accompanies display shift

S/C: 1 = Display shift, 0: Cursor move

R/L: 1: Shift to the right, 0: Shift to the left

DL: 1 = 8 bits, 0 = 4 bits

N: 1 = 2-line, 0 = 1-line

F: 1 = 5 x 10 dots, 0 = 5 x 7 dots

BF: 1 = Internal operation, 0 = Can accept instruction

Table 3-4: List of LCD Instructions

Review Questions

1. The RS pin is an _____ (input, output) pin for the LCD.
2. The E pin is an _____ (input, output) pin for the LCD.

3. The E pin requires an _____ (H-to-L, L-to-H) transition to latch in information at the data pins of the LCD.
4. For the LCD to recognize information at the data pins as data, RS must be set to _____ (high, low).
5. Give the command codes for line 1, first character, and line 2, first character.

Section 3.2: Interfacing the Keyboard to the CPU

To reduce the microcontroller I/O pin usage, keyboards are organized in a matrix of rows and columns. The CPU accesses both rows and columns through ports; therefore, with two 8-bit ports, an 8 × 8 matrix of 64 keys can be connected to a microprocessor. When a key is pressed, a row and a column make a contact; otherwise, there is no connection between rows and columns. In a PC keyboards, an embedded microcontroller in the keyboard takes care of the hardware and software interfacing of the keyboard. In such systems, it is the function of programs stored in the ROM of the microcontroller to scan the keys continuously, identify which one has been activated, and present it to the main CPU on the motherboard. In this section, we look at the mechanism by which the microprocessor scans and identifies the key. For clarity some examples are provided.

Scanning and identifying the key

Figure 3-7 shows a 4 × 4 matrix connected to two ports. The rows are connected to an output port and the columns are connected to an input port.

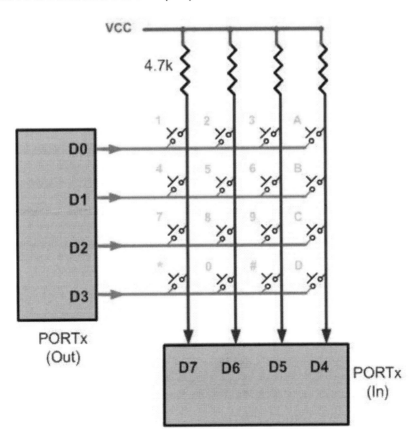

Figure 3-7: Matrix Keyboard Connection to Ports

All the input pins have pull-up resistor connected. If no key has been pressed, reading the input port will yield 1s for all columns. If all the rows are driven low and a key is pressed, the column of that key will read back a 0 since the key pressed shorted that column to the row that is driven low. It is the function of the microprocessor to scan the keyboard continuously to detect and identify the key pressed. How it is done is explained next.

Key press detection

To detect the key pressed, the microprocessor drives all rows low then it reads the columns. If the data read from the columns is D7–D4 = 1111, no key has been pressed and the process continues until a key press is detected. However, if one of the column bits has a zero, this means that a key was pressed. For example, if D7–D4= 1101, this means that a key in the D5 column has been pressed.

The following program detects whether any of the keys is pressed. If a key press is detected, the blue LED is turned on.

Program 3-4: This program turns on the blue LED when a key is pressed.

```
/* p3_4.c: Matrix keypad detect
 *
 * This program checks a 4x4 matrix keypad to see whether
 * a key is pressed or not. When a key is pressed, it turns
 * on the blue LED.
 *
 * Port4 7-4 are connected to the columns and Port4 3-0 are connected
 * to the rows of the keypad.
 *
 * Tested with Keil 5.20 and MSP432 Device Family Pack V2.2.0.
 */

#include "msp.h"

void delay(void);
void keypad_init(void);
char keypad_kbhit(void);

int main(void) {
    keypad_init();
    P2->DIR = 0x04;                 /* make blue LED pins output */

    while(1) {
        if (keypad_kbhit() != 0)    /* if a key is pressed */
            P2->OUT |= 0x04;        /* turn on blue LED */
        else
            P2->OUT &= ~0x04;       /* turn off blue LED */
    }
}

/* this function initializes Port 4 that is connected to the keypad.
 * All pins are configured as GPIO input pin. The column pins have
 * the pull-up resistors enabled.
 */
```

```
void keypad_init(void) {
    P4->DIR = 0;
    P4->REN = 0xF0;         /* enable pull resistor for column pins */
    P4->OUT = 0xF0;         /* make column pins pull-ups */
}

/* This is a non-blocking function.
 * If a key is pressed, it returns 1.
 * Otherwise, it returns a 0 (not ASCII '0'). */

char keypad_kbhit(void) {
    int col;

    P4->DIR |= 0x0F;                /* make all row pins output */
    P4->OUT &= ~0x0F;               /* drive all row pins low */
    delay();                        /* wait for signals to settle */
    col = P4->IN & 0xF0;            /* read all column pins */
    P4->DIR &= ~0x0F;               /* disable all row pins drive */
    if (col == 0xF0)                /* if all columns are high */
        return 0;                   /* no key pressed */
    else
        return 1;                   /* a key is pressed */
}

/* make a small delay */
void delay(void) {
}
```

Key identification

After a key press is detected, the microprocessor will go through the process of identifying the key. Starting from the top row, the microprocessor drives one row low at a time; then it reads the columns. If the data read is all 1s, no key in that row is pressed and the process is moved to the next row. It drives the next row low, reads the columns, and checks for any zero. This process continues until a row is identified with a zero in one of the columns. The next task is to find out which column the pressed key belongs to. This should be easy since each column is connected to a separate input pin. Look at Example 3-1.

Example 3-1

From Figure 3-7, identify the row and column of the pressed key for each of the following.
(a) D3–D0 = 1110 for the row, D7–D4= 1011 for the column
(b) D3–D0 = 1101 for the row, D7–D4= 0111 for the column

Solution:

From Figure 3-7 the row and column can be used to identify the key.
(a)   The row belongs to D0 and the column belongs to D6; therefore, the key number 2 was pressed.

(b)   The row belongs to D1 and the column belongs to D7; therefore, the key number 4 was pressed.

Figure 3-8 is the flowchart for the detection and identification of the key activation.

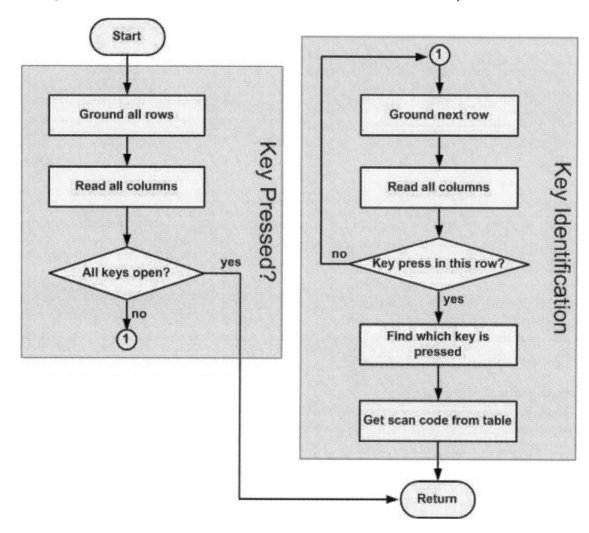

Figure 3-8: The Flowchart for Key Press Detection and Identification

Program 3-5 provides an implementation of the detection and identification algorithm in C language. We will exam it in details here. First for the initialization of the ports, Port 4 pins 3-0 are used for rows. The Port 4 pins 7-4 are used for columns. They are all configured as input digital pin to prevent accidental short circuit of two output pins. If output pins are driven high and low and two keys of the same column are pressed at the same time by accident, they will short the output low to output high of the adjacent pins and cause damages to these pins. To prevent this, all pins are configured as input pin and only one pin is configured as output pin at a time. Since only one pin is actively driving the row, shorting two rows will not damage the circuit. The input pins are configured with pull-up enabled so that when the connected keys are not pressed, they stay high and read as 1.

The key scanning function is a non-blocking function, meaning the function returns regardless of whether there is a key pressed or not. The function first drives all rows low and check to see if any key pressed. If no key is pressed, a zero is returned. Otherwise the code will proceed to check one row at a time by driving only one row low at a time and read the columns. If one of the columns is active, it will find out which column it is. With the combination of the active row and active column, the code will find out the key that is pressed and return a unique numeric code. The program below reads a 4x4 keypad and use the key code returned to set the tri-color LEDs. LED program is borrowed from P2-7 in Chapter 2.

Program 3-5: This program displays the pressed key on the tri-color LED.

```c
/* p3_5.c: Matrix keypad scanning
 *
 * This program scans a 4x4 matrix keypad and returns a unique number
 * for each key pressed.
 *
 * Port 4 7-4 are connected to the columns and Port 4 3-0 are connected
 * to the rows of the keypad.
 *
 * Tested with Keil 5.20 and MSP432 Device Family Pack V2.2.0.
 *
 */

#include "msp.h"

void delay(void);
void keypad_init(void);
char keypad_getkey(void);
void LED_init(void);
void LED_set(int value);

int main(void) {
    unsigned char key;

    keypad_init();
    LED_init();

    while(1) {
        key = keypad_getkey();  /* read the keypad */
        LED_set(key);           /* set LEDs according to the key code */
    }
}

/* this function initializes Port 4 that is connected to the keypad.
 * All pins are configured as GPIO input pin. The column pins have
 * the pull-up resistors enabled.
 */
void keypad_init(void) {
    P4->DIR = 0;
    P4->REN = 0xF0;     /* enable pull resistor for column pins */
    P4->OUT = 0xF0;     /* make column pins pull-ups */
}
```

```c
/*
 * This is a non-blocking function to read the keypad.
 * If a key is pressed, it returns a unique code for the key. Otherwise,
 * a zero is returned.
 * The upper nibble of Port 4 is used as input and connected to the columns.
 * Pull-up resistors are enabled so when the keys are not pressed, these pins
 * are pulled high.
 * The lower nibble of Port 4 is used as output that drives the keypad rows.
 * First all rows are driven low and the input pins are read. If no key is pressed,
 * they will read as all one because of the pull up resistors. If they are not
 * all one, some key is pressed.
 * If some key is pressed, the program proceeds to drive one row low at a time and
 * leave the rest of the rows inactive (float) then read the input pins.
 * Knowing which row is active and which column is active, the program
 * can decide which key is pressed.
 *
 * Only one row is driven so that if multiple keys are pressed and row pins are
 * shorted, the microcontroller will not be damaged. When the row is being
 * deactivated, it is driven high first otherwise the stray capacitance may keep the
 * inactive row low for some time.)
 */
char keypad_getkey(void) {
    int row, col;
    const char row_select[] = {0x01, 0x02, 0x04, 0x08}; /* one row is active */

    /* check to see any key pressed */
    P4->DIR |= 0x0F;              /* make all row pins output */
    P4->OUT &= ~0x0F;             /* drive all row pins low */
    delay();                      /* wait for signals to settle */
    col = P4->IN & 0xF0;          /* read all column pins */
    P4->OUT |= 0x0F;              /* drive all rows high before disable them */
    P4->DIR &= ~0x0F;             /* disable all row pins drive */
    if (col == 0xF0)              /* if all columns are high */
        return 0;                 /* no key pressed */

    /* If a key is pressed, it gets here to find out which key.
     * It activates one row at a time and read the input to see
     * which column is active. */
    for (row = 0; row < 4; row++) {
        P4->DIR &= 0x0F;                  /* disable all rows */
        P4->DIR |= row_select[row];       /* enable one row at a time */
        P4->OUT &= ~row_select[row];      /* drive the active row low */
        delay();                          /* wait for signal to settle */
        col = P4->IN & 0xF0;              /* read all columns */
        P4->OUT |= row_select[row];       /* drive the active row high */
        if (col != 0xF0) break; /* if one of the input is low, some key is pressed. */
    }
    P4->OUT |= 0x0F;                      /* drive all rows high before disable them */
    P4->DIR &= 0x0F;                      /* disable all rows */
    if (row == 4)
        return 0;                         /* if we get here, no key is pressed */

    /* gets here when one of the rows has key pressed, check which column it is */
    if (col == 0xE0) return row * 4 + 1;    /* key in column 0 */
    if (col == 0xD0) return row * 4 + 2;    /* key in column 1 */
    if (col == 0xB0) return row * 4 + 3;    /* key in column 2 */
    if (col == 0x70) return row * 4 + 4;    /* key in column 3 */
```

```
        return 0;    /* just to be safe */
}

/* Initialize tri-color LEDs on the LaunchPad board.
 * P2.0 - red
 * P2.1 - green
 * P2.2 - blue
 */
void LED_init(void) {
    P2->DIR = 0x07;             /* make LED pins output */
    P2->OUT &= ~0x07;           /* turn the LEDs off */
}

/* turn on or off the LEDs according to bit 2-0 of the value */
void LED_set(int value) {
    value &= 0x07;              /* only bit 2-0 are affected */
    P2->OUT = (P2->OUT & ~0x07) | value;
}

/* make a small delay */
void delay(void) {
}
```

Contact Bounce and Debounce

When a mechanical switch is closed or opened, the contacts do not make a clean transition instantaneously, rather the contacts open and close several times before they settle. This event is called contact bounce (see Figure 3-9). So it is possible when the program first detects a switch in the keypad is pressed but when interrogating which key is pressed, it would find no key pressed. This is the reason we have a return 0 after checking all the rows. Another problem manifested by contact bounce is that one key press may be recognized as multiple key presses by the program. Contact bounce also occurs when the switch is released. Because the switch contacts open and close several times before they settle, the program may detect a key press when the key is released.

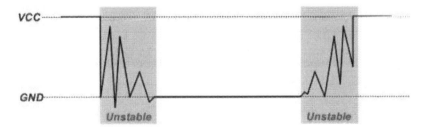

Figure 3-9: Switch contact bounces

For many applications, it is important that each key press is only recognized as one action. When you press a numeral key of a calculator, you expect to get only one digit. A contact bounce results in multiple digits entered with a single key press. A simple software solution is that when a transition of the contact state change is detected such as a key pressed or a key released, the software does a delay for about 10 – 20 ms to wait out the contact bounce. After the delay, the contacts should be settled and stable.

There are IC chips such as National Semiconductor's MM74C923 that incorporate keyboard scanning and decoding all in one chip. Such chips use combinations of counters and logic gates (no microprocessor) to implement the underlying concepts presented in Programs 3-4 and 3-5.

Review Questions

1. True or false. To see if any key is pressed, all rows are driven low.
2. If D3–D0 = 0111 is the data read from the columns, which column does the key pressed belong to?
3. True or false. Key press detection and key identification require two different processes.
4. In Figure 3-7, if the row has D3–D0 = 1110 and the columns are D7–D4 = 1110, which key is pressed?
5. True or false. To identify the key pressed, one row at a time is driven low.

Answers to Review Questions

Section 3-1

1. Input
2. Input
3. H-to-L
4. High
5. 0x80 and 0xC0

Section 3-2

1. True
2. Column 3
3. True
4. A
5. True

Chapter 4: UART Serial Port Programming

Computers transfer data in two ways: parallel and serial. In parallel data transfers, often eight or more lines (wire conductors) are used to transfer data to another device. In serial communication, the data is sent one bit at a time. Years ago, parallel data transfer was preferred for short distance because it may transfer multiple bits at the same time and provides higher throughput. As technology advances, the data rate of serial communication may exceed parallel communication while parallel communication still retains the disadvantages of the size and cost of cable and connector, the crosstalk between the data lines and the difficulty of synchronizing the arrival time of data lines at longer distance.

Serial communication and the study of associated chips are the topics of this chapter.

Section 4.1: Basics of Serial Communication

When a microprocessor communicates with the outside world it usually provides the data in byte-sized chunks. For parallel transfer, 8-bit data is transferred at the same time. For serial transfer, 8-bit data is transferred one bit at a time. Figure 4-1 diagrams serial versus parallel data transfers.

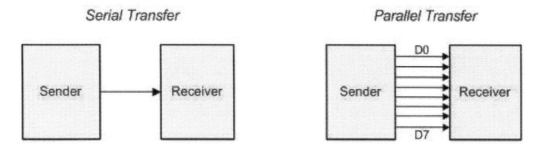

Figure 4-1: Serial vs. Parallel Data Transfer

The fact that in serial communication, a single data line is used instead of the 8-bit data line of parallel communication not only makes it much cheaper but also makes it possible for two computers located in two different cities to communicate.

For serial data communication to work, the byte of data must be grabbed from the 8-bit data bus of the microprocessor and converted to serial bits using a parallel-in-serial-out shift register; then it can be transmitted over a single data line. This also means that at the receiving end there must be a serial-in-parallel-out shift register to receive the serial data, pack it into a byte, and present it to the system at the receiving end. See Figures 4-2 and 4-3.

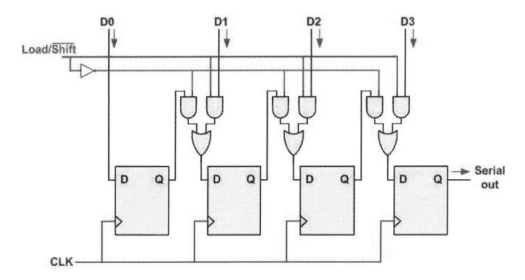

Figure 4-2: Parallel In Serial Out

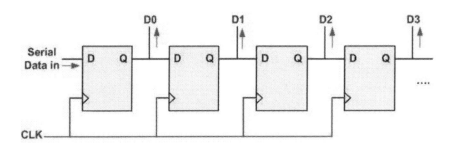

Figure 4-3: Serial In Parallel Out

When the distance is short, the digital signal can be transferred as it is on a simple wire and requires no modulation. This is how PC keyboards transfer data between the keyboard and the motherboard. However, for long-distance data transfers using communication lines such as a telephone, serial data communication requires a modem to modulate the data (convert from 0s and 1s to audio tones) before putting it on the transmission media and demodulate (convert from audio tones to 0s and 1s) at the receiving end.

Serial data communication uses two methods, asynchronous and synchronous. The synchronous method transfers the data with the clock and usually a block of data (characters) at a time while the asynchronous transfers without clock and usually a single byte at a time.

It is possible to write software to use either of these methods, but the programs can be tedious and long. For this reason, special IC chips are made by many manufacturers for serial data communications. These chips are commonly referred to as UART (universal asynchronous receiver-transmitter) and USART (universal synchronous-asynchronous receiver-transmitter). The COM port in the PC uses the UART. When this function incorporated into a microcontroller, it is often referred as SCI (Serial Communication Interface).

Half- and full-duplex transmission

In data transmission, a duplex transmission is one in which the data can be transmitted and received. This is in contrast to a simplex transmission such as printers, in which the computer only sends data. Duplex transmissions can be half or full duplex. If data is transmitted one way at a time, it is referred to as *half duplex*. If the data can go both ways at the same time, it is *full duplex*. Of course, full duplex requires two wire conductors for the data lines (in addition to ground), one for transmission and one for reception, in order to transfer and receive data simultaneously. See Figure 4-4.

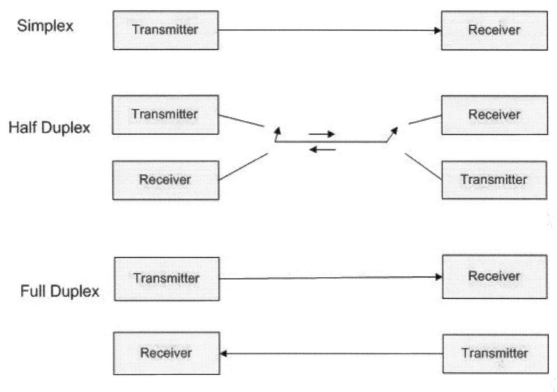

Figure 4-4: Simplex, Half-, and Full-Duplex Transfers

Asynchronous serial communication and data framing

The data coming in at the receiving end of the data line in a serial data transfer is all 0s and 1s; it is difficult to make sense of the data unless the sender and receiver agree on a set of rules, a *protocol*, on how the data is packed, how many bits constitute a character, and when the data begins and ends.

Start and stop bits

Asynchronous serial data communication is widely used for character-oriented transmissions. In the asynchronous method, each character, such as ASCII characters, is packed between start and stop bits. This is called *framing*. The start bit is always one bit but the stop bit can be one or two bits. The start bit is always a 0 (low) and the stop bit(s) is a 1 (high). For example, look at Figure 4-5 where the ASCII character "A", binary 0100 0001, is framed between the start bit and 2 stop bits. Notice that the LSB is sent out first.

81

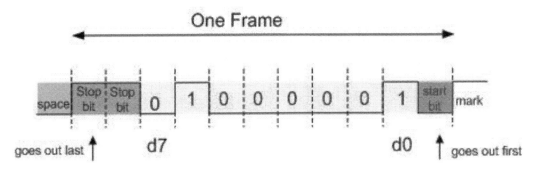

Figure 4-5: Framing ASCII "A" (0x41)

In Figure 4-5, when there is no data transfer, the signal stays at 1 (high), which is referred to as *mark*. The 0 (low) is referred to as *space*. Notice that the transmission begins with a start bit followed by D0, the LSB, then the rest of the bits until the MSB (D7), and finally, the 2 stop bits indicating the end of the character "A".

In asynchronous serial communications, peripheral chips can be programmed for data that is 5, 6, 7, or 8 bits wide. While in older systems ASCII characters were 7-bit, the modern systems usually send 8-bit data. The old Baud code uses 5- or 6-bit characters but they are rarely seen these days even though most of the hardware still supporting them. In some older systems, due to the slowness of the receiving mechanical device, 2 stop bits were used to give the device sufficient time to organize itself before transmission of the next byte. However, in modern PCs the use of 1 stop bit is common. Assuming that we are transferring a text file of ASCII characters using 1 stop bit, we have a total of 10 bits for each character since 8 bits are for the ASCII code, and 2 bits are for start and stop bits, respectively. Therefore, for each 8-bit character there are an extra 2 bits, or 12.5% overhead. (2/8 x100=12.5%)

Parity bit

In some systems in order to maintain data integrity, the parity bit of the character byte is included in the data frame. This means that for each character (7- or 8-bit, depending on the system) we have a single parity bit in addition to start and stop bits. The parity bit may be odd or even. In the case of an odd-parity the number of data bits, including the parity bit, has an odd number of 1s. Similarly, in an even-parity the total number of bits, including the parity bit, is even. For example, the ASCII character "A", binary 0100 0001, has 0 for the even-parity bit. UART chips allow programming of the parity bit for odd-, even-, and no-parity options, as we will see in the next section. If a system requires the parity, the parity bit is transmitted after the MSB, and is followed by the stop bit.

Data transfer rate

The rate of data transfer in serial data communication is stated in *bps* (bits per second). Another widely used terminology for bps is *Baudrate*. However, the baud and bps rates are not necessarily equal. This is due to the fact that baud rate is defined as number of signal changes per second. In modems, it is possible for each signal to transfer multiple bits of data. As far as the conductor wire is concerned, the baud rate and bps are the same, and for this reason in this book we use the terms bps and baud interchangeably.

82

Example 4-1

Calculate the total number of bits used in transferring 50 pages of text, each with 80 × 25 characters. Assume 8 bits per character and 1 stop bit.

Solution:

For each character a total of 10 bits is used, 8 bits for the character, 1 stop bit, and 1 start bit. Therefore, the total number of bits is 80 × 25 × 10 = 20,000 bits per page. For 50 pages, 1,000,000 bits will be transferred.

Example 4-2

Calculate the minimal time it takes to transfer the entire 50 pages of data in Example 4-1 using a baud rate of:

(a) 9600   (b) 57,600

Solution:

(a) 1,000,000 / 9600 = 104 seconds

(b) 1,000,000 / 57,600 = 17 seconds

Example 4-3

Calculate the time it takes to download a movie of 2 gigabytes using a telephone line. Assume 8 bits, 1 stop bit, no parity, and 57,600 baud rate.

Solution:

$2 \times 2^{30} \times 10 / 57,600 = 347,222$ seconds = ~4 days

---

RS232 and other serial I/O standards

To allow compatibility among data communication equipment made by various manufacturers, an interfacing standard called RS232 was proposed by the Electronics Industries Association (EIA) in 1960. It has several revisions through the years with an alphabet at the end to denote the revision number such as RS232C. RS stands for recommended standard. It was finally adopted as an EIA standard and renamed EIA232, later on TIA232 (Telecommunications Industry Association). In this book we refer to it simply as RS232. Today, RS232 is the most widely used serial I/O interfacing standard. However, since the standard was set long before the advent of the TTL logic family, the input and output voltage levels are not TTL compatible. In the RS232 at the receiver, a 1 is represented by −3 to −25 V, while the 0 bit is +3 to +25 V, making −3 to +3 undefined. For this reason, to connect any RS232 to a TTL-level chip (microprocessor or UART) we must use voltage converters such as MAX232 or MAX233 to convert the TTL logic levels to the RS232 voltage level, and vice versa. MAX232 and MAX233 IC chips are commonly referred to as line drivers. This is shown in Figures 4-6 and 4-7. The MAX232 has two sets of line drivers for transferring and receiving data, as shown in Figure 4-6. The line drivers used for TxD are called T1 and T2, while the line drivers for RxD are designated as R1 and R2. In many applications only one of each is used. Notice in MAX232 that the T1 line driver has a designation of T1in and T1out on pin numbers 11 and 14, respectively. The T1in pin is the TTL side and is connected to TxD of the USART, while T1out is the RS232 side that is connected to the RxD pin of the RS232 DB connector. The R1 line driver has a designation of R1in and R1out on pin numbers 13 and 12, respectively. The R1in (pin 13) is the RS232 side that is connected to the TxD pin of the RS232 DB connector, and R1out (pin 12) is the TTL side that is connected to the RxD pin of the USART.

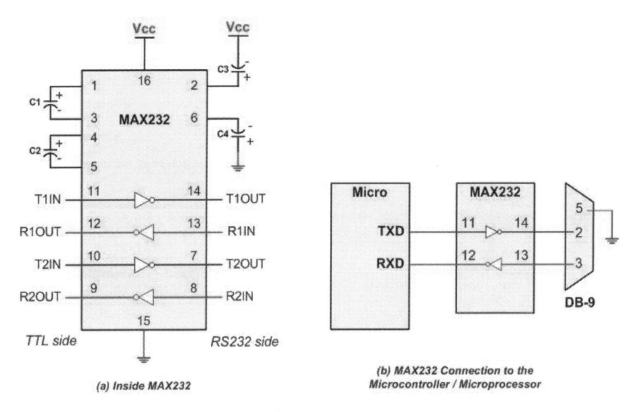

(a) Inside MAX232

(b) MAX232 Connection to the Microcontroller / Microprocessor

Figure 4-6: MAX232

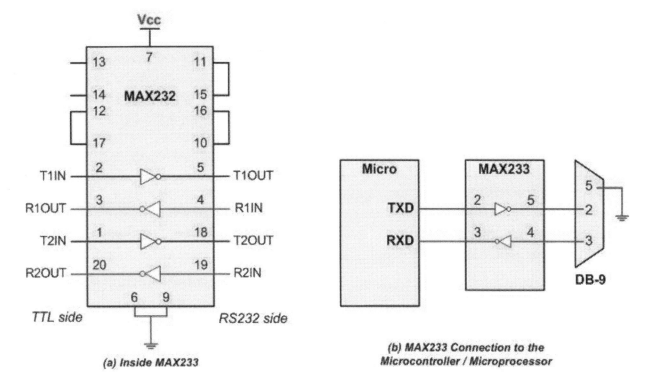

(a) Inside MAX233

(b) MAX233 Connection to the Microcontroller / Microprocessor

Figure 4-7: MAX233

MAX232 requires four capacitors of 1 μF. To save board space, some designers use the MAX233 chip from Maxim. The MAX233 performs the same job as the MAX232 but eliminates the need for capacitors. However, the MAX233 chip is much more expensive than the MAX232. See Figure 4-7 for MAX233 with no capacitor used.

RS232 pins

Table 4-1 provides the pins and their labels for the RS232 cable, commonly referred to as the DB-9 connector. The DB-9 male connector is shown in Figure 4-8.

Pin	Description
1	Data carrier detect (DCD)
2	Received data (RxD)
3	Transmitted data (TxD)
4	Data terminal ready (DTR)
5	Signal ground (GND)
6	Data set ready (DSR)
7	Request to send (RTS)
8	Clear to send (CTS)
9	Ring indicator (RI)

Table 4-1: RS232 Pins

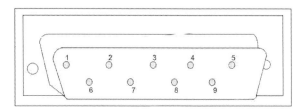

Figure 4-8: 9-Pin Male Connector

Data communication classification

Current terminology classifies data communication equipment as DTE (data terminal equipment) or DCE (data communication equipment). DTE refers to terminals and computers that send and receive data, while DCE refers to communication equipment, such as modems, that is responsible for transferring the data. Notice that all the RS232 pin function definitions of Table 4-1 are from the DTE point of view.

The simplest connection between two PCs (DTE and DTE) requires a minimum of three pins, TxD, RxD, and ground, as shown in Figure 4-9. Notice that the connection between two DTE devices, such as two PCs, requires pins 2 and 3 to be interchanged as shown in Figure 4-9. In looking at Figure 4-9, keep in mind that the RS232 signal definitions are from the point of view of DTE.

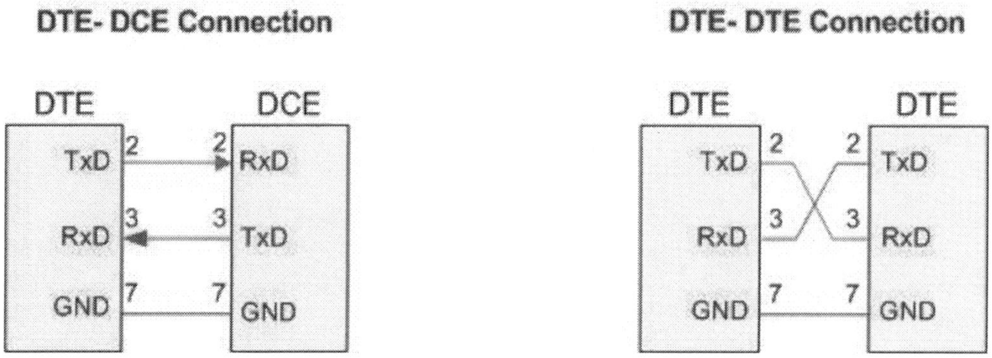

Figure 4-9: DTE-DCE and DTE-DTE Connections

Examining the RS232 handshaking signals

To ensure fast and reliable data transmission between two devices, the data transfer must be coordinated. Some of the pins of the RS-232 are used for handshaking signals. They are described below. Due to the fact that in serial data communication the receiving device may run out of room for more data at times, there must be a way to inform the sender to stop sending data. So some of these handshaking lines may be used for flow control.

1. **DTR (data terminal ready)**: When the terminal (or a PC COM port) is turned on, after going through a self-test, it sends out signal DTR to indicate that it is ready for communication. If there is something wrong with the COM port, this signal will not be activated. This is an active-low signal and can be used to inform the modem that the computer is alive and kicking. This is an output pin from DTE (PC COM port) and an input to the modem.

2. **DSR (data set ready):** When a DCE (modem) is turned on and has gone through the self-test, it asserts DSR to indicate that it is ready to communicate. Therefore, it is an output from the modem (DCE) and an input to the PC (DTE). This is an active-low signal. If for any reason the modem cannot make a connection to the telephone, this signal remains inactive, indicating to the PC (or terminal) that it cannot accept or send data.

3. **RTS (request to send):** When the DTE device (such as a PC) has data to transmit, it asserts RTS to signal the modem. RTS is an active-low output from the DTE and an input to the modem.

4. **CTS (clear to send):** In response to RTS, when the modem is ready to accept data for transmission, it sends out signal CTS to the DTE (PC) to indicate that it can accept data from the PC now. This input signal to the DTE is used by the DTE to start transmission.

5. **CD (carrier detect, or DCD, data carrier detect):** The modem asserts signal DCD to inform the DTE (PC) that a valid carrier signal from the other modem has been detected and that contact between it and the other modem is established. Therefore, DCD is an output from the modem and an input to the PC (DTE).

6. **RI (ring indicator):** An output from the modem (DCE) and an input to a PC (DTE) indicates that the telephone is ringing. It goes on and off in synchronization with the ring tone. Of the six handshake signals, this is the least often used, due to the fact that modems take care of answering the phone. However, if in a given system the PC is in charge of answering the phone, this signal can be used.

From the above description, PC and modem communication can be summarized as follows: While signals DTR and DSR are used by the PC and modem, respectively, to indicate that they are alive and well, it is RTS and CTS that actually control the flow of data. When the PC wants to send data it asserts RTS, and in response, if the modem is ready to accept the data, it sends back CTS. If not, the modem does not activate CTS, and the PC will have to wait until CTS goes active. RTS and CTS are also referred to as *hardware control flow signals*.

This concludes the description of the most important pins of the RS232 handshake signals plus TxD, RxD, and ground. Ground is also referred to as SG (signal ground). In the next section we will see serial communication programming for the microcontroller.

Review Questions

1. The transfer of data using parallel lines is _____ (more expensive, less expensive).
2. In communications between two PCs in New York and Dallas, we use _____ (serial, parallel) data communication.
3. In serial data communication, which method fits block-oriented data?
4. True or false. Sending data to a printer is duplex.
5. True or false. In duplex we must have two data lines.
6. The start and stop bits are used in the _____ (synchronous, asynchronous) method.
7. Assuming that we are transmitting letter "D", binary 100 0100, with odd-parity bit and 2 stop bits, show the sequence of bits transferred.
8. In Question 7, find the overhead due to framing.
9. Calculate the time it takes to transfer 400 characters as in Question 7 if we use 1200 bps. What percentage of time is used due to overhead?
10. True or false. RS232 is not TTL-compatible.

Section 4.2: Programming UART Ports

In this section, we examine the UART serial port registers of MSP432 ARM and show how to program them to transmit and receive data serially. The MSP432 ARM chips come with four on-chip UART ports. They are designated as eUSCI_A (Enhanced Universal Serial Communication Interface A). The eUSCI_A supports both UART and SPI. In this chapter we discuss the UART mode. In the MSP432

LaunchPad, the UART0 port of the MSP432 is connected to the on-board XDS110 emulator, which is connected to a USB connector. This XDS110 emulator performs three distinct functions:

a) The programming (downloading),
b) The debugging using JTAG, and
c) Use as a virtual COM port.

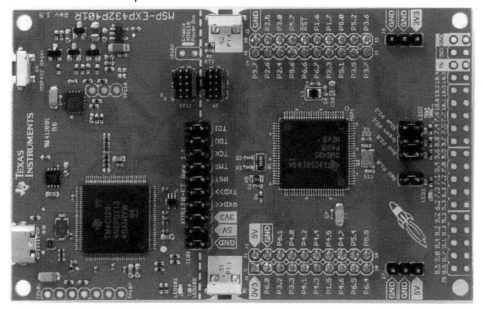

Figure 4-10: MSP432 LaunchPad board

When the USB cable connects the PC to the LaunchPad board, the device driver at the host PC establishes a virtual connection between the PC and the UART of the MSP432 device. On the LaunchPad the connection appears as UART0. On the host PC, it appears as a COM port and will work with communication software on the PC such as a terminal emulator. It is called a virtual connection because there is no need for an additional cable to make this connection.

Examining the datasheet of the MSP432 on LaunchPad board, we see the UART0 uses P1.2 and P1.3 pins as alternate functions for UART0_TXD and UART0_RXD, respectively. See Figure 4-11.

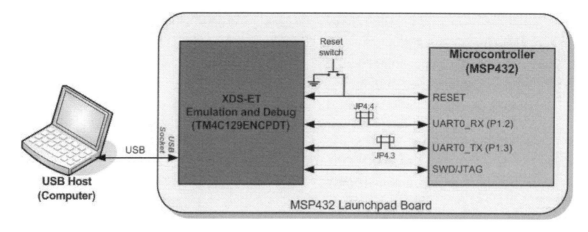

Figure 4-11: XDS110-ET emulator USB Port

As we mentioned earlier, the MSP432 can have up to 4 UART ports. They are designated as UCA0, UCA1, UCA2, and UCA3. For the sake of simplification, we refer to them as UART0 to UAR3. The following shows their Base addresses in the memory map:

- UART0 (UCA0) base address: 0x4000_1000
- UART1 (UCA1) base address: 0x4000_1400
- UART2 (UCA2) base address: 0x4000_1800
- UART3 (UCA3) base address: 0x4000_1C00

The exact address locations for some of the UART0 registers are shown below:

Register Name	Register Function	Register Address
UCA0CTLW0	Control Word 0	4000_1000
UCA0BRW	Baud Rate Control Word	4000_1006
UCA0STATW	Status	4000_100A
UCA0RXBUF	Receive Buffer	4000_100C
UCA0TXBUF	Transfer Buffer	4000_100E
UCA0IFG	Interrupt Flag	4000_101C

Table 4-2: Partial list of UART0 Registers and their addresses

Figure 4-12 shows the simplified block diagram of the UART units.

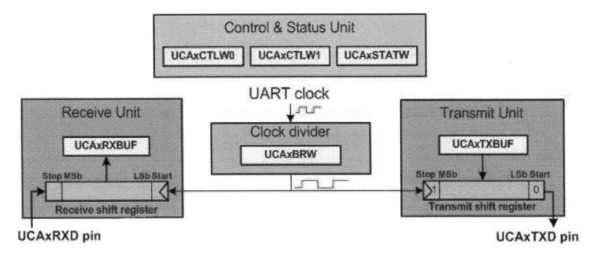

Figure 4-12: a Simplified Block Diagram of UART

In all microcontrollers, there are 4 groups of registers in UART peripherals:

1. **Configuration (Control) registers:** Before using the UART peripheral the configuration registers must be initialized. This sets some parameters of the communication including: Baud rate, word length, stop bit, interrupts (if needed). In MSP432 ARM microcontroller, some of the configuration registers are: UCAxCTLW0 *and UCAxBRW.*

2. ***Transmit and receive register:*** To send data, we simply write to the transmit register. The UART peripheral sends out the contents of the transfer register UCAxTXBUF through the serial transmit pin TX. The received data is stored in the receive register UCAxRXBUF.

3. ***Status register:*** the status register contains some flags which show the error in sending and receiving data including: the framing error, the parity and overrun errors, etc. It also contains the busy flag. The status register is named as UCAxSTATW in the MSP432 ARM.

4. ***Flag register:*** the flag register contains some flags which show the state of sending and receiving data including: the transmitter sent out the entire byte, the transmitter is ready for another byte of data, the receiver received a whole byte of data, etc. The Flag register is named as UCAxIFG in the MSP432 ARMs.

In this section, first, we will be using the UART0 as an example since a virtual connection is available on the MSP432 LaunchPad board.

The eUSCI_A supports both UART and SPI. To use eUSCI_A as UART, we need to clear UCSYNC bit (bit 8) in the Control Word 0 Register. All the registers are shared between UART mode and SPI mode but the bits in the registers may have different functions in different mode. For the rest of this chapter, only the UART functions of the registers are shown.

UART Control Word 0 (UCAxCTLW0) Register

We have several UART Control Registers. The most important among them is UART Control Register word 0 (USCAxCTLW0). It is a 16-bit registers. The Control Register 0 is used to select the data framing size and number of stop bits among other things. See Figure 4-13. The following gives the description of major bits of USCAxCTLW0 Control Word 0 register for UCAx to be used as asynchronous UART.

1. In order to modify some of the bits in the control registers we must place the UART in the software reset mode. This is done by setting D0 bit. Notice upon power-up reset, D0 is 1. After configuring the UART we must make D0=0 to take it out of reset so that it will work.

2. Bit D8 must be cleared to 0 for it to work as UART.

3. Bit D12 selects whether a character is 7 or 8-bit long. In this chapter we will use character size of 8 bits.

4. Bit D15 is used to enable parity generation and verification. Power-up reset default disables the parity and we will leave it at that in this textbook.

5. In transmitting/receiving data serially we use the default setting of D13=0 which means LSB goes out first.

6. The choice of number of stop bits is bit D11. Default is 1 stop bit and we leave it at that.

7. Bits D7-D6 are used to choose the clock source to Baud rate generator. To use 3MHz subsystem master clock (SMCLK) in MSP432, we must set D7-D6=10.

The other bits of the USCIAxCTLW0 registers are not of interest to us since we are using the UART in the Asynchronous mode without any multiprocessor option.

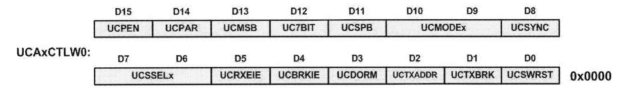

UCAxCTLW0:

Figure 4-13: UART ControlWord0 (UCAxCTLW0) register

Field	Bit	Description
UCPEN	D15	0b = Parity disabled 1b = Parity enabled. Parity bit is generated (UCAxTXD) and expected (UCAxRXD).
UCPAR	D14	0b = Odd parity 1b = Even parity
UCMSB	D13	0b = LSB first 1b = MSB first
UC7BIT	D12	0b = 8-bit data 1b = 7-bit data
UCSPB	D11	0b = One stop bit 1b = Two stop bits
UCMODEx	D10:9	00b = UART mode 01b = Idle-line multiprocessor mode 10b = Address-bit multiprocessor mode 11b = UART mode with automatic baud-rate detection
UCSYNC	D8	0b = Asynchronous mode 1b = Synchronous mode
UCSSELx	D7:6	00b = UCLK 01b = ACLK 10b = SMCLK 11b = SMCLK
UCRXEIE	D5	0b = Erroneous characters rejected and UCRXIFG is not set. 1b = Erroneous characters received set UCRXIFG.
UCBRKIE	D4	0b = Received break characters do not set UCRXIFG. 1b = Received break characters set UCRXIFG.
UCDORM	D3	0b = Not dormant. All received characters set UCRXIFG. 1b = Dormant. Only characters that are preceded by an idle-line or with address bit set UCRXIFG. In UART mode with automatic baud-rate detection, only the combination of a break and synch field sets UCRXIFG.
UCTXADDR	D2	0b = Next frame transmitted is data. 1b = Next frame transmitted is an address.
UCTXBRK	D1	0b = Next frame transmitted is not a break. 1b = Next frame transmitted is a break or a break/synch.
UCSWRST	D0	0b = Disabled. eUSCI_A reset released for operation. 1b = Enabled. eUSCI_A logic held in reset state.

Table 4-3: UART Control 0 Word (UCAxCTLW0) register

UART Control Word 1 (UCAxCTLW1) Register

Control Word 1 Register is used to program the deglitch digital filter. Deglitch is to ignore the small pulses shorter than the duration programmed in Table 4-4. See figure below.

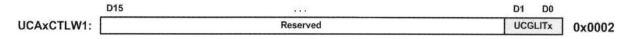

Figure 4-14: UART Control Word 1(UCAxCTLW1) register

Field	Bit	Description
Reserved	D15:1	Reserved
UCGLITx	D0	Deglitch time 00b = Approximately 2 ns 01b = Approximately 50 ns 10b = Approximately 100 ns 11b = Approximately 200 ns

Table 4-4: UART Control Word 1(UCAxCTLW1) register

Transmit clock and receive clock

The transmitter operates on the clock that runs at the Baud rate. For each clock pulse, one bit is transmitted. Because UART is asynchronous, the receiver needs to detect the falling edge of the start bit and sample the input near the center of the bit time so it has to run on a faster clock.

The clock source (BRCLK) of the UART clock circuit (often called Baud Rate Generator) is selected by the UCSSELx bits of UCAxCTLW register. For UART operation, the only valid selections are Auxiliary Clock (ACLK) and Subsystem Master Clock (SMCLK). The power-on reset Clock System configuration provides a 3 MHz SMCLK, which will be used for UART in this chapter.

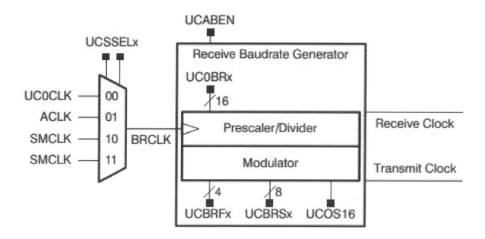

Figure 4-15: Clock Circuit of UART0

The UART clock circuit operates in two modes: Low-Frequency Baud Rate Mode and Oversampling Baud Rate Mode. The Oversampling mode requires complex calculations of the register settings and is meant for better data accuracy under noisy transmission. You may find the details in the MSP432 Technical Reference Manual. In this chapter, we will cover the Low-Frequency mode.

With Low-Frequency mode, the transmit clock is derived by BRCLK divided by the content of UCAxBRW register and the receive clock is the BRCLK.

Baud Rate and UCAxBRW Value

Two registers are used to set the Baud rate: They are UARTx Modulation Control word (UCIAxMCTLW) and UART Baud Rate word (UCIAxBRW) in which x=0, 1, 2, or 3 referring to UART0, UART1, UART2, or UART3. The details of these two registers are shown below:

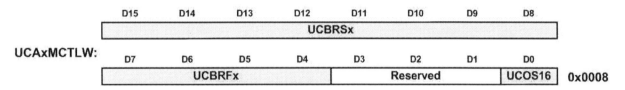

Figure 4-16: UCAxMCTLW (UCOS16=0 for non-oversampling)

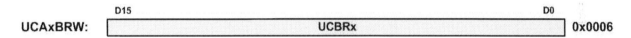

Figure 4-17: UCAxBRW

For the UART0 used in MSP432 LaunchPad board, their physical addresses are located at 0x4000_1006 and 0x4000_1008, respectively. Notice these registers are only 16 bits and each register takes two address locations in the memory map.

To operate in Low-Frequency mode, UCOS16 bit (D0) of UCAxMCTLW register should be cleared to disable the oversampling. When in Low-Frequency mode, the rest of the bits in UCAxMCTLW register are unimportant.

The Baud rate of UARTx is calculated by a simple formula if we disable the Oversampling.

$$Baud\ Rate = \frac{Clock}{UCAxBRW}$$

So if we use the Clock of 3MHz and UCAxBRW = 312, then

$$Baud\ Rate = \frac{3000000}{312} = 9615$$

This is more than the standard 9600 Baud. Because the UCAxBRW register can only hold integer numbers, we don't usually get the precise Baud rate we want. But the UART receiver synchronizes on the start bit of every byte, it will tolerate several percent of Baud rate error. We will discuss the Baud rate error calculation later. See Example 4-4.

Example 4-4

Assume the clock source of 3MHz is fed to UART0 Baud rate generator. Find the values for the divisor registers of UCA0BRW for a) 4800, b) 19,200, 38,400, and 115,200 Baud rates. Assume oversampling is disabled.

Solution:

$$BRW = \frac{Clock}{Baud\ Rate}$$

(a) 3MHz /4800= 625, USCIA0BRW = 625= 0x271

(b) 3MHz / 19200 = 156.25, USCIA0BRW = 156 = 0x9C

(a) 3MHz / 38400= 78.125, USCIA0BRW = 78 = 0x4E

(d) 3MHz / 115200 = 26.04, USCIA0BRW = 26 = 0x1A

Note: It must be noted that we can round up or round down the value loaded into the BRW register. Also notice that not using the oversampling is the default upon Reset.

Some of the standard Baud rates are 4,800, 9,600, 19,200, 38,400, and 115,200. Table 4-5Table 4-5 shows the BRW register values for the different baud rate for UART0 using default USOC16=0 and clock of 3 MHz.

Baud rate	BRW (in decimal)	BRW (in hex)
4,800	625	0x271
9,600	312	0x138
19,200	156	0x9C
38,400	78	0x4E
115,200	26	0x1A

Table 4-5: UART0 BRW Values for Some Standard Baud Rates using default OSCO16=0 and Clock of 3 MHz

Baud rate error calculation

In calculating the baud rate, we have used the integer number for the UCAxBRW register values because UCAxBRW register can only hold integer values. By rounding the decimal fraction portion of the calculated values we run the risk of introducing error into the Baud rate. One way to calculate this error is to use the following formula.

Error = (Calculated value for the BRW – Integer part)/Integer part

See Example 4-5.

Example 4-5

Calculate the Baud rate error for Example 4-4.

Solution:

(a) BRW=3MHz /4800= 625, Error = (625 − 625)/ 625 x100 = 0%

(b) BRW=3MHz / 19200 = 156.25, Error = (156.25 − 156)/ 156 x100 = 0.1%

(a) BRW=3MHz / 38400= 78.125, Error = (78.125 − 78)/ 78 x100 = 0.1%

(d) BRW=3MHz / 115200 = 26.04, Error = (26.04 − 26)/ 26 x100 = 0.15%

(e) BRW=3MHz / 9600 = 312.5, Error = (312.5 − 312)/ 312 x100 = 0.16%

For the transmission to work properly, the error should be no more than few percents.

UART Data Registers

To transmit a byte of data we must place it in UART UCAxTXBUF register. It must be noted that a write to this register initiates a transmission from the UART. The received byte is placed in UCAxRXBUF register and must be retrieved by reading it before it is lost. Notice these are 16-bit registers but only the lower 8 bits are used.

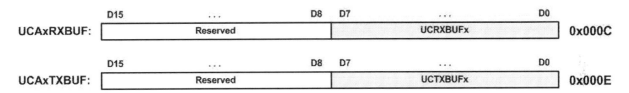

Figure 4-18: UART TX and RX Buffer registers

UART Status (UCAxSTATW) Register

The UART status register UCAxSTATW is a 16-bitregister. The most important bits of UART status register are the receive error bits. Three possible receive errors are posted in the Status Register:

Framing Error – A stop bit was not detected where it should be.

Overrun Error –A character is received before the previous character was read.

Parity Error – When parity is enabled and received character parity bit is in error.

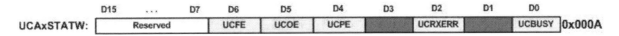

Figure 4- 19: UART Status Register (UCAxSTATW)

95

Field	Bit	Description
Reserved	D15:8	Reserved
UCFE	D6	Framing error flag. UCFE is cleared when UCAxRXBUF is read. 0b = No error 1b = Character received with low stop bit
UCOE	D5	Overrun error flag. This bit is set when a character is transferred into UCAxRXBUF before the previous character was read. UCOE is cleared automatically when UCxRXBUF is read. 0b = No error 1b = Overrun error occurred
UCPE	D4	Parity error flag. When UCPEN = 0, UCPE is read as 0. UCPE is cleared when UCAxRXBUF is read. 0b = No error 1b = Character received with parity error
UCRXERR	D2	Receive error flag. This bit indicates a character was received with one or more errors. When UCRXERR = 1, on or more error flags, UCFE, UCPE, or UCOE is also set. UCRXERR is cleared when UCAxRXBUF is read. 0b = No receive errors detected 1b = Receive error detected
UCBUSY	D0	eUSCI_A busy. This bit indicates if a transmit or receive operation is in progress. 0b = eUSCI_A inactive 1b = eUSCI_A transmitting or receiving

Table 4-6: UART Status Register (UCAxSTATW)

UART Interrupt Flag (UCAxIFG) Register

Although the flags and the register are named interrupt flag, they are useful even when interrupt is not used. In fact, the interrupt flags are status bits that may generate interrupt. For each interrupt flag, there is a corresponding interrupt enable bit in the UCAxIE register. Only when the bit in UCAxIE register is set, an active interrupt flag will generate an interrupt. We will discuss interrupt in Chapter 6. Before that, we will leave the interrupt enable bits in their default disabled state.

We will look into three of the four interrupt flags: UCTXCPTIFG, UCTXIFG, and UCRXIFG.

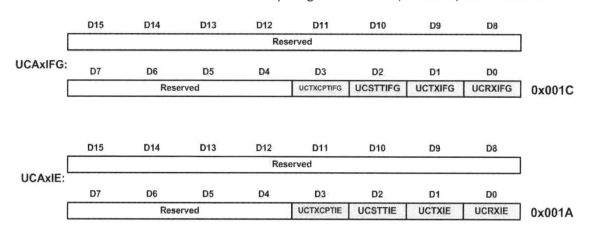

Figure 4-20: UART Interrupt Flag (UCAxIFG) and Interrupt Enable (UCAxIE) Registers

The double buffering of the transmit data

If you study Figure 4-12 carefully, you will see that there are two registers for transmitter, the UART Transmit Buffer Register (UCAxTXBUF) and the transmit shift register. The transmit shift register is an internal register whose job is to get the data from UCAxTXBUF register, frame it with the start and stop bits, and send it out one bit at a time via the UART TxD pin. Notice that the transmit shift register is a parallel-in-serial-out shifter and is not accessible by the program. The program writes the data into UCAxTXBUF register. When the transmit shift register is empty, the content of UCAxTXBUF register is loaded into the shift register automatically and the UCAxTXBUF register becomes empty.

The Transmit Flags

There are two transmit flags: the transmit buffer register empty flag (UCTXIFG) and the transmit complete flag (UCTXCPTIFG). The transmit buffer register empty flag (UCTXIFG) indicates that the transmit buffer register is empty and can take the next byte of data. When transmit buffer register empty flag is set, the transmit shift register may be transmitting the last byte of data. If we monitor this flag and write the next byte of data into the transmit buffer register while the shift register is shifting out the last byte, we could achieve the highest throughput of sending out data bytes back-to-back without a gap in between.

The transmit complete flag (UCTXCPTIFG) specifies that the transmit shift register is empty (so is the transmit buffer register otherwise its content will be loaded into the shift register). This flag is used so that the program does not suspend or shut down the transmitter in the middle of a byte. It is often used in debugging.

The double buffering of the receive data and the Receive Flag

The receiver is double buffered as well. The internal serial-in-parallel-out receive shift register receives data via the UART RxD pin. When the receive shift register is full (a byte of data is received), the start/stop bits are removed and the data is automatically transferred to the UART Receive Buffer Register (UCAxRXBUF) and the receive buffer full flag (UCRXIFG) is set, thus allows the receive shift register to accept the next byte immediately. The program should monitor the receive buffer full flag and read the data received as soon as possible. If the next byte of data is completely shifted into the receive shift register before the last byte of data is read from the receive buffer register, the data is lost and the overrun error (UCOE) bit is set in the Status register (UCAxSTATW).

Enabling UART

The UART is powered up in reset state. To configure the UART properly, you need to put it in the reset state if it is not already in that state. To put the UART in reset state, the UCSWRST bit should be set to 1 in UCAxCTLW0 register. After the UART is properly configured, this bit should be cleared to make the UART operational.

The GPIO pins used for UART TxD and RxD

In addition to the UART registers setup, we must also configure the I/O pins used for UART for their alternate functions. In the case of UART, we need to set up I/O pins for the alternate functions of TXD and RXD signals. In the last two chapters we used GPIO as simple I/O. We showed the minimum configuration for each port as simple I/O. When I/O pins are used for their alternate peripheral functions such as UART, Timer, and ADC, we need to change the values of the PxSEL1:PxSEL0 registers. To use a pin as simple I/O, we must choose PxSEL1:PXSEL0=00 option. Upon reset, all the pins of ports P1-P10 are configured as simple I/O. For the eight pins that may be used for UART, the PxSEL1=0 and PxSEL0=1 option allows them to be used for RXD or TXD signals. See Table 4-7.

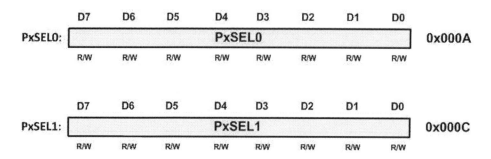

Figure 4-21: PxSEL1 and PxSEL0 Alternate Function Selection registers

I/O pin	Function	PxSEL1=0	PxSEL0=1
P1.2	UCA0RXD	P1SEL1=00000000	P1SEL0=00000100
P1.3	UCA0TXD	P1SEL1=00000000	P1SEL0=00001000
FOR UART0:		P1SEL1=0x00	P1SEL0=00001100=0x0C
P2.2	UCA1RXD	P2SEL1=00000000	P2SEL0=00000100
P2.3	UCA1TXD	P2SEL1=00000000	P2SEL0=00001000
For UART1		P2SEL1=0x00	P2SEL0=00001100=0x0C
P3.2	UCA2RXD	P3SEL1=00000000	P3SEL0=00000100
P3.3	UCA2TXD	P3SEL1=00000000	P3SEL0=00001000
For UART2		P3SEL1=0x00	P3SEL0=00001100=0x0C
P9.6	UCA3RXD	P9SEL1=00000000	P9SEL0=01000000
P9.7	UCA3TXD	P9SEL1=00000000	P9SEL0=10000000
For UART3		P9SEL1=0x00	P9SEL0=11000000=0xC0

Table 4-7: Pins available for UARTs

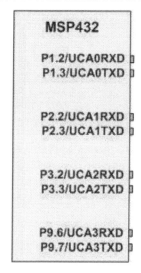

Figure 4-22: UART pins in MSP432

Steps for transmitting data

Here are the steps to configure the UART0 and transmit a byte of data for MSP432 LaunchPad board:

1) Put the UART in software reset state by clearing the D0 bit (UCSWRST=0) of UCA0CTLW0 register.
2) Clear bit 0 of UCA0MTLW register to disable oversampling mode.
3) Set the Baud rate for UART0 by using UCA0BRW register.
4) Configure the control register value for 1 stop bit, no parity, SMCLK clock source, and 8-bit data size by writing 0x0081 for the UCA0CTLW0 register.
5) Select the alternate functions for P1.2 (UCA0RXD) and P1.3 (UCA0TXD) pins for UART.
6) Enable the UART by disabling software reset mode by clearing the D0 (UCSWRST=0) bit of UCA0CTLW0 register. This is the opposite of step 1.
7) Monitor the UCTXIFG flag bit of the UCA0IFG register (for going HIGH) and wait for UART0 transmit buffer empty.
8) Write a byte of data to UCA0TXBUF buffer register to be transmitted.
9) To transmit the next character, go to step 7.

Program 4-1 sends the characters "YES" to the terminal emulator program (TeraTerminal) on a PC. You need to install TeraTerminal (or other terminal emulator program such as HyperTerminal or Putty) on your PC to receive the output. For TeraTerminal download and tutorial see:

http://microdigitaled.com/tutorials/Tera_Terminal.pdf

Program 4-1: UART0 Transmit

```
/* p4_1.c UART0 transmit
 *
 * Sending string "YES" to UART0 on MSP432 LaunchPad.
 * The UART0 is connected to XDS110 on the LaunchPad and it has
 * a virtual connection to the host PC COM port.
 * Use TeraTerm to see the message "YES" on a PC.
 *
 * By default the subsystem master clock is 3 MHz.
 * Setting EUSCI_A0->BRW=26 with oversampling disabled yields 115200 Baud.
 *
 * Tested with Keil 5.20 and MSP432 Device Family Pack V2.2.0.
 */

#include "msp.h"

void UART0_init(void);
void delayMs(int n);

int main(void) {
    UART0_init();
    while (1) {
        while(!(EUSCI_A0->IFG & 0x02)) { }  /* wait for transmit buffer empty */
```

```
        EUSCI_A0->TXBUF = 'Y';              /* send a char */
        while(!(EUSCI_A0->IFG & 0x02)) { }
        EUSCI_A0->TXBUF = 'e';              /* send a char */
        while(!(EUSCI_A0->IFG & 0x02)) { }
        EUSCI_A0->TXBUF = 's';              /* send a char */
        delayMs(2);                         /* leave a gap between messages */
    }
}

void UART0_init(void) {
    EUSCI_A0->CTLW0 |= 1;        /* put in reset mode for config */
    EUSCI_A0->MCTLW = 0;         /* disable oversampling */
    EUSCI_A0->CTLW0 = 0x0081;    /* 1 stop bit, no parity, SMCLK, 8-bit data */
    EUSCI_A0->BRW = 26;          /* 3,000,000 / 115200 = 26 */
    P1->SEL0 |= 0x0C;            /* P1.3, P1.2 for UART */
    P1->SEL1 &= ~0x0C;
    EUSCI_A0->CTLW0 &= ~1;       /* take UART out of reset mode */
}

/* delay milliseconds when system clock is at 3 MHz */
void delayMs(int n) {
    int i, j;

    for (j = 0; j < n; j++)
        for (i = 250; i > 0; i--);          /* Delay */
}
```

Importance of the UCTXIFG (Transmit buffer empty interrupt flag)

To understand the importance of the role of UCTXIFG, look at the following sequence of steps that theMSP432 goes through in transmitting a character via TXD:

1. The byte character to be transmitted is written into the UCAxTXBUF register.
2. The UCTXIFG flag is set to 0 internally to indicate that the UCAxTXBUF register holds a byte of data.
3. The transmit shift register offloads the byte from the UCAxTXBUF register and begins to transfer the byte.
4. The UCTXIFG flag is set to 1 to indicate that the UCAxTXBUF register is ready to accept another byte.

By monitoring the UCTXIFG flag, we make sure that we are not overwriting the UCAxTXBUF register. If we write another byte into the UCAxTXBUF register before the data is transferred to the transmit shift register, the byte that was in the UCAxTXBUF register will be lost.

Steps for receiving data

Here are the steps to receive a byte of data from UART0 in the MSP432 LaunchPad board:

1) Put the UART in software reset state by clearing the D0 bit (UCSWRST=0) of UCA0CTLW0 register.
2) Clear bit 0 of UCA0MTLW register to disable oversampling mode.
3) Set the Baud rate for UART0 by using UCA0BRW register.

4) Configure the control register value for 1 stop bit, no parity, SMCLK clock source, and 8-bit data size by writing 0x0081 for the UCA0CTLW0 register.

5) Select the alternate functions for P1.2 (UCA0RXD) and P1.3 (UCA0TXD) pins for UART.

6) Enable the UART by disabling software reset mode by clearing the D0 (UCSWRST=0) bit of UCA0CTLW0 register. This is the opposite of step 1.

7) Monitor the UCRXIFG flag bit of the UCA0IFG register and wait for UART0 receive buffer is full meaning it has received a byte of data.

8) Read the received byte from UCA0RXBUF data register and save it.

9) To receive another character, go to step 7.

Notice that when UCARXIF goes HIGH, we read a byte of data from UCA0RXBUF data register. By reading this register the Receive flag of UCRXIFG is cleared.

Note

The configuration steps (steps 1 to 6) are identical for receiving and sending data.

Program 4-2 receives the bytes of data via UART0 and displays it on the tri-color LEDs.

Program 4-2: UART0 Receive

```
/* p4_2.c UART0 Receive
 *
 * Receiving any key from terminal emulator (TeraTerm) of the
 * host PC to the UART0 on MSP432 LaunchPad. The UART0 is
 * is connected to XDS110 on the LaunchPad and it has
 * a virtual connection to the host PC COM port.
 * Launch TeraTerm on a PC and hit any key.
 * The LED program from P2_7 of Chapter 2 is used to turn
 * on the tri-color LEDs according to the key received.
 *
 * By default the subsystem master clock is 3 MHz.
 * Setting EUSCI_A0->BRW=26 with oversampling disabled yields 115200 Baud.
 *
 * Tested with Keil 5.20 and MSP432 Device Family Pack V2.2.0.
 */

#include "msp.h"

void UART0_init(void);

int main(void) {
    UART0_init();

    /* initialize P2.2-P2.0 for tri-color LEDs */
    P2->SEL1 &= ~7;          /* configure P2.2-P2.0 as simple I/O */
    P2->SEL0 &= ~7;
    P2->DIR |= 7;            /* P2.2-2.0 set as output */
```

```
    while (1) {
        while(!(EUSCI_A0->IFG & 0x01)) { }  /* wait until receive buffer is full */
        P2->OUT = EUSCI_A0->RXBUF;          /* read the receive char and set the LEDs */
    }
}

void UART0_init(void) {
    EUSCI_A0->CTLW0 |= 1;          /* put in reset mode for config */
    EUSCI_A0->MCTLW = 0;           /* disable oversampling */
    EUSCI_A0->CTLW0 = 0x0081;      /* 1 stop bit, no parity, SMCLK, 8-bit data */
    EUSCI_A0->BRW = 26;            /* 3,000,000 / 115200 = 26 */
    P1->SEL0 |= 0x0C;              /* P1.3, P1.2 for UART */
    P1->SEL1 &= ~0x0C;
    EUSCI_A0->CTLW0 &= ~1;         /* take UART out of reset mode */
}
```

Importance of the UCRXIF (Receive) Flag) bit

In receiving byte via its RXD pin, the MSP432 goes through the following steps:

1. The receiver's shift register receives the start bit indicating that the next bit is the first bit of the character byte it is about to receive.
2. The 8-bit character is received one bit at time. When the last bit is received, a byte is formed and placed in UCA0RXBUF data register and the UCRXIFG is set to 1, indicating that an entire byte has been received and must be picked up before it gets overwritten by another incoming byte.
3. By checking the UCRXIFG flag when it is raised, we know that a character has been received and is sitting in the UCA0RXBUF register. We read the UCA0RXBUF register content and save it to a safe place in some other register or memory before it is lost.

Using UART1, UART2 or UART3 port

The previous two programs showed how to use the UART0 on MSP432 LaunchPad board, which is connected to the host computer through the XDS110 Emulator USB cable. If you like to use UART1, UART2, or UART3 port for communication purpose, you may connect the TXD and RXD pins to the RXD and TXD pins of the other microcontroller directly provided they have the same 3.3V signal level. If you are going to connect them to a PC, you will need a USB-to-Serial module (or cable). One side of the USB-to-Serial module should be 3.3V signal level for TXD and RXD and is connected to the UARTx pins on MSP432 LaunchPad board. The other side is USB port connected to the PC USB port. See these links for some 3.3V compatible products:

https://www.sparkfun.com/products/9893, https://www.sparkfun.com/products/9717,

http://www.adafruit.com/products/284 or http://www.adafruit.com/products/70.

Make sure you are using a 3.3V signal level converter. Many TTL level serial to USB converters produce output higher than 3.6V. They may appear functional for a short time but will damage the MSP432 input pins.

Program 4-3 is modified from Program 4-1 to use UART2. Program 4-3 also demonstrates how to initialize an array of characters and send the character string to UART.

Program 4-3: Sending "Hello" to TeraTerm via UART2

```
/* p4_3.c UART2 transmit
 * Sending a string "Hello\r\n" to UART2 on MSP432 LaunchPad.
 * The UART2 is connected to P3.2 (RXD) and P3.3 (TXD) on the LaunchPad.
 * A 3.3V signal level to USB cable is used to connect to
 * the host PC COM port.
 * Use TeraTerm to see the message "Hello" on a PC.
 *
 * By default the subsystem master clock is 3 MHz.
 * Setting EUSCI_A2->BRW=26 with oversampling disabled yields 115200 Baud.
 *
 * Tested with Keil 5.20 and MSP432 Device Family Pack V2.2.0.
 */

#include "msp.h"

void UART2_init(void);
void delayMs(int n);

int main(void) {
    char message[] = "Hello\r\n";
    int i;

    UART2_init();

    while (1) {
        for (i = 0; i < 7; i++) {
            while(!(EUSCI_A2->IFG & 0x02)) { }  /* wait for transmit buffer empty */
            EUSCI_A2->TXBUF = message[i];       /* send a char */
        }
        delayMs(10); /* leave a gap between messages */
    }
}

void UART2_init(void) {
    EUSCI_A2->CTLW0 |= 1;        /* put in reset mode for config */
    EUSCI_A2->MCTLW = 0;         /* disable oversampling */
    EUSCI_A2->CTLW0 = 0x0081;    /* 1 stop bit, no parity, SMCLK, 8-bit data */
    EUSCI_A2->BRW = 26;          /* 3,000,000 / 115200 = 26 */
    P3->SEL0 |= 0x0C;            /* P1.3, P1.2 for UART */
    P3->SEL1 &= ~0x0C;
    EUSCI_A2->CTLW0 &= ~1;       /* take UART out of reset mode */
}

/* delay milliseconds when system clock is at 3 MHz */
void delayMs(int n) {
    int i, j;
    for (j = 0; j < n; j++)
        for (i = 250; i > 0; i--);   /* Delay */
}
```

Program 4-4 combines the UART transmit with UART receive. When a key on the PC is pressed with a terminal emulator program, the key character is sent to MSP432 LaunchPad board. The received character is sent back out through UART to the terminal emulator.

Program 4-4: Echoing the received data from UART2

```c
/* p4_4.c UART2 echo
 *
 * This program receives a character from UART2 receiver
 * then sends it back through UART2.
 * The UART2 is connected to P3.2 (RXD) and P3.3 (TXD) on the LaunchPad.
 * A 3.3V signal level to USB cable is used to connect to
 * the host PC COM port.
 *
 * By default the subsystem master clock is 3 MHz.
 * Setting EUSCI_A2->BRW=26 with oversampling disabled yields 115200 Baud.
 *
 * Tested with Keil 5.20 and MSP432 Device Family Pack V2.2.0.
 *
 */

#include "msp.h"

void UART2_init(void);

int main(void) {
    char c;

    UART2_init();

    while (1) {
        while(!(EUSCI_A2->IFG & 0x01)) { }      /* wait until receive buffer is full */
        c = EUSCI_A2->RXBUF;                    /* read the receive char */

        while(!(EUSCI_A2->IFG&0x02)) { }        /* wait for transmit buffer empty */
        EUSCI_A2->TXBUF = c;                    /* send the char */
    }
}

void UART2_init(void)
{
    EUSCI_A2->CTLW0 |= 1;          /* put in reset mode for config */
    EUSCI_A2->MCTLW = 0;           /* disable oversampling */
    EUSCI_A2->CTLW0 = 0x0081;      /* 1 stop bit, no parity, SMCLK, 8-bit data */
    EUSCI_A2->BRW = 26;            /* 3,000,000 / 115200 = 26 */
    P3->SEL0 |= 0x0C;              /* P1.3, P1.2 for UART */
    P3->SEL1 &= ~0x0C;
    EUSCI_A2->CTLW0 &= ~1;         /* take UART out of reset mode */
}
```

Interrupt-based data transfer

By now you might have noticed that it is a waste of the microcontroller's time to poll the UCTXIFG and UCRXIFG flags because while the CPU is polling the flags, it is not doing anything productive. In order to avoid wasting the microcontroller's time we use interrupt instead of polling. In Chapter 6, we will show how to use interrupts to program the MSP432's serial communication port.

Review Questions

1. The MSP432 LaunchPad comes with maximum of _____ on-chip UARTs.
2. In MSP432 LaunchPad board, pins ___ and ___ are used for RXD and TXD of UART0.
3. Which register is used to set the data size and number of stop bits?
4. How do we know if the transmit buffer is empty before we load in another byte?
5. How do we know if a new byte has been received?

Section 4.3: Using C Library Console I/O

C library provides some standard console I/O functions that are convenient for use such as getchar(), putchar(), gets(), puts(), printf(), and scanf(). These functions rely on the hardware to provide input and output. In the Keil MDK-ARM, the hardware interface is handled by two functions: fgetc() and fputc(). The embedded programmers are required to implement these two functions for I/O. The implementation of these functions are usually in the part of the software named Board Support Package (BSP). In the example program P4.5 below, we use UART0 as the console and direct fgetc() and fputc() to UART0Rx() and UART0Tx() so all the console I/O will use UART0 which is connected to the host PC by the virtual console of the XDS110 debugger on the MSP432 LaunchPad. Using a terminal emulator like TeraTerm will allow the user interface to the console I/O of the embedded program.

Program 4-5: C library Console I/O using UART0

```
/* p4_5.c C library Console I/O using UART0
 *
 * This program demonstrates the use of C library console I/O.
 * The functions fputc() and fgetc() are implemented using
 * UART0Tx() and UART0Rx() for character I/O.
 * In the fgetc(), the received charater is echoed and if a '\r'
 * is received, it is substituted by a '\n' but both characters are
 * echoed.
 * In fputc() and fgetc(), the file descripter is not checked. All
 * file I/O's are directed to the console.
 *
 * By default the subsystem master clock is 3 MHz.
 * Setting EUSCI_A0->BRW=26 with oversampling disabled yields 115200 Baud.
 *
 * Tested with Keil 5.20 and MSP432 Device Family Pack V2.2.0.
 */

#include "msp.h"
#include <stdio.h>

void UART0_init(void);
```

```c
unsigned char UART0Rx(void);
int UART0Tx(unsigned char c);

int main(void) {
    int n;
    char str[80];

    UART0_init();

    printf("Test stdio library console I/O functions\r\n");
    fprintf(stdout, "    test for stdout\r\n");
    fprintf(stderr, "    test for stderr\r\n");

    while (1) {
        printf("please enter a number: ");
        scanf("%d", &n);
        printf("the number entered is: %d\r\n", n);
        printf("please type a string: ");
        gets(str);
        printf("the string entered is: ");
        puts(str);
        printf("\r\n");
    }
}

/* initialize UART0 to 115200 Baud at 3 MHz system clock */
void UART0_init(void) {
    EUSCI_A0->CTLW0 |= 1;        /* put in reset mode for config */
    EUSCI_A0->MCTLW = 0;         /* disable oversampling */
    EUSCI_A0->CTLW0 = 0x0081;    /* 1 stop bit, no parity, SMCLK, 8-bit data */
    EUSCI_A0->BRW = 26;          /* 3000000 / 115200 = 26 */
    P1->SEL0 |= 0x0C;            /* P1.3, P1.2 for UART */
    P1->SEL1 &= ~0x0C;
    EUSCI_A0->CTLW0 &= ~1;       /* take UART out of reset mode */
}

/* read a character from UART0 */
unsigned char UART0Rx(void) {
    char c;

    while(!(EUSCI_A0->IFG & 0x01)) ;
    c = EUSCI_A0->RXBUF;
    return c;
}

/* write a character to UART */
int UART0Tx(unsigned char c) {
    while(!(EUSCI_A0->IFG&0x02)) ;
    EUSCI_A0->TXBUF = c;
    return c;
}

/* The code below is the interface to the C standard I/O library.
 * All the I/O are directed to the console, which is UART0.
 */
struct __FILE { int handle; };
FILE __stdin = {0};
```

```
FILE __stdout = {1};
FILE __stderr = {2};

/* Called by C library console/file input
 * This function echoes the character received.
 * If the character is '\r', it is substituted by '\n'.
 */
int fgetc(FILE *f) {
    int c;

    c = UART0Rx();        /* read the character from console */

    if (c == '\r') {      /* if '\r', replace with '\n' */
        UART0Tx(c);       /* echo */
        c = '\n';
    }

    UART0Tx(c);           /* echo */

    return c;
}

/* Called by C library console/file output */
int fputc(int c, FILE *f) {
    return UART0Tx(c);  /* write the character to console */
}
```

Answer to Review Questions

Section 4-1

1. more expensive
2. serial
3. synchronous
4. False; it is simplex.
5. True
6. Asynchronous
7. With 100 0100 binary we have 1 as the odd-parity bit. The bits as transmitted in the sequence are:

(a) 0 (start bit)	(b) 0	(c) 0	(d) 1
(e) 0	(f) 0	(g) 0	(h) 1
(i) 1 (parity)	(j) 1 (first stop bit)	(k) 1 (second stop bit)

8. 4 bits (start, parity, stop, stop)
9. $400 \times 11 = 4400$ bits total bits transmitted. $4400/1200 = 3.667$ seconds, 4 bit (overhead) /7 bit (data)= 57%.
10. True

Section 4-2

1. 4
2. RXD is P1.2 and TXD P1.3
3. UCAxCTLW0
4. The UCTXIFG flag in the UCAxIFG register is high when the transmit buffer is empty.
5. The UCRXIFG flag in the UCAxIFG register goes high when a new byte is received.

Chapter 5: MSP432 ARM Timer Programming

In Section 5-0, the counter and timer concepts are reviewed. Section 5-1 covers the System Tick Timer which is available in all ARM Cortex microcontrollers. In Section 5-2, delays are made using Timer32 timers. Section 5-3 shows 16-bit Timer_A timers to make delays. In Section 5-4, input capturing is discussed and the pulse width and frequency measuring are covered. Section 5-5 shows event counter feature. The Output Compare mode is studied in Section 5-6.

Section 5.0: Introduction to counters and timers

In the digital design course you connected many flip flops (FFs) together to create up counter/down counter. For example, connecting 3 FFs together we can count up to 7 (000-111 in binary). This is called *3-bit counter*. The same way, to create a 4-bit counter (counting up to 15, or 0000-1111 in binary) we need 4 FFs. For 16-bit counter, we need 16 FFs and it counts up to $2^{16} - 1$. Figure 5-1 shows the T flip flop connection and pulse outputs for all three flip flops.

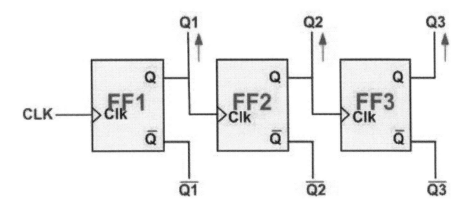

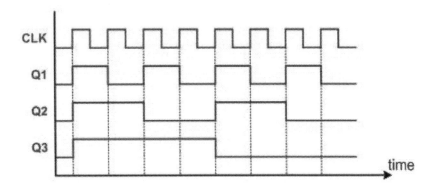

Figure 5-1: A 3-bit Counter

Regarding Figure 5-1, notice the following points:

1) The Q outputs give the down counter.
2) The $\bar{Q}$ (Q not) outputs give us up counter.
3) The frequency on Q3 is 1/8 of the Clock fed to FF1.
4) We can use the circuit in Figure 5-1 to divide clock frequency.
5) We can use the circuit in Figure 5-1 to count the number of pulses fed to CLK pin of FF1.

An up counter begins counting from 0 and its value increases on each clock until it reaches its maximum value. Then, it overflows and rolls over to zero in the next clock. The following figure shows the stages which an 8-bit counter goes through.

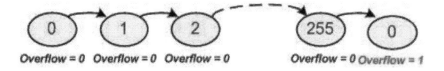

Figure 5-2: an 8-bit Up-Counter Stages

A down counter begins counting from its maximum value and decreases on each clock until it reaches to 0. Then, it underflows and rolls over to its maximum value in the next clock. The following figure shows the stages which an 8-bit down counter goes through.

Figure 5-3: an 8-bit Down-Counter Stages

Counter Usages

Counters have different usages. Some of them are:

1. Counting events
2. Making delays (Using Counter as a Timer)
3. Measuring the time between 2 events

1. Counting events

You might need to count the number of cars going through a street or the number of spaghetti packages which produced in a factory. To do so, you can connect the output of a sensor to a counter, as shown in the following figure.

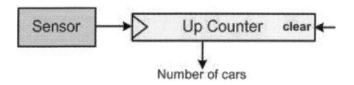

Figure 5-4: Counting Events Using a Counter

2. Making delays (Using Counter as a timer)

While controlling devices, it is a common practice to start or terminate a task when a desired amount of time elapsed. For example, a washing machine or an oven do each task for a determined amount of time. To do timing, we can connect a clock generator to a counter, and wait until a desired amount of time elapses. For example, in the following picture, the clock generator makes a 1 Hz signal and the counter increasing every second. The counter reaches to 60 after 60 seconds.

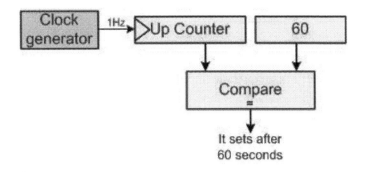

Figure 5-5: Using Counter as a Timer

3. Measuring the time between 2 events

You might need to measure the time between 2 events. For example, the amount of time it takes a marathon runner to go from the start to the finish point. In such cases we can use a circuit similar to the following:

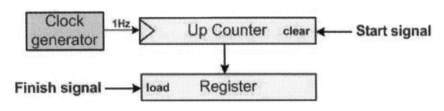

Figure 5-6: Capturing

The counter is cleared at the start. Then, it increases on each clock pulse. The value of the counter is loaded into another register when the runner passes the finish line.

Counters and Timers in microcontrollers

Nowadays, all the microcontrollers come with on-chip Timer/Counter. If the clock to the Timer comes from internal source such as PLL, XTAL, and RC, then it is called a *Timer*. If the clock source comes from external source, such as pulses fed to the CPU pin, then it is called a *Counter*. By Counter it is meant event-counter since it counts the event happening outside the CPU. In many microcontrollers, the Timers can be used as Timer or Counter.

Review Questions

1. With 5 FFs we can count to the maximum value of _____.
2. With 5 FFs we can divide the frequency by maximum of _____.
3. When pulses are fed to a timer from the outside it is called _____.
4. When clocks pulses are fed to a timer from inside it is called _____.
5. If we need to divide a frequency by 512, we need _____ flip flops.

Section 5.1: System Tick Timer

Every ARM Cortex-M comes with a System tick timer. System tick timer allows the system to initiate an action on a periodic basis. This action is performed internally at a fixed rate without external signal. For example, in a given application we can use SysTick to read a sensor every 200 msec. SysTick is used widely by operating systems so that the system software may interrupt the application software periodically (often at 10 ms interval) to monitor and control the system operations. The SysTick is a 24-bit down counter driven by the master clock (MCLK, the clock of the CPU) . It counts down from an initial value to 0. When it reaches 0, in the next clock, it underflows and it raises a flag called COUNT and reloads the initial value and starts all over. We can set the initial value to a value between 0x000000 to 0xFFFFFF. See the following figure.

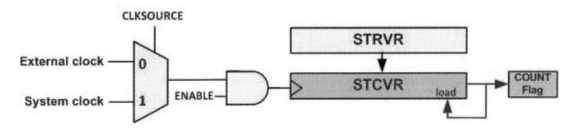

Figure 5-7: System Tick Timer Internal Structure

The down counter is named as STCVR (SysTick Current Value Register) in TI MSP432 ARM products. The counter receives clock from the master clock or the external clock. The clock source is chosen using the CLKSOURCE bit of STCSR (SysTick Control & Status Register) register. In the TI MSP342, no external clock is available for SysTick so the CLKSOURCE bit must be set to 1. The clock is ANDed with the ENABLE bit of STCSR register so it counts down when the ENABLE bit is set. The STCSR register is shown in Figure 5-8.

SysTick Registers

Next, we will describe the SysTick registers. There are three registers in the SysTick module: SysTick Control and Status register, SysTick Reload Value register, and SysTick Current Value register.

The STCTRL (SysTick Control and Status) register is located at 0xE000E010. We use it to start the SysTick counter among other things.

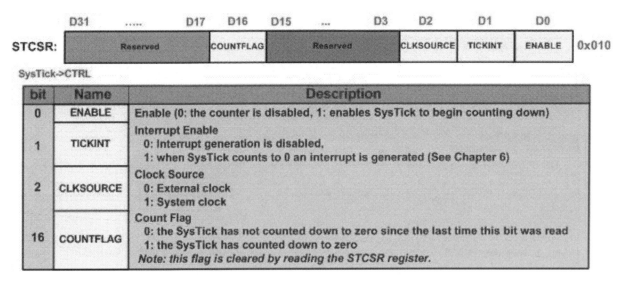

Figure 5-8: STCTRL (System Tick Control)

ENABLE (D0): enables or disables the counter. When the *ENABLE* bit is set the counter initializes the STCVR (*SysTick Current Value Register*) with the value of the *STRVR (SysTick Reload Value Register)* register and it counts down until it reaches to zero. Then, in the next clock, it underflows which sets the *COUNTFLAG* flag to high and the counter reloads the STCVR with the value of the *STRVR* register and then the process is repeated. See the following figure.

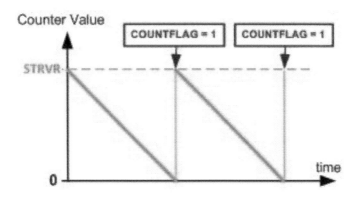

Figure 5-9: System Tick Counting

TICKINT (Tick Interrupt): If TICKINT=1, an interrupt occurs when the COUNTFLAG flag is set. See Chapter 6.

CLKSOURCE (Clock Source): The ARM core provides the choices of clock coming from Master clock or External clock. If CLKSOURCE=0 then the clock comes from External source. If CLKSOURCE=1, then the master clock provides the clock source to SysTick down counter. In the MSP432P401R, when CLKSOURCE=1, the SysTick clock uses the same clock as the one used by the CPU. The external clock source is not implemented so CLKSOURCE must be set to 1 for SysTick to function.

COUNTFLAG: Counter counts down from the initial value and when it reaches 0, the counter is reloaded with the value in STRVR and the COUNTFLAG is set high. See Figure 5-9. The flag remains high until it is cleared by software. The flag can be cleared by reading the STCSR register or writing to the STCVR register.

Example 5-1

Find the value for STCSR register, to start counting down with the internal clock.

Solution:

STCSR:	000000000000000	0	0000000000000	1	0	1
	Reserved	COUNTFLAG	Reserved	CLKSOURCE	TICKINT	Enable

SysTick Reload Value Register (STRVR)

The STRVR (SysTick Reload Value) register is used to program the start value of SysTick down counter, the STCVR register. The STRVR should contain the value N − 1 for the COUNT to fire every N clock cycles because the counter counts down to 0 and stay at 0 for one clock cycle before reloading. For example, if we need 1000 clocks of interval, then we make STRVR = 999. Although this is a 32-bit register, only the lower 24 bits are used. That means the highest value that can be loaded into this register is 0xFFFFFF or 16,777,216 decimal. See Figures 5-7 and 5-10.

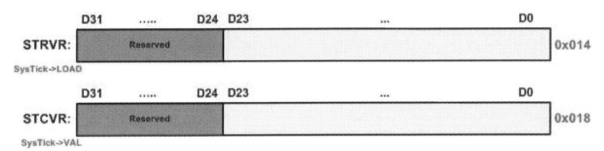

Figure 5-10: STRVR vs. STCVR

Program 5-1 loads the initial value to the maximum and dumps the current value of the SysTick on LEDs connecting to PORT2 as it counts down. The value of STCVR (SysTick->VAL) is shifted 21 places to the right so that the most significant bit is aligned with P2.2, which is connected to the blue LED. SysTick is configured to use default master clock at 3 MHz. The STRVR (SysTick->LOAD) register has 24 bits and is set to the maximal value. So the counter has the frequency of

$$\frac{3000000\ Hz}{2^{24}} = \frac{3000000\ Hz}{16777216} = 0.1788 Hz$$

And that is the frequency of the blue LED at P2.2. The green LED is connected to P2.1 and runs twice as fast as the blue LED. The red LED is connected to P2.0 and runs twice as fast as the green LED.

Program 5-1: Monitoring the value of STCVR of SysTick on LEDs

```
/* p5_1.c Toggling LEDs using SysTick counter
 *
 * This program lets the SysTick counter run freely and dumps
 * the counter values to the tri-color LEDs continuously.
 * The counter value is shifted 21 places to the right so that
 * the changes of LEDs will be slow enough to be visible.
 * SysTick counter has 24 bits.
 * The blue LED is connected to P2.2.
 * The green LED is connected to P2.1.
 * The red LED is connected to P2.0.
 *
 * Tested with Keil 5.20 and MSP432 Device Family Pack V2.2.0.
 */

#include "msp.h"

int main(void) {
    int c;
```

114

```
/* initialize P2.2-P2.0 for tri-color LEDs */
P2->SEL1 &= ~7;               /* configure P2.2-P2.0 as simple I/O */
P2->SEL0 &= ~7;
P2->DIR  |= 7;                /* P2.2-P2.0 set as output */

/* Configure SysTick */
SysTick->LOAD = 0xFFFFFF;     /* reload reg. with max value */
SysTick->VAL = 0;             /* clear current value register */
SysTick->CTRL = 5;            /* enable it, no interrupt, use master clock */

while (1)
{
    c = SysTick->VAL;         /* read current value of down counter */
    P2->OUT = c >> 21;        /* line up counter MSB with LED */
}
}
```

See the following examples.

Example 5-2

In an ARM microcontroller master clock = 8MHz. Calculate the delay which is made by the following function.

```
void delay()
{
SysTick->LOAD = 9;
SysTick->VAL = 0;        /* clear current value register */
SysTick->CTRL = 5;       /*Enable the timer */

while((SysTick->CTRL &0x10000) == 0) /*wait until the COUNTFLAG is set */
{ }
SysTick->CTRL = 0; /*Stop the timer (Enable = 0) */
}
```

Solution:

The timer is initialized with 9. So, it goes through the following 10 stages:

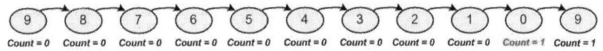

Since the master clock is chosen as the clock source, each clock lasts $\frac{1}{sysclk} = \frac{1}{8MHz} = 0.125\mu s$.

So, the program makes a delay of $9 \times 0.125\mu s = 1.125\mu s$..

Note: *the function call and the instructions execution take a few clock cycles as well. If you want to calculate the exact amount of delay, you should include this overhead, as well. But, in this book we do not consider it since most of the time it is negligible.*

Note: *Because the COUNTFLAG is set when the counter reaches zero, it takes 9 cycles for the COUNTFLAG to set. If periodic (repetitive) operation is used, the period will be equal to 10 cycles because the counter stays at 0 for one clock cycle before reloading.*

Example 5-3

In an ARM microcontroller the master clock is chosen as the clock source for the System tick timer. Calculate the delay which is made by the timer if the STRVR register is loaded with N.

Solution:

The timer is initialized with N. So, it goes through N cycles.
Since the master clock is chosen as the clock source, each clock lasts 1 / MCLK
So, the program makes a delay of N × (1/ MCLK) = N / MCLK.

Example 5-4

Using the SysTick timer, write a function that makes a delay of 1ms. Assume MCLK = 3MHz.

Solution:

From the equation derived in Example 5-2
delay = N / MCLK
N = delay ×MCLK = 0.001 sec × 3 MHz = 3,000
N = 3,000

```
void delay1ms(void) {
SysTick->LOAD = 3000;
SysTick->VAL = 0;     /* clear current value register */
SysTick->CTRL = 0x5;  /* Enable the timer */

while((SysTick->CTRL & 0x10000) == 0) /* wait until the COUNTFLAG is set */
{ }
SysTick->CTRL = 0; /* Stop the timer (Enable = 0) */
}
```

The Program 5-2 uses the SysTick to toggle the P2.0 every second. We need the STRVR (Reload) value of 3,000,000 − 1 since 1 sec × 3MHz =3,000,000. We assume the master clock is 3 MHz. Notice, every 3,000,000 clocks the down counter reaches 0, and COUNTFLAG is raised. Then the STRVR register is loaded with 3,000,000 − 1 automatically. The COUNTFLAG is clear when the STCTRL (SysTick->CTRL) register is read.

Program 5-2: Toggle red LED at 1 Hz using the SysTick Counter

```
/* p5_2.c Toggling red LEDs at 1 Hz using SysTick
 *
 * This program uses SysTick to generate 1000 ms delay to
 * toggle the red LED.
 * Master clock is running at 3 MHz. SysTick is configured
 * to count down from 3,000,000-1 to give a 1s delay.
 * The red LED is connected to P2.0.
 *
 * Tested with Keil 5.20 and MSP432 Device Family Pack V2.2.0.
 *
 */

#include "msp.h"

int main(void) {
    /* initialize P2.0 for red LED */
    P2->SEL1 &= ~1;             /* configure P2.0 as simple I/O */
    P2->SEL0 &= ~1;
    P2->DIR |= 1;               /* P2.0 set as output */

    /* Configure SysTick */
    SysTick->LOAD = 3000000-1;  /* reload reg. with 3,000,000-1 */
    SysTick->VAL = 0;           /* clear current value register */
    SysTick->CTRL = 5;          /* enable it, no interrupt, use master clock */

    while (1) {
        if (SysTick->CTRL & 0x10000)    /* if COUNTFLAG is set */
            P2->OUT ^= 1;               /* toggle red LED */
    }
}
```

In Program 5-3, SysTick is used to generate multiple of 1 millisecond delay. STRVR value of 3,000 − 1 is used since 0.001 sec × 3MHz = 3,000.

Program 5-3: Making delays using SysTick

```
/* p5_3.c Toggling green LED using SysTick delay

 * This program uses SysTick to generate one second delay to
 * toggle the green LED.
 * master clock is running at 3 MHz. SysTick is configure
 * to count down from 3000-1 to 0 to give a 1 ms delay.
 * For every 1000 delays (1 ms * 1000 = 1 sec), toggle the
```

```
 * green LED once. The green LED is connected to P2.1.
 *
 * Tested with Keil 5.20 and MSP432 Device Family Pack V2.2.0.
 *
 */

#include "msp.h"

void delayMs(int n);

int main(void)
{
    /* initialize P2.1 for green LED */
    P2->SEL1 &= ~2;          /* configure P2.1 as simple I/O */
    P2->SEL0 &= ~2;
    P2->DIR |= 2;            /* P2.1 set as output */

    while (1) {
        delayMs(1000);       /* delay 1000 ms */
        P2->OUT ^= 2;        /* toggle green LED */
    }
}

void delayMs(int n)
{
    int i;
    SysTick->LOAD = 3000 - 1;   /* reload with number of clocks per millisecond */
    SysTick->VAL = 0;           /* clear current value register */
    SysTick->CTRL = 0x5;     /* Enable the timer */

    for(i = 0; i < n; i++)
    {
        while((SysTick->CTRL & 0x10000) == 0) /* wait until the COUNTFLAG is set */
            { }
    }
    SysTick->CTRL = 0;          /* Stop the timer (Enable = 0) */
}
```

The System Tick Timer has a very simple structure and is the same across all the ARM Cortex-M chips regardless of who makes them. In contrast, TI MSP432 has its own timers which are covered in the next sections.

Review Questions

1. True or false. The highest number we can place in STRVR register is _____.
2. Assume CPU frequency of 16MHz. Find the value for STRVR register if we want 5 ms elapsed time.
3. The SysTick is _____-bit wide.
4. Which bit of STCSR is used to enable the SysTick.
5. The SysTick is (down or up) counter.

Section 5.2: Delay Generation with Timer32

In addition to SysTick timers, TI MSP432 chips have Timer32 and Timer_A timers. Timer32 is a simple timer which is discussed in this section. Timer_A timers will be discussed in later sections.

Timer32 is similar to SysTick timer with some extra features including:

- Timer32 is 32-bit.
- It can be used as 16-bit timer or 32-bit timer.
- To slow down the speed of timer counting, it has a prescaler.
- It has a free-running mode, in which the counter continuously counting. When the count reaches zero, it wraps around to its maximum count.
- It has a one-shot mode. In one-shot, the timer stops counting when it reaches zero. See the following figure.

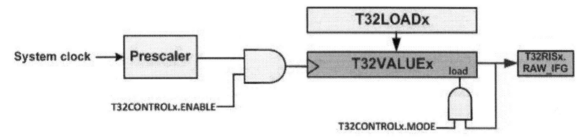

Figure 5-11: System Tick Timer Internal Structure

MSP432 has two Timer32 timers: Timer 1 and Timer 2. In Timer 1, the names of the registers end with 1; e.g. T32LOAD1 and T32VALUE1 while the registers of Timer 2 end with 2. Table 5-1 shows the registers of the Timer32 timers. Since the timers are exactly the same, in this book, we put x to generally refer to the registers. For example, we refer to the load register as T32LOADx. But the exact name of T32LOADx is T32LOAD1 in Timer 1 and T32LOAD2 for Timer 2.

Offset	Acronym	Register Name	Type	Reset Value
00H	T32LOAD1	Timer 1 Load Register	RW	0
04H	T32VALUE1	Timer 1 Current Value Register	R	FFFFFFFFH
08H	T32CONTROL1	Timer 1 Timer Control Register	RW	20H
0CH	T32INTCLR1	Timer 1 Interrupt Clear Register	W	-
10H	T32RIS1	Timer 1 Raw Interrupt Status Register	R	0
14H	T32MIS1	Timer 1 Interrupt Status Register	R	0
18H	T32BGLOAD1	Timer 1 Background Load Register	RW	0
20H	T32LOAD2	Timer 2 Load Register	RW	0
24H	T32VALUE2	Timer 2 Current Value Register	R	FFFFFFFFH
28H	T32CONTROL2	Timer 2 Timer Control Register	RW	20H
2CH	T32INTCLR2	Timer 2 Interrupt Clear Register	W	-
30H	T32RIS2	Timer 2 Raw Interrupt Status Register	R	0
34H	T32MIS2	Timer 2 Interrupt Status Register	R	0
38H	T32BGLOAD2	Timer 2 Background Load Register	RW	0H

Table 5-1: Timer32 Registers

The Timer32 is a 32-bit down counter driven by the master clock (the clock of CPU). It counts down from an initial value to 0. When it reaches 0, the flag RAW_IFG in T32RISx register is raised.

The down counter is named as T32VALUEx (where x is 1 for Timer 1 and 2 for Timer2). The clock is ANDed with the ENABLE bit of T32CONTROL register. So, it counts down when the ENABLE bit is set. The T32CONTROL register is shown in Figure 5-12.

Timer32 Registers

Next, we will describe the Timer32 registers.

T32CONTROLx

	D31 ..... D8	D7	D6	D5	D4	D3 D2	D1	D0
T32CONTROLx:	Reserved	ENABLE	MODE	IE	Reserved	PRESCALE	SIZE	ONESHOT

bit	Name	Description
7	ENABLE	Enable (0: the timer is disabled, 1: enables timer to begin counting down)
6	MODE	Mode bit 0: Free-running mode (The timer rolls over to its maximum value) 1: Periodic mode (The timer is reloaded with the value of the T32LOADx register)
5	IE	Interrupt Enable bit 0: Timer interrupt disabled 1: Timer interrupt enabled
3-2	PRESCALE	Prescale bits 00: clock is divided by 1 01: clock is divided by 16 10: clock is divided by 256 11: Reserved
1	SIZE	Selects 16-bit or 32-bit counter operation 0: 16-bit counter 1: 32-bit counter
0	ONESHOT	Selects one-shot or wrapping counter mode: 0: wrapping mode (The timer continues counting when it reaches to zero) 1: one-shot (The timer stops when it reaches to zero)

Figure 5-12: T32CONTROLx Register

ENABLE (D7): enables or disables the counter. When the *ENABLE* bit is set, the timer counts down until it reaches zero and sets the *RAW_IFG* flag to high.

MODE (D6): As shown in Figure 5-11, the MODE bit is ANDed with underflow signal. If the MODE bit is 0, on underflow, the timer rolls over to the maximum value (which is 0xFFFFFFFF for 32-bit operation and 0x0000FFFF for 16-bit operation depending on the SIZE bit, bit 1, of the same register). This mode of counting is called free-running mode. When the MODE bit is set to 1, on underflow the timer reloads the initial value from the T32LOADx register. This mode is called periodic mode.

See Figure 5-13. The timer reloads the T32VALUEx with the value of the T32LOADx or rolls over to the maximum value depending on the value of the MODE bit.

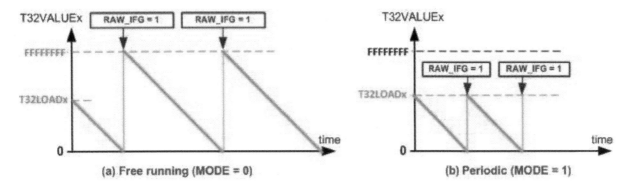

Figure 5-13: Counting in Free-Running Mode vs. Periodic Mode

IE (D5): If IE=1, an interrupt occurs when the RAW_IFG flag is set. See Chapter 6.

PRESCALE (D3-D2): The prescaler slows down the counting speed of the timer by dividing the input clock of the timer.

SIZE (D1): Each Timer32 can work as a 32-bit timer or 16-bit timer. If SIZE=0 then the timer works as a 16-bit timer. If SIZE=1, then the timer works as a 32-bit timer. In 16-bit mode, only the lower 16 bits of the counter is used.

ONESHOT (D0): When the one-shot bit is set to 1, the timer counts down to 0 and then stops counting.

Example 5-5

Find the value for T32CONTROLx register, to start counting down with no prescaler, periodic mode. Disable the interrupt and initialize it as a 32-bit timer.

Solution:

T32CONTROL:	0000000000000000	1	1	0	0	00	1	0
	Reserved	ENABLE	MODE	IE	Reserved	PRESCALER	SIZE	ONE-SHOT

T32RISx (Timer Raw Interrupt Status Register)

The bit 0 of the T32RISx register is used as RAW_IFG flag. The timer counts down and when it reaches 0 the RAW_IFG is set high. The flag remains high until it is cleared by software. The flag can be cleared by writing anything to the T32INTCLRx register.

Figure 5-14: T32RIS Register

T32LOADx (Timer Load Register)

See Figures 5-15. The T32LOADx (Timer Load Register) register is used to program the starting value of the down counter, the T32VALUEx register. The T32VALUEx should contain the value N − 1 for the RAW_IFG to fire every N clock cycles because the counter counts down to 0.

D31 ..... D0

T32LOADx:

D31 ..... D0

T32VALUEx:

Figure 5-15: T32LOAD vs. T32VALUE

For example, if we need 1000 clocks of interval, then we make T32LOADx = 999. The value that can be loaded into this register is between 1 to 0xFFFFFFFF. See the following examples.

Note: about the naming convention of timer registers

To conform to CMSIS (Cortex Microcontroller Software Interface Standard), the register names use *module->register* format in the C programs. Therefore, T32LOAD1 register is called TIMER32_1->LOAD and T32CONTROL1 is called TIMER32_1->CONTROL and so on.

Example 5-6

In an ARM microcontroller master clock = 4MHz. Calculate the delay which is made by the following function. Assume no prescaler was used.

```
void delay(void) {
/* set the reload value */
    TIMER32_1->LOAD = 6;
    /* counting down, no prescaler, periodic mode,
disable interrupt, 32-bit timer. */
TIMER32_1->CONTROL = 0xC2;

while((TIMER32_1->RIS& 1) == 0); /* wait until the RAW_IFG is set */
    TIMER32_1->INTCLR = 0;    /* clear raw interrupt flag */
}
```

Solution:

The timer is initialized with 6. So, it goes through the following 7 stages:

Since the master clock is chosen as the clock source, each clock lasts $\frac{1}{sysclk} = \frac{1}{4MHz} = 0.25\mu s$.

So, the program makes a delay of $6 \times 0.25\mu s = 1.5\mu s$.

Note: the function call and the instructions execution take a few clock cycles as well. If you want to calculate the exact amount of delay, you should include this overhead, as well. But, in this book we do not consider it since most of the time it is negligible.

Note 2: Since the timer is initialized as periodic mode, it rolls over to 6. If T32CONTROL was initialized with 0x42 (free-running mode) the timer would roll over to 0xFFFFFFFF.

Example 5-7

In an ARM microcontroller the master clock is chosen as the clock source for the Timer32. Calculate the delay which is made by the timer if the T32LOADx register is loaded with N and it is in no prescaler mode.

Solution:

The timer is initialized with N. So, it goes through N stages.
Since the master clock is chosen as the clock source, each clock lasts 1 / MCLK
So, the program makes a delay of N × (1 / MCLK) = N / MCLK.

Example 5-8

Using the timer, write a function that makes a delay of 20 ms using Timer32. Assume MCLK = 40MHz.

Solution:

From the equation derived in Example 5-7
delay = N / MCLK
N = delay × MCLK = 0.020 sec × 40 MHz = 800,000
N = 800,000

```
void delay(void) {
/* set the reload value */
    TIMER32_1->LOAD = 800000;
    /* counting down, no prescaler, periodic mode,disable interrupt, 32-bit timer. */
TIMER32_1->CONTROL = 0xC2;

while((TIMER32_1->RIS& 1) == 0); /* wait until the RAW_IFG is set */
    TIMER32_1->INTCLR = 0;    /* clear raw interrupt flag */
}
```

The Program 5-4 uses the Timer32 to toggle the blue LED on P2.2 at 1Hz. We need the reload value of 3,000,000 − 1 since 1 sec × 3 MHz = 3,000,000. We assume the master clock is 3 MHz. Notice, every 3,000,000 − 1 master clocks the down counter reaches 0, and RAW_IFG flag is raised. Then the counter is reloaded with 3,000,000 − 1 automatically. Because the counter stays at 0 for one cycle, the period is 3,000,000. The RAW_IFG flag is clear when the TIMER32_INTCLR1 register is written to.

Program 5-4: Toggle the blue LED every second using Timer32

```
/* p5_4.c Toggling blue LEDs at 1 Hz using Timer32
 *
 * This program uses Timer32 to generate 1 second delay to
 * toggle the blue LED.
 * Master clock is running at 3 MHz. Time32 is configured
 * to count down from 3,000,000-1 to 0 to give a 1 second delay.
 * The blue LED is connected to P2.2.
 *
 * Tested with Keil 5.20 and MSP432 Device Family Pack V2.2.0.
 *
 */

#include "msp.h"

int main(void) {
    /* initialize P2.2 for blue LED */
    P2->SEL1 &= ~4;             /* configure P2.2 as simple I/O */
    P2->SEL0 &= ~4;
    P2->DIR |= 4;               /* P2.2 set as output */

    TIMER32_1->LOAD = 3000000-1; /* set the reload value */
    /* no prescaler, periodic wrapping mode, disable interrupt, 32-bit timer. */
    TIMER32_1->CONTROL = 0xC2;

    while (1) {
        while((TIMER32_1->RIS & 1) == 0); /* wait until the RAW_IFG is set */
        TIMER32_1->INTCLR = 0;  /* clear raw interrupt flag */
        P2->OUT ^= 4;           /* toggle blue LED */
    }
}
```

In Program 5-5, the Timer32 is used to generate multiple of 1 millisecond delay. Reload value of 3,000 − 1 is used since 0.001 sec × 3 MHz = 3000.

Program 5-5: Making millisecond delays using loop and Timer32

```
/* p5_5.c Toggling green LED using Timer32 delay
 *
 * This program uses Timer32 to generate one second delay to
 * toggle the green LED.
 * Master clock is running at 3 MHz. Timer32 is configure
 * to count down from 3000-1 to give a 1 ms delay.
```

```
* For every 1000 delays (1 ms * 1000 = 1 sec), toggle the
* green LED once.  The green LED is connected to P2.1.
*
* Tested with Keil 5.20 and MSP432 Device Family Pack V2.2.0.
*
*/

#include "msp.h"

void delayMs(int n);

int main(void)
{
    /* initialize P2.1 for green LED */
    P2->SEL1 &= ~2;         /* configure P2.1 as simple I/O */
    P2->SEL0 &= ~2;
    P2->DIR |= 2;           /* P2.1 set as output */

    while (1) {
        P2->OUT ^= 2;       /* toggle green LED */
        delayMs(1000);      /* delay 1000 ms */
    }
}

void delayMs(int n)
{
    int i;

    TIMER32_1->LOAD = 3000 - 1; /* reload with number of clocks per millisecond */
    /* no prescaler, periodic wrapping mode, disable interrupt, 32-bit timer. */
    TIMER32_1->CONTROL = 0xC2;

    for(i = 0; i < n; i++) {
        while((TIMER32_1->RIS & 1) == 0); /* wait until the RAW_IFG is set */
        TIMER32_1->INTCLR = 0;            /* clear RAW_IFG flag */
    }
}
```

Periodic mode vs. Free-running mode

The periodic mode can be used to generate periodic interrupts, as we will see in the next chapter. The following example compares the periodic and Free-running modes.

Example 5-9

In the following two programs, show the stages that the timer goes through.

(a) Periodic mode

```
int main(void)
{
    TIMER32_1->LOAD = 5;        /* set the reload value */
    TIMER32_1->CONTROL = 0xC2;/* periodic mode, 32-bit */
```

```
while (1) {
        while((TIMER32_1->RIS& 1) == 0); /* wait until the RAW_IFG is set */
        TIMER32_1->INTCLR = 0;     /* clear raw interrupt flag */
    }
}
```

(b) Free running mode

```
int main(void)
{
    TIMER32_1->LOAD = 5;       /* set the reload value */
    TIMER32_1->CONTROL = 0x82;/* free-running mode, 32-bit */

    while (1) {
        while((TIMER32_1->RIS& 1) == 0); /* wait until the RAW_IFG is set */
        TIMER32_1->INTCLR = 0;     /* clear raw interrupt flag */
    }
}
```

Solution:

The codes are almost the same. Code (a) works in periodic mode. So, when the timer becomes zero, the timer is reloaded with the value of T32LOAD register.

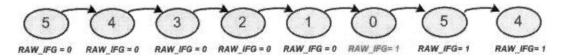

(b) is working in free running mode. So the timer rolls over to 0xFFFFFFFF.

Periodic mode vs. one-shot mode

As discussed above, in periodic mode the timer continues counting after each timeout. But in one-shot mode, the timer stops counting after timeout is reached. When it is in one-shot mode, it counts from T32LOADx to 0 just once and then stops. To restart another one-shot operation, the T32LOADx register needs to be written again.

When the Timer32 is in one-shot mode and the T32LOADx register is loaded with N, it takes N clock cycles to reach 0 and set the RAW_IFG flag in T32RISx register. But with N in T32LOADx register and periodic mode, the period of the timer is N + 1 because the timer counter stays in 0 for one cycle before it is reloaded with the value in T32LOADx. The following program makes a delay of 1 second using one-shot mode. It is almost the same as Program 5-4.

126

```c
/* p5_6.c Toggling blue LEDs at 1 Hz using Timer32 one-shot mode
 *
 * This program uses Timer32 to generate 1 second delay to
 * toggle the blue LED.
 * Master clock is running at 3 MHz. Timer32 is configured
 * as one-shot mode to count down from 3,000,000 to 0 to give
 * a 1 second delay. In order to restart another one-shot,
 * the TIMER32_1->LOAD register is reloaded.
 * The blue LED is connected to P2.2.
 *
 * Tested with Keil 5.20 and MSP432 Device Family Pack V2.2.0.
 *
 */
#include "msp.h"

int main(void) {
    /* initialize P2.2 for blue LED */
    P2->SEL1 &= ~4;             /* configure P2.2 as simple I/O */
    P2->SEL0 &= ~4;
    P2->DIR |= 4;               /* P2.2 set as output */

    TIMER32_1->LOAD = 3000000;  /* set the reload value */

    /* no prescaler, one-shot mode, disable interrupt, 32-bit timer. */
    TIMER32_1->CONTROL = 0xC3;

    while (1) {
        while((TIMER32_1->RIS & 1) == 0); /* wait until the RAW_IFG is set */
        TIMER32_1->INTCLR = 0;            /* clear raw interrupt flag */
        P2->OUT ^= 4;                     /* toggle blue LED */
        TIMER32_1->LOAD = 3000000;   /* reload LOAD register to restart one-shot */
    }
}
```

Prescaler options of timer

The clock of the system could go up to 48 MHz in an MSP432. In some cases, we might need the timer to count slower in order to measure longer intervals such as minutes. In such cases prescalers can be used.

As shown in Figure 5-12, the prescaler sits between the clock source and the timer counter. It can be configured to divide the master clock by a number before feeding it to the timer counter. The bits D2 and D3 of the T32CONTROLx register give the options of the number we can divide by. As shown in Figures 5-12 and 5-16, this number can be 1, 16, or 256.

Notice that the lowest factor is 1 and the highest factor is 256. That means at the lowest number 1, the clock source bypasses the prescaler and is fed into the timer counter directly. Next, we will examine how the prescaler options are programmed.

127

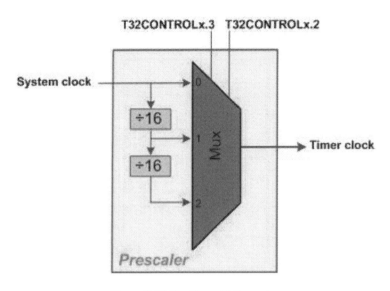

Figure 5-16: The Timer32 Prescaler

How the prescaler works (Case study)

As discussed in Section 5-0, Flip-flops divide the clock by 2. The prescaler is made of an 8-bit counter (8 Flip-flops) and a multiplexer.

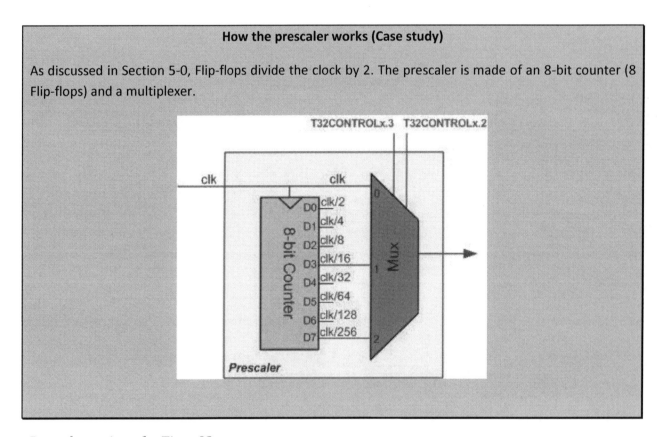

Prescaler register for Timer32

Because T32VALUE register has 32 bits, the time interval is limited to 89 seconds with 48 MHz clock. For longer delay, we will need to incorporate prescaler. The Program 5-7 below sets the prescalers to divide by 256 that will extend the period.

```
/* p5_7.c Toggling blue LED using Timer32 with prescaler
 *
 * This program uses Timer32 with prescaler to generate 1 second delay to toggle
 * the blue LED.
 * Master clock is running at 3 MHz. Timer32 is configured
 * with prescaler divides the incoming clock by 256. The
 * clock feeding the counter has the frequency of
 * 3,000,000 / 256 ~= 11719.
 * Since it is running at periodic mode, the counter reload is set to 11719-1 to
 * give a 1-second delay.
 * The blue LED is connected to P2.2.
 *
 * Tested with Keil 5.20 and MSP432 Device Family Pack V2.2.0.
 */
#include "msp.h"

int main(void) {
    /* initialize P2.2 for blue LED */
    P2->SEL1 &= ~4;             /* configure P2.2 as simple I/O */
    P2->SEL0 &= ~4;
    P2->DIR |= 4;               /* P2.2 set as output */

    TIMER32_1->LOAD = 11719 - 1; /* set the reload value */
    /* prescaler divided by 256, periodic wrapping mode, disable interrupt, 32-bit
timer. */
    TIMER32_1->CONTROL = 0xCA;

    while (1) {
        while((TIMER32_1->RIS & 1) == 0);   /* wait until the RAW_IFG is set */
        TIMER32_1->INTCLR = 0;       /* clear raw interrupt flag */
        P2->OUT ^= 4;                /* toggle blue LED */
    }
}
```

Example 5-10

(a) Show time delay calculation for Program 5-7,
(b) Calculate the largest delay time without prescaler at master clock = 48 MHz.
(c) Calculate the largest delay time with prescaler set to divide by 256 at master clock = 48 MHz.
(d) Find the T32LOAD1 value with master clock = 48 MHz to generate a delay of 2 minutes. Use the prescaler of 16.

Solution:

(a) 3 MHz / 256 = 11718.75 Hz with prescaler of 256.
1 / 11718.75Hz = 85.333 μsec
85.333 μsec x 11719 = 1.000021sec

(b) 48 MHz / 1 = 48 MHz with no prescaler.

   1 / 48 MHz = 20.833 ns.

   The largest possible delay is TIMER32_1->LOAD=0xFFFFFFFF = 4,294,987,295.

   Now, 4,294,987,295 × 20.833 ns = 89,477,470,317 ns = 89.5 sec = 1 minute and 29.5 seconds

(c) 48 MHz / 256 = 187.5kHz with prescaler set to divide by 256.

   1 / 187.5kHz = 5.33μs.

   The largest possible delay is TIMER32_1->LOAD= 0xFFFFFFFF = 4,294,987,295.

   4,294,987,295 × 5.33 μs = 22,892 sec = 6 hours 21 minute and 32 seconds

(d) 48 MHz / 16 = 3MHz with prescaler of 16.

   1 / 3,000,000 Hz = 0.333 μsec

   2 minutes = 120 sec

   120 sec / 0.333 μsec= 360,360,360.

   TIMER32_1->LOAD is 360,360,360 − 1 = 360,360,359.

Example 5-11

Calculate the delay which is made by the Time32 using master clock if the T32LOADx register is loaded with N and the prescaler is set to k (k is 1, 16, or 256).

Solution:

The timer is initialized with N. So, it goes through N+1 stages.
Each master clock lasts 1 / MCLK. So each timer clock lasts k/MCLK.
The program makes a delay of (N + 1) × (k/ MCLK) = (N + 1) × k / MCLK.

Review Questions

1. MSP432 has _____32-bit timers.
2. MSP432 Timer32 is (up, down) _____ counter.
3. What prescaler values can be used for MPS432 Timer32?
4. True or false. One-shot counter counts down and it stops when it reaches zero.
5. True or false. Upon Reset, the timer is ready to go.

Section 5.3: Timer_A 16-bit Timers

MSP432P401R microcontrollers have four 16-bit Timer_A timer modules. Timer_A timers can be used as timers, event counters, capture/compare, and PWM. In this section we use Timer_A as a timer, and in the next sections we program the timer as event counters and capture/compare.

Basic registers of Timer_A

See Figure 5-17. For each of the timers, there is a TAxR register. That means we have TA0R for Timer0, TA1R for Timer1, and so on. The TAxR register is a counter. Upon reset, the TAxR contains zero. It counts up with each clock cycle. You can load a value into the TAxR register or read its value.

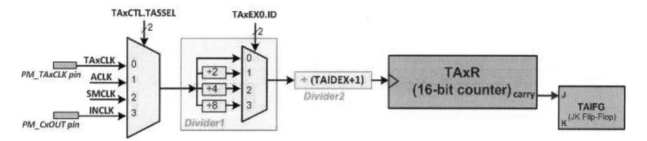

Figure 5-17: Timer_A Simplified Diagram

Each timer has a TAIFG (Timer_A Interrupt Flag) flag, as well. When a timer overflows, its TAIFG flag will be set.

Each timer also has the TAxCTL (Timer_A control register) register for setting modes of operation. For example, you can specify Timer_A0 to work as a timer or a counter by loading proper values into the TA0CTL. Next, we discuss the timer in more detail.

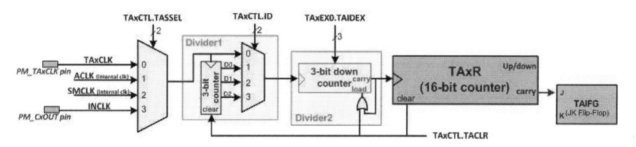

Figure 5-18: A more detailed diagram of Timer_A

Timer_A Registers

TAxR register

TAxR is a 16-bit register as shown in Figure 5-19. You can read the TAxR value or load it with new values.

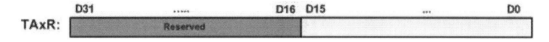

Figure 5-19: TAxR register

TAxCTL (Timer_A Control Register) register

TAxCTL is used for control of Timer_A. The bits for TAxCTL are shown in Figure 5-20 and Table 5-2.

131

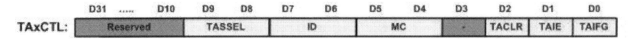

Figure 5-20: TAxCTL register

bit	Name	Description
0	TAIFG	Timer_A Interrupt Flag 0: Timer did not overflow 1: Timer overflowed
1	TAIE	Timer_A Interrupt Enable (0: Disabled, 1: Enabled)
2	TACLR	Timer_A Clear
4-5	MC	Mode Control: 00: Stop mode: timer is halted 01: Up mode: Timer counts up to TAxCCR0 10: Continuous mode: Timer counts up to 0xFFFF 11: Up/down mode: Timer counts up to TAxCCR0 then down to 0.
6-7	ID	Input divider: These bits select the divider for the input clock: 00: divide by 1 01: divide by 2 10: divide by 4 11: divide by 8
8-9	TASSEL	Timer_A clock Source Select: These bits select the Timer_A clock source: 00: TAxCLK (external clock): The timer uses external clock which is fed to the PM_TAxCLK pin. 01: ACLK (internal clock) 10: SMCLK (internal clock) 11: INCLK

Table 5-2: TAxCTL register

TAIFG (Timer_A Interrupt Flag)

The flag is set to 1 when the TAxR counter overflows. It remains set until the software clears it. See Figure 9-18. To clear the TAIFG flag, read the TAxCTL register.

TAIE (Timer_A Interrupt Enable)

If TAIE=1, an interrupt occurs when the TAIFG flag is set. See Chapter 6.

TACLR (Timer_A Clear)

By setting the TACLR bit to 1, you can clear the TAxR counter. As shown in Figure 5-20, setting the TACLR resets the prescaler counter, as well.

MC (Mode Control)

Timer_A can work in 3 different modes: Up mode, Continuous mode, and Up/Down mode. The MC bits are used to choose one of them. The Up and Continuous modes are discussed in this section. We will discuss the Up/Down mode to generate square waves later and in Chapter 11. If MC = 00, the timer is stopped and its power consumption decreases.

ID (Input clock Divider)

As shown in Figures 5-17 and 5-18, there are two dividers (prescalers) in Timer_A which can divide the input clock before feeding to the TAxR counter. They are discussed later in this section.

TASSEL (Timer_A clock source select)

These bits in the TAxCTL register are used to choose the clock source. If TASSEL = 00 or TASSEL=11, then the Timer_A works as a counter. If TASSEL has values 01 or 10, the internal clock sources are used and the Timer_A acts as a timer. See Figure 5-18 and then see Example 5-12.

Example 5-12

(a) Find the value for TAxCTL if we want to program Timer_A in continuous mode with no clock division. Use ACLK for the clock source.

(b) Find the value for TAxCTL if we want to program Timer_A in up mode with no clock division. Use SMCLK for the clock source.

(c) Find the value for TAxCTL if we want to program Timer_A in up mode with clock division of 8. Use SMCLK for the clock source.

Solution:

(a)

000000	01	00	10	0	0	0	1
Reserved	TASSEL	ID	MC	Reserved	TACLR	TAIE	TAIFG

TAxCTL:

TAxCTL = 0x0121

(b)

000000	10	00	01	0	0	0	1
Reserved	TASSEL	ID	MC	Reserved	TACLR	TAIE	TAIFG

TAxCTL:

TA1CTL = 0x0211;

(c)

000000	10	11	01	0	0	0	1
Reserved	TASSEL	ID	MC	Reserved	TACLR	TAIE	TAIFG

TAxCTL:

TA1CTL = 0x02D1;

TAxCCR0 to TAxCCR4 registers

See Figures 5-21 and 5-22. Each timer has five TAxCCRn (Timer_Ax Capture/Compare Register n) registers. In capture mode, the content of TAxR is copied into TAxCCRn when capture is performed. In compare mode, the content of the TAxCCRn is compared with the content of the TAxR. When they are equal, the CCIFG (Capture/Compare Interrupt Flag) flag will be set.

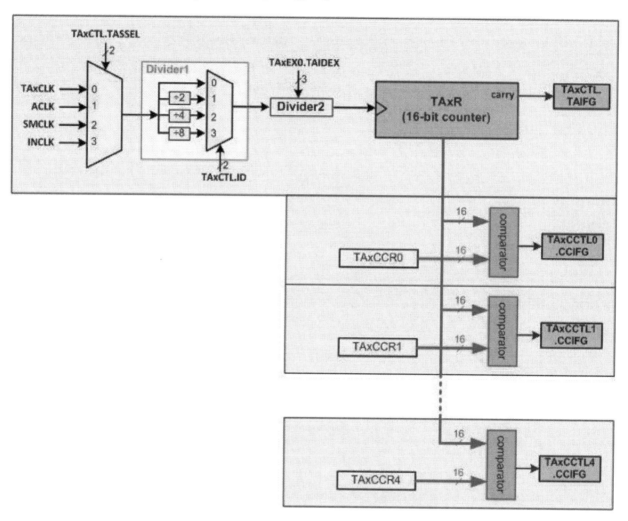

Figure 5-21: TAxCCRn Registers and TAxCCTLn Flags

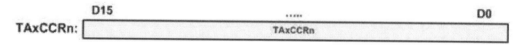

Figure 5-22: TAxCCRn Register

TAxCCTL0 register

For each TAxCCRn register, there is a TAxCCTLn register associated with it. As shown in Figure 5-21, in compare mode the CCIFG bit of the TAxCCTLn register sets when the values of TAxR and TAxCCRn are equal. You will learn more about the TAxCCTL registers in the next sections. See Figure 5-23 and Table 5-3.

134

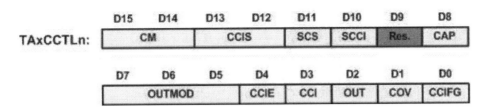

Figure 5-23: TAxCCTLn Register

bit	Name	Description
15-14	CM	Capture mode 00: No capture 01: Capture on rising edge 10: Capture on falling edge 11: Capture on both rising and falling edges
13-12	CCIS	Capture/compare input select. These its select the TAxCCR0 input signal: 00: CCIxA 01: CCIxB 10: GND 11: VCC
11	SCS	Synchronize capture source. This bit is used to synchronize the capture input signal with the timer clock. 0: Asynchronous capture 1: Synchronous capture
10	SCCI	Synchronized capture/compare input. The selected CCI input signal is latched with the EQUx signal and can be read via this bit.
8	CAP	Capture mode 0: Compare mode 1: Capture mode
7-5	OUTMOD	Output mode. Modes 2, 3, 6, and 7 are not useful for TAxCCR0 because EQUx = EQU0 000: OUT bit value 001: Set 010: Toggle/reset 011: Set/reset 100: Toggle 101: Reset 110: Toggle/set 111: Reset/set
4	CCIE	Capture/compare interrupt enable. This bit enables the interrupt request of the corresponding CCIFG flag. 0: Interrupt disabled 1: Interrupt enabled
3	CCI	Capture/compare input. The selected input signal can be read by this bit.
2	OUT	Output. For output mode 0, this bit directly controls the state of the output. 0: Output low

		1: Output high
1	COV	Capture overflow. This bit indicates a capture overflow occurred. COV must be reset with software. 0: No capture overflow occurred 1: Capture overflow occurred
0	CCIFG	Capture/compare interrupt flag 0: No interrupt pending <div align="right">1: interrupt pending</div>

Table 5-3: TAxCCTLn Register (Table 17-6 of the MSP432 reference manual)

TAxEX0 register

TAxEX0 (Timer_Ax Expansion 0) register is used to program the second input clock divider (prescaler). See Figures 5-17, 5-18, and 5-24.

Figure 5-24: TAxEXn Register

Up mode

In the up mode, the timer is incremented with the input clock. It counts up until the content of the TAxR register matches the content of TAxCCR0; then, the CCIFG flag of the TAxCCTL0 will be set and in the next clock, the TAxR value rolls over to zero and the TAIFG flag in TAxCTL register is set. See Figure 5-25 and Examples 5-13 and 5-14. There are potentially seven TAxCCRn registers (only five are implemented in MSP432P401R), TAxCCR0 is the one dedicated for the maximum count of TAxR.

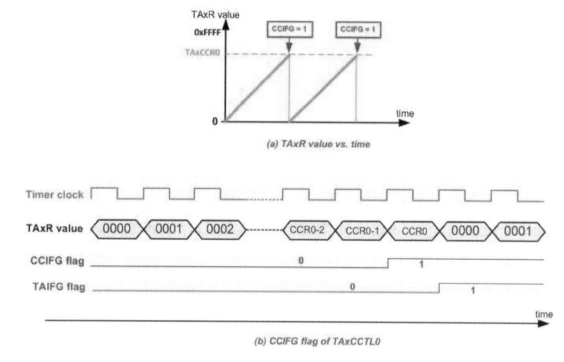

Figure 5-25: Counting in Up Mode

Example 5-13

In the following program, we are creating a square wave of 50% duty cycle (with equal portions high and low) on the P2.0 pin. Timer_A1 is used to generate the time delay.

```
#include "msp.h"
int main(void) {
    /* initialize P2.0 for red LED */
    P2->SEL1 &= ~1;          /* configure P2.0 as simple I/O */
    P2->SEL0 &= ~1;
    P2->DIR |= 1;            /* P2.0 set as output */

TIMER_A1->CTL= 0x0211;      /* SMCLK, ID= /1, up mode, TA clear */
TIMER_A1->EX0= 0;           /* Divider2 = 1/(0+1) = 1/1 */
TIMER_A1->CCR[0]= 30 - 1;

while (1) {
    while((TIMER_A1->CCTL[0]& 1) == 0); /* wait until the CCIFG is set */
    TIMER_A1->CCTL[0]&= ~1;              /* clear interrupt flag */
        P2->OUT ^= 1;                    /* toggle red LED */
    }
}
```

Example 5-14

Find the delay generated by Timer_A1 in Example 5-13. Do not include the overhead due to instructions. (SMCLK = 3 MHz)

Solution:

TA1CCR0 is loaded with 30 − 1. So, after 30 clocks TA0R becomes equal to TA1CCR0 and the CCIFG flag is set. That means the CCIFG is set after 30 clocks. Because SMCLK = 3 MHz, the counter counts up every 1/3 MHz = 0.333 µs. Therefore, we have 30 × 0.333 µs = 10 µs.

The clock sources

See Figure 5-26. Four different sources provide clocks for Timer_A timers: TAxCLK, ACLK, SMCLK, and INCLK. TAxCLK and INCLK clocks are provided through the chip pins and they can be used as counters. Meanwhile the Subsystem Master Clock (SMCLK) and Auxiliary Clock(ACLK) are provided internally. The SMCLK has the frequency of 3 MHz by default and ACLK has the frequency of 32.768kHz. The TASSEL bits of TAxCTL select between the 4 clock sources. Note the previous two times SysTick and Timer32 use the CPU clock (MCLK), Timer_A does not use CPU clock even though the default clock configuration provides the same clock rate for CPU clock and SMCLK.

Then the clock is fed to Divider1 which can divide the clock by 1, 2, 4, and 8. You can select between the divide choices using the ID bits of TAxCTL. The first divider divides the frequency of the clock by 2^{ID}, which means, if the input clock of Divider1 has the frequency of clk, then the output of divider1 has frequency $clk/2^{ID}$.

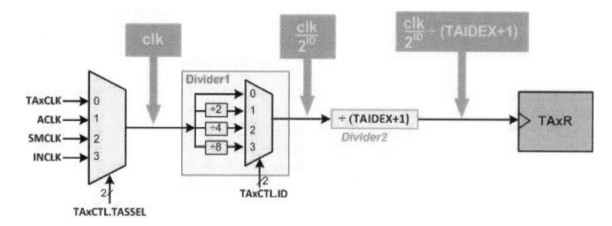

Figure 5-26: Clock in Timer_A

The second divider is in fact a down counter. It is initialized with the value of TAIDEX and then counts down to zero. When it reaches to zero, in the next clock, the carry signal rises for 1 clock which makes the TAxR register count. The carry signal also triggers the load pin of the counter and the counter is initiated with the TAIDEX value. The output of the second divider is (TAIDEX + 1) times slower than its input. So the TAxR register counts with the following frequency:

$$F_{Timer\ clock} = \frac{clk}{2^{ID} \times (TAIDEX + 1)}$$

Example 5-15

Find the delay generated by Timer_A in the following program. Do not include the overhead due to instructions. (SMCLK = 3MHz)

```
void delay(void) {
TIMER_A1->CTL= 0x0211;      /* SMCLK, ID = 0, up mode, TA clear */
TIMER_A1->EX0= ٢;           /* TA1EX0 = 2, Divider2 = 1/٣ */
TIMER_A1->CCR[0]= 2000-1;

while((TIMER_A1->CCTL[0]& 1) == 0); /* wait until the CCIFG is set */
TIMER_A1->CCTL[0]&= ~1;             /* clear interrupt flag */
}
```

Solution:

$$F_{Timer\ clock} = \frac{3\ MHz}{2^0 \times (2 + 1)} = 1\ MHz$$

138

$$T_{Timer\ clock} = \frac{1}{F_{Timer\ clock}} = \frac{1}{1\ MHz} = 1\ \mu s$$

$$Delay = T_{Timer\ clock} \times TAxCCR0 = 1\ \mu s \times 2000 = 2\ ms$$

The generated delay in up mode is as follows:

$$Delay = T_{Timer\ clock} \times TAxCCR0 = \frac{1}{F_{Timer\ clock}} \times TAxCCR0$$

$$Delay = \frac{2^{ID} \times (TAIDEX + 1) \times TAxCCR0}{clk}$$

Example 5-16

Assuming SMCLK = 3MHz, write a program to generate a delay of 25ms. Use up mode, with divider1 = 1/1 and divider2 = 1/3.

Solution:

To make divider1 = 1/1 and divider2 = 1/3, we set ID = 0 and TAIDEX = 2.
Due to divider1 = 1/8 and divider2=1/3, each timer clock lasts:

$$F_{Timer\ clock} = \frac{3\ MHz}{2^0 \times (2 + 1)} = 3\ MHz$$

$$F_{Timer\ clock} = \frac{1}{1\ MHz} = 1\ \mu s.$$

Thus, in order to generate a delay of 25 ms we should wait 25 ms / 1μs = 25,000 μs / 1μs =25,000 timer clocks and the TA0CCR0 register should be loaded with 25,000.

```
void delay(void) {
TIMER_A1->CTL= 0x0211;      /* SMCLK, ID = 0, up mode, TA clear */
TIMER_A1->EX0= 2;           /* TA1EX0 = 2, Divider2 = 1/r */
TIMER_A1->CCR[0]= 25000-1;    /* 25,000 timer clocks */

    while ((TIMER_A1->CCTL[0]& 1) == 0); /* wait until the CCIFG is set */
TIMER_A1->CCTL[0]&= ~1;            /* clear interrupt flag */
}
```

The following program makes a delay of 1 second using the Timer_A.

```
/* p5_8.c Toggling red LED at 1 Hz using Timer_A
 *
 * This program uses Timer_A to generate 1 second delay to
 * toggle the red LED.
 * Subsystem Master Clock (SMCLK) running at 3 MHz is used.
 * Timer_A is configured to count up from 0 to 46,875-1, which
 * is loaded in TIMER_A1->CCR[0].
 * When the counter (TA1R) value reaches TIMER_A1->CCR[0], the CCIFG
 * bit in TIMER_A1->CCTL[0] is set.
 * The clock input dividers are set to divide by 8 and 8.
 * The timer counter roll over interval is:
 * 3,000,000 / 8 / 8 / 46,875 = 1 Hz.
 * The red LED is connected to P2.0.
 *
 * Tested with Keil 5.20 and MSP432 Device Family Pack V2.2.0.
 *
 */

#include "msp.h"

int main(void) {
    /* initialize P2.0 for red LED */
    P2->SEL1 &= ~1;          /* configure P2.0 as simple I/O */
    P2->SEL0 &= ~1;
    P2->DIR |= 1;            /* P2.0 set as output */

    TIMER_A1->CTL = 0x02D1;     /* SMCLK, ID=/8, up mode, TA clear */
    TIMER_A1->EX0 = 7;          /* IDEX = /8 */
    TIMER_A1->CCR[0] = 46875 - 1;   /* for 1 sec */

    while (1) {
        while((TIMER_A1->CCTL[0] & 1) == 0);   /* wait until the CCIFG is set */
        TIMER_A1->CCTL[0] &= ~1;               /* clear interrupt flag */
        P2->OUT ^= 1;                          /* toggle red LED */
    }
}
```

Generating large time delays using Timer_A

Unlike Time32, Timer_A counter is only 16 bit long that limits the range of the timer period. With the addition of two input clock dividers, the clock rate can be reduced by 8 in each divider yield a total of divided by 64. For applications that need much slower time, the Auxiliary Clock (ACLK) is available to the Timer_A. By default, the power up reset configures the Auxiliary Clock to run at 32,768 Hz. The next program example uses Auxiliary Clock as the clock source for Timer_A1.

```
/* p5_9.c Toggling green LEDs at 1 Hz using Timer_A and Auxiliary clock
 *
```

```
* This program uses Timer_A to generate 1 second delay to
* toggle the green LED.
* Auxiliary clock (ACLK) running at 32,768 Hz is used.
* Timer_A is configured to count up from 0 to 512-1,
* which is loaded in TIMER_A1->CCR[0].
* When the counter (TA1R) value reaches TIMER_A1->CCR[0],
* the CCIFG bit in TIMER_A1->CCTL[0] is set.
* The clock input dividers are set to divide by 8 and 8 again.
* The timer counter roll over interval is:
* 32,768 / 8 / 8 / 512 = 1 Hz.
* The green LED is connected to P2.1.
*
* Tested with Keil 5.20 and MSP432 Device Family Pack V2.2.0.
*
*/

#include "msp.h"

int main(void)
{
    /* initialize P2.1 for green LED */
    P2->SEL1 &= ~2;             /* configure P2.1 as simple I/O */
    P2->SEL0 &= ~2;
    P2->DIR |= 2;               /* P2.1 set as output */

    TIMER_A1->CTL = 0x01D1;     /* ACLK, ID = /8, up mode, TA clear */
    TIMER_A1->CCR[0] = 512 - 1; /* for 1 sec */
    TIMER_A1->EX0 = 7;          /* IDEX = /8 */

    while (1)
    {
        while((TIMER_A1->CCTL[0] & 1) == 0); /* wait until the CCIFG flag is set */
        TIMER_A1->CCTL[0] &= ~1;             /* clear interrupt flag */
        P2->OUT ^= 2;                        /* toggle green LED */
    }
}
```

Changing the TAxCCRn register while counting

We are able to change the value of TAxCCRn registers while the timer is counting. In up mode, if we load the TAxCCR0 register with a value that is smaller than TAxR 's value, the TAxR will reset to 0 and will count up until it reaches the TAxCCR0 value. But if the value of TAxCCR0 is bigger than TAxR, the timer continues its counting.

Continuous mode

In this mode, the content of the TAxR counter increments with each clock. It counts up until it reaches its max of 0xFFFF. When it rolls over from 0xFFFF to 0x0000, it sets high the TAIFG flag (Timer_A Interrupt Flag). This flag can be monitored by software. See Figure 5-27.

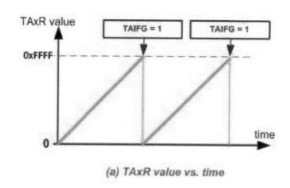

(a) TAxR value vs. time

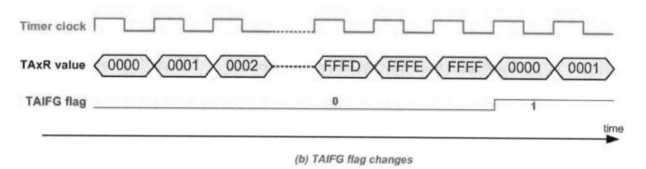

(b) TAIFG flag changes

Figure 5-27: Continuous mode

Up/Down mode

The up/down mode of the timer is used in conjunction with compare mode to generate pulse width modulation (PWM). PWM will be discussed in details in Chapter 11.

Review Questions

1. How many timer_A timers do we have in MSP432?
2. True or false. Timer_A0 is a 16-bit timer.
3. True or false. Timer_A prescalers can divide the clock by 256.
4. In up mode, the counter rolls over when the counter reaches____.
5. In continuous mode, when the counter rolls over it goes from ____ to ____.

Section 5.4: Using Timer for Input Capture

Input capture mode

In input capture mode, an I/O pin is used to capture the signal transition events. When an event occurs, the content of the TAxR register is copied to the TAxCCRn register and the CCIFG flag of the TAxCCTLn register is set. See Figure 5-28.

To configure Timer_A as Input capture mode, bits CM of the TAxCCTLn should be other than 00 (binary). Depending on the value of CM, it captures on rising edge, falling edge, or both edges. See Figure 5-29 and Table 5-4.

142

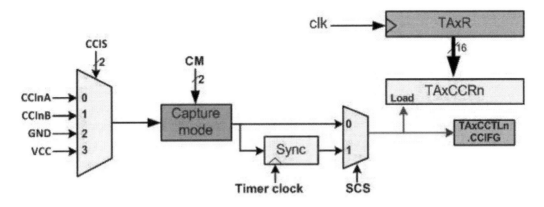

Figure 5-28: Input Edge Time Capturing

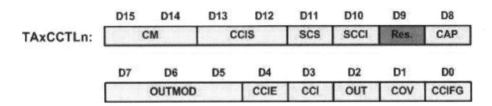

Figure 5-29: TAxCCTLn Register

bit	Name	Description
15-14	CM	Capture mode 00: No capture 01: Capture on rising edge 10: Capture on falling edge 11: Capture on both rising and falling edges
13-12	CCIS	Capture/compare input select. These its select the TAxCCR0 input signal: 00: CCIxA 01: CCIxB 10: GND 11: VCC
11	SCS	Synchronize capture source. This bit is used to synchronize the capture input signal with the timer clock. 0: Asynchronous capture 1: Synchronous capture
10	SCCI	Synchronized capture/compare input. The selected CCI input signal is latched with the EQUx signal and can be read via this bit.
8	CAP	Capture mode 0: Compare mode 1: Capture mode
7-5	OUTMOD	Output mode. Modes 2, 3, 6, and 7 are not useful for TAxCCR0 because EQUx = EQU0

		000: OUT bit value 001: Set 010: Toggle/reset 011: Set/reset 100: Toggle 101: Reset 110: Toggle/set 111: Reset/set
4	CCIE	Capture/compare interrupt enable. This bit enables the interrupt request of the corresponding CCIFG flag. 0: Interrupt disabled 1: Interrupt enabled
3	CCI	Capture/compare input. The selected input signal can be read by this bit.
2	OUT	Output. For output mode 0, this bit directly controls the state of the output. 0: Output low 1: Output high
1	COV	Capture overflow. This bit indicates a capture overflow occurred. COV must be reset with software. 0: No capture overflow occurred 1: Capture overflow occurred
0	CCIFG	Capture/compare interrupt flag 0: No interrupt pending 1: interrupt pending

Table 5-4: TAxCCTLn Register (Table 17-6 of the MSP432 reference manual)

Notice that the channel can be configured to capture on the falling edge, rising edge, or both. To determine the type of edge that is captured, the CM bits of the TAxCCTLn register should be initialized. See Table 5-5. Also notice that capturing has no effect on counting and the timer counter continues counting when the capture event takes place.

CM	Capture mode
00	No capture
01	Capture on rising edge
10	Capture on falling edge
11	Capture on both edges

Table 5-5: Choosing the Capture Edge

Pin Selection for Input Capture

To measure the edge time, we must feed the pulse into the ICCnA or ICCnB pin. The input capture timer channel-pin designation is identical to the output compare timer channel-pin designation. See Table 5-6.

Timer_A	Port Pin	Timer_A	Port Pin	Timer_A	Port Pin	Timer_A	Port Pin
TA0.0	P7.3	TA1.0	P8.0	TA2.0	P8.1	TA3.0	P10.4
TA0.1	P2.4	TA1.1	P7.7	TA2.1	P5.6	TA3.1	P10.5
TA0.2	P2.5	TA1.2	P7.6	TA2.2	P5.7	TA3.2	P8.2
TA0.3	P2.6	TA1.3	P7.5	TA2.3	P6.6	TA3.3	P9.2
TA0.4	P2.7	TA1.4	P7.4	TA2.4	P6.7	TA3.4	P9.3

Table 5-6: Port pin assignement of Timer_A

On the trainer board, the power supply is regulated at 3.3V. Input signal shall not exceed 3.3V otherwise damage to the pin or device may happen. For an input signal to be recognized by the input pin, a high signal should be above 2.31V and below 3.3V, a low signal should be below 1.15V and above 0V. For more details, check out the datasheet.

Input Capture mode usages

The input edge time capturing can be used for many applications; e.g. recording the arrival time of an event, measuring the frequency and pulse width of a signal.

Steps to program the Input Capture function

Perform the following steps to measure the period of a periodic waveform based on the edge arrival time of the Input Capture function.

1) select the CCIx alternate function for the input pin at the PxSEL register,
2) select the clock source for timer counter, prescaler value, counter mode in TAxCTL register,
3) select second prescaler value in TAxEX0register,
4) set the TAxCCTLn register to capture rising edge,
5) clear the CCIFG bit in TAxCCTLn register,
6) wait until the CCIFG bit is set in TAxCCTLn register,
7) read the current counter value captured,
8) clear the CCIFG bit in TAxCCTLn register,
9) wait until the CCIFG bit is set in TAxCCTLn register,
10) read the current counter value captured,
11) calculate the difference between the current value from the last value,

As shown in Figure 5-30, to measure the period of a signal we must measure the time between two falling edges or two rising edges. Program 5-10 measures the period using the difference between two rising edges.

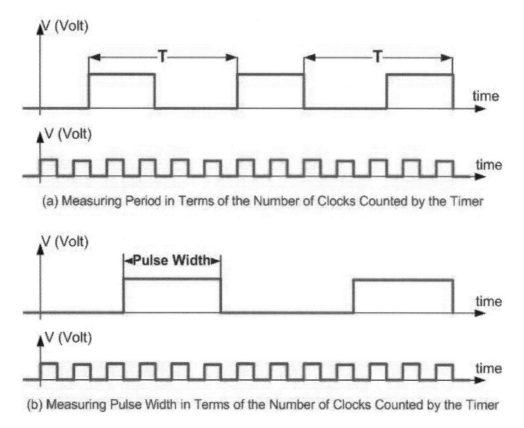

(a) Measuring Period in Terms of the Number of Clocks Counted by the Timer

(b) Measuring Pulse Width in Terms of the Number of Clocks Counted by the Timer

Figure 5-30: Measuring Period and Pulse Width

Program 5-10: Using Timer_A input capture of pin P2.5

```
/* p5_10.c using Timer_A0.2 for capture mode of pin P2.5.
 *
 * This program uses TA0.2 for capture mode of pin P2.5.
 * SMCLK is running at 3 MHz. Timer_A0 is free-running
 * without input clock dividers. When rising edge of P2.5
 * occurs, the content of TA0R is copied into TIMER_A0->CCR[2] and
 * CCIFG flag in TIMER_A0->CCTL[2] is set.
 * Two timestamps are taken and the difference is the
 * period of the input signal. By shifting the difference
 * 13 bits to the right, it is displayed on the tri-color LEDs.
 * It works well up to about 100 Hz with 13-bit shift.
 * To run this program, you need to connect a 0-3V periodic
 * signal to pin P2.5.
 *
 * Tested with Keil 5.20 and MSP432 Device Family Pack V2.2.0.
 *
 */
#include "msp.h"

int main(void) {
    unsigned short last, current, diff;

    /* initialize P2.2-P2.0 for tri-color LEDs */
```

```
P2->SEL1 &= ~7;              /* configure P2.2-P2.0 as simple I/O */
P2->SEL0 &= ~7;
P2->DIR  |= 7;               /* P2.2-P2.0 set as output */

/* configure P2.5 as TA0.CCI1A */
P2->SEL1 &= ~0x20;
P2->SEL0 |= 0x20;
P2->DIR  &= ~0x20;

TIMER_A0->CTL = 0x0224;      /* SMCLK, ID = /1, up mode, TA clear */
TIMER_A0->CCTL[2] = 0x4900;  /* rising edge, CCI2A, SCS, capture mode */
TIMER_A0->EX0 = 0;           /* IDEX = /1 */

while (1) {
    TIMER_A0->CCTL[2] &= ~1;              /* clear interrupt flag */
    while((TIMER_A0->CCTL[2] & 1) == 0);  /* wait until the CCIFG is set */
    last = TIMER_A0->CCR[2];              /* save first timestamp */

    TIMER_A0->CCTL[2] &= ~1;              /* clear interrupt flag */
    while((TIMER_A0->CCTL[2] & 1) == 0);  /* wait until the CCIFG is set */
    current = TIMER_A0->CCR[2];           /* save second timestamp */

    diff = current - last;       /* display the time interval */
    P2->OUT = diff >> 13;
    }
}
```

Review Questions

1. True or false. To capture the input edge time, the CM bits of the TAxCCTLn register must be configured.

2. True or false. To measure the frequency of a signal, the time interval between a falling edge and a rising edge are needed.

3. True or false. If the time interval between two consecutive falling edges is measured, the frequency of the periodic signal can be calculated.

4. True or False. The MSP432 supports both rising and falling edge detection.

Section 5-5: Counter programming using Timer_A

Timer_A can also be used to count events happening outside the microcontroller. We can use this feature to count the events such as the rotary sensor of the wheel for the speed of the bike.

When the timer is used as a timer, an internal clock is used as the source of the frequency. When it is used as a counter, however, it is a pulse outside the microcontroller that increments the TAxR register.

TASSEL bits in the TAxCTL register

Recall from Section 5-3 that the TASSEL bits (clock source select) in the TAxCTL register decide the source of the clock for the timer. If TASSEL is 01 or 10, the timer gets pulses from the internal clock.

In contrast, when TASSEL is 00 or 11, the timer is used as a counter and gets its pulses from a source outside the microcontroller. See Figure 5-18, Table 5-7, and Example 5-28.

Counter Input Clock	Pin Name	PxSEL1	PxSEL0
TA0CLK	P7.1	0	1
TA1CLK	P7.2	0	1
TA2CLK	P4.2	1	0
TA3CLK	P8.3	0	1

Table 5-7: Counters Input Pins

Example 5-28

Find the value for TAxCTL if we want to program Timer_A as an up mode counter. Use the TAxCLK clock for the clock source.

Solution:

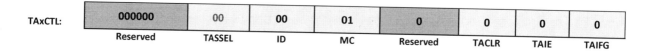

In Program 5-11, we are using Timer_A2 as an event counter that counts up as clock pulses are fed into P4.2. These clock pulses could represent the number of people passing through an entrance, or of wheel rotations, or any other event that can be converted to pulses.

Program 5-11: using Timer_A2 as an event counter on pin P4.2

```
/* p5_11.c using Timer_A2 as an event counter on pin P4.2
 *
 * The Timer_A2 is configured to use P4.2 as the clock.
 * Clock input dividers are disabled. Timer counter TA2R
 * is incremented for every pulse of P4.2. TA2 is configured
 * as up count mode and TIMER_A2->CCR[0] is set to 10. For every 10
 * pulses from P4.2, the CCIFG flag of TIMER_A2->CCTL[0] is set.
 *
 * The content of timer counter TA2R is read and dumped at
 * the tri-color LEDs so for every pulse of P4.2, the LED
 * color changes. For every 10 pulses, the red LED1 is toggled.
 *
 * Connect a 0V-3V low frequency signal to P4.2 and see
 * the result.
 *
 * Tested with Keil 5.20 and MSP432 Device Family Pack V2.2.0.
 *
 */

#include "msp.h"
```

```
int main(void) {
    /* initialize P2.2-P2.0 for tri-color LEDs */
    P2->SEL1 &= ~7;            /* configure P2.2-P2.0 as simple I/O */
    P2->SEL0 &= ~7;
    P2->DIR |= 7;              /* P2.2-P2.0 set as output */
    P2->OUT &= ~7;             /* turn off all LEDs */

    /* initialize P1.0 for red LED1 */
    P1->SEL1 &= ~1;            /* configure P1.0 as simple I/O */
    P1->SEL0 &= ~1;
    P1->DIR |= 1;              /* P1.0 set as output */
    P1->OUT &= ~1;             /* turn off LED1 */

    /* initialize P4.2 as TA2CLK */
    P4->SEL1 |= 4;
    P4->SEL0 &= ~4;
    P4->DIR &= ~4;

    /* Configure TA2 as up counter using external clock, no input divides */
    TIMER_A2->CTL = 0x0014;    /* TA2CLK, ID = /1, up mode, TA clear */
    TIMER_A2->EX0 = 0;         /* IDEX = /1 */
    TIMER_A2->CCR[0] = 10;     /* set the flag every 10 pulses */

    while (1) {
        P2->OUT &= ~7;                            /* turn off tri-color LEDs */
        P2->OUT |= TIMER_A2->R & 7;               /* set tri-color LEDs with counter value */
        if((TIMER_A2->CCTL[0] & 1) == 1) {   /* when the CCIFG is set (10 count) */
            TIMER_A2->CCTL[0] &= ~1;             /* clear the CCIFG flag */
            P1->OUT ^= 1;                         /* toggle red LED1 */
        }
    }
}
```

Before we finish this section, we need to state an important point. You might think monitoring the CCIFG flags is a waste of CPU time. You are right. There is a solution to this: the use of interrupts. Using interrupts enables us to do other things with the microcontroller. When a timer interrupt flag such as TAxCCTLn is raised it will inform us. This important and powerful feature of the microcontroller is discussed in Chapter 6.

Review Questions

1. True or false. The Timer can also be used as event counter.
2. True or false. The MSP432 timer counts both rising and falling edges.
3. True or false. To use the timer as event-counter, we must configure it in capture mode.
4. True or false. Using TASSEL bits, we can choose between timer and counter modes.

Answers to Review Questions

Section 5-0

1. 31
2. 32

3. event counter
4. Timer
5. 9

Section 5.1

1. 0xFFFFFF
2. 1/16MHz=62.5 nsec. Now, 5 msec/62.5nsec=80,000. Therefore, RELOAD=80,000 − 1 =79,999
3. 24
4. The D0 of STCTRL (the Enable)
5. Down counter

Section 5.2

1. 2
2. down
3. 1, 16, 256
4. True
5. False, we need to enable it

Section 5.3

1. 4
2. True
3. True
4. TAxCCR0
5. 0xFFFF to 0

Section 5.4

1. True
2. False, to measure frequency the time between two falling edges or two rising edges is needed
3. True
4. True

Section 5.5

1. True
2. False
3. False
4. True

Chapter 6: Interrupt and Exception Programming

This chapter examines the interrupt handling in ARM Cortex-M processor. We also discuss sources of hardware interrupts in the MSP432P401R ARM chip. In Section 6.1 we discuss the concept of interrupts in the ARM CPU, and then we look at the interrupt assignment of the ARM Cortex-M. Section 6.2 examines the NVIC interrupt controller and discusses the Thread and Handler mode in ARM Cortex-M. The interrupt for I/O ports are discussed in Section 6.3. Section 6.4 examines the interrupt for UART. Timer's interrupts are explored in Section 6.5. The SysTick interrupt is covered in Section 6.6. The interrupt priority is discussed in Section 6.7.

Section 6.1: Interrupts and Exceptions in ARM Cortex-M

In this section, first we examine the difference between polling and interrupt and then describe the various interrupts of the ARM Cortex-M.

Interrupts vs. polling

A single microprocessor can serve several devices. There are two ways to do that: interrupts or polling. In the *interrupt* method, whenever any device needs service, the device notifies the CPU by sending it an interrupt signal. Upon receiving an interrupt signal, the CPU halts whatever it is doing and serves the device. In *polling*, the CPU continuously monitors the status of a given device; when the status condition is met, it performs the service. After that, it moves on to monitor the next device until everyone is serviced. See Figure 6-1.

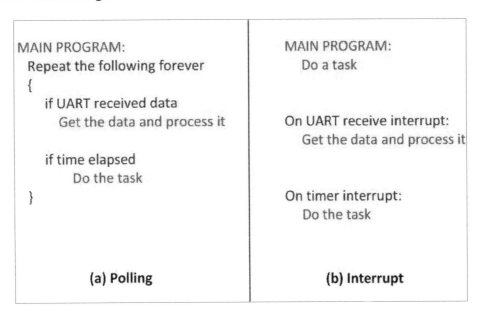

Figure 6-1: Polling vs. Interrupts

Although polling can monitor the status of several devices and serve each of them as certain conditions are met, it is not an efficient use of the CPU time. The polling method wastes much of the CPU's time by polling devices when they do not need service. So, in order to avoid tying down the CPU, interrupts are used. For example, using polling in Timer we might wait until a determined amount of time elapses, and while we were waiting we cannot do anything else. That is a waste of the CPU's time that could have been used to perform some useful tasks. In the case of the Timer, if we use the interrupt

151

method, the CPU can go about doing other tasks, and when the interrupt flag is raised the Timer will interrupt the CPU to let it know that the time is elapsed. See Figure 6-1.

Interrupt service routine (ISR)

For every interrupt there must be a program associated with it. When an interrupt occurs this program is executed to perform certain services for the interrupt. This program is commonly referred to as an *interrupt service routine* (ISR). The interrupt service routine is also called the *interrupt handler*. When an interrupt occurs, the CPU runs the interrupt service routine. Now the question is how the ISR gets executed?

As shown in Figure 6-2, in the ARM CPU there are pins that are associated with hardware interrupts. They are input signals into the CPU. When the signals are triggered, CPU pushes the PC register onto the stack and loads the PC register with the address of the interrupt service routine. This causes the ISR to get executed.

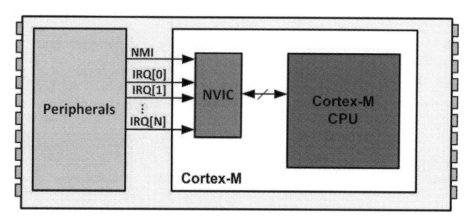

Figure 6-2: NVIC in ARM Cortex-M

Interrupt Vector Table

As can be seen from Table 6-1:, for every interrupt there are four bytes allocated in the memory. These four bytes of memory, called interrupt vector, provide the address of the interrupt service routine for which the interrupt was invoked.

The interrupt vectors are usually allocated in a table in the memory. This look-up table is called the *interrupt vector table*. In the ARM, the lowest 1024 bytes ($256 \times 4 = 1024$) of memory space are set aside for the interrupt vector table and must not be used for any other function. Table 6-1 provides a list of interrupts and their designated functions as defined by ARM Cortex-M products. Of the 256 interrupts, some are used for software interrupts and some are for hardware IRQ interrupts.

Nested Vectored Interrupt Controller (NVIC) In ARM Cortex-M

The ARM Cortex-M core comes with a circuit called Nested Vectored Interrupt Controller (NVIC) to handle the external interrupt lines. It is capable of handling 240 external interrupts but only the first 64 of them are implemented in MSP432P401 controllers and only 41 of them are used.

152

The NVIC may assign one of the eight interrupt levels to each interrupt. It has registers to indicate whether an interrupt is active and to mask (block) the interrupts. All these functions will be discussed in more details later.

Interrupt and Exception assignments in ARM Cortex-M

The NVIC of the ARM Cortex-M has room for the total of 255 interrupts and exceptions. The interrupt numbers are also referred to INT type (or INT #) in which the type can be from 1 to 255 or 0x01 to 0xFF. That is INT 01 to INT 255 (or INT 0x01 to INT 0xFF.) The NVIC in ARM Cortex-M assigns the first 15 interrupts for internal use. The memory locations 0-3 are used to store the value to be loaded into the stack pointer when the device is coming out of reset. See Table 6-1.

Interrupt #	Interrupt	Memory Location (Hex)
	Stack Pointer initial value	0x00000000
1	Reset	0x00000004
2	NMI	0x00000008
3	Hard Fault	0x0000000C
4	Memory Management Fault	0x00000010
5	Bus Fault	0x00000014
6	Usage Fault (undefined instructions, divide by zero, unaligned memory access,...)	0x00000018
7	Reserved	0x0000001C
8	Reserved	0x00000020
9	Reserved	0x00000024
10	Reserved	0x00000028
11	SVCall	0x0000002C
12	Debug Monitor	0x00000030
13	Reserved	0x00000034
14	PendSV	0x00000038
15	SysTick	0x0000003C
16	IRQ 0 for peripherals	0x00000040
17	IRQ 1 for peripherals	0x00000044
...	...	...
255	IRQ 239 for peripherals	0x000003FC

Table 6-1: Interrupt Vector Table for ARM Cortex-M

The predefined Interrupts (INT 0 to INT 15)

The followings are the first 15 interrupts in ARM Cortex-M:

The ARM devices have a reset pin. It is usually tied to a circuit that keeps the pin low for a while when the power is coming on. This is the power-up reset or power-on reset (POR). On the ARM trainer board, there is often a push-button switch to lower the signal. The reset signal is normally high during operation. Right after the power is turned on or when the reset button is pressed, it goes low and the CPU goes to a known state with all the registers loaded with the predefined values. When the device is coming out of reset, the ARM Cortex-M loads the program counter from memory location 0x00000004.

153

In ARM Cortex-M system we must place the starting address of the program at the 0x00000004 to get the program running. Notice in Table 6-1, the addresses 0x00000000 to 0x00000003 are set aside for the initial stack pointer value. This ensures that the ARM has access to stack immediately coming out of the reset.

Reset

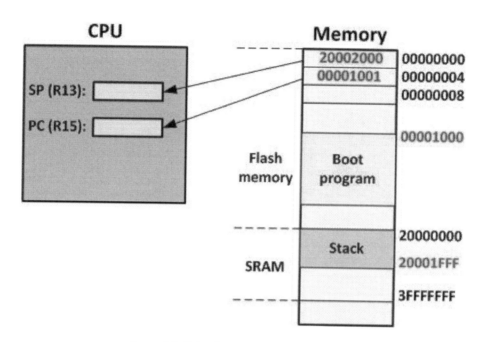

Figure 6-3: Going from Reset to Boot Program

Non-maskable interrupt

As shown in Figure 6-2, there are pins in the ARM chip that are associated with hardware interrupts. They are IRQs (interrupt request) and NMI (non-maskable interrupt). IRQ is an input signal into the CPU, which can be masked (ignored) and unmasked through the use of software. However, NMI, which is also an input signal into the CPU, cannot be masked by software, and for this reason it is called a *non-maskable interrupt*. ARM Cortex-M NVIC has embedded "INT 02" into the ARM CPU to be used only for NMI. Whenever the NMI pin is activated, the CPU will go to memory location 0x0000008 to get the address of the interrupt service routine (ISR) associated with NMI. Memory locations 0x00000008 to 0x0000000B contain the 4 bytes of address associated with the ISR belonging to NMI.

Exceptions (Faults)

There is a group of interrupts belongs to the category referred to as *fault* or exception *interrupts*. Internally, they are invoked by the microprocessor whenever there are conditions (exceptions) that the CPU is unable to handle. One such situation is an attempt to execute an instruction that is not implemented in this CPU. Since the result is undefined, and the CPU has no way of handling it, it automatically invokes the invalid instruction exception interrupt. This is commonly referred to as *exception or fault* in the ARM literature. Whenever an invalid instruction is executed, the CPU will go to memory location 0x00000018 to get the address of the ISR to handle the situation. The undefined instruction fault is part of the *Usage Fault* exceptions. There are many exceptions in the ARM Cortex. See Table 6-1. They are:

Hard Fault

The hard fault is an exception that occurs when the CPU having difficulties executing the ISR for any of the exceptions.

Memory Management Fault

The memory manager unit fault is used for protection of memory from unwanted access. An example of memory management exception fault is when the access permission in MPU is violated by attempting to write into a region of memory designated as read-only. In an ARM chip with an on-chip MMU, the page fault can also be mapped into the memory management fault. See Chapter 15.

Bus Fault

The bus fault is an exception that occurs when there is an error in accessing the buses. This can be due to memory access problem during the fetch stage of an instruction or reading and writing to data section of memory. For example, if you try to access memory address location that has not been mapped to a memory chip or peripheral device the Bus Fault exception will occur.

Usage Fault

The ARM Cortex-M chip has implemented the undefined instruction, access to coprocessor that's not ready and so on as part of the Usage Fault exception. See your ARM Cortex-M data sheet.

SVCall

An ISR can be called upon as a result of the execution of SVC (supervisor call) instruction. This is referred to as a *software interrupt* since it was invoked from software, not from a fault exception, external hardware, or any peripheral interrupt. Whenever the SVC instruction is executed, the CPU will go to memory location 0x0000002C to get the address of the ISR associated with SVC. The SVC is widely used by the application software to call the operating system kernel functions and services that can be provided only by the privileged access mode of the OS. In many systems, the API and function calls needed by various user applications are handled by the SVCall to make sure the OS is protected. In the classical ARM literature, SVC was called SWI (software interrupt), but the ARM Cortex-M has renamed it as SVC.

PendSV (pendable service call)

The PendSV (pendable service call) can be used to do the same thing as the SVC to get the OS services. However, the SVC is an instruction and is executed right away just like all ARM instructions. The PendSV is an interrupt initiated by setting a bit in a register and will wait until NVIC has time to service it when other higher priority interrupts are being taken care. Examine the concept of nested interrupt and pending interrupts at the end of this section to see how NVIC handles multiple pending interrupts.

Debug Monitor

In executing a sequence of instructions, there is a need to examine the contents of the CPU's registers and system memory. This is often done by executing the program one instruction at a time and then inspecting registers and memory. This is commonly referred to as *single-stepping*, or performing a trace. ARM has designated INT 12, debug monitor, specifically for implementation of single-stepping.

SysTick

In the multitasking OS we need a real time interrupt clock to notify the CPU that it needs to service the task. The clock tick happens at a regular interval and is used mainly by the OS system. The SysTick in ARM Cortex is designed for this purpose.

IRQ Peripheral interrupts

An ISR can be launched as a result of an event at the peripheral devices such as timer timeout or analog-to-digital converter (ADC) conversion complete. The largest number of the interrupts in the ARM Cortex-M belongs to this category. Notice from Table 6-1 that ARM Cortex-M NVIC has set aside the first 15 interrupts (INT 1 to INT 15) for internal use and exceptions and is not available to chip designer. The Reset, NMI, undefined instructions, and so on are part of this group of exceptions. The rest of the interrupts can be used for peripherals. Many of the INT 16 to INT 255 are used by the chip manufacturer to be assigned to various peripherals such as timers, ADC, serial communication, external hardware interrupts, and so on. There is no standard in assigning the INT 16 to INT 255 to the peripherals. Different manufacturers assign different interrupts to different peripherals and you need to examine the datasheet for your ARM Cortex-M chip. Each peripheral device has a group of special function registers that must be used to access the device for configuration. For a given peripheral interrupt to take effect, the interrupt for that peripheral must be enabled. The special function registers for that device provide the way to enable the interrupts. For MSP432P401 controllers, only 41 peripheral interrupts are used.

Fast context saving in task switching

Most of the interrupts are asynchronous, that means they may happen any time in the middle of program execution. When the interrupt is acknowledged and the interrupt service routine is launched, the interrupt service routine will need some CPU resource, mainly the CPU registers, to execute the code. In order not to corrupt the register content of the program that was running before interrupt occurs, these CPU registers need to be preserved. This saving of the CPU contents before switching to interrupt handler is called context switching (or context saving). The use of the stack as a place to save the CPU's contents is tedious and time consuming. In executing an interrupt service routine, each task generally needs some key registers such as PC (R15), LR (R14), and CPSR (flag register), in addition to some working registers. For that reason, the ARM Cortex-M automatically saves the registers of CPSR, PC, LR, R12, R3, R2, R1, and R0 on stack when an interrupt is acknowledged. See Figure 6-4. If the interrupt service routine needs to use more registers than those preserved, the program has to save the content before using the other registers. The choice of the registers automatically saved adheres to the ARM Architecture Procedure Call Standard (AAPCS) so that an interrupt handler may be written as a plain C function without the need of any special provision.

When floating-point coprocessor is present, the FPU registers need to be saved too. If the interrupt handler does not use floating point coprocessor, saving FPU registers is a waste of time. The ARM chip allows enabling lazy stacking of the FPU registers. When lazy stacking is enabled, the stack pointer will be moved as if the FPU registers are saved for compatibility reason but the content of the

FPU registers are not actually saved. This is very useful if no floating point instructions are used in the interrupt handler. Even with lazy stacking enabled, the interrupt handler still has the option to save the FPU registers before performing floating point instructions.

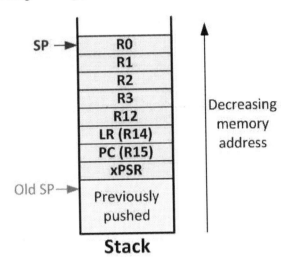

Figure 6-4: ARM Cortex-M Stack Frame upon Interrupt

Processing interrupts in ARM Cortex-M

When the ARM Cortex-M processes any interrupt (from either Fault Exceptions or peripheral IRQs), it goes through the following steps:

1. The current processor status register (CPSR) is pushed onto the stack and SP is decremented by 4, since CPSR is a 4-byte register.
2. The current PC (R15) is pushed onto the stack and SP is decremented by 4.
3. The current LR (R14) is pushed onto the stack and SP is decremented by 4.
4. The current R12 is pushed onto the stack and SP is decremented by 4.
5. The current R3 is pushed onto the stack and SP is decremented by 4.
6. The current R2 is pushed onto the stack and SP is decremented by 4.
7. The current R1 is pushed onto the stack and SP is decremented by 4.
8. The current R0 is pushed onto the stack and SP is decremented by 4.
9. Save Floating point coprocessor registers or move SP if lazy stacking is enabled.
10. The CPU goes into the Handler Mode (details will be described later). LR is loaded with a number with bit 31-5 all 1s.
11. The INT number (type) is multiplied by 4 to get the address of the location within the vector table to fetch the program counter of the interrupt service routine (interrupt handler).
12. From the memory locations pointed to by this new PC, the CPU starts to fetch and execute instructions belonging to the ISR program.
13. When one of the return instructions is executed in the interrupt service routine, the CPU recognizes that it is in the Handler Mode from the value of the LR. It then restores the registers saved when entering ISR including the program counter from the stack and makes the CPU run the code where it left off when interrupt occurred. See Figure 6-5.

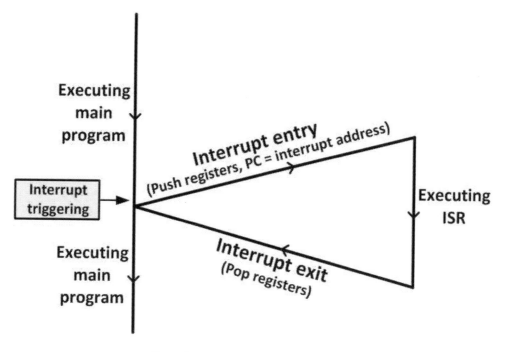

Figure 6-5: Main Program gets interrupted

Interrupt priority

The next topic in this section is the concept of priority for exceptions and IRQs. What happens if two interrupts want the attention of the CPU at the same time? Which has priority? In the ARM Cortex-M the Reset, NMI and Hard Fault exceptions have fixed priority levels and are set by the ARM itself and not subject to change. Among the Reset, NMI and Hard Fault, the Reset has the highest priority. As we can see from Table 6-2, the NMI and Hard Fault have lower priority than Reset, meaning if all three of them are activated at the same time, the Reset will be executed first. If both NMI and an IRQ are activated at the same time, NMI is responded to first since NMI has a higher priority than IRQ. The rest of the exceptions and IRQs have lower priority and are configurable, meaning their priority levels can be set by the programmer. Programmable priority levels are values between 0 and 7 with 7 has the lowest priority.

Interrupt #	Interrupt	Priority Level
0	*Stack Pointer initial value*	
1	Reset	-3 Highest
2	NMI	-2
3	Hard Fault	-1
4	Memory Management Fault	Programmable
5	Bus Fault	Programmable
6	Usage Fault (undefined instructions, divide by zero, unaligned memory access,....)	Programmable
7	Reserved	Programmable
8	Reserved	Programmable
9	Reserved	Programmable
10	Reserved	Programmable

11	SVCall	Programmable
12	Debug Monitor	Programmable
13	Reserved	Programmable
14	PendSV	Programmable
15	SysTick	Programmable
16	IRQ 0 for peripherals	Programmable
17	IRQ 1 for peripherals	Programmable
...	...	Programmable
255	IRQ 239 for peripherals	Programmable

Table 6-2: Interrupt Priority for ARM Cortex-M

Table 6-2 shows standard interrupt assignment for ARM Cortex. Not all Cortex-M chips have all the first 15 interrupts. In some ARM Cortex-M chips if there is no memory management unit then its interrupt is reserved. Make sure you examine your ARM Cortex-M chip manual before you start using it. Again it must be emphasized that for the hardware IRQs coming through NVIC, the NVIC resolves priority depending on the way the NVIC is programmed. Also, not all the interrupts are used in all the chips.

Interrupt latency

The time from the moment the event that triggers an interrupt flag to the moment the CPU starts to execute the ISR code is called the interrupt latency. The duration of interrupt latency can also be affected by the type of the instruction which the CPU was executing when the interrupt occurs. It takes longer in cases where the instruction being executed lasts for many clock cycles compared to the instructions that last for only one clock cycle time. In the ARM Cortex-M, we also have extra clocks added to the latency due to the fact that it takes time to save the content of registers CPSR, PC, LR, R12, and R0-R3 on stack. See your ARM Cortex-M manual for the timing data sheet.

Another source of the interrupt latency is the interrupt priority. As mentioned earlier, when several interrupts occur at the same time, the interrupt with the highest priority is acknowledged first, all other interrupts have to wait. The impact of interrupt priority is more than when the interrupts occur at the same time as we will see next.

Interrupt inside an interrupt handler (nested interrupt)

What happens if the ARM is executing an ISR belonging to an interrupt and another interrupt is activated? In such cases, a preemption happens, the higher priority interrupt will stop the lower priority interrupt handler and launch the higher priority interrupt handler. When the higher priority interrupt handler is finished, the lower priority interrupt handler that was preempted will resume its execution.

In the ARM Cortex-M systems, it is up to the software engineer to configure the priority level for each exception and IRQ device and set the policy of how to support nested interrupt. In many older CPUs when an interrupt service routine is launched, all other interrupts are masked. All interrupts happened at this time have to wait. If the interrupt service routine runs too long, there is a risk some interrupts may be lost. The interrupt service routine may unmask the interrupts. But in doing so, it will allow all the interrupts to preempt itself.

The ARM Cortex-M allows only the higher priority interrupts to preempt the lower priority interrupt service routine. The programmer is responsible to assign the proper priority to each IRQ in the NVIC registers. The NVIC in ARM Cortex-M has the ability to capture the pending interrupts and keeps track of each one until all are serviced.

Review Questions

1. True or false. When any interrupt is activated, the CPU jumps to a fixed and unique address.
2. There are _____ bytes of memory in the interrupt vector table for each interrupt.
3. How many K bytes of memory are used by the interrupt vector table, and what are the beginning and ending addresses of the table for the first 256 interrupts?
4. The program associated with an interrupt is also referred to as _____.
5. What is the function of the interrupt vector table?
6. What memory locations in the interrupt vector table hold the address for INT 16 ISR?
7. The ARM Cortex-M has assigned INT 2 to NMI. Can that be changed?
8. Which interrupt is assigned to divide error exception handling?

Section 6.2: ARM Cortex-M Processor Modes

In this section we examine various operation modes in ARM Cortex-M.

ARM Cortex Thread (application) and Handler (exception) modes

The ARM Cortex-M can run in one of the two modes at any given time. They are: (1) Thread (Application) mode and (2) Handler (Exception) mode. The differences can be stated as follows:

1. When the ARM Cortex-M is powered on and coming out of reset, it automatically goes to the Thread mode. The Thread mode is the mode that vast majority of the applications programs are executed in. The CPU spends most of its time in Thread mode and gets interrupted only to execute ISR for exception faults or peripheral IRQs.

2. The ARM Cortex-M switches to Handler mode only when an exception fault (of course other than the Reset) or an IRQ interrupt from a peripheral is activated to get the attention of the CPU to execute an ISR (interrupt handler). Upon returning from ISR, the CPU automatically changes from Handler mode back to Thread mode. It must be noted that of all the exceptions and IRQs in the Table 6-1, only the Reset forces the CPU into Thread mode and the rest are executed in Handler mode.

A big advantage of having Handler mode is that when returning from Handler mode, the CPU will pop the stack and restore the registers saved during entry to Handler mode. With this, an interrupt handlers are written just like any other functions as we will see in the examples soon.

There are two Stacks in ARM Cortex

The classical ARM has a single stack pointer (R13) to be used to point to RAM area for the purpose of stack. With a multi-threaded operating system, every thread should have their own stack so does the operating system itself. It is much more efficient to have separate stack pointers for the system and the thread. The ARM Cortex-M has two stack pointer registers. They are called PSP (processor stack pointer) and MSP (main stack pointer). Threads running in Thread mode should use the process stack and the kernel and exception handlers should use the main stack.

The bit 1, ASP (active stack pointer), of the special function register called CONTROL register gives the option of choosing MSP or PSP for stack pointer. Upon Reset the ASP=0, meaning that R13 is the Main Stack pointer (MSP) and its value come from the first 4 bytes of the interrupt vector table starting at 0x00000000 address location. By making the ASP=1, the R13 is the same as PSP (processor stack pointer). Next, we examine the privilege levels in ARM Cortex-M.

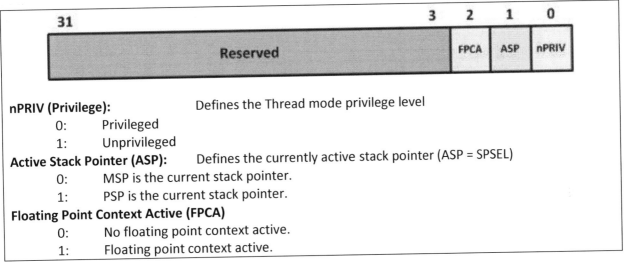

Figure 6-6: CONTROL Register in ARM Cortex-M4

Processor Mode	Software	Privilege level
Thread	Applications	Privileged and Unprivileged
Handler	ISR for Exceptions and IRQs	Always Privileged
In Thread mode, use bit 0 of the CONTROL register to select Privileged or Unprivileged		

Table 6-3: Privileged level Execution and Processor Modes in ARM Cortex-M

Privileged and Unprivileged levels in ARM Cortex-M

The ARM Cortex-M series has a new feature that did not exist in the previous ARM products. This new feature is called privileged level. There are two privilege levels in ARM Cortex-M. They are called Privileged and Unprivileged. The Privileged level in ARM Cortex-M can be used to limit the CPU access to special registers and protected memory area to prevent the system from getting corrupted due to error in coding or malicious user. Here are summary of the Privileged level software:

1. Privileged level software has access to all registers including the special function registers for interrupts.
2. Privileged level software has access to every region of memory.
3. Privileged level software has access to system timer, NVIC, and system resources.

4. The Privileged level software can execute all the ARM Cortex-M instructions including the MRS, MSR, and CPS.

5. The Handlers for fault exceptions and IRQs can be executed only in Privileged level.

6. Only the Privileged software can access the CONTROL register to see whether execution is in Privileged or Unprivileged mode. In Unprivileged mode one can switch from Unprivileged level to Privileged level by using SVC instruction.

Processor Mode	Software	Stack Usage
Thread	Applications	MSP or PSP
Handler	ISR for Exceptions and IRQs	MSP
Note: In Thread mode, use bit 1 of the Control register to select MSP or PSP for stack pointer.		

Table 6-4: Processor Modes and Stack Usage in ARM Cortex-M

Here are summary of the Unprivileged level software:

1. Unprivileged level software has no access to some registers such the special function registers for interrupts.

2. Unprivileged level software has limited access to some regions of memory.

3. Unprivileged level software is blocked from accessing system timer, NVIC, and system control block and resources.

4. The Unprivileged level software cannot execute some of the ARM instructions such as CPS. It has limited access to the MRS and MSR instructions.

5. While Handler mode is always executed in the Privileged level, the Thread mode software can be executed in Privileged or Unprivileged level. The bit 0 of the special a function register called CONTROL register gives the option of running the software in Privileged or Unprivileged mode.

6. In Unprivileged mode, one can use SVC instruction to make a supervisor call to switch from Unprivileged level to Privileged level.

Mode	Privilege	Stack Pointer	Typical Example usage
Handler	Privileged	Main	Exception Handling
Handler	Unprivileged	Any	Reserved since Handler is always Privileged
Thread	Privileged	Main	Operating system kernel
Thread	Privileged	Process	
Thread	Unprivileged	Main	
Thread	Unprivileged	Process	Application threads

Table 6-5: Processor Mode, Privilege, and Stack in ARM Cortex

Special Function register in ARM Cortex

Beside the traditional general purpose registers of R0–R15, the ARM Cortex has many new special function registers. These registers are widely used in programs written for the Cortex-M based embedded systems. See Figure 6-7.

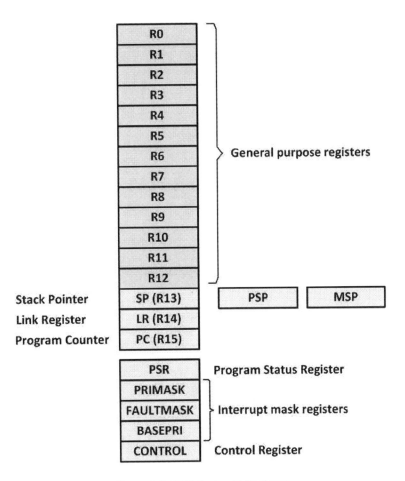

Figure 6-7: ARM Cortex-M Registers

While the general purpose registers of R0–R15 can be accessed using the MOV, LDR, and STR instructions, these new special function registers can be accessed only with the two new instructions MSR and MRS. To manipulate (clear or set) the bits of special function registers, first we must use the MSR to move them to a general purpose register and after changing their values they are moved back by using MRS instruction. Table 6-6 shows special function registers.

Register name	Privilege Usage
MSP (main stack pointer)	Privileged
PSP (processor stack pointer)	Privileged or Unprivileged
PSR (Processor status register)	Privileged
APSR (application processor status register)	Privileged or Unprivileged
ISPR (interrupt processor status register)	Privileged
EPSR (execution processor status register)	Privileged
PRIMASK (Priority Mask register)	Privileged
FAULTMASK(fault mask register)	Privileged
BASEPRI (base priority register)	Privileged
CONTROL (control register)	Privileged
Note: We must use MSR and MRS instructions to access the above registers	

Table 6-6: Special function registers of ARM Cortex-M

163

Review Questions

1. True or false. When a Reset pin is activated, the ARM CPU wakes up in Thread mode.
2. There are only _____ processor modes in the ARM Cortex. Give their names.
3. How many bytes of data are fetched into CPU from interrupt vector table when ARM Cortex-M is Reset, and what are they?
4. Another name for ISR is _____.
5. True or false. When an interrupt comes in from exception fault or IRQ, the ARM CPU switches to Handler mode automatically.

Section 6.3: MSP432 I/O Port Interrupt Programming

MSP432 is an ARM Cortex-M4 chip. In Chapter 2, we showed how to use GPIO ports for simple I/O. We also showed a simple program getting (polling) an input switch status and using it to turn on or off an LED. In this section, we show how to program the interrupt capability of the I/O ports in MSP432P401Rchip.

PORTx Interrupt Registers

In this section, we will use a switch to show an example of external interrupt programming using GPIO pins. However, before we do that, we need to examine the interrupt vector table for the MSP432 microcontroller. Table 6-7 shows interrupt assignment in MSP432P401R. See Section 6.6.2 of MSP432P401R reference manual.

INT#	IRQ#	Vector location	Device
1-15	None	0000 0000 to 0000 003C	CPU Exception(set by ARM)
16	0	0000 0040	PSS
17	1	0000 0044	CS
18	2	0000 0048	PCM
19	3	0000 004C	WDT_A
20	4	0000 0050	FPU_INT
21	5	0000 0054	Flash Controller
22	6	0000 0058	COMP_E1
23	7	0000 005C	COMP_E2
24	8	0000 0060	TIMERA0
25	9	0000 0064	TIMERA0
26	10	0000 0068	TIMERA1
27	11	0000 006C	TIMERA1
28	12	0000 0070	TIMERA2
29	13	0000 0074	TIMERA2
30	14	0000 0078	TIMERA3
31	15	0000 007C	TIMERA3
32	16	0000 0080	eUSCI_A0
33	17	0000 0084	eUSCI_A1
34	18	0000 0088	eUSCI_A2
35	19	0000 008C	eUSCI_A3
36	20	0000 0090	eUSCI_B0

37	21	0000 0094	eUSCI_B1
38	22	0000 0098	eUSCI_B3
39	23	0000 009C	eUSCI_B4
40	24	0000 00A0	ADC14
41	25	0000 00A4	TIMER32_INT1
42	26	0000 00A8	TIMER32_INT2
43	27	0000 00AC	TIMER32_INTC
44	28	0000 00B0	AES256
45	29	0000 00B4	RTC_C
46	30	0000 00B8	DMA_ERR
47	31	0000-00BC	DMA_INT3
48	32	0000 00C0	DMA_INT2
49	33	0000 00C4	DMA_INT1
50	34	0000 00C8	DMA_INT0
51	35	0000-00CC	I/O Port P1
52	36	0000 00D0	I/O Port P2
53	37	0000 00D4	I/O Port P3
54	38	0000 00D8	I/O Port P4
55	39	0000-00DC	I/O Port P5
56	40	0000 00E0	I/O Port P6
57-79	41-63	0000 00E4 – 0000 013C	reserved

Table 6-7: IRQ assignment in MSP432P401R

Notice from Table 6-7 that interrupt numbers 16 to 255 are allocated for the peripherals. In the MSP432P401R, only INT16 to INT56 are assigned. The INT 51 to INT 56 are assigned to the Digital I/O ports of P1 to P6. See Table 6-7. Although each Digital I/O port has up to 8 pins, there is only one interrupt assigned to the entire port. In other words, there is only one interrupt vector associated with port Px. When any one of the Px.y pins trigger an interrupt, they all use the same address in the interrupt vector table for Px. PxIFG register indicates which pin or pins triggered the interrupt. It is the job of the Interrupt Service Routine (ISR or interrupt Handler) to find out which pin caused the interrupt. Next, we examine the registers associated with the Digital I/O port interrupt.

Upon Reset, all the interrupts are disabled at the peripheral modules and NVIC but enabled globally. To enable any interrupt, we need to enable the interrupt for a specific peripheral module and enable the interrupts at the NVIC module.

Next, we look at the details of each one.

We need to enable the interrupt capability of a given peripheral at the module level. This should be done after other configurations of that peripheral are done. In the case of the Digital I/O ports, each pin can be used as a source of external hardware interrupt. This is done with the PxIE (Portx Interrupt Enable) register, as we will see next.

165

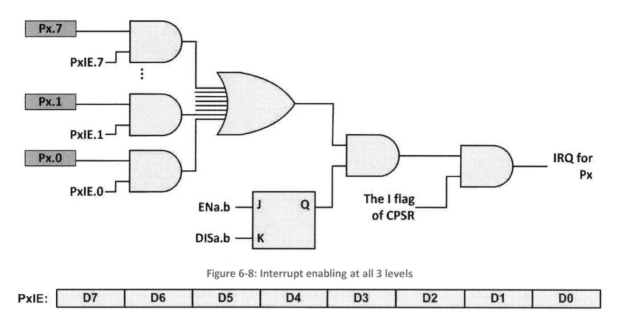

Figure 6-8: Interrupt enabling at all 3 levels

PxIE:	D7	D6	D5	D4	D3	D2	D1	D0

Figure 6-9: PxIE register

Notice that, in the PxIE register bits D7-D0 are used to enable the interrupt capability of each pin of the Digital I/O port, which is D0 for Px.0, D1 for Px.1 pin and so on. For example, to enable the interrupts for P1.4 pin, we will need the following:

P1->IE |= 0x10; /* enable P1.4 pin interrupt */

In ARM Cortex, there is an interrupt enable bit for each entry in the interrupt vector table. These enable bits are controlled by the registers in NVIC. There is a set of registers setting the enable bits (*Interrupt Set Enable Registers* or ENx registers) and there is a set of registers clearing the enable bits (*Interrupt Clear Enable Registers* or DISx registers). Each register covers 32 IRQ interrupts. For example, register EN0 controls the enable for interrupts IRQ0 to IRQ31, EN1 for IRQ32 to IRQ63, and so on. See Figure 6-10.

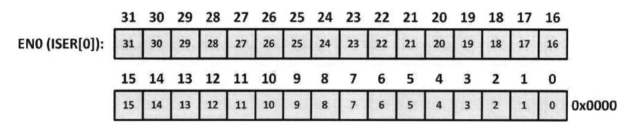

Figure 6-10: Interrupts 0~31 Set Enable (EN0)

Notice, the Interrupt Set Enable Registers are called EN0, EN1, and so on while they are configured as an array in the header file as ISER[0], ISER[1]. The MSP432P401R has a total of 41 IRQs and only ISER[0] and ISER[1] are used.

As we can see in the interrupt vector table in Table 6-7, the PORT1 interrupt is assigned to IRQ35. It corresponds to bit 3 of ISER[1]. Therefore, to enable the interrupts associated with PORT1, we need the following:

NVIC->ISER[1] = 4;   /* enable IRQ35 (bit 3 of ISER[1]) */

Calculating which bit in which register to use is not a trivial task and is prone to errors. The interrupts can be enabled using the following function, as well:

void NVIC_EnableIRQ (IRQn_Type IRQn);

This function is defined in the core_cm4.h file which is included in the *msp432p401r.h* header file. To enable an interrupt using this function, the IRQ number of the interrupt should be passed as the argument to the function. For example, the following statement enables PORT1 interrupt:

NVIC_EnableIRQ(35);

Since the IRQ numbers of all the interrupts are defined in the *msp432p401r.h*, we can use their names instead of their numbers. For example, to enable PORT1 interrupt the following can be used as well:

NVIC_EnableIRQ(PORT1_IRQn);

For more information, open the msp432p401r.h file and find "typedef enum IRQn" in the file.

To disable interrupts there are other registers: ICER0 to ICER1. Again because MSP432P401R device has 41 IRQs, only ISER[0] and ISER[1] are used. See the Figure 6-11.

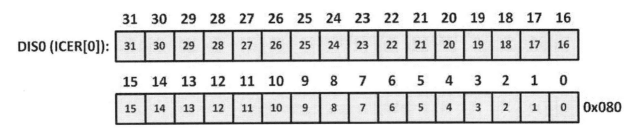

Figure 6-11: Interrupts 0–31 Clear Enable (DIS0)

Each interrupt can be disabled by writing a 1 to the corresponding bit in the ICER registers. Writing 0 to the ICER registers has no effect on their values. For example, the following instruction disables UART0 interrupt, keeping the other interrupts unchanged:

NVIC->ICER[0] = 0x00010000;   /*disable EUSCIA0Interrupt */

The interrupts can be disabled using the following function, as well:

void NVIC_DisableIRQ(IRQn_Type IRQn);

For example, the following instruction disables the UART0 interrupt:

NVIC_DisableIRQ(EUSCIA0_IRQn);

167

In fact, each bit of the ISER register together with its corresponding bit in the ICER register is connected to a J-K Flip-Flop, as shown below:

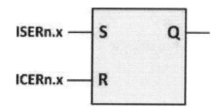

Figure 6-12: Enabling and Disabling an Interrupt

Global interrupt enable/disable allows us with a single instruction to mask all interrupts during the execution of some critical task such as manipulating a common pointer shared by multiple threads. In ARM Cortex M, we do the global enable/disable of interrupts with assembly language instructions of CPSID I (Change processor state-disable interrupts) and CPSIE I (Change processor state-enable interrupts). In C language we use pseudo-functions:

__enable_irq();   /* Enable interrupt Globally */

and

__disable_irq();   /* Disable interrupt Globally */

It is a good idea to disable all interrupts during the initialization of the program and enable interrupts after all the initializations are complete. Now, using the following lines of code, we enable the interrupts for P1.1 pin at all three levels:

```
P1->IE |= 0x02;          /* enable interrupt from P1.1 */
NVIC->ISER[1] = 4;       /* enable IRQ35 (bit 3 of ISER[1]) */
__enable_irq();          /* global enable IRQs */
```

IRQ Priority

As describe earlier, since ARM Cortex-M supports higher priority interrupt to preempt the lower interrupt handler, it is important that each interrupt be assigned a proper priority before they are enabled. The IRQ interrupt priorities are controlled by the NVIC IPR registers. For each IRQ number, there is one byte corresponding to that IRQ to assign its priority. The allowed priority levels are ranging from 0 to 7 in a MSP432P401R device and they are defined by three bits left justified in that byte. There are eleven IPR registers to hold the priority of 41 IRQs. One needs to identify the byte and the register to set the IRQ priority. We will describe it in more details in Section 6.7.

Interrupt trigger point

When an input pin is connected to an external device to be used for interrupt, we have 2 choices for trigger point. They are:

1) rising-edge trigger (positive-edge going from Low to High),
2) falling-Edge trigger (negative-edge going from High to Low),

In MSP432, we must use PxIES (Portx Interrupt Edge Select) to select the trigger point of an interrupt.

| PxIES: | D7 | D6 | D5 | D4 | D3 | D2 | D1 | D0 | 0x0018 |

Figure 6-13: PxIES Interrupt edge activation bits

From above figure, we see the D7-D0 bits are used to decide falling-edge or rising-edge activation. If the bit is cleared to 0, the interrupt is activated on a low-to-high transition. If the bit is set to 1, the interrupt is activated on a high-to-low transition.

Now, the following lines of code make the P1.4 interrupt trigger on falling edge.

P1->IES= 0x10; /* enable falling edge interrupt */

In program 6-1, the main program toggles the red LED on P2.0 continuously. When an interrupt comes from external switches connected to P1.1 or P1.4, it toggles the green LED on P2.1 for a short period of time then it returns back to the main. The delay function is called several times in the interrupt handler to make the LED blink. This is done only for demonstration purpose. It is generally a poor practice to do delay or to wait for some event to happen in the interrupt service routine because when interrupt service routine is active, the main program is halted as you can see that when the green LED is blinking, the red LED ceases to blink.

With Keil µVision IDE, a new project will get an assembly startup code **startup_msp432p401r_uvision.s** created by the project wizard. For all the undefined interrupts, there is one dummy interrupt handler written that does not perform anything and will never return from the handler. The addresses of these interrupt handlers are listed in the interrupt vector table named **__Vectors** in the file. To write an interrupt handler, one has to find out the name of the dummy interrupt handler in the interrupt vector table and reuse the name of the dummy interrupt handler. The linker will overwrite the interrupt vector table with the address of the new interrupt handler. In the case of P1 interrupt, the interrupt handler name is **PORT1_IRQHandler**. The interrupt handler is written with a format of a function in C language.

It is critical that the interrupt handler clears the interrupt flag before returning from the interrupt handler. Otherwise the interrupt appears as if it is still pending and the interrupt handler will be executed again and again forever and the program hangs. The PORT pin interrupt posts an interrupt flag at its corresponding bit in the Interrupt Flag Register (PxIFG). For example, P1.1 interrupt posts the interrupt flag in bit 1 of P1IFG. To clear the interrupt flag, the program writes a 0 to the location of the flag. So to clear the interrupt flag of P1.1, the following statement is used:
P1->IFG&= ~0x02;   /* clear interrupt flag of P1.1 */

The program 6.1 configures P1.1 and P1.4 pin as external interrupt sources. The pins are set to trigger on the falling edge of the signal and the internal pull-up is enabled. The MSP432 LaunchPad has two push button switches connected from P1.1 and P1.4 pins to ground. Pressing either of the push button switches will generate a falling edge and trigger a PORT1 interrupt. The interrupt handler blinks the green LED three times. It does not distinguish which switch is pressed. The infinite loop in main blinks the red LED continuously but when the interrupt is acknowledged and the green LED is blinking, the blinking of the red LED is halted.

Note

All the programs in this chapter except P6-3 may work with TI Code Composer Studio (CCS) with additional editing of msp432_startup_ccs.c. In Keil MDK-ARM, the dummy interrupt handler names are declared as [weak] which could be overwritten by the interrupt handler in our programs. With TI CCS, we need to edit the interrupt vector table to point to our interrupt handler. For example, in Program 6-1 we need to add the function prototype `void PORT1_IRQHandler(void);` in msp432_startup_ccs.c then find the entry in the interrupt vector table that has the comment `/* PORT1 ISR */` and replace `defaultISR` with `PORT1_IRQHandler`.

Program 6-1: P1 interrupt from a switch on MSP432 LaunchPad

```c
/* p6_1: Toggle red LED on P2.0 continuously. Upon pressing either
 * SW1 or SW2, the green LED of P2.1 should toggle for three times.
 * main program toggles red LED while waiting for interrupt from SW1 or SW2.
 * When green LED is blinking, the red LED ceases to blink.
 *
 * Tested with Keil 5.20 and MSP432 Device Family Pack V2.2.0.
 */

#include "msp.h"

void delayMs(int n);

int main(void) {
    __disable_irq();     /* global disable IRQs */

    /* configure P1.1, P1.4 for switch inputs */
    P1->SEL1 &= ~0x12;   /* configure P1.1, P1.4 as simple I/O */
    P1->SEL0 &= ~0x12;
    P1->DIR  &= ~0x12;   /* P1.1, P1.4 set as input */
    P1->REN  |= 0x12;    /* P1.1, P1.4 pull resistor enabled */
    P1->OUT  |= 0x12;    /* Pull up/down is selected by P1->OUT */
    P1->IES  |= 0x12;    /* make interrupt trigger on high-to-low transition */
    P1->IFG   = 0;       /* clear pending interrupt flags */
    P1->IE   |= 0x12;    /* enable interrupt from P1.1, P1.4 */

    /* configure P2.2-P2.0 for tri-color LEDs */
    P2->SEL1 &= ~7;      /* configure P2.2-P2.0 as simple I/O */
    P2->SEL0 &= ~7;

    P2->DIR  |= 7;       /* P2.2-2.0 set as output */
    P2->OUT  &= ~7;      /* turn all three LEDs off */

    NVIC_SetPriority(PORT1_IRQn, 3); /* set priority to 3 in NVIC */
    NVIC_EnableIRQ(PORT1_IRQn);      /* enable interrupt in NVIC */
    __enable_irq();                  /* global enable IRQs */
```

```
    /* toggle the red LED (P2.0) continuously */
    while(1) {
        P2->OUT |= 0x01;
        delayMs(500);
        P2->OUT &= ~0x01;
        delayMs(500);
    }
}

/* SW1 is connected to P1.1 pin, SW2 is connected to P1.4
 * Both of them trigger PORT1 interrupt */
void PORT1_IRQHandler(void) {
    int i;
    volatile int readback;
    /* toggle green LED (P2.1) three times */
    for (i = 0; i < 3; i++) {
        P2->OUT |= 0x02;
        delayMs(500);
        P2->OUT &= ~0x02;
        delayMs(500);
    }
    P1->IFG &= ~0x12; /* clear the interrupt flag before return */
}

/* delay n milliseconds (3 MHz CPU clock) */
void delayMs(int n) {
    int i, j;

    for (j = 0; j < n; j++)
        for (i = 250; i > 0; i--);   /* do nothing for 1 ms */
}
```

Notice in Program 6-1, if we have two switches connected to P1.1 and P1.4, the program does not make any distinction which switch is pressed. The reason is that only one interrupt (IRQ35) is associated with the entire PORT1. In other words, whichever pin of PORT1 interrupt is activated it goes to the same interrupt handler belonging to PORT1. Next, we will modify the program to distinguish between various pins of P1. That means, by pressing SW1 (P1.1) we can blink the green LED (P2.1) and when SW2 (P1.4) is pressed, the blue LED (P2.2) is blinked.

Each of the PORT1 pin interrupt, sets a bit in the P1IFG register. By reading P1IFG register, the interrupt handler will be able to discern the source pin of the interrupt.

Program 6-2: Rewrite of the interrupt handler in Program 6-1 to distinguish the interrupt pin

```
/* p6_2: Toggle red LED on P2.0 continuously. Upon pressing
 * SW1, the green LED on P2.1 blinks three times.
 * If SW2 is pressed, the blue LED on P2.2 blinks three times.
 * main program toggles red LED while waiting for interrupt from SW1 or SW2.
 * When green LED is blinking, the red LED ceases to blink.
 *
```

```
 * Tested with Keil 5.20 and MSP432 Device Family Pack V2.2.0.
 */

#include "msp.h"

void delayMs(int n);

int main(void)
{
    __disable_irq();

    /* configure P1.1, P1.4 for switch inputs */
    P1->SEL1 &= ~0x12;     /* configure P1.1, P1.4 as simple I/O */
    P1->SEL0 &= ~0x12;
    P1->DIR  &= ~0x12;     /* P1.1, P1.4 set as input */
    P1->REN  |= 0x12;      /* P1.1, P1.4 pull resistor enabled */
    P1->OUT  |= 0x12;      /* Pull up/down is selected by P1->OUT */
    P1->IES  |= 0x12;      /* make interrupt trigger on high-to-low transition */
    P1->IFG   = 0;         /* clear all pending interrupt from PORT1 */
    P1->IE   |= 0x12;      /* enable interrupt from P1.1, P1.4 */

    /* configure P2.2-P2.0 for tri-color LEDs */
    P2->SEL1 &= ~7;        /* configure P2.2-P2.0 as simple I/O */
    P2->SEL0 &= ~7;

    P2->DIR  |= 7;         /* P2.2-2.0 set as output */
    P2->OUT  &= ~7;        /* turn all three LEDs off */

    NVIC_SetPriority(PORT1_IRQn, 3); /* set priority to 3 in NVIC */
    NVIC_EnableIRQ(PORT1_IRQn);      /* enable interrupt in NVIC */
    __enable_irq();                  /* global enable IRQs */

    /* toggle the red LED (P2.0) continuously */
    while(1) {
        P2->OUT |= 0x01;
        delayMs(500);
        P2->OUT &= ~0x01;
        delayMs(500);
    }
}

/* SW1 is connected to P1.1 pin, SW2 is connected to P1.4
 * Both of them trigger PORT1 interrupt */
void PORT1_IRQHandler(void) {
    int i;

    if (P1->IFG & 2) {     /* from SW1 (P1.1) */
        /* toggle green LED (P2.1) three times */
        for (i = 0; i < 3; i++) {
            P2->OUT |= 0x02;
            delayMs(500);
            P2->OUT &= ~0x02;
            delayMs(500);
        }
        P1->IFG &= ~2;     /* clear interrupt flag */
    }
```

```
    if (P1->IFG & 0X10) { /* from SW2 (P1.4) */
        /* toggle blue LED (P2.2) three times */
        for (i = 0; i < 3; i++) {
            P2->OUT |= 0x04;
            delayMs(500);
            P2->OUT &= ~0x04;
            delayMs(500);
        }
        P1->IFG &= ~0x10;  /* clear interrupt flag */
    }
}

/* delay n milliseconds (3 MHz CPU clock) */
void delayMs(int n)
{
    int i, j;
    for(i = 0 ; i < n; i++)
        for(j = 0; j < 250; j++)
            {}  /* do nothing for 1 ms */
}
```

Review Questions

1. IRQ35 is assigned to INT number____.
2. True or false. There is an interrupt assigned to each pin of every Digital I/O port.
3. True or false. The I/O ports in MSP432 support both level and edge trigger interrupts.
4. We use _____ in C to enable the interrupts globally.
5. Show 3 levels of interrupt enabling we must go through before we start using it.

Section 6.4: UART Serial Port Interrupt Programming

In Chapter 4, we showed the programming of UART0 in MSP432 ARM using polling. This chapter shows how to do the same thing using interrupt. Using interrupt frees up the CPU from having to poll the status of UART.

UART0 Interrupt Programming to receive data

Program 4-2 in Chapter 4 showed how UART0 receives data by polling Receive Transmit Interrupt (UCRXIFG) flag. The disadvantage with that program is that it ties down the CPU while polling the flag. We can modify it to make it an interrupt driven program. Examining the UCAxIE (UARTx Interrupt Enable) register, we see bit 0 (UCRXIE) allows us to enable the receive interrupt. If the receive interrupt for UART is enabled when a byte is received, the receiver UCRXIFG flag (bit 0 in UCAxIFG Interrupt Flag register) goes high and that in turn is directed to NVIC and causes the interrupt handler associated with the UARTx to be executed. In the UARTx handler we must read the received character. Reading the received character from the UCAxRXBUF data register clears the UCRXIFG flag.

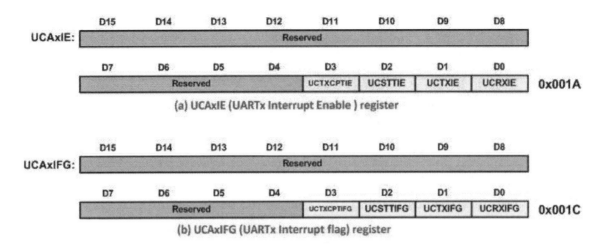

Figure 6-14: UART Interrupt Registers

Field	Bit	Description
UCTXCPTIE	D3	Transmit complete interrupt enable 0 = Interrupt disabled 1 = Interrupt enabled
UCSTTIE	D2	Start bit interrupt enable 0 = Interrupt disabled 1 = Interrupt
UCTXIE	D1	Transmit interrupt enable 0 = Interrupt disabled 1 = Interrupt enabled
UCRXIE	D0	Receive interrupt enable 0 = Interrupt disabled 1 = Interrupt enabled

Table 6-8: UCAxIE (UARTx Interrupt Enable) register

From Table 6-7 we see IRQ16 is assigned to UART0. We enable the receiver interrupt in UART0 as follow:

EUSCI_A0->IE |= 1;   /* enable receive interrupt */
NVIC_EnableIRQ(EUSCIA0_IRQn); /* enable EUSCIA0 interrupt in NVIC */
__enable_irq();   /* global enable IRQs */

In Program 6-3, pressing a key at the terminal emulator causes the PC to send the ASCII code of the key to the MSP432 LaunchPad. When the character is received by UART0, the interrupt handler reads the character and writes it to LEDs.

Program 6-3: Using the UART0 interrupt

```
/* p6_3.c UART0 Receive Interrupt Handling
 *
 * This program modifies p4_2.c to use interrupt to handle the UART0 receive.
 * It receives any key from terminal emulator (TeraTerm) of the host PC to the UART0
 * on MSP432 LaunchPad. The UART0 is connected to the XDS110 debug interface on the
 * LaunchPad and it has a virtual connection to the host PC COM port.
 *
 * Launch a terminal emulator (TeraTerm) on a PC and hit any key.
```

```
 * The tri-color LEDs are turned on or off according to the key received.
 *
 * By default the subsystem master clock is 3 MHz.
 * Setting EUSCI_A0->BRW=26 with oversampling disabled yields 115200 Baud.
 *
 * Tested with Keil 5.20 and MSP432 Device Family Pack V2.2.0.
 */
#include "msp.h"

void UART0_init(void);

int main(void) {
    __disable_irq();

    UART0_init();

    /* initialize P2.2-P2.0 for tri-color LEDs */
    P2->SEL1 &= ~7;            /* configure P2.2-P2.0 as simple I/O */
    P2->SEL0 &= ~7;
    P2->DIR |= 7;              /* P2.2-2.0 set as output */

    NVIC_SetPriority(EUSCIA0_IRQn, 4); /* set priority to 4 in NVIC */
    NVIC_EnableIRQ(EUSCIA0_IRQn);      /* enable interrupt in NVIC */
    __enable_irq();                    /* global enable IRQs */

    while (1) {
    }
}

void UART0_init(void) {
    EUSCI_A0->CTLW0 |= 1;      /* put in reset mode for config */
    EUSCI_A0->MCTLW = 0;       /* disable oversampling */
    EUSCI_A0->CTLW0 = 0x0081;  /* 1 stop bit, no parity, SMCLK, 8-bit data */
    EUSCI_A0->BRW = 26;        /* 3000000 / 115200 = 26 */
    P1->SEL0 |= 0x0C;          /* P1.3, P1.2 for UART */
    P1->SEL1 &= ~0x0C;
    EUSCI_A0->CTLW0 &= ~1;     /* take UART out of reset mode */
    EUSCI_A0->IE |= 1;         /* enable receive interrupt */
}

void EUSCIA0_IRQHandler(void) {
    P2->OUT = EUSCI_A0->RXBUF; /* read the receive char and set the LEDs */
                               /* interrupt flag is cleared by reading RXBUF */
}
```

Review Questions

1. In MSP432, Which IRQ is assigned to UART0?
2. True or false. There is only one interrupt for both Receiver and Transmitter.
3. Which pins are assigned to UART0_TXD and UART0_RXD of MSP432 LaunchPad?
4. We use register _____ to enable the interrupt associated with UART0.
5. True or false. Upon Reset, UART0 is enabled and ready to go.

Section 6.5: SysTick Programming and Interrupt

Another useful interrupt in ARM is the SysTick. The SysTick timer was discussed in Chapter 5. Next, you learn how to use the SysTick interrupt. See Figure 6-15.

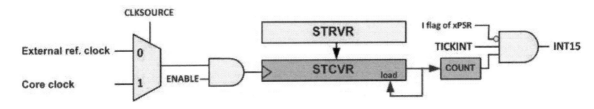

Figure 6-15: SysTick Internal Structure

If TICKINT=1, when the COUNT flag is set, it generates an interrupt. TICKINT is D1 of the STCTRL register, as shown in Figure 6-16.

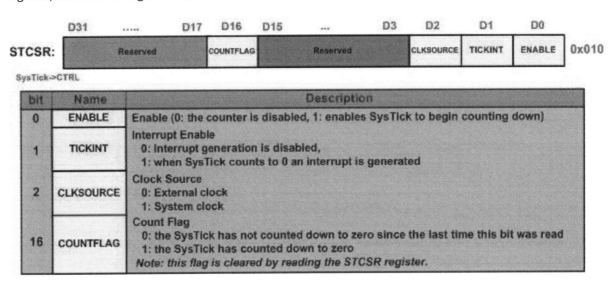

Figure 6-16: SysTick Control and Status Register (STCTRL)

The SysTick interrupt can be used to initiate an action on a periodic basis. This action is performed internally at a fixed rate without external signal. For example, in a given application we can use SysTick to read a sensor every 200 msec. SysTick is used widely for an operating system so that the system software may interrupt the application software periodically (often at 10 ms interval) to monitor and control the system operations.

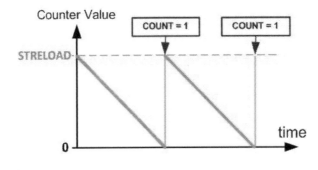

Figure 6-17: SysTick Counting

Using SysTick with Interrupt

Examining interrupt vector table for ARM Cortex, we see the SysTick is the interrupt #15.

The Program 6-4 uses the SysTick to toggle the red LED of P2.0 every second. We need the RELOAD value of 3,000,000-1. The CLK_SRC bit of CTRL register is set so system clock is used as the clock source of SysTick. The system clock is running at 3 MHz. The COUNT flag is raised every 3,000,000 clocks and an interrupt occurs. Then the RELOAD register is loaded with 3,000,000-1 automatically.

Notice the interrupt is enabled in SysTick Control register. Because SysTick is an interrupt below interrupt #16, the enable/disable and the priority are not managed by the registers in the NVIC. Its priority is controlled in the most significant byte of System Handler Priority 3 register (SHPR3) of System Control Block (SCB->SHP[1]). We used NVIC_SetPriority() function defined in core_cm4.h to change the priority. Although the function name has NVIC in it, it modifies SHP registers for interrupts below 16. There is no need to clear interrupt flag in the interrupt handler for SysTick.

Program 6-4: SysTick interrupt

```
/* p6_4.c: Toggle the blue LED using the SysTick interrupt
 * This program sets up the SysTick to interrupt at 1 Hz.
 * The system clock is running at 3 MHz, so 3,000,000-1 for RELOAD register.
 * In the interrupt handler, the blue LED is toggled.
 *
 * Tested with Keil 5.20 and MSP432 Device Family Pack V2.2.0.
 */

#include "msp.h"

int main(void) {
    __disable_irq();

    /* initialize P2.2 for tri-color LEDs */
    P2->SEL1 &= ~4;             /* configure P2.2 as simple I/O */
    P2->SEL0 &= ~4;
    P2->DIR |= 4;               /* P2.2 set as output */

    /* Configure SysTick */
    SysTick->LOAD = 3000000-1;  /* reload with number of clocks per second */
    SysTick->CTRL = 7;              /* enable SysTick interrupt, use system clock */
    NVIC_SetPriority (SysTick_IRQn, 2); /* set priority to 2 */

    __enable_irq();             /* global enable interrupt */

    while (1) {
    }
}

void SysTick_Handler(void){
    P2->OUT ^= 4;     /* toggle the blue LED */
}
```

Review Questions

1. Which interrupt is assigned to SysTick in MSP432 chip?
2. We use register _____ to enable the interrupt associated with SysTick.
3. True or false. We use EN0 register to enable SysTick interrupt.

Section 6.6: Timer Interrupt Programming

In Chapter 5, we showed how to program the timers. In those programming examples, we used polling to see if a timeout event occurred. In this section, we give interrupt-based version of those programs.

Timer32 Interrupt

Examine the programs in Section 5.2 of Chapter 5. Notice, we could only run those programs one at a time since we have to monitor the timer flag continuously. By using interrupt, we can run several of timer programs all at the same time. To do that, we need to enable the timer interrupt using the IE (Interrupt Enable) bit in the in T32CONTROLx register. See Figure 6-18 and Table 6-9.

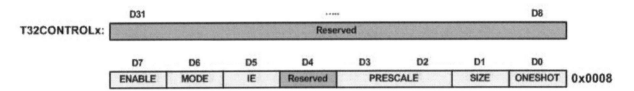

Figure 6-18: IE (Interrupt Enable) bit (d5) in T32CONTROLx (T32 Control) register

INT#	IRQ#	Vector location	Device
1-15	None	0000 0000 to 0000 003C	CPU Exception(set by ARM)
16	0	0000 0040	PSS
17	1	0000 0044	CS
18	2	0000 0048	PCM
19	3	0000 004C	WDT_A
20	4	0000 0050	FPU_INT
21	5	0000 0054	Flash Controller
22	6	0000 0058	COMP_E1
23	7	0000 005C	COMP_E2
24	8	0000 0060	TIMERA0
25	9	0000 0064	TIMERA0
26	10	0000 0068	TIMERA1
27	11	0000 006C	TIMERA1
28	12	0000 0070	TIMERA2
29	13	0000 0074	TIMERA2
30	14	0000 0078	TIMERA3
31	15	0000 007C	TIMERA3
32	16	0000 0080	eUSCI_A0
33	17	0000 0084	eUSCI_A1
34	18	0000 0088	eUSCI_A2
35	19	0000 008C	eUSCI_A3

178

36	20	0000 0090	eUSCI_B0
37	21	0000 0094	eUSCI_B1
38	22	0000 0098	eUSCI_B3
39	23	0000 009C	eUSCI_B4
40	24	0000 00A0	ADC14
41	25	0000 00A4	TIMER32_INT1
42	26	0000 00A8	TIMER32_INT2
43	27	0000 00AC	TIMER32_INTC
44	28	0000 00B0	AES256
45	29	0000 00B4	RTC_C
46	30	0000 00B8	DMA_ERR
47	31	0000-00BC	DMA_INT3
48	32	0000 00C0	DMA_INT2
49	33	0000 00C4	DMA_INT1
50	34	0000 00C8	DMA_INT0
51	35	0000-00CC	I/O Port P1
52	36	0000 00D0	I/O Port P2
53	37	0000 00D4	I/O Port P3
54	38	0000 00D8	I/O Port P4
55	39	0000-00DC	I/O Port P5
56	40	0000 00E0	I/O Port P6
57-79	41-63	0000 00E4 – 0000 013C	reserved

Table 6-7: IRQ assignment in MSP432P401R

Bit	Field	Description
7	ENABLE	Enable bit (0: Timer disabled, 1: Timer enabled)
6	MODE	Mode bit (0: free-running mode, 1: periodic mode)
5	IE	Interrupt enable bit (0: disabled, 1: enabled)
3-2	PRESCALE	Prescale bits: <table><tr><td>00</td><td>clock is divided by 1</td></tr><tr><td>01</td><td>clock is divided by 16</td></tr><tr><td>10</td><td>clock is divided by 256</td></tr><tr><td>11</td><td>Reserved</td></tr></table>
1	SIZE	Selects 16 or 32 bit counter operation <table><tr><td>0</td><td>16-bit counter</td></tr><tr><td>1</td><td>13-bit counter</td></tr></table>
0	ONESHOT	Selects one-shot or wrapping counter mode <table><tr><td>0</td><td>Wrapping mode</td></tr><tr><td>1</td><td>One-shot mode</td></tr></table>

Table 6-9: T32CONTROLx

Notice that IRQ25 and IRQ26 are assigned to Timer32_INT1 and Timer32_INT2, respectively. Timer32_INTC is the combined interrupt request of Timer32_INT1 and Timer32_INT2 and is assigned IRQ27.

The following will enable these timers in NVIC:

NVIC->ISER[0] |= 0x02000000;   /* enable IRQ25(D25of ISER[0]) */
NVIC->ISER[0] |= 0x04000000;   /* enable IRQ26 (D26 of ISER[0]) */
NVIC->ISER[0] |= 0x08000000;   /* enable IRQ27 (D27 of ISER[0]) */

The priority of these three interrupts may be assigned by:

NVIC->IP[25] |= prio << 5;   /* set priority of IRQ25 to the value of prio */
NVIC->IP[26] |= prio << 5;   /* set priority of IRQ26 to the value of prio*/
NVIC->IP[27] |= prio << 5;   /* set priority of IRQ27 to the value of prio*/

In Program 6-5, the main program toggles the blue LED of P2.2 continuously. Using interrupts, Timer32_INT1 Toggles red LED (P2.0) and Timer32_INT2 toggles green LED (P2.1), every so often. We used the function defined in core_cm4.h to enable the interrupts and change the priorities.

Program 6-5: Toggling the LEDs using the Timer32 interrupts

```
/* p6_5.c Toggling LEDs independently using Timer32 interrupts
 *
 * This program uses Timer32.1 and Timer32.2 to generate interrupts.
 * In the interrupt handlers, the red and green LEDs are toggled.
 * In the infinite loop the blue LED is toggled.
 * All three LEDs are blinked independently.
 *
 * Tested with Keil 5.20 and MSP432 Device Family Pack V2.2.0.
 */

#include "msp.h"
void delayMs(int n);

int main(void) {
    __disable_irq();

    /* initialize P2.2-P2.0 for tri-color LEDs */
    P2->SEL1 &= ~7;               /* configure P2.2-P2.0 as simple I/O */
    P2->SEL0 &= ~7;
    P2->DIR |= 7;                 /* P2.2-P2.0 set as output */

    /* configure Timer32.1 */
    TIMER32_1->CONTROL = 0xC2;          /* no prescaler, periodic mode, 32-bit timer. */
    TIMER32_1->LOAD = 2300000-1;        /* set the reload value */
    TIMER32_1->CONTROL |= 0x20;         /* enable interrupt */
    NVIC_SetPriority(T32_INT1_IRQn, 3); /* set priority to 3 in NVIC */
    NVIC_EnableIRQ(T32_INT1_IRQn);      /* enable interrupt in NVIC */

    /* configure Timer32.2 */
    TIMER32_2->CONTROL = 0xC2;          /* no prescaler, periodic mode, 32-bit timer. */
```

```
    TIMER32_2->LOAD = 1900000-1;           /* set the reload value */
    TIMER32_2->CONTROL |= 0x20;            /* enable interrupt */
    NVIC_SetPriority(T32_INT2_IRQn, 4);    /* set priority to 4 in NVIC */
    NVIC_EnableIRQ(T32_INT2_IRQn);         /* enable interrupt in NVIC */

    __enable_irq();                        /* global enable IRQs */

    while (1) {
        P2->OUT ^= 4;                      /* blink blue LED */
        delayMs(1000);
    }
}

void T32_INT1_IRQHandler(void) {
    TIMER32_1->INTCLR = 0;           /* clear raw interrupt flag */
    P2->OUT ^= 1;                    /* toggle red LED */
}

void T32_INT2_IRQHandler(void) {
    TIMER32_2->INTCLR = 0;           /* clear raw interrupt flag */
    P2->OUT ^= 2;                    /* toggle green LED */
}

/* delay milliseconds when system clock is at 3 MHz */
void delayMs(int n) {
    int i, j;

    for (j = 0; j < n; j++)
        for (i = 250; i > 0; i--);       /* wait 1 ms */
}
```

Timer_A Interrupt

As mentioned in Chapter 5, there are four Timer_A modules and each Timer_A module has five capture/compare blocks in a MSP432P401R device. Each Timer_A module has six sources of interrupt, one for the timer counter (TAxR) overflow and five for each of the five capture/compare blocks. There are two interrupt vectors for each Timer_A module. One interrupt vector is for the capture/compare block 0, the other vector is for the rest of the interrupts including the timer counter overflow.

The Timer counter overflow sets the TAIFG flag in TAxCTL register. The TAIE bit of the same register enables the interrupt.

The capture event or a compare event occurs, the CCIFG flag of the corresponding TAxCCTLy register is set. The CCIE bit of the same register enables the interrupt.

In the Keil MDK-ARM, the compare/capture block 0 interrupt is named TAx_0_IRQ. The interrupt for the rest is named TAx_N_IRQ.

In Program 6-6, Timer_A1 is configured for up count mode. When the timer counter matches the value in TA1CCR0, the timer counter is rest to 0 and the CCIFG bit in TA1CCTL0 is set. With CCIE bit in

TA1CCTL0 set, it generates a TA1_0_IRQ interrupt. In the interrupt handler, the CCIFG is cleared and the red LED is toggled.

Program 6-6: Toggling the red LED using the Timer_A interrupt

```c
/* p6_6.c Toggling red LED at 1 Hz using Timer_A1 interrupt
 * System clock running at 3 MHz is used. Timer_A1 is configured
 * to count up from 0 to 46,875-1, which is loaded in TIMER_A1->CCR[0].
 * When the counter (TA1R) value reaches TIMER_A1->CCR[0], CCIFG
 * bit in TIMER_A1->CCTL[0] is set and an interrupt is generated.
 * The clock input dividers are set to divide by 8 and 8.
 * The timer counter roll over interval is: 3,000,000 / 8 / 8 / 46,875 = 1 Hz.
 * In the interrupt handler, the red LED is toggled.
 * The red LED is connected to P2.0.
 *
 * Tested with Keil 5.20 and MSP432 Device Family Pack V2.2.0.
 */
#include "msp.h"

int main(void) {
    __disable_irq();

    /* initialize P2.0 for red LED */
    P2->SEL1 &= ~1;            /* configure P2.0 as simple I/O */
    P2->SEL0 &= ~1;
    P2->DIR |= 1;              /* P2.0 set as output */

    TIMER_A1->CTL = 0x02D1;        /* SMCLK, ID=/8, up mode, TA clear */
    TIMER_A1->CCR[0] = 46875 -1;    /* for 1 sec */
    TIMER_A1->EX0 = 7;             /* IDEX = /8 */
    TIMER_A1->CCTL[0] |= 0x10;     /* enable TA1.0 interrupt */

    NVIC_SetPriority(TA1_0_IRQn, 3);    /* set priority to 3 in NVIC */
    NVIC_EnableIRQ(TA1_0_IRQn);         /* enable interrupt in NVIC */
    __enable_irq();                     /* global enable IRQs */

    while (1) {
    }
}

void TA1_0_IRQHandler(void) {
    TIMER_A1->CCTL[0] &= ~1;       /* clear interrupt flag */
    P2->OUT ^= 1;                  /* toggle red LED */
}
```

Using Compare Mode to Generate Periodic Signals

In Chapter 5, we discussed using compare mode of Timer_A to generate a periodic output signal. Generating output signal using timer hardware instead of toggling the output pin in interrupt handler has the advantage of precision timing that is not affected by the jittering of the interrupt latency. But the method used in Chapter 5 (Program 5-11) requires two Capture/Compare blocks and one of them must be block 0, where TAxCCR0 is used to determine the period of the signal. That means even though a timer module may generate five output signals, they must all have the same frequency.

The other way to generate precision output signals using compare mode is demonstrated in Program 6-7. TA0CCR4 is loaded with 11,719 after TA0R is cleared. It takes 11,719 timer clock cycles for the compare circuit to match. When there is a match, the output toggles and an interrupt is generated. In the interrupt handler, 11,719 is added to the value of TA0CCR4. That means the compare circuit will have another match 11,719 timer clock cycles after the last match when the output toggled. See Figure 6-19.

None of the Timer_A output is connected to the LEDs of the MSP432 LaunchPad. To demonstrate the Program 6-7 output, we use the Port Mapping function of the Digital I/O modules (see Section 2.6) to map the Timer_A0 block 4 output to pin P2.1.

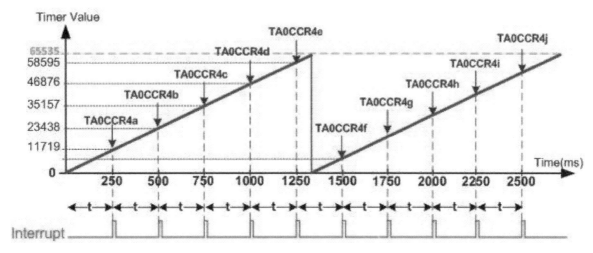

Figure 6-19: Making Periodic Interrupts using Timer_A

Program 6-7: Waveform generation using Timer_A compare mode

```
/* p6_7.c Waveform generation using Timer_A0.4 compare
 *
 * This program uses TA0.4 in compare mode to generate
 * periodic signal on pin P2.7.
 * System clock is running at 3 MHz. Clock input dividers are
 * set to divide by 8 and 8. TA0 is set to continuous mode.
 * TA0.4 is configured for compare mode. When the
 * TA0R counter value matches TIMER_A0->CCR[4], the output is set to toggle.
 * It also triggers an interrupt. In the interrupt handler,
 * 11719 is added to TIMER_A0->CCR[4] so that the next toggle occurs
 * 11719 cycles (250 ms) later. Both P2.7 and P2.1 toggle at 250 ms period.
 *
 * Since none of the LEDs is connected to a Timer_A output,
 * Port Map is used to connect the TA0.4 output to P2.1, which
 * is connected to the green LED.
 *
 * Tested with Keil 5.17 and MSP432 CMSIS Update
 */

#include "msp.h"
```

```
void redirect(void);

int main(void)
{
    __disable_irq();

    /* set up TA0.4 to do compare */
    TIMER_A0->CTL = 0x02E4;      /* SMCLK, ID = /8, continuous mode, TA clear */
    TIMER_A0->EX0 = 7;           /* IDEX = /8 */
    TIMER_A0->CCTL[4] = 0x80;    /* OUTMOD = toggle */
    TIMER_A0->CCR[4] = 11719;    /* toggle point */
    TIMER_A0->CCTL[4] |= 0x10;   /* enable CC interrupt */

    /* Configure P2.7 as Timer A0.4 compare output */
    P2->SEL0 |= 0x80;
    P2->SEL1 &= ~0x80;
    P2->DIR |= 0x80;

    redirect();             /* connect TA0.4 output to pin P2.1 */

    NVIC_SetPriority(TA0_N_IRQn, 3);    /* set priority to 3 in NVIC */
    NVIC_EnableIRQ(TA0_N_IRQn);         /* enable interrupt in NVIC */
    __enable_irq();                     /* global enable IRQs */

    while (1) {
    }
}

void TA0_N_IRQHandler(void) {
    TIMER_A0->CCTL[4] &= ~1;        /* clear interrupt flag */
    TIMER_A0->CCR[4] += 11719;      /* schedule next toggle */
}

/* This function connects the output of TA0.4 to pin P2.1 */
void redirect(void) {
    PMAP->KEYID = 0x2D52;       /* unlock PMAP */
    P2MAP->PMAP_REGISTER1 = PMAP_TA0CCR4A;  /* 23, map P2.1 to TA0.4 */
    P2->DIR |= 2;               /* set up P2.1 to take TA0.4 output */
    P2->SEL0 |= 2;
    P2->SEL1 &= ~2;
    PMAP->CTL = 1;              /* lock PMAP */
    PMAP->KEYID = 0;
}
```

Review Questions

1. For MSP432 chip, which IRQ is assigned to Timer32_INT1?
2. For MSP432 chip, which IRQ is assigned to Timer32_INT2?
3. True or false. There is only one interrupt for both Timer32_INT1 and Timer32_INT2.
4. True or false. Upon Reset, Timer32_INT1 is enabled and ready to go.
5. Which bit of IE register is used to enable the Timer32_INT1 interrupt?

Section 6.7: Interrupt Priority Programming in MSP432 ARM

The implementation of interrupts varies from vendor to vendor. While ARM Holdings Co. has control over the standardization of the first 3 interrupts (INT0, INT1, and INT2), the ARM licensees are free to implement the interrupts of INT3-INT255. The first three interrupts are Reset, NMI, and Hard Fault. For these three interrupts, Reset has the highest priority (with -3 priority number), then NMI (with -2), and Hard Fault (with -1). In ARM, the lower priority number has the higher priority. All other interrupts have the priority number 0 meaning they have lower priority than Reset, NMI, and Hard Fault. In the case of ARM Cortex-M, it groups several interrupts together with specific interrupt priority. There are several special function registers dealing with the interrupts belonging to system exceptions of 4 to 15. You can explore them by reading the ARM Cortex-M data sheet. In this section, we deal with the priority of peripheral interrupts of INT16 (IRQ0) to INT56 (IRQ40).

IRQ0 to IRQ41 in MSP432 ARM

The INT16 is assigned to IRQ0 since the first 15 interrupts (INT1-INT15) are used by the ARM core itself. Not all the IRQs are implemented in all ARM chips. For example, The MSP432 ARM chip implements up to IRQ40 (or INT56). In other words, MSP432 has IRQ0 to IRQ40. Notice that if we add 16 to IRQ# we get its INT#. We learned in Section 6.1 that, by multiplying the INT# by 4 we get its address in the interrupt vector table. Now, as far as peripherals are concerned, we must pay special attention to the IRQ# since this is used in the priority scheme used by the NVIC.

When more than one interrupts are pending, the interrupt with the highest priority is acknowledged first. While an interrupt handler is running, another interrupt with higher priority will interrupt the current interrupt handler and start its own interrupt handler (nested interrupts).

The IPR registers and Priority Grouping in ARM Cortex

The priority of an IRQ is assigned in one of the interrupt priority registers called *IPRx (Interrupt PRiorityx)* in NVIC. If we do not assign a priority to an IRQ, by default, it has priority 0. Each IRQ uses one byte in an interrupt priority register. Therefore, each interrupt priority register holds priorities for four IRQ. For example, IPR0 (IPR zero) holds the priorities of IRQ0, IRQ1, IRQ2 and IRQ3. In the same way, the priorities of IRQ4, IRQ5, IRQ6 and IRQ7 are assigned in IPR1. See Figure 6-20. For 41 IRQs, eleven interrupt priority registers are used. The MSP432 devices use only the three most significant bits of the byte in the interrupt priority register. With three bits, there can be eight different priorities, 0 to 7. The lower the number the higher the priority is.

Notice, there is a pattern in the IPR# and IRQ# assignments. It follows the following formula:

IPRn   IRQ(4n), IRQ(4n+1), IRQ(4n+2), and IRQ(4n+3)

In other words, we multiply the IPR# number by 4 to get the first IRQ and from there we add 1, 2, and 3 to get all the four IRQs it supports. Because only the highest three bits are used, we need to multiply the priority number by 32 before loading it into the proper byte. For example, for priority 5, the value 160 should be loaded. To ease the calculation of finding the correct bits of the correct register to set the proper value for the priority, Keil MDK-ARM has a function NVIC_SetPriority(IRQ#) defined in core_cm4.h for programmers to set the priority of an IRQ.

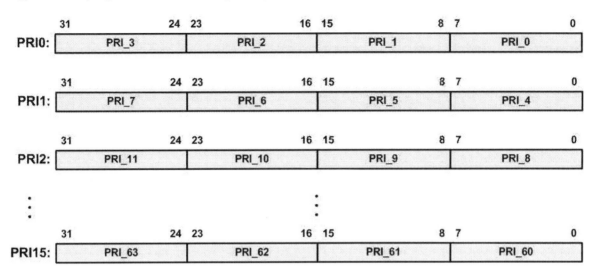

Figure 6-20: IPRn Registers

For example, if we want to set the T32_INT2 interrupt priority to 3, first we need to find out the IRQ number of T32_INT2 interrupt, which is 26. To locate the register for IRQ26, we will divide 26 by 4, which results in a quotient of 6 and remainder of 2. The byte that holds the priority of T32_INT2 is byte 2 of IPR6. To get to byte 2, we need to shift the priority 16 bits (8 x 2) to the left and to get the three most significant bits, we need to shift it 5 more bits to the left. To make the task a little easier, the priority registers are defined as an array of 8-bit bytes, NVIC->IP[IRQn]. We can use the interrupt number as index of IP[ ] to access the priority byte. So the statement will look like:

NVIC->IP[IRQn] = PRIO << 5;

    or

NVIC->IP[26] = 3 << 5;

This is tedious and error prone. It would be easier to use the function:

NVIC_SetPriority (T32_INT2_IRQn, 3);

    T32_INT2_IRQn is defined in msp432p401r.h.

Program 6-8 illustrates two interrupts with different priority. In this example, delay function is called in the interrupt handler to demonstrate the preemption by higher priority interrupt. (In real applications, it is a bad practice to call delay function in interrupt handler.) T32_INT1 is programmed to interrupt at 1 second interval. In the interrupt handler, the red LED is turned on for 500 ms. T32_INT2 is programmed to interrupt at 100 ms interval and in its interrupt handler, the blue LED is turned on for 20 ms. Since T32_INT1 has higher priority, you will observe that the blue LED is not blinking when T32_INT2 interrupt handler is running (when the red LED is on). Now change the priority of the T32_INT2 to be higher than T32_INT1 by changing the lines from

186

```
#define PRIO_TMR1 2
#define PRIO_TMR2 3
```

to

```
#define PRIO_TMR1 3
#define PRIO_TMR2 2
```

You will see that the blue LED is blinking all the time so is the red LED because the T32_INT2 (blue LED) preempts T32_INT1 interrupt handler (red LED).

Program 6-8: Interrupt priority demonstration

```c
/* P6_8.c Testing nested interrupts
 * Timer1 is setup to interrupt at 1 Hz. In timer interrupt handler,
 * the red LED is turned on and a delay function of 350 ms is called.
 * The red LED is turned off at the end of the delay.
 *
 * Timer2 is setup to interrupt at 10 Hz. In timer interrupt handler,
 * the blue LED is turned on and a delay function of 20 ms is called.
 * The blue LED is turned off at the end of the delay.
 *
 * When Timer1 has higher priority (the way this code is), the Timer2
 * interrupts are blocked by Timer1 interrupt handler. You can see
 * that when the red LED is on, the blue LED stops blinking.
 *
 * When Timer2 has higher priority (you need to switch the priority of
 * the two timers at the #defines), the Timer1 interrupt handler is
 * preempted by Timer2 interrupts and the blue LED is blinking all the time.
 *
 * Tested with Keil 5.20 and MSP432 Device Family Pack V2.2.0.
 */

#include "msp.h"

void Timer1_init(void);
void Timer2_init(void);
void delayMs(int n);

int main (void) {
    __disable_irq();

    /* initialize P2.2, P2.0 for blue and red LED */
    P2->SEL1 &= ~5;         /* configure P2.2, P2.0 as simple I/O */
    P2->SEL0 &= ~5;
    P2->DIR |= 5;           /* P2.2, P2.0 set as output */

    Timer1_init();
    Timer2_init();

    __enable_irq();

    while(1) { /*wait here for interrupt */
    }
}
```

```
void T32_INT1_IRQHandler(void) {
    P2->OUT |= 4;               /* turn on blue LED */
    delayMs(350);
    P2->OUT &= ~4;              /* turn off blue LED */
    TIMER32_1->INTCLR = 0;      /* clear raw interrupt flag */
}

void T32_INT2_IRQHandler(void) {
    P2->OUT |= 1;               /* turn on red LED */
    delayMs(20);
    P2->OUT &= ~1;              /* turn off red LED */
    TIMER32_2->INTCLR = 0;      /* clear raw interrupt flag */
}

/* priority of Timer1 and Timer2 should be between 0 and 7 */
#define PRIO_TMR1 2
#define PRIO_TMR2 3

void Timer1_init(void) {
    TIMER32_1->CONTROL = 0xC2;       /* no prescaler, periodic mode, 32-bit timer. */
    TIMER32_1->LOAD = 3000000-1;     /* set the reload value for 1 Hz */
    TIMER32_1->CONTROL |= 0x20;      /* enable interrupt */

    NVIC_SetPriority(T32_INT1_IRQn, PRIO_TMR1);
    NVIC_EnableIRQ(T32_INT1_IRQn);       /* enable interrupt in NVIC */
}

void Timer2_init(void) {
    TIMER32_2->CONTROL = 0xC2;       /* no prescaler, periodic mode, 32-bit timer. */
    TIMER32_2->LOAD = 300000-1;       /* set the reload value for 10 Hz */
    TIMER32_2->CONTROL |= 0x20;      /* enable interrupt */

    NVIC_SetPriority(T32_INT2_IRQn, PRIO_TMR2);
    NVIC_EnableIRQ(T32_INT2_IRQn);   /* enable interrupt in NVIC */
}

/* delay n milliseconds (3 MHz CPU clock) */
void delayMs(int n) {
    int i, j;
    for(i = 0 ; i < n; i++)
        for(j = 0; j < 250; j++)
            {}  /* do nothing for 1 ms */
}
```

Review Questions

1. In ARM, which interrupt has the highest priority?
2. True or false. Upon Reset, all the IRQs have the same priority.
3. We use register _____ to modify the interrupt priority of IRQ8.
4. To assign priority to IRQ21, we need to program the IPR__ register.

Answer to Review Questions

Section 6.1
1. True
2. 4
3. 1K byte beginning at 00000000 and ending at 000003FFH
4. Interrupt service routine (ISR) or interrupt handler
5. To hold the starting address of each ISR
6. 0x00000040, 41, 42, and 43
7. No; it is internally embedded into the NVIC.
8. INT 6

Section 6.2
1. True
2. 2. Thread and Handler
3. 8 bytes. 4 bytes for the address of the stack and 4 bytes for the address of boot ROM
4. Interrupt handler
5. True

Section 6.3
1. INT51
2. False
3. False (only on the rising edge or falling edge)
4. __enable_irq();
5. (a) on the peripheral device level. (b) on the system level with ISER register in NVIC. (c) on the global level with the __enable_irq(); statement.

Section 6.4
1. IRQ16
2. True
3. P1.3 and P1.2
4. UCA0IE
5. False

Section 6-5
1. INT15
2. STCTRL
3. False. NVIC_EN0 register is used for IRQs (external interrupts) and SysTick is not part of them.

Section 6-6
1. IRQ25
2. IRQ26
3. False
4. False

5. D5

Section 6-7
1. Reset
2. False
3. IPR2
4. IPR5

Chapter 7: ADC, DAC, and Sensor Interfacing

This chapter explores more real-world devices such as ADCs (analog-to-digital converters), DACs (digital-to-analog converters), and sensors. We will also explain how to interface the MSP432 ARM to these devices. In Section 7.1, we describe analog-to-digital converter (ADC) chips. We will program the ADC module of the MSP432P401R chip in Section 7.2. In Section 7.3, we show the interfacing of sensors and discuss the issue of signal conditioning. The characteristics and programming of DAC chips are discussed in Section 7.4.

Section 7.1: ADC Characteristics

This section will explore ADC generally. First, we describe some general aspects of the ADC itself, then focus on the functionality of some important pins in ADC.

ADC devices

Analog-to-digital converters are among the most widely used devices for data acquisition. Digital computers use binary (discrete) values, but in the physical world everything is analog (continuous). Temperature, pressure (wind or liquid), humidity, and velocity are a few examples of physical quantities that we deal with every day. A physical quantity is converted to electrical (voltage, current) signals using a device called a *transducer*. Transducers used to generate electrical outputs are also referred to as *sensors*. Sensors for temperature, velocity, pressure, light, and many other natural physical quantities produce an output that is voltage (or current). Therefore, we need an analog-to-digital converter to translate the analog signals to digital numbers so that the microcontroller can read and process the numbers. See Figures 7-1 and 7-2.

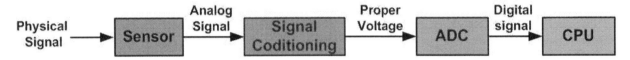

Figure 7-1: Microcontroller Connection to Sensor via ADC

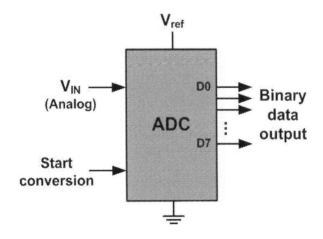

Figure 7-2: An 8-bit ADC Block Diagram

Some of the major characteristics of the ADC

Resolution

The ADC has n-bit resolution, where n can be 8, 10, 12, 16, or even 24 bits. Higher-resolution ADCs provide a smaller step size, where *step size* is the smallest change that can be discerned by an ADC. Some widely used resolutions for ADCs are shown in Table 7-1. Although the resolution of an ADC chip is decided at the time of its design and cannot be changed, we can control the step size with the help of what is called V_{ref}. This is discussed below.

n-bit	Number of steps	Step size
8	256	5V /256 = 19.53 mV
10	1024	5V /1024 = 4.88 mV
12	4096	5V /4096 = 1.2 mV
16	65,536	5V /65,536 = 0.076 mV
	Note: V_{ref} = 5V	

Table 7-1: Resolution versus Step Size for ADC (Vref = 5V)

Vref

Vref is an input voltage used for the reference voltage. The voltage connected to this pin, along with the resolution of the ADC chip, determine the step size. For an 8-bit ADC, the step size is Vref / 256 because it is an 8-bit ADC, and 2 to the power of 8 gives us 256 steps. See Table 7-1. For example, if the analog input range needs to be 0 to 4 volts, Vref is connected to 4 volts. That gives 4 V / 256 = 15.62 mV for the step size of an 8-bit ADC. In another case, if we need a step size of 10 mV for an 8-bit ADC, then V_{ref} = 2.56 V, because 2.56 V / 256 = 10 mV. For the 10-bit ADC, if the V_{ref} = 5V, then the step size is 4.88 mV as shown in Table 7-1. Tables 7-2 and 7-3 show the relationship between the V_{ref} and step size for the 8- and 10-bit ADCs, respectively.

V_{ref} (V)	V_{in} in Range (V)	Step Size (mV)
5.00	0 to 5	5 / 256 = 19.53
4.00	0 to 4	4 / 256 = 15.62
3.00	0 to 3	3 / 256 = 11.71
2.56	0 to 2.56	2.56 / 256 = 10
2.00	0 to 2	2 / 256 = 7.81
1.28	0 to 1.28	1.28 / 256 = 5
1.00	0 to 1	1 / 256 = 3.90
Note: In an 8-bit ADC, step size is V_{ref}/256		

Table 7-2: Vref Relation to Vin Range for an 8-bit ADC

Vref (V)	V_{in} Range (V)	Step Size (mV)
5.00	0 to 5	5 / 1024 = 4.88
4.96	0 to 4.096	4.096 / 1024 = 4
3.00	0 to 3	3 / 1024 = 2.93
2.56	0 to 2.56	2.56 / 1024 = 2.5
2.00	0 to 2	2 / 1024 = 2
1.28	0 to 1.28	1.28 / 1024 = 1.25
1.024	0 to 1.024	1.024 / 1024 = 1
Note: In a 10-bit ADC, step size is V_{ref}/1024		

Table 7-3: Vref Relation to Vin Range for an 10-bit ADC

In some applications, we need the differential reference voltage where $V_{ref} = V_{ref(+)} - V_{ref(-)}$. Often the $V_{ref(-)}$ pin is connected to ground and the $V_{ref(+)}$ pin is used as the V_{ref}.

Conversion time

In addition to resolution, conversion time is another major factor in selecting an ADC. *Conversion time* is defined as the time it takes the ADC to convert the analog input to a digital number.

The conversion time is dictated by the clock source connected to the ADC in addition to the method used for data conversion and technology used in the fabrication of the ADC.

Digital data output

In an 8-bit ADC we have an 8-bit digital data output of D0–D7, while in the 10-bit ADC the data output is D0–D9. To calculate the output voltage, we use the following formula:

$$D_{OUT} = V_{IN} / StepSize$$

Where D_{out} = digital data output (in decimal), V_{in} = analog input voltage, and step size (resolution) is the smallest change, which is $V_{ref}/256$ for an 8-bit ADC.

Figure 7-3 shows a simple 2-bit ADC. In the circuit, the voltage between Vref(+) and Vref(-) is divided into 4 since resistors have the same values. As a result, the step size is $(V_{ref(+)} - V_{ref(-)}) / 4$.

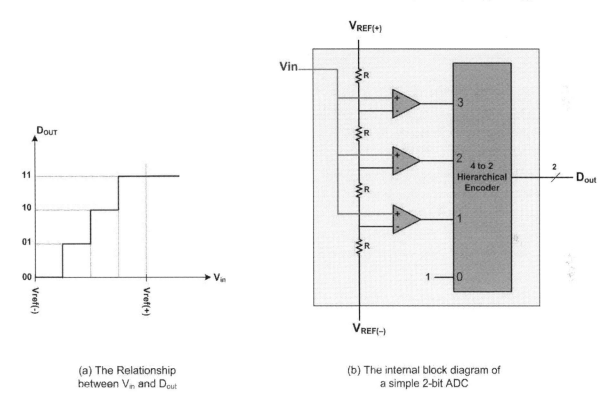

(a) The Relationship between V_{in} and D_{out}

(b) The internal block diagram of a simple 2-bit ADC

Figure 7-3: A Simultaneous 2-bit ADC

If V_{in} is below step size all the comparators send out zeros. When V_{in} is between step size and step size × 2, the lowest comparator sends out 1 and the encoder gives 01.

If V_{in} is between step size × 2 and step size × 3, the second comparator and the first comparator sends out 1. Since the encoder is hierarchical priority, it sends out the highest value in cases that more than 1 input is high. As a result, 2 (10 in binary) will be sent out.

When V_{in} is bigger than step size × 3, the third comparator becomes high and 3 will be sent out.

See Example 7-1. This data is brought out of the ADC chip either one bit at a time (serially), or in one chunk, using a parallel line of outputs. This is discussed next.

Example 7-1

For a given 8-bit ADC (e.g. ADC0848), we have V_{ref} = 2.56 V. Calculate the D0–D7 output if the analog input is: (a)1.7 V, and (b) 2.1 V.

Solution:

Since the step size is 2.56/256 = 10 mV, we have the following.
(a)D_{OUT} = 1.7V/10 mV = 170 in decimal, which gives us 10101011 in binary for D7–D0.
(b)D_{OUT} = 2.1V/10 mV = 210 in decimal, which gives us 11010010 in binary for D7–D0.

Parallel versus serial ADC

The ADC chips are either parallel or serial. In parallel ADC, we have 8 or more pins dedicated to bringing out the binary data, but in serial ADC we have only one pin for data out. The D0–D7 data pins of the 8-bit ADC provide an 8-bit parallel data path between the ADC chip and the CPU. In the case of the 16-bit parallel ADC chip, we need 16 pins for the data path. In order to save pins, many 12- and 16-bit ADCs use pins D0–D7 to send out the upper and lower bytes of the binary data. In recent years, for many applications where space is a critical issue, using such a large number of pins for data is not feasible. For this reason, serial devices such as the serial ADC are becoming widely used. While the serial ADCs use fewer pins and their smaller packages take much less space on the printed circuit board, more CPU time is needed to get the converted data from the ADC because the CPU must get data one bit at a time, instead of in one single read operation as with the parallel ADC. ADC0848 is an example of a parallel ADC with 8 pins for the data output, while the MAX1112 is an example of a serial ADC with a single pin for D_{out}. Figures 7-4 and 7-5 show the block diagram for ADC0848 and MAX1112, respectively.

Analog input channels

Many data acquisition applications need more than one analog input for ADC. For this reason, we see ADC chips with 2, 4, 8, or even 16 channels on a single chip. Multiplexing of analog inputs is widely used as shown in the ADC848 and MAX1112. In these chips, we have 8 channels of analog inputs, allowing us to monitor multiple quantities such as temperature, pressure, flow, and so on. Nowadays, some ARM microcontroller chips come with 16-channel on-chip ADC.

Start conversion and end-of-conversion signals

For the conversion to be controlled by the CPU, there are needs for start conversion (SC) and end-of-conversion (EOC) signals. When SC is activated, the ADC starts converting the analog input value of V_{in} to a digital number. The amount of time it takes to convert varies depending on the conversion method. When the data conversion is complete, the end-of-conversion signal notifies the CPU that the converted data is ready to be picked up.

194

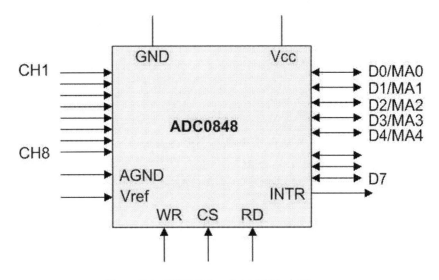

Figure 7-4: ADC0848 Parallel ADC Block Diagram

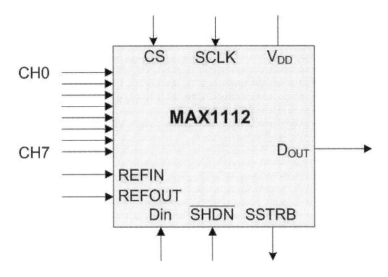

Figure 7-5: MAX1112 Serial ADC Block Diagram

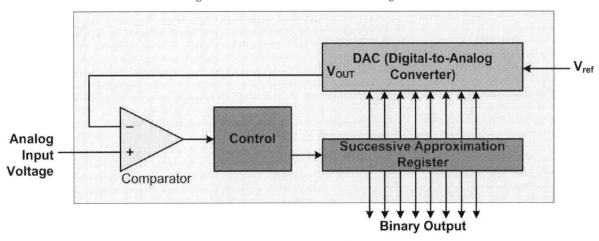

Figure 7-6: Successive Approximation ADC

Successive Approximation ADC

Successive Approximation is a widely used method of converting an analog input to digital output. It has three main components: (a) successive approximation register (SAR), (b) comparator, and (c) control unit. See the Figure 7-6.

The successive approximation register is loaded with only the most significant bit set at the start. An internal digital-to-analog converter converts the value of SAR to an analog voltage which is used to compare to the input voltage. If the input voltage is higher, the bit is kept. If the voltage is lower, the bit is cleared. The next bit is tried and the DAC and compare are exercised. This process is repeated for all bits of the SAR. Assuming a step size of 10 mV, the 8-bit successive approximation ADC will go through the following steps to convert an input of 1 Volt:

(1) It starts with binary number 10000000. Since 128 × 10 mV = 1.28 V is greater than the 1 V input, bit 7 is cleared (dropped).

(2) 01000000 gives us 64 × 10 mV = 640 mV and bit 6 is kept since it is smaller than the 1 V input.

(3) 01100000 gives us 96 × 10 mV = 960 mV and bit 5 is kept since it is smaller than the 1 V input,

(4) 01110000 gives us 112 × 10 mV = 1120 mV and bit 4 is dropped since it is greater than the 1 V input.

(5) 01101000 gives us 108 × 10 mV = 1080 mV and bit 3 is dropped since it is greater than the 1 V input.

(6) 01100100 gives us 100 × 10 mV = 1000 mV = 1 V and bit 2 is kept since it is equal to input. Even though the answer is found it does not stop.

(7) 011000110 gives us 102 × 10 mV = 1020 mV and bit 1 is dropped since it is greater than the 1 V input.

(8) 01100101 gives us 101 × 10 mV = 1010 mV and bit 0 is dropped since it is greater than the 1 V input.

Notice that the Successive Approximation method goes through all the steps even if the answer is found in one of the earlier steps. The advantage of the Successive Approximation method is that the conversion time is fixed since it has to go through all the steps.

Review Questions
1. Give two factors that affect the step size calculation.
2. The ADC0848 is a(n) _____-bit converter.
3. True or false. While the ADC0848 has 8 pins for Dout, the MAX1112 has only one Dout pin.
4. Find the step size for an 8-bit ADC, if Vref = 1.28 V.
5. For question 4, calculate the output if the analog input is: (a) 0.7 V, and (b) 1 V.

Section 7.2: ADC Programming with MSP432

Because the ADC is widely used in data acquisition, in recent years an increasing number of microcontrollers have on-chip ADC modules. In this section, we discuss the ADC feature of the MSP432 and show how it is programmed.

The MSP432P401R ARM chip has a single ADC module which can support up to 24 ADC channels. These ADC channels have 14-bit resolution. To program them, we need to understand some of the major registers. Figure 7-7 shows a simplified block diagram of an MSP432P401R chip.

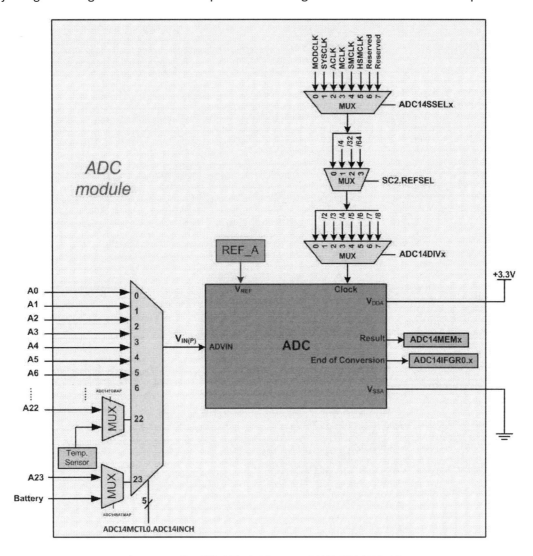

Figure 7-7: Simplified Block Diagram of MSP432P401R chip

In this section, we examine some of these registers and show how to program the ADC. Below are some major registers of MSP432P401R ADC from MSP432P401R reference manual.

Absolute Address	Register
4001 2000	ADC Control Registers 0 (ADC14CTL0)
4001 2004	ADC Control Registers 1 (ADC14CTL1)
4001 2018	ADC Memory Control Register0 (ADC14MCTL0, there are 32 of them)
4001 2098	ADC Memory Register0 (ADC14M0, there are 32 of them)
4001 213C	ADC IER0 Register (ADC14 Interrupt Enable 0)
4001 2144	ADC IFGR0 (ADC14 Interrupt Flag 0)

Table 7-4: Some of the MSP432P401R ADC Registers (See reference manual table 20-3)

The configurations of the ADC shall not change when it is enabled. The configuration bits of ADC14CTL0 register cannot be modified when ADC14ENC=1.

Turning on the ADC14

First thing we need to do is to turn on the power of ADC14 module. In order to conserve energy, the ADC14 is "off" upon reset. Bit D4 of ADC14CTL0 register is used to turn on the ADC14 module. The ADC14CTL0 is located at physical address 0x4001 2000 + 0 = 0x4001 2000. Notice 0x4001 2000 is the base address of the ADC14 in MSP432P401R. See Table 7-4 and Figure 7-8.

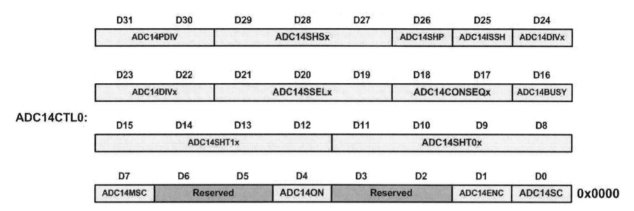

Figure 7-8: ADC14CTL0 (ADC14 Control 0) register

Bit	Field	Descriptions
31-30	ADC14PDIV	ADC14 predivider. These bits pre-divide the selected ADC14 clock source. Can be modified only when ADC14ENC = 0. 00b = Predivide by 1 01b = Predivide by 4 10b = Predivide by 32 11b = Predivide by 64
29-27	ADC14SHSx	ADC14 sample-and-hold source select. Can be modified only when ADC14ENC = 0. 000b = ADC14SC bit 001b = TA0_C1 010b = TA0_C2 011b = TA1_C1 100b = TA1_C2 101b = TA2_C1 110b = TA2_C2 111b = TA3_C1
26	ADC14SHP	ADC14 sample-and-hold pulse-mode select. This bit selects the source of the sampling signal (SAMPCON) to be either the output of the sampling timer or the sample-input signal directly. Can be modified only when ADC14ENC = 0. 0b = SAMPCON signal is sourced from the sample-input signal. 1b = SAMPCON signal is sourced from the sampling timer
25	ADC14ISSH	ADC14 invert signal sample-and-hold.

		Can be modified only when ADC14ENC = 0.
		0b = The sample-input signal is not inverted.
		1b = The sample-input signal is inverted.
		Setting ADC14ISSH=1 and triggering a conversion using ADC14SC is not recommended. ADC14SC bit gets reset to 0 automatically at the end of conversion and if ADC14ISSH=1, the 1->0 transition on ADC14SC will trigger another conversion.
24-22	ADC14DIVx	ADC14 clock divider. Can be modified only when ADC14ENC = 0. 000b = /1 001b = /2 010b = /3 011b = /4 100b = /5 101b = /6 110b = /7 111b = /8
21-19	ADC14SSELx	ADC14 clock source select. Can be modified only when ADC14ENC = 0. 000b = MODCLK 001b = SYSCLK 010b = ACLK 011b = MCLK 100b = SMCLK 101b = HSMCLK 110b = Reserved 111b = Reserved
18-17	ADC14CONSEQx	ADC14 conversion sequence mode select Can be modified only when ADC14ENC=0. 00b = Single-channel, single-conversion 01b = Sequence-of-channels 10b = Repeat-single-channel 11b = Repeat-sequence-of-channels
16	ADC14BUSY	ADC14 busy. This bit indicates an active sample or conversion operation. 0b = No operation is active. 1b = A sequence, sample, or conversion is active
15-12	ADC14SHT1x	ADC14 sample-and-hold time. These bits define the number of ADC14CLK cycles in the sampling period for registers ADC14MEM8 to ADC14MEM23. Can be modified only when ADC14ENC = 0. 0000b = 4 0001b = 8 0010b = 16 0011b = 32 0100b = 64 0101b = 96 0110b = 128 0111b = 192

		1000b to 1111b = Reserved
11-8	ADC14SHT0x	ADC14 sample-and-hold time. These bits define the number of ADC14CLK cycles in the sampling period for registers ADC14MEM0 to ADC14MEM7 and ADC14MEM24 to ADC14MEM31. Can be modified only when ADC14ENC = 0. 0000b = 4 0001b = 8 0010b = 16 0011b = 32 0100b = 64 0101b = 96 0110b = 128 0111b = 192 1000b to 1111b = Reserved
7	ADC14MSC	ADC14 multiple sample and conversion. Valid only for sequence or repeated modes. 0b = The sampling timer requires a rising edge of the SHI signal to trigger each sample-and-convert. 1b = The first rising edge of the SHI signal triggers the sampling timer, but further sample-and-conversions are performed automatically as soon as the prior conversion is completed
6-5	Reserved	Reserved. Always reads as 0.
4	ADC14ON	ADC14 on 0b = ADC14 off 1b = ADC14 on. ADC core is ready to power up when a valid conversion is triggered.
3-2	Reserved	Reserved. Always reads as 0.
1	ADC14ENC	ADC14 enable conversion 0b = ADC14 disabled 1b = ADC14 enabled ADC14ENC low pulse width must be at-least 3 ADC14CLK cycles.
0	ADC14SC	ADC14 start conversion. Software-controlled sample-and-conversion start. ADC14SC and ADC14ENC may be set together with one instruction. ADC14SC is reset automatically. 0b = No sample-and-conversion-start 1b = Start sample-and-conversion

Table 7-5: ADC14CTL0 (ADC14 Control 0) Register of MSP432P401R

Conversion Clock

The ADC has a wide selection of clock source, which may be selected by ADC14SSELx bits in ADC14CTL0 register. The clock source may be divided by the "predivider" chosen by ADC14PDIV bits then further divided by the clock divider selected by ADC14DIVx bits in ADC14CTL0 register. The output of the clock divider is the ADC14CLK. It is used to clock the ADC core and the sample timer.

ADC Conversion Time

The conversion time for the ADC has two parts. They are as follows:

1) In the first phase the sampling timer holds off the conversion while the input signal buffer and the reference buffer settle. The number of clock cycles of the sampling timer can be 4, 8, 16, 32, 64, 96, 128, or 192. This number is programmed via the ADC14SHT1x, ADC14SHT0x bits in ADC14CTL0 register depending on the conversion result memory used. Longer sampling time ensures that the voltage of the sample buffer is brought closer to the input voltage. This is important when the input voltage differs significantly from sample to sample. But it prolongs the conversion time of each sample.

2) In the second phase, the analog input is converted to binary numbers using the successive approximation method. In this phase, the number of clocks used depends on how many bits are set for the binary output. The conversion takes 9, 11, 14, 16 ADC14CLK cycles for 8, 10, 12, 14 bit output.

ADC Conversion Result Memory Registers

Upon the completion of conversion, the result is placed in the ADC14MEMx registers. There are 32 ADC14MEMx (ADC14MEM0-ADC14MEM31) registers. Although the ADC14MEMx register is a 32-bit wide but only the lower 16 bits are used and upper 16 bits are reserved. For the ADC14, we have the options of 8-, 10-, 12-, and 14-bit for single-ended unsigned result. When ADC is configured for unsigned binary format (ADC14DF=0 in ADC14CTL1 register), the result is right-justified and the unused bits are filled with 0s. That means for 14-bit option the bits D13-D0 hold the binary output result of ADC conversion and D14 and D15 bits are zeros. In the same way, for 12-bit, bits D12 to D15 are zeros while D11-D0 has the ADC data result. In the case of 10-bit, D15-D10 bits are zeros, and D9-D0 has the result. For 8-bit the D7-D0 is our converted data while D15-D8 are all 0s. If the result is in 2's complement format (ADC14DF=1) the results are left-aligned and the unused bits on the right are filled with 0's.

Conversion Memory Control

Again there are 32 ADC14MEM registers, ADC14MEM0 to ADC14MEM31. The purpose of having 32 conversion result memory registers is that the ADC can be configured to do multiple conversions in one sequence for up to 32 samples. Each result memory register has a corresponding control register (ADC14MCTL0 to ADC14MCTL31), in which the analog input channel, the reference voltages, whether the input is single-ended or differential are determined. Because each result memory register has its own control register to select the input channel, a conversion sequence may convert a set of different input channels or multiple conversions of the same channel and perform signal averaging to reduce noise for high precision applications.

Conversion sequence may run once after it is started or it may repeat continuously. Each sequence may be started with a single trigger or each conversion may need a trigger. Bits D18-D17 (ADC14CONSEQx) and bit D7 (ADC14MSC) of ADC14CTL0 register are used to select these options. In this section we will only cover single conversion of a single channel. The multi-channel conversion will be covered later.

When a conversion starts, the bits D20-D16 (ADC14CSTARTADDx) of ADC14CTL1 (ADC14 Control 1) register is used to determine which ADC14MEMx register is used and the input of the analog multiplexer will choose the input channel using the control register associated with that ADC14MEMx register.

Choosing input channel

As mentioned earlier, the channel selection is done through the ADC14MCTLx register. In addition, the pins selected as analog input pin must have their pin multiplexing (discussed in Chapter 2) set as analog input.

The lowest 5 bits of ADC14MCTLx register are used to select one of the 24 single-ended channels to be converted. See Figure 7-10.

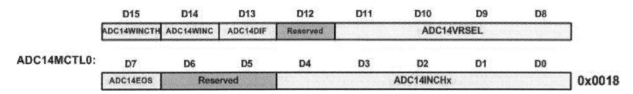

Figure 7-9: ADC14MCTL0 Register

Bit	Field	Description
13	ADC14DIF	Differential mode (0= single-ended, 1=Differential)
11-18	ADCVRSEL	ADC14 Vref selection. 0000 = Vref+= AVCC (analog VCC) and Vref-=AVSS 1110 = Vref+= External Source connected to pin P5.6 Vref- =External Source connected to pin P5.7
4-0	ADC14INCH	ADC14 input channel: The field selects the input channel. When DIFF = 0 (single-ended mode), values 0 to 23 choose between the 24 ADC input channels. When DIFF = 1 (Differential mode), values 0 to 15 select between the 12 differential channels. See the reference manual for more information. 00000 = A0 00001 = A1 00010 = A2 00011 = A3 00100 = A4 00101 = A5 00110 = A6 00111 = A7 01000 = A8 01001 = A9 01010 = A10 01011 = A11 01100 = A12 01101 = A13 01110 = A14

```
01111 = A15
10000 = A16
10001 = A17
10010 = A18
10011 = A19
10100 = A20
10101 = A21
10110 = A22
10111 = A23
```

Table 7-6: ADC14MCTL0 Register

Not all the channels are connected to the input pins. In the case of MSP432401R chip used in the LaunchPad board, there are 24 channels connected to the input pins and additional 4 channels are connected internally. See Table 7-7.

Pin Function	ADC Channel Input	Pin Name	PxSEL1 : PxSEL0
A0	ADC input 0	P5.5	P5SEL0=00100000=0x20 P5SEL1=00100000=0x20
A1	ADC input 1	P5.4	P5SEL0=00010000=0x10 P5SEL1=00010000=0x10
A2	ADC input 2	P5.3	P5SEL0=00001000=0x08 P5SEL1=00001000=0x08
A3	ADC input 3	P5.2	P5SEL0=00000100=0x04 P5SEL1=00000100=0x04
A4	ADC input 4	P5.1	P5SEL0=00000010=0x02 P5SEL1=00000010=0x02
A5	ADC input 5	P5.0	P5SEL0=00000001=0x01 P5SEL1=00000001=0x01
A6	ADC input6	P4.7	P4SEL0=10000000=0x80 P4SEL1=10000000=0x80
A7	ADC input 7	P4.6	P4SEL0=01000000=0x40 P4SEL1=01000000=0x40
A8	ADC input 8	P4.5	P4SEL0=00100000=0x20 P4SEL1=00100000=0x20
A9	ADC input 9	P4.4	P4SEL0=00010000=0x10 P4SEL1=00010000=0x10
A10	ADC input 10	P4.3	P4SEL0=00001000=0x08 P4SEL1=00001000=0x08
A11	ADC input 11	P4.2	P4SEL0=00000100=0x04 P4SEL1=00000100=0x04
A12	ADC input 12	P4.1	P4SEL0=00000010=0x02 P4SEL1=00000010=0x02
A13	ADC input 13	P4.0	P4SEL0=00000001=0x01 P4SEL1=00000001=0x01
A14	ADC Input 14	P6.1	P6SEL0=00000010=0x02 P6SEL1=00000010=0x02

A15	ADC Input 15	P6.0	P6SEL0=00000001=0x01
			P6SEL1=00000001=0x01
A16	ADC Input 16	P9.1	P9SEL0=00000010=0x02
			P9SEL1=00000010=0x02
A17	ADC Input 17	P9.0	P9SEL0=00000001=0x01
			P9SEL1=00000001=0x01
A18	ADC Input 18	P8.7	P8SEL0=10000000=0x80
			P8SEL1=10000000=0x80
A19	ADC Input 19	P8.6	P8SEL0=01000000=0x40
			P8SEL1=01000000=0x40
A20	ADC Input 20	P8.5	P8SEL0=00100000=0x20
			P8SEL1=00100000=0x20
A21	ADC Input 21	P8.4	P8SEL0=00010000=0x10
			P8SEL1=00010000=0x10
A22	ADC Input 22	P8.3	P8SEL0=00001000=0x08
			P8SEL1=00001000=0x08
A23	ADC Input 23	P8.2	P8SEL0=00000100=0x04
			P8SEL1=00000100=0x04

Table 7-7: Analog input pin assignment in MSP432P401R chip for LaunchPad

Differential versus Single-Ended

In some applications, our interest is in the differences between two analog signal voltages (the differential voltages). Rather than converting two channels and calculate the differences between them, the MSP432 has the option of converting the differential voltages of two analog channels. The bit D13 (ADC14DIFF) of ADC14MCTLx register allows us to enable the differential option. Upon Reset, the default is the single-ended input and we will leave it at that for the discussion here. See the MSP432P401R reference manual for further information on differential options.

Selecting Bit Resolution

We use ADC14RES bits (D5-D4) of ADC14CTL1 (ADC14 Control 1) register to select 8, 10, 12, or 14-bit ADC resolution. The default is 8-bit.

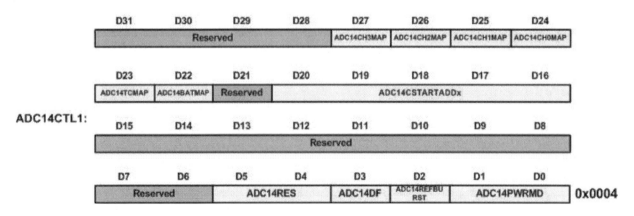

Figure 7-10: ADC14CTL1 (ADC14 Control 1) Register

Bit	Name	Description
31-28	Reserved	Reserved
27	ADC14CH3MAP	0b = ADC input channel internal 3 is not selected 1b = ADC input channel internal 3 is selected for ADC input channel MAX-5
26	ADC14CH2MAP	0b = ADC input channel internal 2 is not selected 1b = ADC input channel internal 2 is selected for ADC input channel MAX-4
25	ADC14CH1MAP	0b = ADC input channel internal 1 is not selected 1b = ADC input channel internal 1 is selected for ADC input channel MAX-3
24	ADC14CH0MAP	0b = ADC input channel internal 0 is not selected 1b = ADC input channel internal 0 is selected for ADC input channel MAX-2
23	ADC14TCMAP	0b = ADC internal temperature sensor channel is not selected for ADC 1b = ADC internal temperature sensor channel is selected for ADC input channel
22	ADC14BATMAP	0b = ADC internal 1/2 x AVCC channel is not selected for ADC 1b = ADC internal 1/2 x AVCC channel is selected for ADC input channel MAX
21	Reserved	Reserved
20-16	ADC14CSTARTADDx	0h to 1Fh, corresponding to ADC14MEM0 to ADC14MEM31
15-6	Reserved	Reserved
5-4	ADC14RES	00b = 8 bit (9 clock cycle conversion time) 01b = 10 bit (11 clock cycle conversion time) 10b = 12 bit (14 clock cycle conversion time) 11b = 14 bit (16 clock cycle conversion time)
3	ADC14DF	0b = Binary unsigned. Theoretically, for ADC14DIF = 0 and 14-bit mode, the analog input voltage - V(REF) results in 0000h, and the analog input voltage + V(REF) results in 3FFFh. 1b = Signed binary (2s complement), left aligned. Theoretically, for ADC14DIF = 0 and 14-bit mode, the analog input voltage - V(REF) results in 8000h, and the analog input voltage + V(REF) results in 7FFCh.
2	ADC14REFBURST	0b = ADC reference buffer on continuously 1b = ADC reference buffer on only during sample-and-conversion
1-0	ADC14PWRMD	00b = Regular power mode for use with any resolution setting. Sample rate can be up to 1 Msps. 01b = Reserved 10b = Low-power mode for 12-bit, 10-bit, and 8-bit resolution settings. Sample rate must not exceed 200 ksps. 11b = Reserved

Table 7-8: ADC14CTL1 (ADC14 Control 1) Register

Start Conversion trigger options

There are two ways to start an A-to-D conversion in MSP432. They are timer trigger and software trigger. The selection of trigger option is done via the bits ADC14SHSx of ADC14CTL0 register. The default trigger is software and that is what we will use in this section. After turning on the ADC with bit D4 (ADC14ON), we need to enable the ADC by setting D1 (ADC14ENC) then setting bit D0 (ADC14SC) to start the conversion. While using software trigger, the ADC may be left enabled (ADC14ENC) all the time. Each time the Start Conversion (ADC14SC) bit is set while enable is high, a new A-to-D conversion is started.

Polling or interrupt

The end-of-conversion is indicated by a flag bit in the ADC14IFGR0 (ADC14 Interrupt Flag 0) register. See Figure 7-11 and Table 7-9.

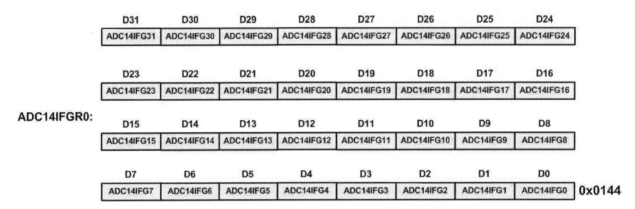

Figure 7-11: ADC14IFGR0 (ADC14 Interrupt Flag Register 0) Register for End-of-Conversion

Bit	Field	Descriptions
X	ADC14IFGx	ADC14MEMx interrupt flag. This bit is set to 1 when ADC14MEMx is loaded with a conversion result. This bit is reset to 0 when the ADC14MEMx register is read, or when the ADC14IV register is read, or when the corresponding bit in the ADC14CLRIFGR0 register is set to 1. 0b = No interrupt pending 1b = Interrupt pending

Table 7-9: ADC14IFGR0 Register

ADC14IFGR0 is a 32-bit register. Each bit represents an end-of-conversion flag for a conversion result memory register. Upon the completion of a conversion for a given result memory register, the corresponding flag bit goes high indicating that the conversion result memory register is loaded with a new value. By polling this flag, we know if the conversion is complete and we can read the value in ADC14MEMx result memory register. This flag bit is cleared (goes LOW) when the ADC14MEMx data result register is read. The following figure shows the ADC14MEMx register.

Figure 7-12: ADC14MEMx (ADC14 memoryx) holding ADC14 conversion result (x=0- 31)

In this section, we use polling to see if the conversion result is ready. We can also use an interrupt to inform us that the conversion is complete. By default, the interrupt option is not enabled.

Clearing conversion complete flag

The flag bit in ADC14IFGR0 indicates conversion is complete and result is ready to be read in ADC14MEMx register. You may write a '1' to the corresponding bit in ADC14CLRIFGR0 register to clear the flag or the flag is cleared automatically when the data from the respective ADC14MEMx register is read.

V_{ref} in MSP432

In the MSP432 ARM chip, the reference voltage for A-to-D conversion (Vref) can be programmed. We can also connect Vref+ (pin P5.7) and Vref- (pin P5.6) to an external reference voltage. Notice even if we connect the Vref+ to an external voltage other than the V_{DD} of the chip, it cannot go beyond the V_{DD} voltage. With Vref+=3.3V, we have the step size of 3.3V / 16,384 = 0.2 mV since the maximum ADC resolution for MSP432P401R is 14 bits. See Example 7-2.

Example 7-2

Give the digital converted output if the ADC input channel voltage is 1.2V for the MSP432 with Vref+ = 3.3V and Vref- = 0.

Solution:

Since the step size is 3.3V / 16,384 = 0.20 mV, we have 1.2V / 0.20 mV = 6,000 = 0x1770 as ADC output.

Configuring ADC and reading ADC channel

The following steps are used to configure the ADC14 to perform A-to-D conversion on analog channel 6 (pin P4.7). These steps are implemented in Program 7-1.

1. Power on the ADC14 module by setting ADC14ON=1 in ADC14CTL0 register.
2. Disable the ADC14 with ADC14ENC=0 in ADC14CTL0 register. Most of the bits in the ADC14 registers can only be modified when ADC14ENC is 0.
3. Choose sample/hold pulse mode, clock source, clock division, trigger source, and sampling time using ADC14CTL0 register.
4. Select the ADC resolution using ADC14CTL1 register.
5. Choose a result memory register for this conversion. Use the corresponding ADC14MCTLx register to select the ADC channel to be converted, single-ended input, and Vref option.
6. Using PxSEL1:PxSEL0 to configure input pin for analog input channel.
7. Select the result memory register to be used in ADC15CTL1.

8. Enable the ADC14 by making ADC14ENC=1 after ADC configuration is completed.

9. Set the ADC14SC bit (D0) in ADC14CTL0 register to start the conversion.

10. Monitor the flag in the ADC14IFGR0 for end-of-conversion.

11. When the interrupt flag goes HIGH, read the ADC result from the ADC14MEMx and save it.

12. Repeat steps 9 through 11 for the next conversion.

Program 7-1 illustrates the steps for ADC conversion shown above. Figure 7-13 shows the hardware connection for Program 7-1.

Program 7-1: Using ADC14 to convert input from channel 6 pin P4.7

```c
/* p7_1.c ADC14 software trigger conversion
 *
 * In this example, conversion result memory register 5 is used.
 * Analog input channel 6 using pin P4.7 is configured for result
 * memory register 5. Conversion is started by software trigger.
 * The bits 10-8 of the 12-bit conversion result are displayed on
 * the tri-color LEDs.
 *
 * Connect a potentiometer to P4.7 and see the color changes when
 * the potentiometer is turned.
 *
 * Tested with Keil 5.20 and MSP432 Device Family Pack V2.2.0.
 *
 */

#include "msp.h"

int main(void) {
    int result;

    /* Configure P2.2-P2.0 as output for tri-color LEDs */
    P2->SEL0 &= ~7;
    P2->SEL1 &= ~7;
    P2->DIR  |= 7;

    ADC14->CTL0 =  0x00000010;   /* power on and disabled during configuration */
    ADC14->CTL0 |= 0x04080300;   /* S/H pulse mode, sysclk, 32 sample clocks,
software trigger */
    ADC14->CTL1 =  0x00000020;   /* 12-bit resolution */
    ADC14->MCTL[5] = 6;          /* A6 input, single-ended, Vref=AVCC */
    P4->SEL1 |= 0x80;            /* Configure P4.7 for A6 */
    P4->SEL0 |= 0x80;
    ADC14->CTL1 |= 0x00050000;   /* convert for mem reg 5 */
    ADC14->CTL0 |= 2;            /* enable ADC after configuration*/

    while (1) {
        ADC14->CTL0 |= 1;         /* start a conversion */
        while (!ADC14->IFGR0);    /* wait till conversion complete */
        result = ADC14->MEM[5];   /* read conversion result */
        P2->OUT = result >> 8;    /* display bits 10-8 on tri-color LEDs */
    }
}
```

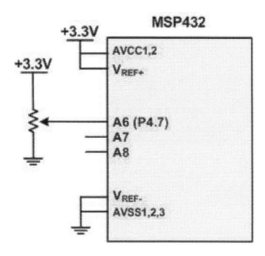

Figure 7-13: ADC Connection for Program 7-1

Internal Temperature sensor

The MSP432P401R chip comes with an internal temperature sensor. Channel A22 (for 100 pin package or the second to the last analog input channel of all packages) normally connects to pin P8.3 but can be redirect to the temperature sensor. This is done by setting ADC14TCMAP to 1 in the ADC14CTL1 register. The on-chip temperature sensor is built in the Reference Module. In order to use the temperature sensor, we need to power on the Reference Module by setting REFON bit in REFCTL0 register and enable the sensor by clearing REFTCOFF bit (bit D3) of REFCTL0 register to 0.

The next program shows how to convert the internal temperature sensor output.

Program 7-2: Converting the on-chip temperature sensor with timer trigger

```
/* p7_2.c ADC14 conversion of internal temperature sensor
 *
 * In this example, conversion result memory register 3 is used.
 * The internal temperature sensor in the REF_A module is used.
 * It requires that the REF_A module is powered up and the
 * temperature sensor is enabled.
 * The sensor is connected to channel 22 and mapped by bit 23
 * of ADC14->CTL1 register. Conversion is started by software trigger.
 * The bits 3-0 of the 10 bit conversion result are displayed on
 * the tri-color LEDs.
 *
 * Heat the MSP432 MCU with a hot air blower or put your finger on the chip
 * and see the LED color change.
 *
 * Tested with Keil 5.20 and MSP432 Device Family Pack V2.2.0.
 *
 */

#include "msp.h"

int main(void) {
    int result;
```

```
/* Configure P2.2-P2.0 as output */
P2->SEL0 &= ~7;
P2->SEL1 &= ~7;
P2->DIR  |= 7;

REF_A->CTL0 |= 1;    /* power up REF for temperature sensor */
REF_A->CTL0 &= ~8;   /* enable temperature sensor */

ADC14->CTL0 =  0x00000010;    /* power on and disabled during configuration */
ADC14->CTL0 |= 0x04883000;    /* S/H pulse mode, use int. temp, sysclk, 32 sample
clocks, software trigger */
ADC14->CTL1 =  0x00000010;    /* 10-bit resolution */
ADC14->CTL1 |= 0x00800000;    /* select internal temperature sensor */
ADC14->MCTL[3] |= 22;         /* internal temp sensor */
ADC14->CTL1 |=  0x00030000;   /* start at mem reg 3 */
ADC14->CTL0 |=  0x00000002;   /* enable ADC */

while (1) {
    ADC14->CTL0 |= 1;          /* start a conversion */
    while (!ADC14->IFGR0);     /* wait till conversion complete */
    result = ADC14->MEM[3];    /* read conversion result */
    P2->OUT = result;          /* dump it at the LEDs */
}
}
```

Multiple Channel Conversion Sequence

The ADC14 module is capable of performing sequence of multiple conversions of different channels or the same channel. To do so, first in the ADC14CTL0 register, the ADC14CONSEQx bits are set to 2 and ADC14MSC bit is set to 1. These configure the ADC14 to perform multiple conversions on different result memory registers for each trigger signal. When the trigger is active, the ADC14 looks in the ADC14CSTARTADDx bits of ADC14CTL1 register to find the starting memory register and used the channel selection bits (ADC14INCHx) of the ADC14MCTLx register to set the analog input multiplexer for sampling. When the conversion of that channel is complete, the conversion for the consecutive ADC14MEMx will start automatically on the channel designated by the associated ADC14MCTLx register. This repeats until the ADC14MCTLx register marked with end of sequence is reached. In the program 7-3, we set the starting address at MEM4. MEM4 is configured to sample and convert channel A8 (P4.5). MEM5 is configured to sample and convert channel A6 (P4.7). MEM6 is configured to sample and convert channel A10 (P4.3). The ADC14EOS bit of ADC14MCTL6 is set for the end of the conversion sequence. The ADC14 will start sample and convert channel A8. When A8 conversion is complete, it starts sample and convert A6 then A10. When conversion of A10 is complete, the sequence is complete and stop because the ADC14EOS bit is detected. When the conversion result is loaded into the result memory register, the corresponding interrupt flag bit is set in ADC14IFGR0 register for each conversion. The program monitors the bit corresponding to the last of the sequence MEM6. When ADC14IFG6 bit is set, the sequence has completed.

UART0 is used to display the conversion result.

```
/* p7_3.c Multiple analog input conversions in a sequence
 *
 * This program is an example of performing a sequence of
 * multiple channel conversion. The sequence starts at result
 * memory register 4 and ends at result memory register 6.
 * The assignments of input channels are as follows:
 * MEM4 - A8  - P4.5
 * MEM5 - A6  - P4.7
 * MEM6 - A10 - P4.3
 *
 * Once the conversions are started by software, the program
 * polls for the completion flag of MEM6, the last channel.
 * When the last channel conversion is completed, the conversion
 * results are read and displayed using UART0.
 * Using a terminal emulator (putty, tera term) set at 115200 Baud,
 * you should be able to see the conversion results on the terminal.
 *
 * Tested with Keil 5.20 and MSP432 Device Family Pack V2.2.0.
 */

#include "msp.h"
#include "stdio.h"

void UART0_init(void);
void UART0_putchar(char c);
void UART0_puts(char* s);

int main(void) {
    char buffer[80];
    int data[3] = {0};

    ADC14->CTL0 =  0x00000010;    /* power on and disabled during configuration */
    ADC14->CTL0 |= 0x040A0380;    /* S/H pulse mode, sysclk, 32 sample clocks,
multiple channel conversion sequence, software trigger */
    ADC14->CTL1 =  0x00040020;    /* 12-bit resolution, starting from result memory 4
*/

    ADC14->MCTL[4] |= 8;                /* select A8 input; Vref=AVCC */
    P4->SEL1 |= 0x20;                   /* Configure P4.5 for A8 */
    P4->SEL0 |= 0x20;

    ADC14->MCTL[5] |= 6;                /* select A6 input; Vref=AVCC */
    P4->SEL1 |= 0x80;                   /* Configure P4.7 for A6 */
    P4->SEL0 |= 0x80;

    ADC14->MCTL[6] |= 10 | 0x80;    /* select A10 input; Vref=AVCC; end of sequence */
    P4->SEL1 |= 0x08;                   /* Configure P4.3 for A10 */
    P4->SEL0 |= 0x08;

    ADC14->CTL0 |=  0x00000002;   /* enable the converter */
    UART0_init();
```

```
    while (1) {
        ADC14->CTL0 |= 1;          /* start a conversion sequence */
        while (!(ADC14->IFGR0 & 0x00000040)); /* wait till last channel in the
sequence complete */
        data[0] = ADC14->MEM[4];    /* read the conversion results */
        data[1] = ADC14->MEM[5];
        data[2] = ADC14->MEM[6];
        /* convert to an ASCII string for UART0 output */
        sprintf(buffer, "\r\nA8: %d, A6: %d, A10:%d", data[0], data[1], data[2]);
        UART0_puts(buffer);
    }
}

/* UART0 is connected to virtual COM port through the USB debug connection */
void UART0_init(void) {
    EUSCI_A0->CTLW0 |= 1;              /* put in reset mode for config */
    EUSCI_A0->MCTLW = 0;               /* disable oversampling */
    EUSCI_A0->CTLW0 = 0x0081;          /* 1 stop bit, no parity, SMCLK, 8-bit data */
    EUSCI_A0->BRW = 26;                /* 3000000 / 115200 = 26 */
    P1->SEL0 |= 0x0C;                  /* P1.3, P1.2 for UART */
    P1->SEL1 &= ~0x0C;
    EUSCI_A0->CTLW0 &= ~1;             /* take UART out of reset mode */
}

void UART0_putchar(char c) {
    while(!(EUSCI_A0->IFG&0x02)) { }   /* wait for transmit buffer empty */
    EUSCI_A0->TXBUF = c;               /* send a char */
}

void UART0_puts(char* s) {
    while (*s != 0)                    /* if not end of string */
    UART0_putchar(*s++);               /* send the character through UART0 */
}
```

Analog Comparator unit

Many microcontrollers come with analog comparator for monitoring an analog input voltage. Using the analog comparator, we can monitor an analog input against two threshold values to determine whether the analog input value is above the high threshold, between the two threshold values, or below the low threshold. When the analog input falls in the selected region, the comparator may generate an interrupt or trigger an A-to-D conversion and let the conversion completion generate an interrupt. Using analog comparator, the software does not have to continuously monitor the analog input.

For example, we may program the comparator for the on-chip temperature sensor. When the temperature exceeds a preset threshold, the cooling fan is turned on. When the temperature drops below the threshold, the cooling fan is turned off. The software only has to set the thresholds once and handle the interrupts. It does not have to use the ADC to monitor the temperature continuously. If the microcontroller has no other tasks to run, it may go into the low power mode to conserve energy.

For the details of programming the analog comparator unit, we will leave it to the reader.

Review Questions

1. The ADC in MSP432P401R is _____bit.
2. In MSP432P401R, the highest number we can get for the ADC output is_____ in hex.
3. Assume Vref+= 3.3V. Find the ADC output in decimal and hex if V_{in} of analog input is 1.9V. Assume 12-bit resolution.
4. In MSP432P401R, which register provides the ADC output converted data?
5. In MSP432P401R, we have resolution choices of _____.

Section 7.3: Sensor Interfacing and Signal Conditioning

This section will show how to interface external sensors to the microcontroller. We examine some popular temperature sensors and then discuss the issue of signal conditioning. Although we concentrate on temperature sensors, the principles discussed in this section are the same for other types of sensors such as light or pressure sensors.

Temperature sensors

Sensors convert physical data such as temperature, light intensity, flow, and speed to electrical signals. Depending on the sensor, the output produced is in the form of voltage, current, resistance, or capacitance. For example, temperature may be converted to electrical signals using a sensor called thermistor. A thermistor responds to temperature change by changing its resistance, but its response is not linear, as seen in Table 7-10 and Figure 7-14.

Temperature ('C)	Tf (K ohms)
0	29.490
25	10.000
50	3.893
75	1.700
100	0.817

Table 7-10: Thermistor Resistance vs. Temperature

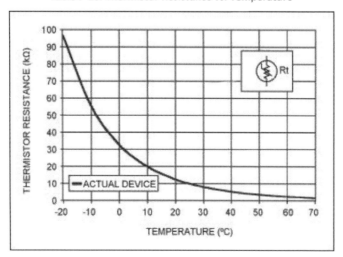

Figure 7-14: Thermistor (Copied from http://www.maximintegrated.com)

The resistance of a thermistor is typically modeled by Steinhart-Hart equation and requires a logarithmic amplifier to produce a linear output. The complexity associated with the circuit for such nonlinear devices has led some manufacturers to market linear temperature sensors. Simple and widely used linear temperature sensors include the LM34 and LM35 from Texas Instruments. They are discussed next.

LM34 and LM35 temperature sensors

The LM34 sensor is a precision integrated-circuit temperature sensor whose output voltage is linearly proportional to the temperature in Fahrenheit. See Figure 7-15. The LM34 requires no external calibration because it is internally calibrated. It outputs 10 mV for each degree of Fahrenheit temperature.

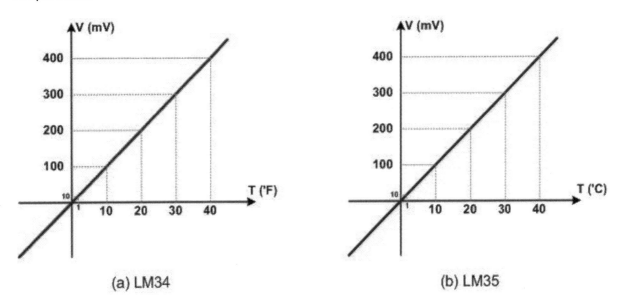

(a) LM34   (b) LM35

Figure 7-15: LM34 and LM35

The LM35 sensor is similar to LM34 except that the output voltage is linearly proportional to the temperature in Celsius (centigrade). It outputs 10 mV for each degree of centigrade temperature. See Figure 7-15.

Signal conditioning

The common transducers produce an output in the form of voltage, current, charge, capacitance, or resistance. In order to perform A-to-D conversion on these signals, they need to be converted to voltage unless the transducer output is already voltage. In addition to the conversion to voltage, the signal may also need gain and offset adjustment to achieve optimal dynamic range. A low-pass analog filter is often incorporated in the signal conditioning circuit to eliminate the high frequency to avoid aliasing. Figure 7-16 shows a block diagram of the input of a data acquisition system.

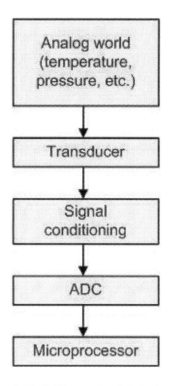

Figure 7-16: Getting analog data to the CPU

Interfacing the LM34 to the TI MSP432 ARM Microcontroller

The A/D of TI MSP432 ARM Microcontroller has 14-bit resolution with a maximum of 16,384 steps, and the LM34 produces 10 mV for every degree of temperature change. The maximum operating temperature of the LM34 is 300 degrees F, so the highest output will be 3000 mV (3.00 V), which is below 3.3V of V_{ref}. The LM34/35 can be connected to the microcontroller as shown in Figure 7-17.

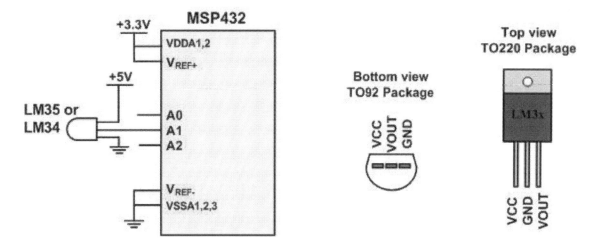

Figure 7-17: LM34/35 Connection to ARM and Its Pin Configuration

To convert the ADC result to temperature in degree, use the following equation:

$$temperature = result * 330 / 16384 ;$$

215

Reading and displaying temperature

Programs 7-3 shows code for reading and displaying temperature in C. Notice that in Figure 7-17, the LM34 (or LM35) is connected to channel 1 (A1 pin P5.4). 14-bit conversion is used to enhance the precision. At 14-bit, the noise is much more apparent so we turn on the hardware averaging to reduce the output fluctuation.

Program 7-4: Reading Temperature Sensor of LM34 or LM35

```c
/* p7_4.c ADC14 conversion of external temperature sensor
 *
 * In this example, conversion result memory register 2 is used.
 * Input channel A1 using P5.4 is connected to an external temperature
 * sensor. Assuming we use LM34 or LM35, which produces 10mV per degree,
 * the conversion result is scaled to degree and displayed through
 * UART0 and a terminal emulator (putty, tera term) on the PC.
 *
 * Tested with Keil 5.20 and MSP432 Device Family Pack V2.2.0.
 */

#include "msp.h"
#include <stdio.h>

void UART0_init(void);
void UART0_putchar(char c);
void UART0_puts(char* s);

int main(void) {
    int result;
    char buffer[20];

    UART0_init();

    ADC14->CTL0 =  0x00000010;       /* power on and disabled during configuration */
    ADC14->CTL0 |= 0x04080300;       /* S/H pulse mode, sysclk, 32 sample clocks,
software trigger */
    ADC14->CTL1 =  0x00000030;       /* 14-bit resolution */
    ADC14->MCTL[2] = 1;              /* A1 input, single-ended, Vref=AVCC */
    P5->SEL1 |= 0x10;                /* Configure P5.4 for A1 */
    P5->SEL0 |= 0x10;
    ADC14->CTL1 |= 0x00020000;       /* convert for mem reg 2 */
    ADC14->CTL0 |= 2;                /* enable ADC after configuration*/

    while (1) {
        ADC14->CTL0 |= 1;            /* start a conversion */
        while (!ADC14->IFGR0);       /* wait till conversion complete */
        result = ADC14->MEM[2];      /* read conversion result */
        result = result * 330 / 16384; /* scale to degree for display */
        sprintf(buffer, "%d\r\n", result);  /* convert it to char string */
        UART0_puts(buffer);          /* send it out through UART0 */
    }
}

void UART0_init(void) {
    EUSCI_A0->CTLW0 |= 1;       /* put in reset mode for config */
    EUSCI_A0->MCTLW = 0;        /* disable oversampling */
```

216

```
    EUSCI_A0->CTLW0 = 0x0081;  /* 1 stop bit, no parity, SMCLK, 8-bit data */
    EUSCI_A0->BRW = 26;        /* 3000000 / 115200 = 26 */
    P1->SEL0 |= 0x0C;          /* P1.3, P1.2 for UART */
    P1->SEL1 &= ~0x0C;
    EUSCI_A0->CTLW0 &= ~1;     /* take UART out of reset mode */
}

void UART0_putchar(char c) {
    while(!(EUSCI_A0->IFG&0x02)) { }  /* wait for transmit buffer empty */
    EUSCI_A0->TXBUF = c;              /* send a char */
}

void UART0_puts(char* s) {
    while (*s != 0)      /* if not end of string */
    UART0_putchar(*s++);        /* send the character through UART0 */
}
```

Review Questions

1. True or false. The transducer must be connected to signal conditioning circuitry before its signal is sent to the ADC.
2. The LM35 provides _____ mV for each degree of _____ (Fahrenheit, Celsius) temperature.
3. The LM34 provides _____ mV for each degree of _____ (Fahrenheit, Celsius) temperature.
4. What is the temperature if the ADC output is 0000 0011 1110?

Section 7.4: Interfacing to a DAC

This section will discuss the fundamentals of a digital-to-analog converter (DAC). Then we demonstrate how to generate a sawtooth wave and a sine wave using the DAC.

Digital-to-analog (DAC) converter

The digital-to-analog converter (DAC) is a device widely used to convert digital signals to analog signals. In this section we discuss the basics of a DAC.

Recall from your digital electronics book the two methods of making a DAC: binary weighted and R/2R ladder. The vast majority of integrated circuit DACs, including the DAC0808 used in this section, use the R/2R method since it can achieve a much higher degree of precision. The first criterion for selecting a DAC is its resolution, which is a function of the number of bits of the digital input. The common ones are 8, 10, and 12 bits. The number of digital input bits decides the resolution of the DAC since the number of analog output levels is equal to 2^n, where n is the number of digital input bits. Therefore, the 8-bit DAC such as the DAC0808 provides 256 discrete voltage (or current) levels of output. See Figure 7-18.

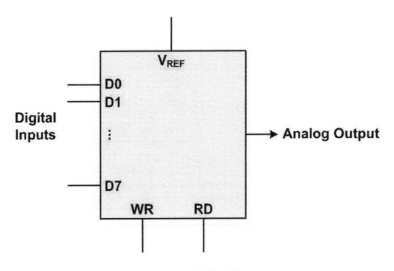

Figure 7-18: DAC Block Diagram

Similarly, the 12-bit DAC provides 4096 discrete voltage levels. Although there are 16-bit DACs, they are much more expensive.

DAC0808

In the DAC0808, the digital inputs are converted to current (I_{OUT}). By connecting a resistor to the I_{OUT} pin, we convert the conversion result current to voltage. The total current provided by the I_{OUT} is a function of the binary numbers at the D0–D7 inputs of the DAC0808 and the reference current (I_{ref}), and is as follows:

$$I_{OUT} = I_{ref} \times (D7 / 2 + D6 / 4 + D5 / 8 + D4 / 16 + D3 / 32 + D2 / 64 + D1 / 128 + D0 / 256) = I_{ref} \times Data / 256$$

where D0 is the LSB, D7 is the MSB for the inputs, and I_{ref} is the reference input current that must be applied to pin 14. The I_{ref} current is generally set to 2.0 mA. Figure 7-19 shows the generation of current reference (setting I_{ref} = 2 mA) by using the standard 5-V power supply and 5K ohm resistors.

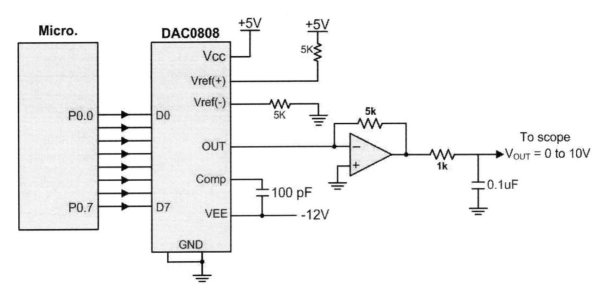

Figure 7-19: Microcontroller Connection to DAC0808

Some also use the zener diode reference voltage device (LM336), which overcomes fluctuations associated with the power supply voltage. Now assuming that I_{ref} = 2 mA, if all the input bits to the DAC are high, the maximum output current is 1.99 mA (verify this for yourself).

Converting I_{out} to voltage in DAC0808

We connect the output pin I_{OUT} to a resistor, convert this current to voltage, and monitor the output on the scope. However, in real life this can cause inaccuracy since the input resistance of the load where it is connected will also affect the output voltage. For this reason, the I_{ref} current output is buffered by connecting it to an op amp such as the 741 with R_f = 5K ohms for the feedback resistor. Assuming that R = 5K ohms, by changing the binary input, the output voltage changes as shown in Example 7-3.

Example 7-3

Assuming that R = 5K and I_{ref} = 2 mA, calculate V_{out} for the following binary inputs:
(a) 10011001 binary (0x99)   (b) 11001000 (0xC8)

Solution:

(a) I_{out} = 2 mA (153/255) = 1.195 mA and V_{out} = 1.195 mA × 5K = 5.975 V
(b) I_{out} = 2 mA (200/256) = 1.562 mA and V_{out} = 1.562 mA × 5K = 7.8125 V

Generating a sawtooth ramp

In order to generate a stair-step ramp, you can set up a circuit similar to Figure 7-19 and load Program 7-5 on the microcontroller. Instead of DAC in Figure 7-19 we can use DAC TLC7524 chip. To see the result wave, connect the output to an oscilloscope. Figure 7-20 shows the output.

Program 7-5: Generating Sawtooth Waveform

```
/* p7_5.c Use DAC to generate a saw tooth waveform

 * This program uses a for loop to generate a saw tooth
 * waveform output through a DAC. An 8-bit parallel input
 * DAC (TLC7524) is connected to P4. The DAC input latch
 * is put in transparent mode by grounding /CS and /WR.
 *
 * Tested with Keil 5.20 and MSP432 Device Family Pack V2.2.0.
 */

#include "msp.h"

void delayMs(int n);

int main(void) {
    int i;
```

```
    /* Configure P4 as output */
    P4->SEL0 &= ~0xFF;
    P4->SEL1 &= ~0xFF;
    P4->DIR |= 0xFF;

    while (1) {
        for (i = 0; i < 0xFF; i++) {
            /* write value of i to DAC0 */
            P4->OUT = i;
            delayMs(1);              /* delay 1ms */
        }
    }
}

/* delay milliseconds when system clock is at 3 MHz */
void delayMs(int n) {
    int i, j;

    for (j = 0; j < n; j++)
        for (i = 250; i > 0; i--);        /* Delay 1 ms */
}
```

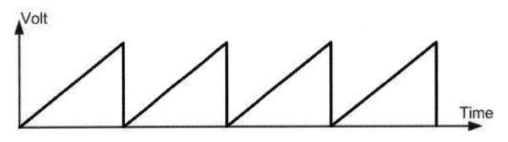

Figure 7-20: Saw Tooth Wave Form

Generating a sine wave

To generate a sine wave, we first need a table whose values represent the magnitude of the sine of angles between 0 and 360 degrees. The values for the sine function vary from -1.0 to +1.0 for 0 to 360 degree angles. Therefore, the table values are integer numbers representing the voltage magnitude for the sine of the angle. This method ensures that only integer numbers are output to the DAC by the processor. Table 7-11 shows the angles, the sine values, the voltage magnitudes, and the integer values representing the voltage magnitude for each angle with 30-degree increments.

To generate Table 7-11, we assumed the full-scale voltage of 10V for the DAC output. Full-scale output of the DAC is achieved when all the data input bits of the DAC are high. Therefore, to achieve the full-scale 10V output, we use the following equation:

$$V_{out} = 5V + (5V \times sin\theta)$$

220

Angle Θ (degrees)	Sin Θ	V_{OUT} (Voltage Magnitude) 5V + (5V × sin Θ)	Values Sent to DAC (decimal) (Voltage Mag. × 25.6)
0	0	5	128
30	0.5	7.5	192
60	0.866	9.33	238
90	1.0	10	255
120	0.866	9.33	238
150	0.5	7.5	192
180	0	5	128
210	-0.5	2.5	64
240	-0.866	0.669	17
270	-1.0	0	0
300	-0.866	0.669	17
330	-0.5	2.5	64
360	0	5	128

Table 7-11: Angle vs. Voltage Magnitude for Sine Wave

To find the value sent to the DAC for various angles, we simply multiply the V_{OUT} voltage by 25.6 because there are 256 steps and full-scale V_{OUT} is 10 volts. Therefore, 256 steps / 10 V = 25.6 steps per volt. To further clarify this, look at Example 7-4.

Example 7-4

Verify the values of Table 7-11 for the following angles: (a) 30 (b) 60.

Solution:

(a) V_{OUT} = 5 V + (5 V × sin Θ) = 5 V + 5 × sin 30 = 5 V + 5 × 0.5 = 7.5 V
   DAC input values = 7.5 V × 25.6 = 192 (decimal)
(b) V_{OUT} = 5 V + (5 V × sin Θ) = 5 V + 5 × sin 60 = 5 V + 5 × 0.866 = 9.33 V
   DAC input values = 9.33 V × 25.6 = 238 (decimal)

The following program sends the values of Table 7-11 to the DAC.

Program 7-6: Generating Sine Wave

```
/* p7_6.c Use DAC to generate sine wave
 * This program uses a pre-calculated lookup table to generate a
 * sine wave output through a DAC. An 8-bit parallel input
 * DAC (TLC7524) is connected to P4. The DAC input latch
 * is put in transparent mode by grounding /CS and /WR.
 *
 * Tested with Keil 5.20 and MSP432 Device Family Pack V2.2.0.
 *
 */
```

```
#include "msp.h"

void delayMs(int n);

int main(void) {
    int i;
    const static int sineWave[] =
        {116, 175, 217, 233, 217, 175,
         116,  58,  16,   0,  16,  58};

    /* Configure P4 as output */
    P4->SEL0 &= ~0xFF;
    P4->SEL1 &= ~0xFF;
    P4->DIR  |= 0xFF;

    while (1) {
        for (i = 0; i < 12; i++) {
            /* write value of i to DAC0 */
            P4->OUT = sineWave[i];
            delayMs(1);              /* delay 1ms */
        }
    }
}

/* delay milliseconds when system clock is at 3 MHz */
void delayMs(int n) {
    int i, j;

    for (j = 0; j < n; j++)
        for (i = 250; i > 0; i--);        /* delay 1 ms */
}
```

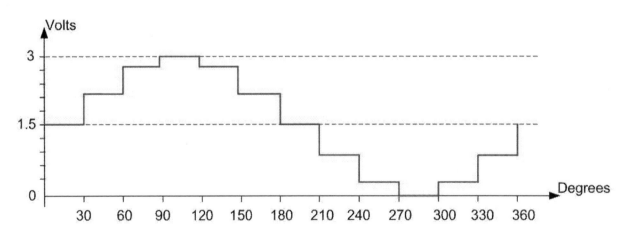

Figure 7-21: Angle vs. Voltage Magnitude for Sine Wave

Program 7-7 uses the C math library functions to generate sine wave.

```c
/* p7_7.c Use DAC to generate sine wave

 * This program calculates the lookup table to generate a
 * sine wave output through a DAC. An 8-bit parallel input
 * DAC (TLC7524) is connected to P4. The DAC input latch
 * is put in transparent mode by grounding /CS and /WR.
 *
 * Tested with Keil 5.20 and MSP432 Device Family Pack V2.2.0.
 */

#include "msp.h"
#include <math.h>

void delayMs(int n);
#define WAVEFORM_LENGTH 256
int sinewave[WAVEFORM_LENGTH];

int main(void) {
    int i;
    float fRadians;
    const float M_PI = 3.1415926535897;

    /* construct data table for a sine wave */
    fRadians = ((2 * M_PI) / WAVEFORM_LENGTH);

    for (i = 0; i < WAVEFORM_LENGTH; i++) {
        sinewave[i] = 127 * (sinf(fRadians * i) + 1);
    }

    /* Configure P4 as output */
    P4->SEL0 &= ~0xFF;
    P4->SEL1 &= ~0xFF;
    P4->DIR  |= 0xFF;

    while (1) {
        for (i = 0; i < WAVEFORM_LENGTH; i++) {
            /* write value of i to DAC0 */
            P4->OUT = sinewave[i];
            delayMs(1);             /* delay 1ms */
        }
    }
}

/* delay milliseconds when system clock is at 3 MHz */
void delayMs(int n) {
    int i, j;

    for (j = 0; j < n; j++)
        for (i = 250; i > 0; i--);      /* delay 1 ms */
}
```

See Chapter 8 for the ARM connection and programming of LTC1661 DAC using SPI bus.

Review Questions

1. In a DAC, input is _____ (digital, analog) and output is _____ (digital, analog).
2. DAC0808 is a(n) _____-bit D-to-A converter.
3. The output of DAC808 is in _____ (current, voltage).

Answers to Review Questions

Section 7.1

1. Number of steps and V_{ref} voltage
2. 8
3. True
4. 1.28 V / 256 = 5 mV
5.
   (a) 0.7 V / 5 mV = 140 in decimal and D7–D0 = 10001100 in bin
   (b) 1 V/ 5 mV = 200 in decimal and D7–D0 = 11001000 in binary.

Section 7.2

1. 14
2. 0x3FF
3. Step size is 3.3V / 4096 = 0.8057 mV and 1.9V / 0.8057mv = 2,358 in decimal or 0x936.
4. ADC14MEMx
5. 8-,10-,12-, and 14-bit.

Section 7.3

1. True
2. 10, Celsius
3. 10, Fahrenheit
4. 00111110 (binary) = 62 → Temperature = 62 × 330 / 4096 = 5

Section 7.4

1. Digital, analog
2. 8
3. current

Chapter 8: SPI Protocol and DAC Interfacing

The SPI (serial peripheral interface) is a bus interface incorporated in many devices such as ADC, DAC, and EEPROM. In Section 8.1 we will examine the signals of the SPI bus and show how the read and write operations in the SPI work. Section 8.2 examines the TI MSP432 ARM SPI registers. In Section 8.3 we show LTC1661 DAC interfacing to ARM using SPI bus.

Section 8.1: SPI Bus Protocol

The SPI bus was originally started by Motorola (later became Freescale), but in recent years has become widely used by many semiconductor chip companies. SPI devices use only 2 pins for data transfer, called SDI (Din) and SDO (Dout), instead of the 8 or more pins used in traditional buses. This reduction of data pins reduces the package size and power consumption drastically, making them ideal for many applications in which space or pin count is a major concern. The SPI bus has the SCLK (serial clock) pin to synchronize the data transfer between two chips. The last pin of the SPI bus is CE (chip enable), which is used to initiate and terminate the data transfer. These four pins, SDI, SDO, SCLK, and CE, make the SPI a 4-wire interface. See Figure 8-1.

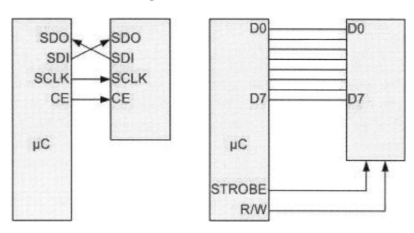

Figure 8-1: SPI Bus vs. Traditional Parallel Bus Connection to Microcontroller

In many chips, the SDI, SDO, SCLK, and CE signals are alternatively named as MOSI, MISO, SCK, and SS as shown in Figure 8-2 (compared with Figure 8-1). There is also a widely used standard called a 3-wire interface bus. In a 3-wire interface bus, we have SCLK and CE, and only a single pin for data transfer. The SPI 4-wire bus can become a 3-wire interface when the SDI and SDO data pins are tied together. However, there are some major differences between the SPI and 3-wire devices in the data transfer protocol. For that reason, a device must support the 3-wire protocol internally in order to be used as a 3-wire device. Many devices support both SPI and 3-wire protocols.

How SPI works

SPI consists of two shift registers, one in master and the other in the slave side. Also there is a clock generator in the master side that generates the clock for the shift registers.

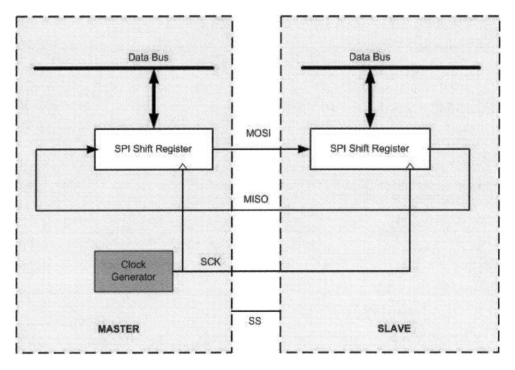

Figure 8-2: SPI Architecture

As you can see in Figure 8-2, serial-out pin of the master shift register is connected to the serial-in pin of the slave shift register by MOSI (Master Out Slave In) and the serial-in pin of the master shift register is connected to the serial-out pin of the slave shift register by MISO (Master In Slave Out). The master clock generator provides clock to shift register in both master and slave shift registers. The clock input of the shift registers can be falling- or rising-edge triggered. This will be discussed shortly.

In SPI, the shift registers are 8 bits long. It means that after 8 clock pulses, the contents of the two shift registers are interchanged. When the master wants to send a byte of data, it places the byte in its shift register and generates 8 clock pulses. After 8 clock pulses, the byte is transmitted to the slave shift register. When the master wants to receive a byte of data, the slave side should place the byte in its shift register and after 8 clock pulses the data will be received by the master shift register. It must be noted that SPI is full duplex meaning that it may send and receive data at the same time.

Clock polarity and phase in SPI device

As we mentioned before in UART communication, transmitter and receiver must agree on a clock frequency (baud rate). In SPI communication, both master and slave use the same clock but the master and slave must agree on the clock polarity and phase with respect to the data. Clock polarity implies the clock signal level when the clock is idling. Each clock pulse has two edges, the leading edge and the trailing edge. Clock phase determines whether leading edge or trailing edge is used to sample the data.

With clock polarity as 0 the idle value of the clock is zero while with clock polarity as 1 the idle value of the clock is one. When clock phase is 0, data is sampled on the leading (first) clock edge; while clock phase is 1, data is sampled on the trailing (second) clock edge. Notice that if the idle value of the clock is zero the leading (first) clock edge is a rising edge but if the idle value of the clock is one, the leading (first) clock edge is a falling edge. See

Clock Polarity	Clock Phase	Data read and change time	SPI Mode
0	0	read on falling edge, changed on a rising edge	0
0	1	read on rising edge, changed on a falling edge	1
1	0	read on rising edge, changed on a falling edge	2
1	1	read on falling edge, changed on a rising edge	3

Table 8-1: SPI Clock Polarity and phase

and Figure 8-3.

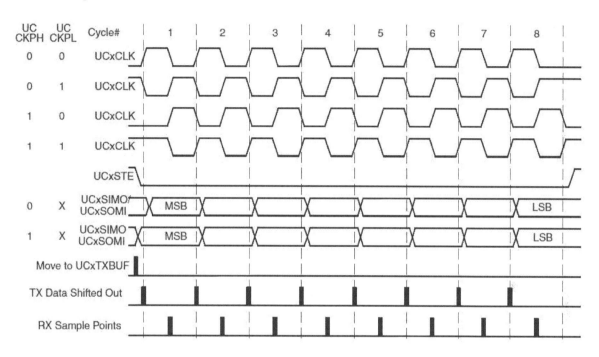

Figure 8-3: SPI Clock Polarity and phase

Clock Polarity	Clock Phase	Data read and change time	SPI Mode
0	0	read on falling edge, changed on a rising edge	0
0	1	read on rising edge, changed on a falling edge	1
1	0	read on rising edge, changed on a falling edge	2
1	1	read on falling edge, changed on a rising edge	3

Table 8-1: SPI Clock Polarity and phase

Review Questions

1. True or false. SPI is an Asynchronous protocol.
2. True or false. In the SPI protocol, the clock is always generated by the master device.

Section 8.2: SPI programming in MSP432

The MSP432P401R chip comes with up to 8 eUSCI (enhanced universal serial communication interface) modules. The four eUSCI_Ax modules support UART that we discussed in Chapter 4. The other four eUSCI_Bx modules support I2C protocol. All eight of them support SPI function. In this section, we examine the SPI mode of eUSCI modules. The eUSCI modules are located at the following base addresses:

USCI_Ax Module	Base Address
eUSCI_A0	0x4000_1000
eUSCI_A1	0x4000_1400
eUSCI_A2	0x4000_1800
eUSCI_A3	0x4000_1C00

Table 8-1A: eUSCI_A Module Base Address (Shared with UART)

USCI_Bx Module	Base Address
eUSCI_B0	0x4000_2000
eUSCI_B1	0x4000_2400
eUSCI_B2	0x4000_2800
eUSCI_B3	0x4000_2C00

Table 8-1B: eUSCI_B Module Base Address (Shared with I2C)

SPI Register

To program the SPI mode of the eUSCI, we need to examine the registers associated with it. Table 8-2 shows some of the registers. Notice that the names of the registers and their addresses are identical to the UART registers we covered in Chapter 4. The 4 SPI modules of eUSCIAx (x=0, 1, 2, 3) can be used for SPI or UART but not at the same time. In the same way, the 4 SPI modules of eUSCIBx (x=0, 1, 2, 3) can be used for SPI or I2C but not at the same. Now, if the registers are the same, how the CPU distinguishes between the SPI and UART? This is done with the UCSYNC (bit D8) bits of the UCAxCTLW0 (UCAx Control Word 0) register. Upon Reset, UCSYNC=0 meaning all the bits of UCAxCTLW0 are used to set the UART parameters. By making UCSYNC=1, the bits of UCAxCTLW0 registers are used to set parameters for SPI. Notice that SPI (UCSYNC=1) is called synchronous since a clock used to synchronize the data transfer between the MSP432 and SPI devices such as DAC, as we will see soon. Recall from Chapter 4 that there was no such a clock for UART. UART used TXD and RXD and common ground between the MSP432 and the PC for terminal emulator such as TeraTerminal.

Register Name	Register Function
UCAxCTLW0 (UCAx Control Word 0)	Control 0
UCAxBRW (UCAx Baud Rate Control Word)	Baud Rate
UCAxSTATW (UCAx Status)	Status
UCAxRXBUF (UCAx Receive Buffer)	Receive Register
UCAxTXBUF (UCAx Transmit Buffer)	Transmit Register
UCAxIE (UCAx Interrupt Enable)	Interrupt Enable
UCAxIFG (UCAx Interrupt Flag)	Interrupt Flags
UCAxIV (UCAx Interrupt Vector)	Interrupt Vector

Table 8-2: eUSCI Registers

Configuring the SPI Module

The UCAxCTLW0 (UCAx Control Word 0) sets SPI configuration. Figure 8-4 shows the bits of UCAxCTLW0 and Table 8-3 describes the function of each bit. Although the conventional SPI uses only 8-bit data, the SPI module allows transfer of data for 7 bits too.

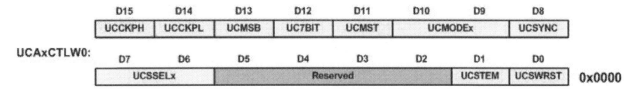

Figure 8-4: SPI Control Word 0 (UCAxCTLW0) Registers in MSP432

Bits	Name	Function	Description
0	UCSWRST	Software reset enable	0b = Disabled. eUSCI reset released for operation. 1b = Enabled. eUSCI logic held in reset state
1	UCSTEM	STE mode select in master mode.	0b = STE pin is used to prevent conflicts with other masters 1b = STE pin is used to generate the enable signal for a 4-wire slave
7-6	UCSSELx	eUSCI clock source select	00b = Reserved 01b = ACLK 10b = SMCLK 11b = SMCLK
8	UCSYNC	Synchronous mode enable	0b = Asynchronous mode (UART) 1b = Synchronous mode (SPI or I2C)
10-9	UCMODEx	eUSCI mode.	00b = 3-pin SPI 01b = 4-pin SPI with UCxSTE active high: Slave enabled when UCxSTE = 1 10b = 4-pin SPI with UCxSTE active low: Slave enabled when UCxSTE = 0 11b = I2C mode
11	UCMST	Master mode select	0b = Slave mode 1b = Master mode
12	UC7BIT	Character length	0b = 8-bit data 1b = 7-bit data
13	UCMSB	MSB first select.	0b = LSB first 1b = MSB first
14	UCCKPL	Clock polarity select	0b = The inactive state is low. 1b = The inactive state is high.
15	UCCKPH	Clock phase select	0b = Data is changed on the first UCLK edge and captured on the following edge. 1b = Data is captured on the first UCLK edge and changed on the following edge.

Table 8-3: UCAxCTLW0 (UCAx Control Word 0) register

An important bit is the UCSWRST bit (Software Reset) in UCAxCTLW0 register. We must make UCSWRST = 1 during configuration. After the initialization of all the registers are done we make UCSWRST = 0 to transmit and receive data. When UCSWRST is set, it clears UCRXIE and UCTXIE. If interrupt will be used, the interrupt enable must be done after UCSWRST is cleared.

Clock Polarity and Clock Phase

As discussed in Section 8.1, we need to choose clock polarity and clock phase that agree with the other devices connected to the SPI. In the MSP432, the clock polarity is determined by UCCKPL bit D14 and the clock phase is determined by UCCKPH bit D15 in UCAxCTLW0 register.

Master or Slave

The SPI Module inside the MSP432 chip can be Master or Slave. Master is the device that generate clock and drives the UCxCLK pin. Slave is the device that uses the UCxCLK pin as the SPI clock. We use UCMST (UC Master, bit D11) in SPI control register 0 (UCAxCTLW0) to designate the MSP432 chip as master or slave. See Figures 8-4 and 8-5.

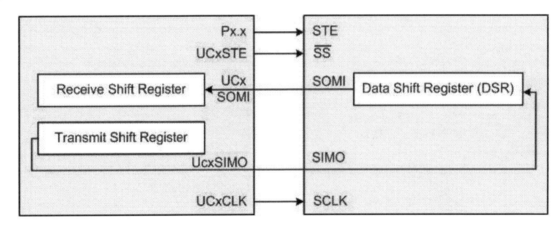

Figure 8-5: Using MSP432 SPI module as Master

3-pin SPI or 4-pin SPI

The UCMODEx bits (bits 10, 9) determine the operation mode of SPI. When these two bits are set to 01b or 10b, the hardware generates a slave select signal (UCxSTE) and is called 4-pin SPI (UCxSIMO, UCxSOMI, UCxCLK, UCxSTE). If these two bits are 00b, there is no hardware generated slave select, only three pin signals are generated by the hardware (UCxSIMO, UCxSOMI, UCxCLK). Hardware generated slave select signal simplifies the software but can only support one slave on the SPI connection. If there are more than one slave device hanging on the same SPI connection, software controlled slave select is the only way to go. Also, hardware generated slave select is activated for each byte of data transmission. Some slave device operations require more than 8-bit of data for each transaction while the slave select signal is active. In that case, we have to use software controlled slave select.

Setting Bit Rate

SPI module baud rate register (UCAxBRW) is the same as the one we saw in the UART chapter. The clock source of SPI module is divided by the content of UCBRx for the SPI clock. The clock source is selected by the UCSSELx bits in UCAxCTLW0 register. By default, the MSP432 LaunchPad SMCLK is running at 3 MHz and it can be selected by setting UCSSELx bits to 10b or 11b.

D15		D0	
UCAxBRW:	UCBRx		**0x0006**

Figure 8-6: UCAxBRW Register SPI Baud Rate

See Examples 8-1, 8-2, and 8-3.

Example 8-1

Assume the system clock frequency is 3MHz. Find the values for the UCAxBRW register for the bit rate of (a) 1M, (b) 750K, and (c) 500K.

Solution

(a) 3 MHz/1MHz = 3,
(b) 3 MHz/750KHz = 4,
(c) 3 MHz/ 500KHz = 6.

Example 8-2

In a given MSP432 board, The UCAxBRW=12 and the system clock is 3MHz. What is the baud rate for the SPI?

Solution:

3MHz/12=250K

Example 8-3

(a) Find the value for UCAxCTLW0 for MSB first, 8-bit, master, 4-pin SPI, STE low active, synchronous mode, SMCLK as clock and SPI as slave. Set the phase and polarity as 11.

(b) Find the same configuration for 3-pin SPI

Solution:

    (a) UCAxCTLW0 = 0xEDC3
    (b) UCAxCTLW0 = 0xE9C1

Data Register

The data is placed in UCAxTXDBUF (UCAx Transmit Buffer) register for transmission. We use the UCAxRXDBUF register for the received data buffer. In 8-bit data size selection, the data must be placed into the lower 8-bits of the register and the rest of the register is unused. In the receive mode, the received data is held in the lower 8-bit of the register. In this regard it is the same as UART.

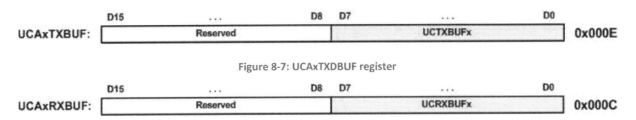

Figure 8-7: UCAxTXDBUF register

Figure 8-8: UCAxRXDBUF register

Status Flag Register

We monitor the UCBUSY flag in the UCAxSTATW (UCAx Status Word) register to see whether the SPI module is busy transmitting or receiving data. Because the slave select signal needs to be held active while data transmission is going on, this status flag should be used to wait on until the data transmission is over before removing slave select by software.

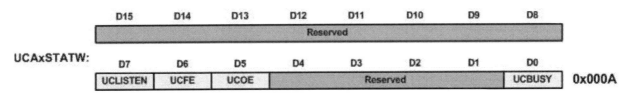

Figure 8-9: UCAx Status (UCAxSTATW) Register

Bits	Name	Function	Description
0	UCBUSY	SPI Busy Bit	The bit is 1 when the SPI is currently busy transmitting or receiving
5	UCOE	Overrun error flag.	0b = No error 1b = Overrun error occurred
6	UCFE	Framing error flag.	0b = No error 1b = Bus conflict occurred
7	UCLISTEN	Listen enable.	0b = Disabled 1b = Enabled. The transmitter output is internally fed back to the receiver.

Table 8-4: UCAx Status (UCAxSTATW) Register

Interrupt Flag Register

We monitor the UCTXIFG (D1 bit) flag in the UCAxIFG (UCAx Interrupt Flag) register to see whether TXBUF is empty so we can write another byte for transmission. To see whether a byte has been received in the RXDBUF, we check the UCRXIFG (D0 bit). See Figure 8-10 and Table 8-5.

D15	......	D2	D1	D0	
UCAxIFG:	Reserved		UCTXIFG	UCRXIFG	0x001C

Figure 8-10: UCAx Interrupt Flag (UCAxIFG) Register

Bits	Name	Function	Description
0	UCRXIFG	RX Receive Interrupt flag	The bit is 1 when the receive BUF is empty
1	UCTXIFG	TX Transmit Interrupt flag	The bit is 1 when the transmit BUF is empty

Table 8-5: UCAx Interrupt Flag (UCAxIFG) Register

Configuring GPIO for SPI

In using SPI, we must also configure the GPIO pins to allow the connection of SPI module signals to the external pins of the device. See Tables 8-7 and 8-8. In this regard, it is the same as all other peripherals. Notice that the MSP432 designates the SPI pins as STE, CLK, SOMI, and SIMO. Not all the pins are needed and not all the pins need to be configured. For example, if the program only writes to the slave device and never reads it, the SOMI pin does not need to be configured.

SPI Module Pin	IO Pin	SPI Module Pin	IO Pin
STE(UCA0)	P1.0	STE(UCA1)	P2.0
CLK(UCA0)	P1.1	CLK(UCA1)	P2.1
SOMI(UCA0)	P1.2	SOMI(UCA1)	P2.2
SIMO(UCA0)	P1.3	SIMO(UCA1)	P2.3
STE(UCA2)	P3.0	STE(UCA3)	P9.4
CLK(UCA2)	P3.1	CLK(UCA3)	P9.5
SOMI(UCA2)	P3.2	SOMI(UCA3)	P9.6
SIMO(UCA2)	P3.3	SIMO(UCA3)	P9.7

Table 8-6A: IO Pin Assignment for all 4 UCAx Modules

SPI Module Pin	IO Pin	SPI Module Pin	IO Pin
STE(UCB0)	P1.4	STE(UCB1)	P6.2
CLK(UCB0)	P1.5	CLK(UCB1)	P6.3
SIMO(UCB0)	P1.6	SIMO(UCB1)	P6.4
SOMI(UCB0)	P1.7	SOMI(UCB1)	P6.5
STE(UCB2)	P3.4	STE(UCB3)	P10.0
CLK(UCB2)	P3.5	CLK(UCB3)	P10.1
SIMO(UCB2)	P3.6	SIMO(UCB3)	P10.2
SOMI(UCB2)	P3.7	SOMI(UCB3)	P10.3

Table 8-6B: IO Pin Assignment for all 4 UCBx Modules

I/O pin	Function	PxSEL1=0	PxSEL0=1
P1.0	STE(UCA0)	P1SEL1=00000000	P1SEL0=00000001
P1.1	CLK(UCA0)	P1SEL1=00000000	P1SEL0=00000010
P1.2	SOMI(UCA0)	P1SEL1=00000000	P1SEL0=00000100
P1.3	SIMO(UCA0)	P1SEL1=00000000	P1SEL0=00001000
For SPI0:		P1SEL1=0x00	P1SEL0=00001111=0x0F
P2.0	STE(UCA1)	P2SEL1=00000000	P2SEL0=00000001

P2.1	CLK(UCA1)	P2SEL1=00000000	P2SEL0=00000010
P2.2	SOMI(UCA1)	P2SEL1=00000000	P2SEL0=00000100
P2.3	SIMO(UCA1)	P2SEL1=00000000	P2SEL0=00001000
For SPI1:		P2SEL1=0x00	P2SEL0=00001111=0x0F
P3.0	STE(UCA2)	P3SEL1=00000000	P3SEL0=00000001
P3.1	CLK(UCA2)	P3SEL1=00000000	P3SEL0=00000010
P3.2	SOMI(UCA2)	P3SEL1=00000000	P3SEL0=00000100
P3.3	SIMO(UCA2)	P3SEL1=00000000	P3SEL0=00001000
For SPI2:		P3SEL1=0x00	P3SEL0=00001111=0x0F
P9.4	STE(UCA3)	P9SEL1=00000000	P9SEL0=00010000
P9.5	CLK(UCA3)	P9SEL1=00000000	P9SEL0=00100000
P9.6	SOMI(UCA3)	P9SEL1=00000000	P9SEL0=01000000
P9.7	SIMO(UCA3)	P9SEL1=00000000	P9SEL0=10000000
For SPI3:		P9SEL1=0x00	P9SEL0=11110000=0xF0

Table 8-7A: Pins available for UCAs

I/O pin	Function	PxSEL1=0	PxSEL0=1
P1.4	STE(UCB0)	P1SEL1=00000000	P1SEL0=00010000
P1.5	CLK(UCB0)	P1SEL1=00000000	P1SEL0=00100000
P1.6	SIMO(UCB0)	P1SEL1=00000000	P1SEL0=01000000
P1.7	SOMI(UCB0)	P1SEL1=00000000	P1SEL0=10000000
For SPI0:		P1SEL1=0x00	P1SEL0=11110000=0XF0
P6.2	STE(UCB1)	P2SEL1=00000000	P2SEL0=00000100
P6.3	CLK(UCB1)	P6SEL1=00000000	P6SEL0=00001000
P6.4	SIMO(UCB1)	P6SEL1=00000000	P6SEL0=00010000
P6.5	SOMI(UCB1)	P6SEL1=00000000	P6SEL0=00100000
For SPI1:		P6SEL1=0x00	P6SEL0=00111100=0x3C
P3.4	STE(UCB2)	P3SEL1=00000000	P3SEL0=00010000
P3.5	CLK(UCB2)	P3SEL1=00000000	P3SEL0=00100000
P3.6	SIMO(UCB2)	P3SEL1=00000000	P3SEL0=01000000
P3.7	SOMI(UCB2)	P3SEL1=00000000	P3SEL0=10000000
For SPI2:		P3SEL1=0x00	P3SEL0=11110000=0xF0
P10.0	STE(UCB3)	P10SEL1=00000000	P10SEL0=00000001
P10.1	CLK(UCB3)	P10SEL1=00000000	P10SEL0=00000010
P10.2	SIMO(UCB3)	P10SEL1=00000000	P10SEL0=00000100
P10.3	SOMI(UCB3)	P10SEL1=00000000	P10SEL0=00001000
For SPI3:		P10SEL1=0x00	P10SEL0=00001111=0x0F

Table 8-7B: Pins available for UCBs

Steps for transmitting data in 4-pin mode

Here are the steps to configure the UCA1 as SPI and transmit a byte of data for MSP432 LaunchPad board. There is a twist in configuration for a 4-pin mode of SPI. None of the modules has all CLK, SIMO, SOMI, and STE pins brought out to the 40-pin headers. In the following example, we use the pin map function to redirect the UCA1 output pins to P2.3, P2.4, and P2.5.

1) Disable the SPI by setting the software reset (UCSWRST, D0) bit of UCA1CTLW0 register to 1.

2) Configure the control register value for clock phase and clock polarity, MSB first, 8-bit data size, master mode, 4-pin SPI, synchronous mode, clock source, and set STE for slave enable in the UCA1CTLW0 register.

3) Set the Baud rate for SPI by using UCB0BRW register.

4) Use pin map to map P2.3 to PM_UCA1CLK, P2.4 to PM_UCA1SIMO, and P2.5 to PM_UCA1STE.

5) Select the alternate function as pin map for P2.3, P2.4, and P2.5 pins using the P2->SEL1~=0x38 and P2->SEL0|=0x38.

6) Enable the SPI by clearing software reset bit of UCA1CTLW0 register. This is the opposite of step 1.

7) Wait for the UCTXIFG flag bit of the UCA1IFG register to go high for transmit buffer empty.

8) Write a byte to UCA1TXDBUF buffer register to be transmitted.

9) To transmit another character, go to step 7.

Program 8-1: sending A to Z characters via UCA1

```
/* p8_1.c: Using SPI to send A to Z characters via SPI
 * UCA1 is configured as 4-pin SPI.
 * Because MSP432 has no SPI with all 4 pins brought out
 * to the 40-pin headers, Pin Map is used to redirect them:
 * P2.3 CLK
 * P2.4 SIMO
 * P2.5 STE
 *
 * Tested with Keil 5.20 and MSP432 Device Family Pack V2.2.0.
 */

#include "msp.h"

void delayMs(int n);

int main(void)
{
    int i;

    EUSCI_A1->CTLW0 = 0x0001;          /* disable UCA1 during config */
    /* clock phase/polarity:11, MSB first, 8-bit, master, 4-pin SPI, STE low active,
       synchronous mode, use SMCLK as clock source, STE for slave enable */
    EUSCI_A1->CTLW0 = 0xEDC3;
    EUSCI_A1->BRW = 1;                 /* 3 MHz / 1 = 3 MHz */
    EUSCI_A1->CTLW0 &= ~0x0001;        /* enable UCA1 after config */

    PMAP->KEYID = 0x2D52;        /* unlock PMAP */
    P2MAP->PMAP_REGISTER[1] = 0x0800;    /* map P2.3 to PM_UCA1CLK */
    P2MAP->PMAP_REGISTER[2] = 0x070A;    /* map P2.4 to PM_UCA1SIMO, map P2.5 to
PM_UCA1STE */
    P2->SEL0 |= 0x38;                  /* set alternate function to pinmap */
    P2->SEL1 &= ~0x38;                 /* for P2.3, P2.4, P2.5 */
    PMAP->CTL = 0;                     /* lock PMAP */
    PMAP->KEYID = 0;

    while(1) {
```

```
        for (i = 'A'; i <= 'Z'; i++) {
            while(!(EUSCI_A1->IFG & 2)) ; /* wait for transmit buffer empty */
            EUSCI_A1->TXBUF = i;         /* write the character */
            delayMs(10);
        }
    }
}

/* system clock at 3 MHz */
void delayMs(int n) {
    int i, j;

    for (j = 0; j < n; j++)
        for (i = 250; i > 0; i--);       /* delay */
}
```

Second set of SPI Modules

As we stated earlier, the MSP432 has total of 8 SPI modules. The first four are called UCAx (x=0, 1, 2, and 3) and the second set is called UCBx (x = 0, 1, 2, and 3). See Tables 8-9A and 8-9B. Notice the designation of letter A and B. While the UCAx modules are shared with the UART, the UCBx modules can be used either by SPI or I2C. Although there are differences between UCAx modules and UCBx modules, when it comes to SPI, the configurations are identical. First, the UCSYNC bit in UCAxCTLW0 must be set to 1 then the UCMODEx bits are set to 00b, 01b, or 10b. There are additional registers of UCBx for I2C configuration and operations but they are irrelevant to SPI functions.

USCI_Bx Module	Base Address
eUSCI_B0	0x4000_2000
eUSCI_B1	0x4000_2400
eUSCI_B2	0x4000_2800
eUSCI_B3	0x4000_2C00

Table 8-8A: eUSCI_B Module Base Address (Shared with I2C)

SPI Module Pin	IO Pin	SPI Module Pin	IO Pin
STE(UCB0)	P1.4	STE(UCB1)	P6.2
CLK(UCB0)	P1.5	CLK(UCB1)	P6.3
SIMO(UCB0)	P1.6	SIMO(UCB1)	P6.4
SOMI(UCB0)	P1.7	SOMI(UCB1)	P6.5
STE(UCB2)	P3.4	STE(UCB3)	P10.0
CLK(UCB2)	P3.5	CLK(UCB3)	P10.1
SIMO(UCB2)	P3.6	SIMO(UCB3)	P10.2
SOMI(UCB2)	P3.7	SOMI(UCB3)	P10.3

Table 8-8B: IO Pin Assignment for all 4 UCBx Modules

236

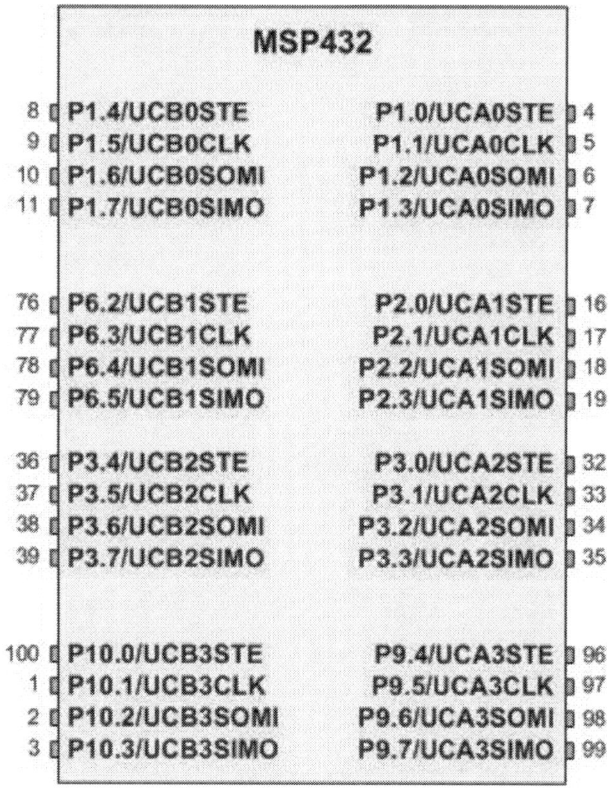

```
                        MSP432

    8 ◻ P1.4/UCB0STE          P1.0/UCA0STE ◻ 4
    9 ◻ P1.5/UCB0CLK          P1.1/UCA0CLK ◻ 5
   10 ◻ P1.6/UCB0SOMI         P1.2/UCA0SOMI ◻ 6
   11 ◻ P1.7/UCB0SIMO         P1.3/UCA0SIMO ◻ 7


   76 ◻ P6.2/UCB1STE          P2.0/UCA1STE ◻ 16
   77 ◻ P6.3/UCB1CLK          P2.1/UCA1CLK ◻ 17
   78 ◻ P6.4/UCB1SOMI         P2.2/UCA1SOMI ◻ 18
   79 ◻ P6.5/UCB1SIMO         P2.3/UCA1SIMO ◻ 19


   36 ◻ P3.4/UCB2STE          P3.0/UCA2STE ◻ 32
   37 ◻ P3.5/UCB2CLK          P3.1/UCA2CLK ◻ 33
   38 ◻ P3.6/UCB2SOMI         P3.2/UCA2SOMI ◻ 34
   39 ◻ P3.7/UCB2SIMO         P3.3/UCA2SIMO ◻ 35


  100 ◻ P10.0/UCB3STE         P9.4/UCA3STE ◻ 96
    1 ◻ P10.1/UCB3CLK         P9.5/UCA3CLK ◻ 97
    2 ◻ P10.2/UCB3SOMI        P9.6/UCA3SOMI ◻ 98
    3 ◻ P10.3/UCB3SIMO        P9.7/UCA3SIMO ◻ 99
```

Figure 8-11: SPI pins for UCAx and UCBx

Steps for transmitting data in 3-pin mode

Here are the steps to configure the UCB0 as SPI and transmit a byte of data for MSP432 LaunchPad board. In this example, we use P2.3 as a software controlled slave select pin.

1) Disable the SPI by setting the software reset (UCSWRST, D0) bit of UCB0CTLW0 register to 1.
2) Configure the control register value for clock phase and clock polarity, MSB first, 8-bit data size, master mode, 3-pin SPI, synchronous mode, and clock source in the UCB0CTLW0 register.
3) Set the Baud rate for SPI by using UCB0BRW register.
4) Select the alternate functions for P1.5 (UCB0CLK) and P1.6 (UCB0SIMO) pins using the P1SEL1~=0x60 and P1SEL0|=0x60.
5) Enable the SPI by clearing software reset bit of UCB0CTLW0 register. This is the opposite of step 1.
6) Configure a general purpose I/O pin P2.3 as slave select pin.
7) Keep the slave select pin idle high.
8) Assert slave select pin by driving it low.
9) Wait for the UCTXIFG flag bit of the UCB0IFG register to go high for transmit buffer empty.
10) Write a byte to UCB0TXDBUF buffer register to be transmitted.
11) To transmit another character, go to step 9.
12) After all the characters are transmitted, wait for the BUSY flag in UCB0STATW register to go low (transmit complete) then deassert the slave select signal by driving it high.

```c
/* p8_2.c: Using SPI to send A to Z characters via SPI
 * UCB0 is configured as SPI. Software controlled slave select.
 *
 * P1.5 UCB0CLK
 * P1.6 UCB0SIMO
 * P2.3 Slave Select
 *
 * Tested with Keil 5.20 and MSP432 Device Family Pack V2.2.0.
 */

#include "msp.h"

void delayMs(int n);

int main(void) {
    int c;

    EUSCI_B0->CTLW0 = 0x0001;     /* disable UCB0 during config */
    /* clock phase/polarity:11, MSB first, 8-bit, master, 3-pin SPI,
       synchronous mode, use SMCLK as clock source */
    EUSCI_B0->CTLW0 = 0xE9C1;
    EUSCI_B0->BRW = 1;            /* 3 MHz / 1 = 3 MHz */
    EUSCI_B0->CTLW0 &= ~0x0001;   /* enable UCB0 after config */

    P1->SEL0 |= 0x60;          /* P1.5, P1.6 for UCB0CLK, UCB0SIMO */
    P1->SEL1 &= ~0x60;

    P2->DIR |= 8;              /* P2.3 set as output for slave select */
    P2->OUT |= 8;              /* slave select idle high */

    while(1)
    {
        for (c = 'A'; c <= 'Z'; c++) {
            P2->OUT &= ~8;                  /* assert slave select */

            while(!(EUSCI_B0->IFG & 2)) ;    /* wait for transmit buffer empty */
            EUSCI_B0->TXBUF = c;             /* write to SPI transmit buffer */

            while(EUSCI_B0->STATW & 1) ;     /* wait for transmit done */
            P2->OUT |= 8;                    /* deassert slave select */
            delayMs(10);
        }
    }
}

/* system clock at 3 MHz */
void delayMs(int n) {
    int i, j;

    for (j = 0; j < n; j++)
        for (i = 250; i > 0; i--);       /* delay 1 ms */
}
```

Review Questions

1. True or false. The UCAx module in MSP432 does not support SPI protocol.
2. True or false. UCAx modules support both UART and SPI.
3. In MSP432, the CS of the SPI module is called _____.
4. In MSP432, which register is used to enable the SPI mode?
5. In MSP432, which register is used to set the data size?

Section 8.3: LTC1661 SPI DAC

In Chapter 7 we examined DAC concepts. In this section we show an SPI-based DAC and its interfacing to MSP432 ARM MCU. LTC1661 is a 10-bit SPI serial DAC from Linear Technology. It has two separate output channels, named A and B, as shown in Figure 8-12.

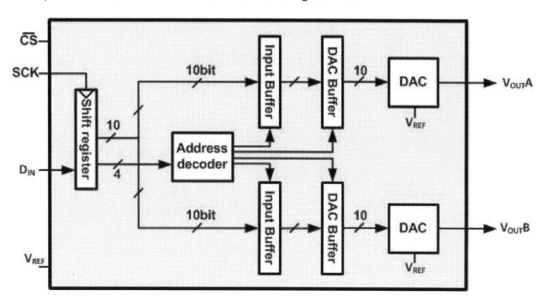

Figure 8-12: LTC1661 Internal Block Diagram

The relation between the input number and the output voltage is as follows:

$$VOUT = \frac{(VREF \times DIN)}{1024}$$

We can control the LTC1661 by sending 2 bytes of data. As shown in Figure 8-14, the 16-bit is made of 3 parts: control code (4 bits), data (10 bits), and not used (2 bits). The control codes are used to control the internal parts of the LTC1661.

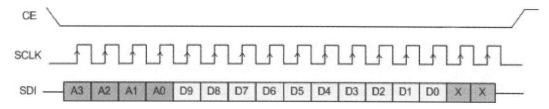

Figure 8-13: Sending a Packet of Data to LTC166x

As shown in Figure 8-12, each DAC is double buffered to provide simultaneous update. To do so, we load input buffers with proper values in two transactions and then load the DAC buffers from the input buffers simultaneously. Table 8-10 shows the list of available control codes. To decrease power consumption, the DAC has a sleep mode, as well. We can switch between sleep and awake modes using proper control code.

A3 A2 A1 A0	Interrupt Register	DAC Register	Power Down Status	Comments
0 0 0 0	No Change	No Update	No Change	No operation. power-down status unchanged
0 0 0 1	Load DAC A	No Update	No Change	Load input register A with data. DAC outputs unchanged. power-down Status unchanged
0 0 1 0	Load DAC B	No Update	No Change	Load input register B with data. DAC outputs unchanged. power-down status unchanged
0 0 1 1	-	-	-	Reserved
0 1 0 0	-	-	-	Reserved
0 1 0 1	-	-	-	Reserved
0 1 1 0	-	-	-	Reserved
0 1 1 1	-	-	-	Reserved
1 0 0 0	No Change	Update Outputs	Wake	Load both DAC Regs with existing contents of input Regs. Outputs update. Part wakes up
1 0 0 1	Load DAC A	Update Outputs	Wake	Load input Reg A. Load DAC Regs with new contents of input Reg A and existing contents of Reg B. Outputs update.
1 0 1 0	Load DAC B	Update Outputs	Wake	Load input Reg B. Load DAC Regs with existing contents of input Reg A and new contents of Reg B. Outputs update
1 0 1 1	-	-	-	Reserved
1 1 0 0	-	-	-	Reserved
1 1 0 1	No Change	No Update	Wake	Part wakes up. Input and DAC Regs unchanged. DAC outputs reflect existing contents of DAC Regs
1 1 1 0	No Change	No Update	Sleep	Part goes to sleep. Input and DAC Regs unchanged. DAC outputs set to high impedance state
1 1 1 1	Load ADCs A, B with same 10-bit code	Update Outputs	Wake	Load both input Regs. Load both DAC Regs with new contents of input Regs. Outputs update. Part wakes up

Table 8-10: LTC1661 DAC Control Functions

See Examples 8-4 and 8-5.

Example 8-4

Assuming that V_{REF}= 3.3 V, find the result of sending the following packets to LTC1661:

a) 0001 0001 0000 0000 binary   (0x1100)
b) 1010 1000 1111 1100 binary   (0xA8FC)

240

Solution:

a) In 0001 0001 0000 0000, control code is 0001. As a result, it loads data = 0001000000 (decimal 64) to the input buffer register for channel A. Note the output is not updated with this control code. The output will be updated after a control code of 1000 is sent. Therefore, $V_{OUTA} = V_{REF} *$ $D_{IN}/ 1024 = 3.3 * 64 / 1024 = 0.206V$.

b) In 1010 1000 1111 1100, the control code is 1010. As a result, it loads data 1000111111 (decimal 575) to the input buffer register of channel B and also updates the output. Therefore, $V_{OUTB} =$ $V_{REF} * D_{IN} / 1024 = 3.3 * 575 / 1024 = 1.853V$.

Example 8-5

Assuming that V_{REF}= 3.3 V, find the packets that should be sent to LTC1661 to:

a) send out 0.5V from channel A
b) send out 1.0V from channel B
c) send out 0.5V and 1.0V from channels A and B, simultaneously

Solution:

a) $V_{OUTA} = V_{REF} \times D_{IN} / 1024$
$0.5V = 3.3 \times D_{IN} / 1024$
$D_{IN} = 155$ (binary 0010011011).
We send 1001 0010 0110 1100 binary (0x926C) since control code 9 loads input buffer register of channel A and updates the channel output.

b) $V_{OUTB} = V_{REF} \times D_{IN} / 1024$
$1.0V = 3.3 \times D_{IN} / 1024$
D_{IN}= 310 (binary 0100110110)
We send 1010 0100 1101 1000 binary (0xA4D8) since control code A loads input buffer register of channel B and updates the channel output.

c) In order to change the outputs simultaneously, we need to load the input buffer register for channel A without updating the output first then load the input buffer register for channel B and update the outputs at the same time.
First, we load channel A input buffer register using control code 0001 0010 0110 1100 binary (0x126C). Note it is the same code as (*Part a*) without the most significant bit set.
Then, we load channel B input buffer register, and update the outputs using control code 1010 0100 1101 1000 binary (0xA4D8)

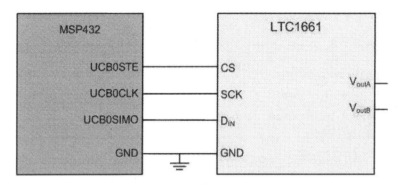

Figure 8-14: Connecting LTC1661 to the Microcontroller

In the following program, we demonstrate a program to generate a sawtooth waveform using LTC1661 via SPI. The LTC1661 expects the chip select to stay low for the duration of the whole 16-bit transmission, so we have to use the 3-pin SPI mode and use a GPIO pin P2.3 as the chip select signal. From the timing diagram (Figure 8-13), we see the clock is idling low and the low to high transition (the leading edge) of the clock latches the data bit, so the clock polarity is set to 0 and the clock phase is 1.

The loop count i of the for-loop is counting from 0 to 1023 and the values are sent to LTC1661 DAC. For each transmission of the value, first the chip select is asserted, the command 9 (write to register A and update the analog output) with the most significant four bits (i >> 6) are sent first, then the least significant six bits padded with two 0s ((i << 2) & 0xFF) are sent. The program waits for the transmission to complete before removing the chip select.

Program 8-3: Generating a saw tooth waveform at LTC1661 DAC through SPI

```
/* p8_3.c Generate sawtooth waveform using DAC LTC1661 on SPI
 * UCB0 is configured as SPI and connected to DAC LTC1661.
 * Software control slave select is used.

 * P1.5 UCB0CLK
 * P1.6 UCB0SIMO
 * P2.3 Slave Select
 *
 * Tested with Keil 5.20 and MSP432 Device Family Pack V2.2.0.
 */

#include "msp.h"

int main(void) {
    int i;

    EUSCI_B0->CTLW0 = 0x0001;      /* disable UCB0 during config */
    /* clock phase/polarity:10, MSB first, 8-bit, master, 3-pin SPI,
        synchronous mode, use SMCLK as clock source */
    EUSCI_B0->CTLW0 = 0xA9C1;
    EUSCI_B0->BRW = 1;                  /* 3 MHz / 1 = 3 MHz */
    EUSCI_B0->CTLW0 &= ~0x0001;    /* enable UCB0 after config */

    P1->SEL0 |= 0x60;           /* P1.5, P1.6 for UCB0CLK, UCB0SIMO */
    P1->SEL1 &= ~0x60;
```

242

```
    P2->DIR |= 8;                   /* P2.3 set as output for slave select */
    P2->OUT |= 8;                   /* slave select idle high */

    while(1)
    {
        for (i = 0; i < 1024; i++) {
            P2->OUT &= ~8;                      /* assert slave select */

            while(!(EUSCI_B0->IFG & 2)) ;       /* wait for transmit buffer empty */
            EUSCI_B0->TXBUF = 0x90 | (i >> 6); /* write command and upper 4 bits of
data */
            while(!(EUSCI_B0->IFG & 2)) ;       /* wait for transmit buffer empty */
            EUSCI_B0->TXBUF = (i << 2) & 0xFF; /* write lower 6 bits of data */

            while(EUSCI_B0->STATW & 1) ;        /* wait for transmit complete */
            P2->OUT |= 8;                       /* deassert slave select */
        }
    }
}
```

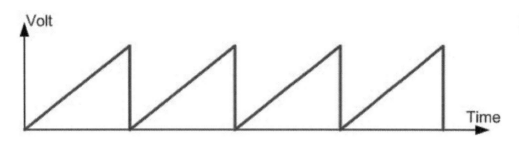

Figure 8-15: The Generated Sawtooth waveform

Review Questions

1. True or false. LTC1661 is an ADC.
2. True or false. LTC1661 is a 10-bit DAC.
3. True or false. There are 4 output channels in the LTC1661.

Answers to Review Questions

Section 8.1

1. False
2. True

Section 8.2

1. False
2. True
3. STE
4. UCAxCTLW0
5. UCAxCTLW0

Section 8.3
1. False
2. True
3. False, it has only two analog output channels

Chapter 9: I2C Protocol and RTC Interfacing

This chapter covers I2C bus interfacing and programming. Section 9.1 examines the I2C bus protocol. Section 9.2 shows the inner working of I2C module in MSP432 ARM devices. The DS1337 RTC and its I2C interfacing and programming are covered in Section 9.3.

Section 9.1: I2C Bus Protocol

The IIC (Inter-Integrated Circuit) is a bus interface connection incorporated into many devices such as sensors, RTC, and EEPROM. The IIC is also referred to as I2C or I square C in many technical literatures. In this section, we examine the signals of the I2C bus and focus on I2C terminology and protocols.

I2C Bus

The I2C bus was originally started by Philips, but in recent years has become a widely used standard adopted by many semiconductor companies. I2C is ideal to attach low-speed peripherals to a motherboard or embedded system or anywhere that a reliable communication over a short distance is required. As we will see in this chapter, I2C provides a connection oriented communication with acknowledgement. I2C devices use only 2 pins for data transfer, instead of the 8 or more pins used in traditional parallel buses. These two signals are called SCL (Serial Clock) which synchronizes the data transfer between two chips, and SDA (Serial Data). This reduction of communication pins reduces the package size and power consumption drastically, making them ideal for many applications in which space is a major concern. These two pins, SDA, and SCK, make the I2C a 2-wire interface. In some application notes, I2C is referred to as Two-Wire Serial Interface (TWI).

I2C line electrical characteristics

I2C devices use only 2 bidirectional open-drain pin for data communication. To implement I2C, a 4.7k ohm pull-up resistor for each of bus lines is needed (see Figure 9-1). This implements a wired-AND which is needed to implement I2C protocols. It means that if one or more devices pull the line to low (zero) level, the line state is zero. The level of line will be 1 only if none of devices pull the line to low level.

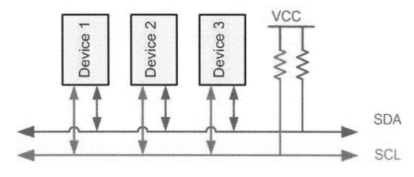

Figure 9-1: I2C Bus Characteristics

I2C Nodes

In I2C protocol, more than 100 devices can share an I2C bus. Each of these devices is called a *node*. In I2C terminology, each node can operate as either master or slave. Master is a device that generates the Clock for the system, it also initiates and terminates a transmission. Slave is a node that receives the clock and is addressed by the master. In I2C, both master and slave can receive or transmit data. So there are 4 modes of operation for each node. They are: master transmitter, master receiver, slave transmitter and slave receiver. Notice that each node can have more than one mode of operation at different times but it has only one mode of operation at any given time. See Example 9-1

Example 9-1

Give an example to show how a device (node) can use more than one mode of operation.

Solution:

If you connect a microcontroller to an EEPROM with I2C, the microcontroller does master transmit operation to write to EEPROM and master receive operation to read from EEPROM

In next sections, you will see that a node can do the operations of master and slave at different time.

Bit Format
I2C is a synchronous serial protocol; each data bit transferred on the SDA line is synchronized by a high to low pulse of clock on SCL line. According to I2C protocols the data line cannot change when the clock line is high, it can change only when the clock line is low. See Figure 9-2. STOP and START condition are the only exceptions to this rule.

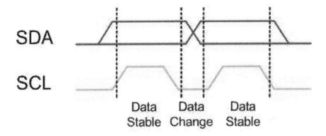

Figure 9-2: I2C Bit Format

START and STOP conditions
As we mentioned before, I2C is a connection oriented communication protocol, it means that each transmission is initiated by a START condition and is terminated by STOP condition. Between the START and STOP, a connection is established between the master and the slave. Remember that the START and STOP conditions are generated by the master.

STOP and START conditions must be distinguished from bits of address or data and that is why they do not obey the bit format rule that we mentioned before.

START and STOP conditions are generated by keeping the level of the SCL line to high and then changing the level of the SDA line. START condition is generated by a high-to-low change in SDA line when SCL is high. STOP condition is generated by a low-to-high change in SDA line when SCL is high. See Figure 9-3.

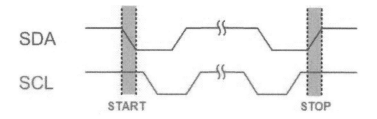

Figure 9-3: START and STOP Conditions

The bus is considered busy between each pair of START and STOP conditions and no other master tries to take control of the bus when it is busy. If a master, which has the control of the bus, wishes to initiate a new transfer and does not want to release the bus before starting the new transfer, it issues a new START condition between a pair of START and STOP condition. It is called REPEATED START condition or simply RESTART condition. See Figure 9-4.

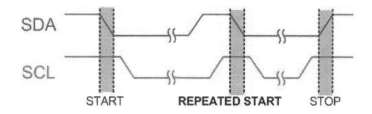

Figure 9-4: REPEATED START Condition

Example 9-2 shows why REPEATED START condition is necessary.

Example 9-2

Give an example to show when a master must use REPEATED START condition. What will happen if the master does not use it?

Solution:

If you connect two microcontrollers (uA and uB) and an EEPROM with I2C, and the uA wants to display the sum of the contents at address 0x34 and 0x35 of EEPROM, it has to use REPEATED START condition. Let's see what may happen if the uA does not use REPEATED START condition. uA transmit a START condition, reads the content of address 0x34 of EEPROM and transmit a STOP condition to release the bus. Before uA reads the contents of address 0x35, the uB seize the bus and change the contents of address 0x34 and 0x35 of EEPROM. Then uA reads the content of address 0x35, adds it to last content of address 0x34 and display the result to LCD. The result on the LCD is neither the sum of old values of address 0x34 and 0x35 nor the sum of the new values of address 0x34 and 0x35 of EEPROM!

Message format in I2C

In I2C, each address or data to be transmitted must be framed in 9 bit long. The first 8 bits are put on SDA line by the transmitter and the 9th bit is the acknowledgement by the receiver or it may be NACK (negative acknowledge). Notice that the clock is always generated by the master, regardless of it being transmitter or receiver. To allow acknowledge, the transmitter release the SDA line during the 9th clock so the receiver can pull the SDA line low to indicate an ACK. If the receiver doesn't pull the SDA line low, it is considered as NACK. See Figure 9-5.

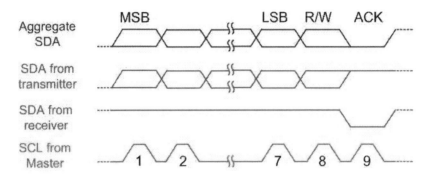

Figure 9-5: Byte Format in I2C

In I2C, each byte may contain either address or data. Also notice that: **START condition + slave address byte + one or more data byte + STOP condition** together form a complete data transfer. Next we will study slave address and data byte formats and how to combine them to make a complete transmission.

Address Byte Format

Like any other bytes, all address bytes transmitted on the I2C bus are nine bits long. It consists of seven address bits, one READ/WRITE control bit and an acknowledge bit. (See Figure 9-6)

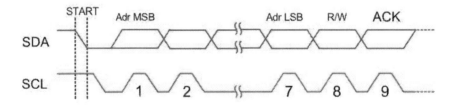

Figure 9-6: Address Byte Format in I2C

Slave address bits are used to address a specific slave device on the bus. Seven bit address let the master to address maximum of 128 slaves on the bus. Although address 0000 000 is reserved for general call and all address of the format 1111 xxx are reserved in many devices. There are 8 more reserved addresses. That means 111 (128-1-8-8) devices can share an I2C bus. In I2C bus the MSB of the address is transmitted first. The I2C bus also supports 10-bit address where the address is split into two frames at the beginning of the transmission. For the rest of the discussion, we will focus on 7 bit address only.

The 8th bit in the address byte is READ/WRITE control bit. If this bit is high, the master will read the next byte from the slave, otherwise, the master will write the next byte on the bus to the slave.

When a slave detects its address on the bus, it knows that it is being addressed and it should acknowledge in the ninth clock cycle by pulling SDA to low. If the addressed slave is not ready or for any reason does not want to respond to the master, it should leave the SDA line high in the 9th clock cycle. It is considered as NACK. In case of NACK, the master can transmit a STOP condition to terminate the transmission, or a REPEATED START condition to initiate a new transmission.

Example 9-3 shows how a master says that it wants to write to a slave.

Example 9-3

Show how a master initiates a write to a slave with address 1001101?
Solution:

The following actions are performed by the master:
1) The master put a high to low pulse on SDA while SCL is high to generate a start condition to start the transmission
2) The master transmit 1001101 0 into the bus. The first seven bits (1001101) indicates the slave address and the 8th bit (0) indicates write operation and the master will write the next byte (data) to the slave.

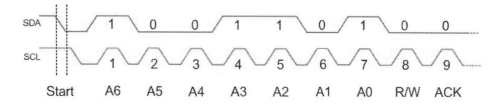

An address byte consisting of a slave address and a READ is called SLA+R while an address byte consisting of a slave address and a WRITE is called SLA+W.

As we mentioned before, address 0000 000 is reserved for general call. It means that when a master transmit address 0000 000 all slaves respond by changing the SDA line to zero for one clock cycle for an ACK and wait to receive the data byte. It is useful when a master wants to transmit the same data byte to all slaves in the system. Notice that the general call address cannot be used to read data from slaves because no more than one slave is able to write to the bus at a given time. Also not all the devices respond to a general call.

Data Byte Format
Like other bytes, data bytes are 9 bits long too. The first 8 bits are a byte of data to be transmitted and the 9th bit, is for ACK. If the receiver has received the last byte of data and does not wish to receive more data, it may signal a NACK by leaving the SDA line high. The master should terminate the transmission with a STOP after a NACK appears. In data bytes, like address bytes, MSB is transmitted first.

Combining Address and Data Bytes into a Transmission

In I2C, normally, a transmission is started by a START condition, followed by an address byte (SLA+R/W), one or more data bytes and finished by a STOP condition. Figure 9-7 shows a typical data transmission. Try to understand each element in the figure. (See Example 9-4)

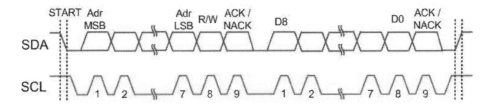

Figure 9-7: Typical Data Transmission

Example 9-4

Show how a master writes data value 1111 0000 to a slave with an address 1001 101?

Solution:

The following actions are performed by the master:

1) The master puts a high to low transition on SDA while SCL is high to generate a START condition to start the transmission

2) The master transmits 1001 101 0 on the bus. The first seven bits (1001 101) indicate the slave address and the 8th bit (0) indicates a write operation and says that the master will write the next byte (data) to the slave.

3) The slave pulls the SDA line low at the 9th clock pulse to signal an ACK to say that it is ready to receive data

4) After receiving the ACK, the master will transmit the data byte (1111 0000) on the SDA line. (MSB first)

5) When the slave device receives the data, it leaves the SDA line high to signal NACK and inform the master that the slave received the last data byte and does not need any more data

6) After receiving the NACK, the master will know that no more data should be transmitted. The master changes the SDA line from low to high when the SCL line is high to transmit a STOP condition and then releases the bus.

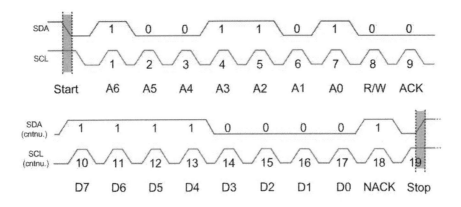

Clock stretching

One of the features of the I2C protocol is clock stretching. It is used by a slow slave device to synchronize with the master. If an addressed slave device is not ready to process more data it will stretch the clock by holding the clock line (SCL) low after receiving (or sending) a bit of data so the master will not be able to raise the clock line (because devices are wire-ANDed) and will wait until the slave releases the SCL line to show it is ready for the next bit. See Figure 9-8. Clock stretching can be used to slow down the clock for each bit or it can be used to temporarily halt the clock at the end of a byte while the receiver is processing the data.

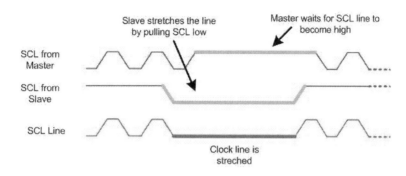

Figure 9-8: Clock Stretching

Arbitration

I2C protocol supports multi-master bus system. It doesn't mean that more than one master can use the bus at the same time. Each master waits for the current transmission to finish and then start to use the bus. But it is possible that two or more masters initiate a transmission at about the same time. In this case the arbitration happens.

Each master has to check the level of the bus and compare it with the levels it is driving; if it doesn't match, that master has lost the arbitration, and will switches to slave mode. In the case of arbitration, the winning master will continue the transmission. Notice that neither the bus is corrupted nor the data is lost. See Example 9-5

Example 9-5

If two master A and B start at about the same time, what happens if master A wants to write to slave 0010 000 and master B wants to write to slave 0001 111?

Solution:

Master A will lose the arbitration in the third clock because the SDA line is different from output of master A at the third clock. Master A switches to slave mode and stops driving the bus after losing the arbitration.

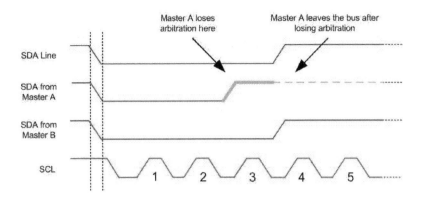

Multi-byte burst write

Burst mode writing is an effective means of loading data into consecutive memory locations. It is supported in I2C, SPI, and many other serial protocols. In burst mode, we provide the address of the first memory location, followed by the data for that location. From then on, consecutive bytes are written to consecutive memory locations. In this mode, the I2C device internally increments the address location as long as STOP condition is not detected. The following steps are used to send (write) multiple bytes of data in burst mode for I2C devices.

1. The master generates a START condition.
2. The master transmits the slave address followed by a zero bit (for write).
3. The master transmits the memory address of the first location.
4. The master transmits the data for the first memory location and from then on, the master simply provides consecutive bytes of data to be placed in consecutive memory locations in the slave.
5. The master generates a STOP condition.

Figure 9-9 shows how to write 0x05, 0x16, and 0x0B to 3 consecutive locations starting from location 00001111 of slave 1111000.

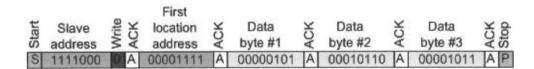

Figure 9-9: Multi-byte Burst Write

Multi-byte burst read

Burst mode reading is an effective means of bringing out the contents of consecutive memory locations. In burst mode, we provide the address of the first memory location only. From then on, contents are brought out from consecutive memory locations. In this mode, the I2C device internally increments the address location as long as STOP condition is not detected. The following steps are used to get (read) multiple bytes of data using burst mode for I2C devices.

1. The master generates a START condition.
2. The master transmits the slave address followed by a zero bit (for writing the memory address).
3. The master transmits the memory address of the first memory location.
4. The master generates a RESTART condition to switch the bus direction from write to read.
5. The master transmits the slave address followed by a one bit (for read).
6. The master clocks the bus 8 times and the slave device provides the data for the first location.
7. The master provides an ACK.
8. The master reads the consecutive locations and provides an ACK for each byte.
9. The master gives a NACK for the last byte received to signal the slave that the read is complete.
10. The master generates a STOP condition.

Figure 9-10 shows how to read three consecutive locations starting from location 00001111 of slave number 1111000.

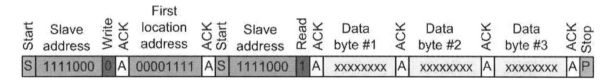

Figure 9-10: Multi-byte Burst Read

Review Questions
1. True or false. I2C protocol is ideal for short distance.
2. How many bits are there in a frame? Which bit is for acknowledgement?
3. True or false. START and STOP conditions are generated when the SDA is high.
4. What is the name of the procedure a slow slave device uses to synchronize with a fast master?
5. True or false. After arbitration of two masters, both of them must start transmission from beginning.

Section 9.2: I2C Programming in MSP432 ARM

The MSP432 chip comes with four on-chip I2C modules. In this section, we examine the registers and features of I2C module. As we mentioned in Chapter 8, the four UCBx (x=0,1,2, and 3) can be used either as SPI or I2C. The I2C modules are located at the following base addresses:

I2C Module(UCBx)	Base Address
UCB0(eUSCI0)	0x4000_2000
UCB1(eUSCI1)	0x4000_2400
UCB2(eUSCI2)	0x4000_2800
UCB3(eUSCI3)	0x4000_2C00

Table 9-1: I2C Module Base Address for MSP432 (shared with SPI)

I2C Register

To program the I2C mode of the eUSCI, we need to examine the registers associated with it. Table 9-2 shows some of the registers. Notice that most of the names of the registers and their addresses are identical to the SPI registers we covered in Chapter 8. The 4 SPI modules of eUSCIBx (x=0,

1,2,3) can be used for SPI or I2C but not at the same time. Now, if the registers are the same, how the CPU distinguishes between the SPI and I2C? This is done with the UCMODEx (bits D9:D10) bits of the UCBxCTLW0 (UCBx Control Word 0) register. Upon Reset, UCMODx=00 meaning all the bits of UCBxCTLW0 are used to set the SPI parameters. By making UCMODx=11, the bits of UCBxCTLW0 registers are used to set parameters for I2C. Notice that I2C and SPI (UCSYNC=1, bit D8) are called synchronous since a single clock is used to synchronize the data transfer between the MSP432 and I2C (or SPI) devices. Recall from Chapter 4 that there was no such a clock for asynchronous UART. UART used TXD and RXD and common ground between the MSP432 and other devices.

Register Name	Register Function	Register Address
UCB0 Control Word 0	Control 0	4000_1000
UCB0 Baud Rate Control Word	Baud Rate	4000_1006
UCB0 Status	Status	4000_1008
UCB0 RXBUF	Receive Buffer	4000_100C
UCB0 TXBUF	Transmit Buffer	4000_100E
UCB0 I2CSA	I2C Slave Address	4000_1020
UCB0 IE	Interrupt Enable	4000_102A
UCB0 IFG	Interrupt Flag	4000_102C

Table 9-2: Some I2C Registers

Configuring the I2C Module

The UCBxCTLW0 (UCBx Control Word 0) sets I2C configuration. Figure 9-11 shows the bits of UCAxCTLW0 and Table 9-3 describes the functions of each bit.

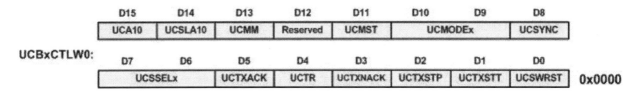

Figure 9-11: I2C Control Word 0 (UCBxCTLW0) Registers in MSP432

Bits	Name	Function	Description
0	UCSWRST	Software reset enable	0b = Disabled. eUSCI_B released for operation. 1b = Enabled. eUSCI_B logic held in reset state.
1	UCTXSTT	Transmit START condition	0b = Do not generate START condition 1b = Generate START condition
2	UCTXSTP	Transmit STOP condition	0b = No STOP generated 1b = Generate STOP
3	UCTXNACK	Transmit a NACK	0b = Acknowledge normally 1b = Generate NACK
4	UCTR	Transmitter/receiver	0b = Receiver

			1b = Transmitter
5	UCTXACK	Transmit ACK condition	0b = Do not acknowledge the slave address 1b = Acknowledge the slave address
7-6	UCSSELx	eUSCI clock source select	00b = Reserved 01b = ACLK 10b = SMCLK 11b = INCLK
8	UCSYNC	Synchronous mode enable	Always 1b 1b = Synchronous mode
10-9	UCMODEx	eUSCI mode.	00b = 3-pin SPI 01b = 4-pin SPI with UCxSTE active high: Slave enabled when UCxSTE = 1 10b = 4-pin SPI with UCxSTE active low: Slave enabled when UCxSTE = 0 11b = I2C mode
11	UCMST	Master mode select	0b = Slave mode 1b = Master mode
13	UCMM	Multi-master environment select.	0b = Single master environment. There is no other master in the system. The address compare unit is disabled. 1b = Multi-master environment
14	UCSLA10	Slave addressing mode select	0b = Address slave with 7-bit address 1b = Address slave with 10-bit address
15	UCA10	Own addressing mode select.	0b = Own address is a 7-bit address. 1b = Own address is a 10-bit address.

Table 9-3: UCBxCTLW0 (UCBx Control Word 0) register bit description

I2C Clock speed

The I2C clock source (BRCLK) may be selected from two difference clocks (ACLK and SMCLK) by UCSSELx bits of UCBxCTLW0 register.

The selected clock source BRCLK is divided by the value in UCBxBRW (I2C Baud Rate Word) register.

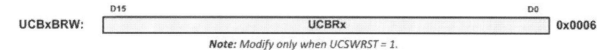

Note: *Modify only when UCSWRST = 1.*

Figure 9-12: UCBxBRW Register to Set I2C Baud Rate

We use the following formula to set the I2C baud rate:

$$I2C\ Baud\ Rate\ = \frac{BRCLK}{UCBRx}$$

The MSP432 supports I2C baud rate up to 100 kHz for Standard Mode or up to 400 kHz for Fast Mode.

See Examples 9-6.

Example 9-6

Assume the clock source frequency is 8MHz. Find the values for the UCBxBRW register if we want I2C clock of (a) 100Kbps and (b) 400Kbps.

Solution:

Using 8MHz for the clock source frequency, we have:

I2C Baud Rate = BRCLK / UCBRx

(a) 100,000 = 8MHz / 80

(b) 400,000 = 8MHz / 20

Master or Slave

The I2C Module can be either the master or the slave. UCMST bit of UCBxCTLW0 register is used to select the mode. When this bit is 0, the I2C module acts as a slave. When this bit is 1, it acts as a master. See Figure 9-11 and Table 9-3.

Slave Address

When the I2C module is designated as a master, it needs to have a calling address to address the slave device. The UCBxI2CSA register holds the slave address, which is put out at the beginning of each transaction. See Figure 9-13. The MSP432 I2C supports either 7-bit address or 10-bit address. The register holds 10 bits. When 7-bit address is used, it should be placed right justified.

Figure 9-13: UCBx I2C Slave Address Register

Transmit and Receive Address

In transmit mode, we place a byte of data in UCBxTXBUF register for transmission. This is a 16-bit register but only the lowest 8 bits are used.

In receive mode, the data received is placed in UCBxRXBUF register. Reading this register gets the last byte of data received.

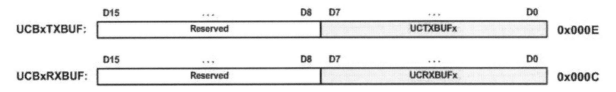

Figure 9-14: UCBxTXBUF and UCBxRXBUF Registers

256

Status Register

The UCBxSTATW register reflects the status of the I2C module. Among others, it indicates the number of bytes transmitted or received since the last START/RESTART and whether the bus is busy or not. See Figure 9-15 and Table 9-4.

After a START occurs on the bus, the bus goes busy (UCBBUSY bit 4) until a STOP is sent.

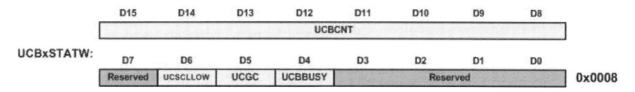

Figure 9-15: UCBxSTATW Status Word Register

Bit	Field	Description
15-8	UCBCNTx	Returns the number of bytes received or transmitted on the I2C-Bus since the last START or RESTART.
7	Reserved	Reserved
6	UCSCLLOW	0b = SCL is not held low 1b = SCL is held low
5	UCGC	General call address received. UCGC is automatically cleared when a START condition is received. 0b = No general call address received 1b = General call address received
4	UCBBUSY	0b = Bus inactive 1b = Bus busy
3-0	Reserved	Reserved

Table 9-4: UCBxSTATW Status Word Register bit description

I2C Interrupt Flag Register

The Interrupt Flag Register (UCBxIFG) contains flags indicating the events that may be used to trigger interrupts. Even if the interrupt is not used, the flags are important to the operations of the I2C module.

- UCTXIFG0 flag is used to indicate that UCBxTXBUF is empty and the I2C module is ready to transmit a byte of data.

- UCRXIFG0 flag is used to indicate that UCBxRXBUF contains a complete byte received.

Figure 9-16: UCAxIFG Register

Configuring GPIO for I2C

In using I2C, we must configure the GPIO pins to allow the connections of the I2C SCL and SDA functions to two GPIO pins of the device. In this regard, it is same as other peripherals. To assign GPIO pins to I2C module, the PxSEL1 should be 0 and the PxSEL0 should be 1. See Tables 9-5 and 9-6.

I2C Module Pin	IO Pin	I2C Module Pin	IO Pin
SCL(UCB0)	P1.5	SCL(UCB1)	P6.3
SDA(UCB0)	P1.6	SDA(UCB1)	P6.4
SCL(UCB2)	P3.5	SCL(UCB3)	P10.1
SDA(UCB2)	P3.6	SDA(UCB3)	P10.2

Table 9-5: IO Pin Assignment for all 4 I2C UCBx Modules

I/O pin	Function	PxSEL1=0	PxSEL0=1
P1.5	SCL(UCB0)	P1SEL1=00000000	P1SEL0=00100000
P1.6	SDA(UCB0)	P1SEL1=00000000	P1SEL0=01000000
P6.3	SCL(UCB1)	P6SEL1=00000000	P6SEL0=00001000
P6.4	SDA(UCB1)	P6SEL1=00000000	P6SEL0=00010000
P3.5	SCL(UCB2)	P3SEL1=00000000	P3SEL0=00100000
P3.6	SDA(UCB2)	P3SEL1=00000000	P3SEL0=01000000
P10.1	SCL(UCB3)	P10SEL1=00000000	P10SEL0=00000010
P10.2	SDA(UCB3)	P10SEL1=00000000	P10SEL0=00000100

Table 9-6: Pins available for I2C

Configuring I2C for master data transmission

After the GPIO configuration, we need to take the following steps to configure the I2C before sending a byte of data to an I2C slave device.

1. Disable the I2C module by writing a 1 to the UCSWRST bit of UCBxCTLW0 register.
2. Configure UCBxCTLW0 register bits to be an I2C master using 7-bit slave address and select clock source.
3. Set the I2C clock speed using UCBxBRW Baud rate register.
4. Enable I2C module by clearing the UCSWRST bit of UCBxCTLW0 register.

Send a byte of data to a slave device

1. Write the slave address in UCBxI2CSA register.
2. Enable transmitter by writing a 1 to UCTR bit of UCBxCTLW0 register.
3. Generate a start and send the slave address by writing a 1 to UCTXSTT bit of UCBxCTLW0 register.
4. Wait until UCTXIFG0 bit of UCxIFG register is set indicating that the transmitter is ready to accept the data.
5. Write the byte of data to UCBxTXBUG register.
6. Wait until UCTXIFG0 bit of UCxIFG register is set indicating that the byte of data is sent.

258

7. Write a 1 to UCTXSTP bit of UCBxCTLW0 register to generate a STOP condition.
8. Wait until UCTXSTP bit of UCBxCTLW0 register goes to 0 indicating the STOP condition is done.

Review Questions
1. True or false. The I2C module in MSP432 can be used as SPI too.
2. True or false. The I2C module in MSP432 can be used as UART at the same time.
3. True or false. There is no CS (chip select) pin in I2C.
4. In MSP432, which register is used to select I2C mode?
5. In MSP432, which register is used to set the I2C baud rate?

Section 9.3: DS1337 RTC Interfacing and Programming

The real-time clock (RTC) is a widely used device that provides accurate time and date information for many applications. Many systems such as the PC come with such a chip on the motherboard. The RTC chip in the PC provides the time components of hour, minute, and second, in addition to year, month, and day. Many RTC chips use an external battery, which keeps the time and date even when the power of the system is off. Although some microcontrollers come with the RTC already embedded into the chip, we have to interface the vast majority of them to an external RTC chip. The DS1337 is a serial RTC with an I2C bus. In this section, we interface and program the DS1337 RTC. According to the DS1337 data sheet from Maxim, "The clock/calendar provides seconds, minutes, hours, day, date, month, and year information. The end of the month date is automatically adjusted for months with fewer than 31 days, including corrections for leap year. The clock operates in either the 24-hour or 12-hour format with AM/PM indicator. The DS1337 has a built-in power-sense circuit that detects power failures and automatically switches to the battery supply." The DS1337 does not support the Daylight Savings Time option. Next, we describe the pins of the DS1337. See Figure 9-17.

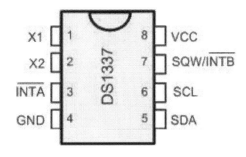

Figure 9-17: DS1337 Pins

The DS1337 is used as replacement for popular DS1307 if system voltage is 3.3V.

X1–X2

These are input pins that allow the DS1337 connection to an external crystal oscillator to provide the clock source to the chip. We must use a 32.768 kHz quartz crystal. The accuracy of the clock depends on the quality of this crystal oscillator.

VCC

Pin 8 is used as the primary voltage supply to the chip. The voltage source can be between 1.3 V to 5.5 V. When Vcc is above 1.3 V, the DS1337 starts working and keeps the time. But the I2C interface is disabled unless the Vcc is above 1.8 V.

Vcc can be connected to an external battery, thereby providing the power source to the chip when the external supply voltage is not available.

GND

Pin 4 is the ground.

SDA (Serial Data)

Pin 5 is the SDA pin and must be connected to the SDA line of the I2C bus.

SCL (Serial Clock)

Pin 6 is the SCL pin and must be connected to the SCL line of the I2C bus.

INTA# (Interrupt A)

The DS1337 has two Alarms: Alarm 1 and Alarm 2. If the alarm 1 is enabled, the INTA pin is asserted when the current time and date matches the values of Alarm 1 registers.

SWQ/INTB

Pin 7 is an output pin providing 1 kHz, 4 kHz, 8 kHz, or 32 kHz frequency if enabled. This pin needs an external pull-up resistor to generate the frequency because it is open drain. If you do not want to use this pin you can omit the external pull-up resistor. The pin can be used as the output for INTB, as well. For more information, see the DS1337 datasheet.

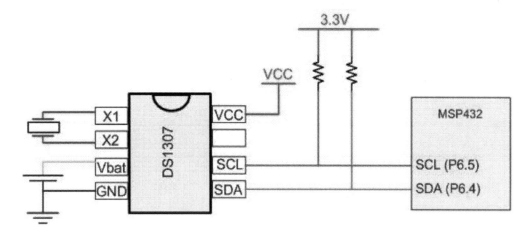

Figure 9-18: MSP432 Connections

Address map of the DS1337

The DS1337 has a total of 15 bytes of space with addresses 00–0FH. The first seven locations, 00–06, are set aside for RTC values of time, date, and year. Locations 07H-0DH are set aside for Alarm 1 and Alarm 2 registers. The next bytes are used for control and status registers. Table 9-7 shows the address map of the DS1337. Next, we study the control register, and time and date access in DS1337.

Address	Bit7	Bit6	Bit5	Bit4	Bit3	Bit2	Bit1	Bit0	Function	Range
00H	0	10 Seconds			Seconds				Seconds	**00-59**
01H	0	10 Minutes			Minutes				Minutes	**00-59**
02H	0	12/24	10 hour PM/AM	10hour	Hours				Hours	1-12 / 0-23
03H	0	0	0	0	0	Day			Day	0-7
04H	0	0	10 Date		Date				Date	01-31
05H	Century	0	0	10Mnt	Month				Month / Century	1-12+ Century
06H	10 Year				Year				Year	00-99
07H	A1M1	10 Seconds			Seconds				Alarm 1 Seconds	**00-59**
08H	A1M2	10 Minutes			Minutes				Alarm 1 Minutes	**00-59**
09H	A1M3	12/24	AM/PM 10 Hour	10 Hour	Hour				Alarm 1 Hours	1-12 / 00-23
0AH	A1M4	DY/DT	10 Date		Day / Date				Alarm 1 Day / Alarm 1 Date	1-7 / 01-31
0BH	A2M2	10 Minutes			Minutes				Alarm 2 Minutes	**00-59**
0CH	A2M3	12/24	AM/PM 10 Hour	10 Hour	Hour				Alarm 2 Hours	1-12 / 00-23
0DH	A2M4	DY/DT	10 Date		Day / Date				Alarm 2 Day / Alarm 2 Date	1-7 / 01-31
0EH	EOSC	0	0	RS2	RS1	INTCN	A2IE	A1IE	Control	-
0FH	OSF	0	0	0	0	0	A2F	A1F	Status	-

Table 9-7: DS1337 Address Map

Time and date address locations and modes

The byte addresses 0–6 are set aside for the time and date, as shown in Table 9-7. The DS1337 provides data in BCD format only. Notice the data range for the hour mode. We can select 12-hour or 24-hour mode with bit 6 of Hours register at location 02. When bit 6 is 1, the 12-hour mode is selected, and bit 6 = 0 provides us the 24-hour mode. In the 12-hour mode, bit 5 indicates whether it is AM or PM. If bit 5 = 0, it is AM; and if bit 5 = 1, it is PM. See Example 9-8.

Example 9-8

What value should be placed at location 02 to set the hour to: (a) 21, (b) 11AM, (c) 12 PM.

Solution:

(a) For 24-hour mode, we have D6 = 0. Therefore, we place 0010 0001 (or 0x21) at location 02, which is 21 in BCD.

(b) For 12-hour mode, we have D6 = 1. Also, we have D5 = 0 for AM. Therefore, we place 0101 0001 at location 02, which is 51 in BCD.

(c) For 12-hour mode, we have D6 = 1. Also, we have D5 = 1 for PM. Therefore, we place 0111 0010 at location 02, which is 72 in BCD.

The DS1337 control register

As shown in Table 9-7, the control register has an address of 0EH. In the DS1337 control register, the bits control the function of the SQW/INTB and INTA pins. Figure 9-19 shows the simplified diagram for SQW/INTB pin.

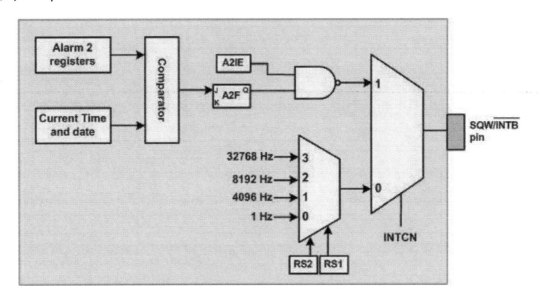

Figure 9-19: Simplified Structure of SQW/INTB Pin

The SQW/INTB pin can be used as a square wave generator or an interrupt generator. When the INTCN bit of control register is 0, the pin works as a wave generator. Using the RS2 and RS1 bits, the frequency of the generated wave is chosen. RS2-RS1 (rate select) bits select the output frequency of the generated wave according to Table 9-8.

RS2	RS1	Output Frequency
0	0	1 Hz
0	1	4.096 kHz
1	0	8.192 kHz
1	1	32.768 kHz

Table 9-8: RS bits

When INTCN = 1, the SQW/INTB works as an interrupt generator. Locations 0BH-0DH of DS1337 memory are related to Alarm 2. The contents of the Alarm 2 registers are compared with the values current time and date (locations 00H-06H). When the current date and time matches the alarm 2 values, the A2F flag of status register (location 0FH) goes high. If the A2IE (Alarm2 Interrupt Enable) bit of the control register is set, the INTB becomes 0. The pin remains 0 until the A2F flag is cleared by software. To clear the A2F flag, write 0 into it.

It can make an interrupt every minute, hour, day, or date. The bit 7 of alarm registers, are mask registers. If it is 0, the value of the register is compared with the timekeeping registers; otherwise, it is masked. Table 9-9 shows how to make interrupts every minute, hour, day, or date.

262

DY/DT	A2M4	A2M3	A2M2	Alarm Rate
X	1	1	1	Alarm once per minute
X	1	1	0	Alarm when minutes match
X	1	0	0	Alarm when hours and minutes match
0	0	0	0	Alarm when date, hours, and minutes match
1	0	0	0	Alarm when day, hours, and minutes match

Table 9-9: Alarm 2 Register Mask Bits

The bit 7 of the control register is EOSC (Enable Oscillator) bit. This bit is active low. If it is 0, the oscillator works.

Register pointer

In DS1337, there is a register pointer that specifies the byte that will be accessed in the next read or write command. The first read or write operation sets the value of the pointer. After each read or write operation, the content of the register pointer is automatically incremented to point to the next location. This is useful in multi-byte read or write. When it points to location 0x0F, in the next read/write it rolls over to 0.

Writing to DS1337

To set the value of the register pointer and write one or more bytes of data to DS1337, you can use the following steps:

1. To access the DS1337 for a write operation, after sending a START condition, you should transmit the address of DS1337 (1101 000) followed by 0 to indicate a write operation.
2. The first byte of data in the write operation will set the register pointer. For example, if you want to write to the control register you should send 0x07.
3. Check the acknowledgement bit to be sure that DS1337 responded.
4. If you want to write one or more bytes of data, you should transmit them one byte at a time and check the acknowledgement bit at the end of each byte sent. Remember that the register pointer is automatically incremented and you can simply transmit bytes of data to consecutive locations in a multi-byte burst write.
5. Transmit a STOP bit condition.

Reading from DS1337

Notice that before reading a byte, you should load the address of the byte to the register pointer by doing a write operation as mentioned before.

To read one or more bytes of data from the DS1337 you should do the following steps:

1. To access the DS1337 for a read operation, you need to set the register pointer first. After sending a START condition, you should transmit the address of DS1337 (1101 000) followed by 0 to indicate a write operation (writing the register pointer).
2. Check the acknowledgement bit to be sure that DS1337 responded.

3. The byte of data in the write operation will set the register pointer. For example, if you want to read from the control register you should send 0x07. Check the acknowledgement bit to be sure that DS1337 responded.

4. Now you need to change the bus direction from transmit to receive. Send a START condition (a REPEATED START), then transmit the address of DS1337 (1101 000) followed by 1 to indicate a read operation. Check the acknowledgement bit to be sure that DS1337 responded.

5. You can read one or more bytes of data. Remember that the register pointer inside the DS1337 indicates which location will be read. The register pointer is automatically incremented and you can receive consecutive bytes of data in a multi-byte burst read.

6. Transmit a STOP bit condition.

Setting the Square Wave Output of DS1337

Program 9-1 initializes the square wave output pin (SQW) with 1Hz using single-byte write operation. SQW pin is open-drain and needs a pull-up resistor. You may connect an LED to it. The pin is rated at 5V and 3mA.

The program generates a START condition then sends the slave address and write flag. Following that, the address of the control register (0x0E) and the byte with control bits are sent. The transaction is terminated with a STOP condition.

Program 9-1: I2C single byte write

```
/* p9_1.c : write a byte to DS1337
 *
 * This program writes a byte to DS1337 to initialized the SQW pin
 * to generate a 1Hz output. SQW pin is open-drain and needs a pull-up resistor.
 * No error checking is done in the I2C code.
 *
 * Tested with Keil 5.20 and MSP432 Device Family Pack V2.2.0.
 */
#include <stdio.h>
#include "msp.h"

void I2C1_init(void);
int I2C1_Write(int slaveAddr, unsigned char memAddr, unsigned char data);

#define SLAVE_ADDR 0x68     // 1101 000.    DS1337

int main(void) {
    I2C1_init();
    I2C1_Write(SLAVE_ADDR, 0x0E, 0);     /* write 0 to location 0x0E */

    for (;;) {
    }
}

/* configure UCB1 as I2C */
void I2C1_init(void) {
    EUSCI_B1->CTLW0 |= 1;                /* disable UCB1 during config */
    EUSCI_B1->CTLW0 = 0x0F81;     /* 7-bit slave addr, master, I2C, synch mode, use
SMCLK */
```

264

```
    EUSCI_B1->BRW = 30;                    /* set clock prescaler 3MHz / 30 = 100kHz */
    P6->SEL0 |= 0x30;                      /* P6.5, P6.4 for UCB1 */
    P6->SEL1 &= ~0x30;
    EUSCI_B1->CTLW0 &= ~1;                 /* enable UCB1 after config */
}

/* Write a single byte at memAddr
 * write: S-(slaveAddr+w)-ACK-memAddr-ACK-data-ACK-P
 */
int I2C1_Write(int slaveAddr, unsigned char memAddr, unsigned char data) {
    EUSCI_B1->I2CSA = slaveAddr;           /* setup slave address */
    EUSCI_B1->CTLW0 |= 0x0010;             /* enable transmitter */
    EUSCI_B1->CTLW0 |= 0x0002;             /* generate START and send slave address */
    while(!(EUSCI_B1->IFG & 2));           /* wait till it's ready to transmit */
    EUSCI_B1->TXBUF = memAddr;             /* send memory address to slave */
    while(!(EUSCI_B1->IFG & 2));           /* wait till it's ready to transmit */
    EUSCI_B1->TXBUF = data;                /* send data to slave */
    while(!(EUSCI_B1->IFG & 2));           /* wait till last transmit is done */
    EUSCI_B1->CTLW0 |= 0x0004;             /* send STOP */
    while(EUSCI_B1->CTLW0 & 4) ;           /* wait until STOP is sent */
    return 0;                              /* no error */
}
```

Reading the Second Counter of DS1337

Program 9-2 reads the second counter of the DS1337 using single byte read and write the least significant three bits to the onboard tri-color LEDs of the LaunchPad. The LED color should change every second.

After sending the slave address, the address of the second counter (0x00) with the write bit is sent then a RESTARAT with the same slave address with a read bit is send to change the bus direction to read from the slave. A STOP condition is sent at the end of transaction.

Program 9-2: I2C single byte read

```
/* p9_2.c : single byte read from DS1337
 *
 * This program uses single byte read to get the second counter
 * of the DS1337 RTC chip. The three least significant bits of
 * the second counter are used to turn on/off the tri-color LEDs
 * on the LaunchPad board.
 * No error checking is done in the I2C code.
 *
 * Tested with Keil 5.20 and MSP432 Device Family Pack V2.2.0.
 */
#include <stdio.h>
#include "msp.h"

void delayMs(int n);
void I2C1_init(void);
int I2C1_Read(int slaveAddr, unsigned char memAddr, unsigned char* data);

#define SLAVE_ADDR 0x68     // 1101 000.    DS1337
```

```c
int main(void) {
    unsigned char data;

    P2->DIR |= 7;     /* P2.2, P2.1 ,P2.0 set as output for tri-color LEDs */
    I2C1_init();

    for (;;)
    {
        I2C1_Read(SLAVE_ADDR, 0, &data);    /* read second counter */
        P2->OUT = data;                     /* write to LEDs */
        delayMs(237);                       /* delay arbitrary time */
    }
}

/* configure UCB1 as I2C */
void I2C1_init(void) {
    EUSCI_B1->CTLW0 |= 1;          /* disable UCB1 during config */
    EUSCI_B1->CTLW0 = 0x0F81;      /* 7-bit slave addr, master, I2C, synch mode, use
SMCLK */
    EUSCI_B1->BRW = 30;            /* set clock prescaler 3MHz / 30 = 100kHz */
    P6->SEL0 |= 0x30;              /* P6.5, P6.4 for UCB1 */
    P6->SEL1 &= ~0x30;
    EUSCI_B1->CTLW0 &= ~1;         /* enable UCB1 after config */
}

/* Read a single byte at memAddr
 * read: S-(slaveAddr+w)-ACK-memAddr-ACK-R-(saddr+r)-ACK-data-NACK-P
 */
int I2C1_Read(int slaveAddr, unsigned char memAddr, unsigned char* data) {
    EUSCI_B1->I2CSA = slaveAddr;      /* setup slave address */
    EUSCI_B1->CTLW0 |= 0x0010;        /* enable transmitter */
    EUSCI_B1->CTLW0 |= 0x0002;        /* generate START and send slave address */

    while(!(EUSCI_B1->IFG & 2));      /* wait till it's ready to transmit */
    EUSCI_B1->TXBUF = memAddr;        /* send memory address to slave */
    while(!(EUSCI_B1->IFG & 2));      /* wait till it's ready to transmit */
    EUSCI_B1->CTLW0 &= ~0x0010;       /* enable receiver */
    EUSCI_B1->CTLW0 |= 0x0002;        /* generate RESTART and send slave address */
    while(EUSCI_B1->CTLW0 & 2);       /* wait till restart is finished */
    EUSCI_B1->CTLW0 |= 0x0004;        /* setup to send STOP after the byte is received
*/
    while(!(EUSCI_B1->IFG & 1));      /* wait till data is received */
    *data = EUSCI_B1->RXBUF;          /* read the received data */
    while(EUSCI_B1->CTLW0 & 4) ;      /* wait until STOP is sent */
    return 0;                         /* no error */
}

/* system clock at 3 MHz */
void delayMs(int n) {
    int i, j;

    for (j = 0; j < n; j++)
        for (i = 250; i > 0; i--);       /* delay 1 ms */
}
```

Setting the date of DS1337 in MSP432

Program 9-3 shows how to setup the DS1337 RTC chip. It uses multi-byte burst mode for writing time, day (of the week), date, month, and year, which occupy the first seven registers of the device. The program first set the register address to 0 and writes the first register. The register address pointer automatically incremented to point to the next register and the subsequent write goes to the next register. A STOP condition is generated after the last byte of data is transmitted. For simplicity, this code does not check for error conditions.

Program 9-3:
Setting the date/time/year of DS1337 using burst write

```
/* p9_3.c: burst write to DS1337
 *
 * This program writes the first seven registers of DS1337 using
 * burst write. After the first write, the register address pointer
 * automatically incremented to point to the next register and the
 * subsequent write goes to the next register. When the last byte
 * is written, a STOP is generated.
 *
 * No error checking is done in I2C code.
 *
 * Tested with Keil 5.20 and MSP432 Device Family Pack V2.2.0.
 */

#include <stdio.h>
#include "msp.h"

void I2C1_init(void);
int I2C1_burstWrite(int slaveAddr, unsigned char memAddr, int byteCount, unsigned
char* data);

#define SLAVE_ADDR 0x68      // 1101 000.    DS1337

int main(void)
{
    /*                              00    01    02    03    04    05    06 */
    unsigned char timeDateToSet[15] = {0x55, 0x58, 0x16, 0x05, 0x19, 0x11, 0x15, 0};
// 2015 November 19, Thu, 16:58:55

    P2->DIR |= 7;    /* P2.2, P2.1 ,P2.0 set as output for tri-color LEDs */

    I2C1_init();

    /* write the first seven bytes of the registers */
    I2C1_burstWrite(SLAVE_ADDR, 0, 7, timeDateToSet);

    for (;;) {
    }
}

/* configure UCB1 as I2C */
void I2C1_init(void) {
    EUSCI_B1->CTLW0 |= 1;                /* disable UCB1 during config */
```

```
        EUSCI_B1->CTLW0 = 0x0F81;           /* 7-bit slave addr, master, I2C, synch mode, use
SMCLK */
        EUSCI_B1->BRW = 30;                      /* set clock prescaler 3MHz / 30 = 100kHz */
        P6->SEL0 |= 0x30;                  /* P6.5, P6.4 for UCB1 */
        P6->SEL1 &= ~0x30;
        EUSCI_B1->CTLW0 &= ~1;              /* enable UCB1 after config */
}

/* Use burst write to write multiple bytes to consecutive locations
 * burst write: S-(slaveAddr+w)-ACK-memAddr-ACK-data-ACK...-data-ACK-P
 */
int I2C1_burstWrite(int slaveAddr, unsigned char memAddr, int byteCount, unsigned
char* data)
{
    if (byteCount <= 0)
        return -1;                  /* no write was performed */

    EUSCI_B1->I2CSA = slaveAddr;        /* setup slave address */
    EUSCI_B1->CTLW0 |= 0x0010;          /* enable transmitter */
    EUSCI_B1->CTLW0 |= 0x0002;          /* generate START and send slave address */
    while(!(EUSCI_B1->IFG & 2));        /* wait till it's ready to transmit */
    EUSCI_B1->TXBUF = memAddr;          /* send memory address to slave */

    /* send data one byte at a time */
    do {
        while(!(EUSCI_B1->IFG & 2));    /* wait till it's ready to transmit */
        EUSCI_B1->TXBUF = *data++;      /* send data to slave */
        byteCount--;
     } while (byteCount > 0);

    while(!(EUSCI_B1->IFG & 2));        /* wait till last transmit is done */
    EUSCI_B1->CTLW0 |= 0x0004;          /* send STOP */
    while(EUSCI_B1->CTLW0 & 4) ;        /* wait until STOP is sent */

    return 0;                   /* no error */
}
```

Reading the date and time of DS1337 in MSP432

Program 9-4 shows how to read the date, time and year from DS1337 using multi-byte burst mode for reading. As you can see in the program, the register pointer is set to 0 and then you can use multi-byte burst read to read the values of second, minute, hour, day, date, month and year in the consecutive locations. During the reception of the last byte, a STOP condition is setup to be generated at the end. For simplicity, this code does not check for error conditions.

Program 9-4: Reading date/time/year of DS1337 using burst read

```
/* p9_4.c: burst read from DS1337
 *
 * This program reads the first seven registers of DS1337 using
 * burst read.
 * After the first read, the register address pointer automatically
 * incremented to point to the next register and the
 * subsequent read comes from the next register. Before the last
```

268

```
 * read, a STOP is setup to be generated when the read is complete.
 * The three least significant bits of the second counter are used to
 * turn on/off the tri-color LEDs on the LaunchPad board.
 *
 * You can modify this program to send data via serial COM port
 * to the PC screen (Teraterminal) or display it on the text LCD.
 *
 * No error checking is done in I2C code.
 *
 * Tested with Keil 5.20 and MSP432 Device Family Pack V2.2.0.
 */

#include <stdio.h>
#include "msp.h"

void delayMs(int n);
void I2C1_init(void);
int I2C1_burstRead(int slaveAddr, unsigned char memAddr, int byteCount, unsigned char*
data);

#define SLAVE_ADDR 0x68      // 1101 000.    DS1337

int main(void) {
    unsigned char timeDateReadback[7];

    P2->DIR |= 7;    /* P2.2, P2.1 ,P2.0 set as output for tri-color LEDs */

    I2C1_init();

    for (;;) {
        /* read the first seven bytes of the registers */
        I2C1_burstRead(SLAVE_ADDR, 0, 7, timeDateReadback);
        P2->OUT = timeDateReadback[0];    /* write second count to LEDs */
        delayMs(237);                     /* delay arbitrary time */
    }
}

/* configure UCB1 as I2C */
void I2C1_init(void) {
    EUSCI_B1->CTLW0 |= 1;            /* disable UCB1 during config */
    EUSCI_B1->CTLW0 = 0x0F81;       /* 7-bit slave addr, master, I2C, synch mode,
use SMCLK */
    EUSCI_B1->BRW = 30;             /* set clock prescaler 3MHz / 30 = 100kHz */
    P6->SEL0 |= 0x30;               /* P6.5, P6.4 for UCB1 */
    P6->SEL1 &= ~0x30;
    EUSCI_B1->CTLW0 &= ~1;          /* enable UCB1 after config */
}

/* Use burst read to read multiple bytes from consecutive locations
 * read: S-(slaveAddr+w)-ACK-memAddr-ACK-R-(slaveAddr+r)-ACK-data-ACK-...-data-NACK-P
 */
int I2C1_burstRead(int slaveAddr, unsigned char memAddr, int byteCount, unsigned char*
data) {
    if (byteCount <= 0)
        return -1;               /* no read was performed */

    EUSCI_B1->I2CSA = slaveAddr;        /* setup slave address */
```

```c
    EUSCI_B1->CTLW0 |= 0x0010;          /* enable transmitter */
    EUSCI_B1->CTLW0 |= 0x0002;          /* generate START and send slave address */

    while(!(EUSCI_B1->IFG & 2));        /* wait till it's ready to transmit */
    EUSCI_B1->TXBUF = memAddr;          /* send memory address to slave */
    while(!(EUSCI_B1->IFG & 2));        /* wait till last transmit is done */
    EUSCI_B1->CTLW0 &= ~0x0010;         /* enable receiver */
    EUSCI_B1->CTLW0 |= 0x0002;          /* generate RESTART and send slave address */
    while(EUSCI_B1->CTLW0 & 2);         /* wait till RESTART is finished */

    /* receive data one byte at a time */
    do {
        if (byteCount == 1)      /* when only one byte of data is left */
            EUSCI_B1->CTLW0 |= 0x0004; /* setup to send STOP after the last byte is
received */

        while(!(EUSCI_B1->IFG & 1));  /* wait till data is received */
        *data++ = EUSCI_B1->RXBUF;    /* read the received data */
        byteCount--;
    } while (byteCount);

    while(EUSCI_B1->CTLW0 & 4) ;       /* wait until STOP is sent */

    return 0;                          /* no error */
}

/* system clock at 3 MHz */
void delayMs(int n) {
    int i, j;

    for (j = 0; j < n; j++)
        for (i = 250; i > 0; i--);        /* delay 1 ms */
}
```

Review Questions

1. How many bytes in the DS1337 are set aside for the time, date, and year?

   (a) 7 bytes

   (b) 8 bytes

   (c) 56 bytes

   (d) 64 bytes

2. True or false. The DS1337 has a single pin for data.

3. Which pin of the DS1337 is used for clock in I2C connection?

4. What is the common voltage for Vbat in the DS1337?

5. True or false. The value of the CH bit is zero at power-up time.

6. What is the address location for the control register?

   (a) 07H

   (b) 08H

   (c) 56H

   (d) 64H

Answers to Review Questions

Section 9-1

1. True
2. 9, the 9th bit is for acknowledge
3. False, START and STOP conditions are generated when the SCL is high.
4. Clock stretching.
5. False, the master who won the arbitration will continue.

Section 9-2

1. True
2. False
3. True
4. UCMODEx bits and UCSYNC bit of UCBxCTLW0 register
5. UCBxBRW

Section 9-3

1. a
2. True
3. SCL
4. 3V
5. False
6. a

Chapter 10: Relay, Optoisolator, and Stepper Motor Interfacing

Microcontrollers are widely used in motor control. We also use relays and optoisolators in motor control. This chapter discusses motor control and shows ARM interfacing with relays, optoisolators, and stepper motors.

Section 10.1: Relays and Optoisolators

This section begins with an overview of the basic operations of electromechanical relays, solid-state relays, reed switches, and optoisolators. Then we describe how to interface them to the ARM. We use the C language programs to demonstrate their control.

Electromechanical relays

A *relay* is an electrically controllable switch widely used in industrial controls, automobiles, and appliances. It allows the isolation of two separate sections of a system with two different voltage sources. For example, a +5 V system can be isolated from a 120 V system by placing a relay between them. One such relay is called an *electromechanical* (or *electromagnetic*) *relay* (EMR) as shown in Figure 10-1. The EMRs have three components: the coil, spring, and contacts.

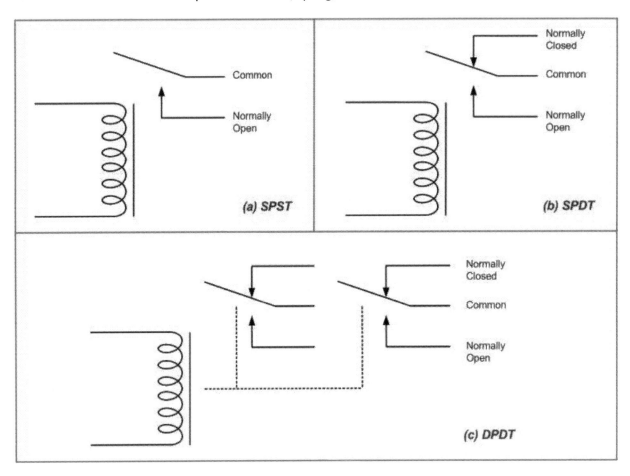

Figure 10-1: Relay Diagrams

In Figure 10-1, a digital +5 V on the left side can control a 12 V motor on the right side without any physical contact between them. When current flows through the coil, a magnetic field is created around the coil (the coil is energized), which causes the armature to be attracted to the coil. The armature's contact acts like a switch and closes or opens the circuit. When the coil is not energized, a spring pulls the armature to its normal state of open or closed. In the block diagram for electromechanical relays (EMR) we do not show the spring, but it does exist internally. There are all types of relays for all kinds of applications. In choosing a relay the following characteristics need to be considered:

1. The contacts can be normally open (NO) or normally closed (NC). In the NC type, the contacts are closed when the coil is not energized. In the NO type, the contacts are open when the coil is unenergized.
2. There can be one or more contacts. For example, we can have SPST (single pole, single throw), SPDT (single pole, double throw), and DPDT (double pole, double throw) relays.
3. The voltage and current needed to energize the coil. The voltage can vary from a few volts to 50 volts, while the current can be from a few mA to 20 mA. The relay has a minimum voltage, below which the coil will not be energized. This minimum voltage is called the "pull-in" voltage. In the datasheets for relays we might not see current, but rather coil resistance. The V/R will give you the pull-in current. For example, if the coil voltage is 5 V, and the coil resistance is 500 ohms, we need a minimum of 10 mA (5 V/500 ohms = 10 mA) pull-in current.
4. The maximum DC/AC voltage and current that can be handled by the contacts. This is in the range of a few volts to hundreds of volts, while the current can be from a few amps to 40 A or more, depending on the relay. Notice the difference between this voltage/current specification and the voltage/current needed for energizing the coil. The fact that one can use such a small amount of voltage/current on one side to handle a large amount of voltage/current on the other side is what makes relays so widely used in industrial controls. Examine Table 10-1 for some relay characteristics.

Part No.	Contact Form	Coil Volts	Coil Ohms	Contact Volts	Current
106462CP	SPST-NO	5 VDC	500	100 VDC	0.5 A
138430CP	SPST-NO	5 VDC	500	100 VDC	0.5 A
106471CP	SPST-NO	12 VDC	1000	100 VDC	0.5 A
138448CP	SPST-NO	12 VDC	1000	100 VDC	0.5 A
129875CP	DPDT	5 VDC	62.5	30 VDC	1 A

Table 10-1: Selected DIP Relay Characteristics (www.Jameco.com)

Driving a relay

Digital systems and microcontroller pins lack sufficient current to drive the relay. While the relay's coil needs around 10 mA to be energized, the microcontroller's pin can provide a maximum of 8 mA current. For this reason, we place a driver, such as the ULN2803, or a transistor between the microcontroller and the relay as shown in Figure 10-2. In the circuit we can turn the lamp on and off by setting and clearing the P4.0.

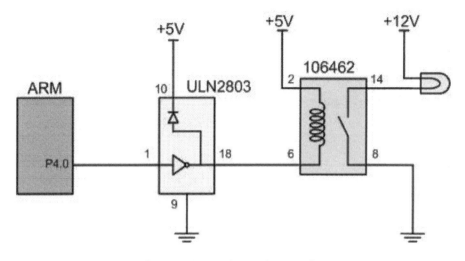

Figure 10-2: ARM Connection to Relay

Program 10-1 turns the lamp shown in Figure 10-2 on and off by energizing and de-energizing the relay every second.

Program 10-1 Turning relay on and off

```
/* p10_1: Relay control
 * This program turns the relay connected to P4.0 on and off every second.
 *
 * Tested with Keil 5.20 and MSP432 Device Family Pack V2.2.0.
 */
#include "msp.h"

void delayMs(int n);

int main(void) {
    P4->SEL1 &= ~1;             /* configure P4.0 as simple I/O */
    P4->SEL0 &= ~1;
    P4->DIR |= 1;               /* P4.0 set as output pin */

    while (1) {
        P4->OUT |= 1;           /* turn on P4.0 */
        delayMs(1000);
        P4->OUT &= ~1;          /* turn off P4.0 */
        delayMs(1000);
    }
}

/* delay milliseconds when system clock is at 3 MHz */
void delayMs(int n) {
    int i, j;

    for (j = 0; j < n; j++)
        for (i = 250; i > 0; i--);      /* delay 1 ms */
}
```

Solid-state relay

Another widely used relay is the solid-state relay. See Table 10-2.

Part No.	Contact Style	Control Volts	Contact Volts	Contact Current
143058CP	SPST	4-32 VDC	240 VAC	3 A
139053CP	SPST	3-32 VDC	240 VAC	25 A
162341CP	SPST	3-32 VDC	240 VAC	10 A
172591CP	SPST	3-32 VDC	60 VAC	2 A
175222CP	SPST	3-32 VDC	60 VAC	4 A
176647CP	SPST	3-32 VDC	120 VAC	5 A

Table 10-2: Selected Solid-State Relay Characteristics (www.Jameco.com)

In this relay, there is no coil, spring, or mechanical contact switch. The entire relay is made out of semiconductor materials. Because no mechanical parts are involved in solid-state relays, their switching response time is much faster than that of electromechanical relays. Another advantage of the solid-state relay is its greater life expectancy. The life cycle for the electromechanical relay can vary from a few hundred thousand to a few million operations. Wear and tear on the contact points can cause the relay to malfunction after a while. Solid-state relays, however, have no such limitations. Extremely low input current and small packaging make solid-state relays ideal for microcontroller and logic control switching. They are widely used in controlling pumps, solenoids, alarms, and other power applications. Some solid-state relays have a phase control option, which is ideal for motor-speed control and light-dimming applications. Figure 10-3 shows control of a fan using a solid-state relay (SSR).

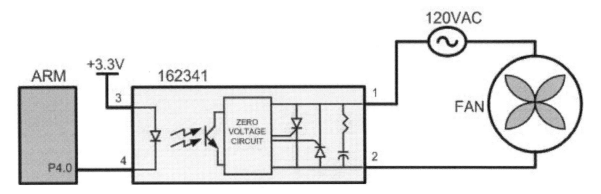

Figure 10-3: ARM Connection to a Solid-State Relay

Reed switch

Another popular switch is the reed switch. When the reed switch is placed in a magnetic field, the contact is closed. When the magnetic field is removed, the contact is forced open by its spring. See Figure 10-4. The reed switch is ideal for moist and marine environments where it can be submerged in fuel or water. Reed switches are also widely used in dirty and dusty atmospheres because they are tightly sealed.

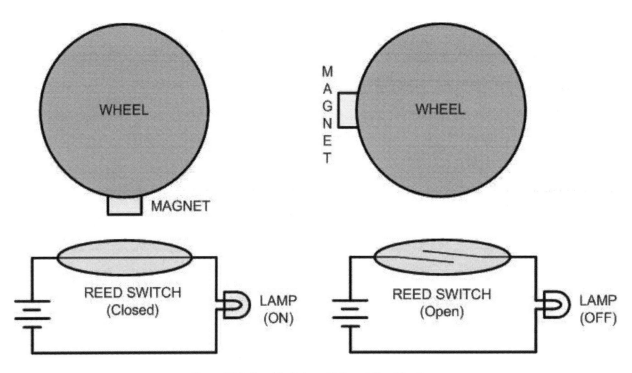

Figure 10-4: Reed Switch and Magnet Combination

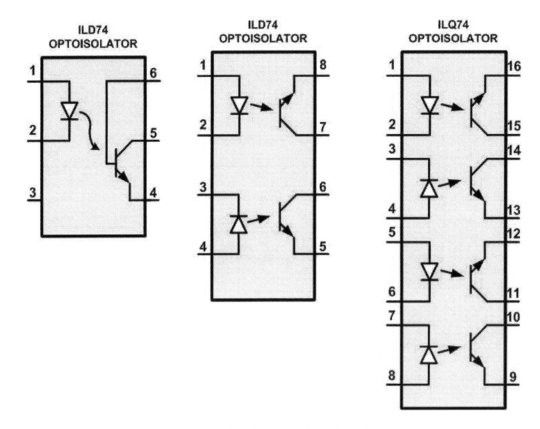

Figure 10-5: Optoisolator Package Examples

Optoisolator

In some applications we use an optoisolator (also called optocoupler) to isolate two parts of a system. An example is driving a motor. Motors can produce what is called *back EMF*, a high-voltage spike produced by a sudden change of current as indicated in the formula V = Ldi/dt. In situations such as printed circuit board design, we can reduce the effect of this unwanted voltage spike (called *ground bounce*) by using decoupling capacitors (see Appendix A). In systems that have inductors (coil winding), such as motors, a decoupling capacitor or a diode will not do the job. In such cases we use optoisolators. An optoisolator has an LED (light-emitting diode) transmitter and a photosensor receiver, separated from each other by a gap. When current flows through the diode, it transmits a signal light across the gap and the receiver produces the same signal with the same phase but a different current and amplitude. See Figure 10-5. Optoisolators are also widely used in communication equipment such as modems. This device allows a computer to be connected to a telephone line without risk of damage from high voltage of telephone line. The gap between the transmitter and receiver of optoisolators prevents the electrical voltage surge from reaching the system.

Interfacing an optoisolator

The optoisolator comes in a small IC package with four or more pins. There are also packages that contain more than one optoisolator. When placing an optoisolator between two circuits, we must use two separate voltage sources, one for each side, as shown in Figure 10-6. Unlike relays, no drivers need to be placed between the microcontroller/digital output and the optoisolators.

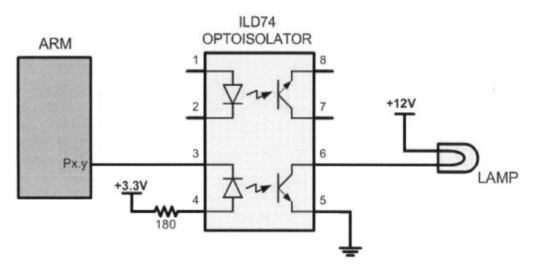

Figure 10-6: Controlling a Lamp via an Optoisolator

Review Questions

1. Give one application where would you use a relay.
2. Why do we place a driver between the microcontroller and the relay?
3. What is an NC relay?
4. Why are relays that use coils called electromechanical relays?
5. What is the advantage of a solid-state relay over EMR?
6. What is the advantage of an optoisolator over an EMR?

Section 10.2: Stepper Motor Interfacing

This section begins with an overview of the basic operation of stepper motors. Then we describe how to interface a stepper motor to the ARM. Finally, we use C language programs to demonstrate control of the rotation of stepper motor.

Stepper motors

A *stepper motor* is a widely used device that translates electrical pulses into mechanical movement. In applications such as dot matrix printers and robotics, the stepper motor is used for position control. Stepper motors commonly have a permanent magnet *rotor* (also called the *shaft*) surrounded by a stator (see Figure 10-7).

There are also steppers called *variable reluctance stepper motors* that do not have a permanent magnet rotor. The most common stepper motors have four stator windings that are paired with a center-tapped common as shown in Figure 10-8.

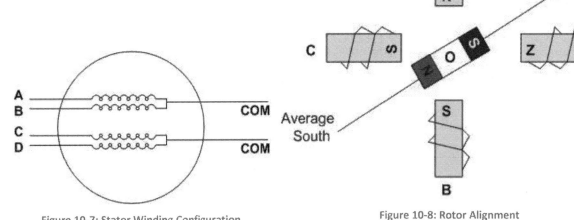

Figure 10-7: Stator Winding Configuration

Figure 10-8: Rotor Alignment

This type of stepper motor is commonly referred to as a four-phase or unipolar stepper motor. The center tap allows a change of current direction in each of two coils when a winding is grounded, thereby resulting in a polarity change of the stator. Notice that while a conventional motor shaft runs freely, the stepper motor shaft moves in a fixed repeatable increment, which allows it to move to a precise position. This repeatable fixed movement is possible as a result of basic magnetic theory where poles of the same polarity repel and opposite poles attract. The direction of the rotation is dictated by the stator poles. The stator poles are determined by the current sent through the wire coils. As the direction of the current is changed, the polarity is also changed causing the reverse motion of the rotor. The stepper motor discussed here has a total of six leads: four leads representing the four stator windings and two commons for the center-tapped leads. As the sequence of power is applied to each stator winding, the rotor will rotate. There are several widely used sequences, each of which has a different degree of precision. Table 10-3 shows a two-phase, four-step stepping sequence.

Clockwise	Step #	Winding A	Winding B	Winding C	Winding D	Counter Clockwise
	1	1	0	0	1	
	2	1	1	0	0	
	3	0	1	1	0	
	4	0	0	1	1	

Table 10-3: Normal Four-Step Sequence

Note that although we can start with any of the sequences in Table 10-3, once we start we must continue in the proper order. For example, if we start with step 3 (0110), we must continue in the sequence of steps 4, 1, 2, and so on.

Step angle

How much movement is associated with a single step? This depends on the internal construction of the motor, in particular the number of teeth on the stator and the rotor. The step angle is the minimum degree of rotation associated with a single step. Various motors have different step angles. Table 10-4 shows some step angles for various motors. In Table 10-4, notice the term steps per revolution. This is the total number of steps needed to rotate one complete rotation or 360 degrees (e.g., 180 steps × 2 degrees = 360).

Step Angle	Step per Revolution
0.72	500
1.8	200
2.0	180
2.5	144
5.0	72
7.5	48
15	24

Table 10-4: Stepper Motor Step Angles

It must be noted that perhaps contrary to one's initial impression, a stepper motor does not need more terminal leads for the stator to achieve smaller steps. All the stepper motors discussed in this section have four leads for the stator winding and two COM wires for the center tap. Although some manufacturers set aside only one lead for the common signal instead of two, they always have four leads for the stators. See Example 10-1. Next we discuss some associated terminology in order to understand the stepper motor further.

Example 10-1

Describe the ARM connection to the stepper motor of Figure 10-9.

Solution:

The following steps show the ARM connection to the stepper motor and its programming:

1. Use an ohmmeter to measure the resistance of the leads. This should identify which COM leads are connected to which winding leads.
2. The common wire(s) are connected to the positive side of the motor's power supply. In many motors, +5 V is sufficient.
3. The four leads of the stator winding are controlled by four bits of the ARM port. Because the microcontroller lacks sufficient current to drive the stepper motor windings, we must use a driver such as the ULN2003 (or ULN2803) to energize the stator. Instead of the ULN2003, we could have used transistors as drivers, as shown in Figure 10-11. However, notice that if transistors are used as drivers, we must also use diodes to take care of inductive current generated when the coil is turned off. One reason that using the ULN2003 is preferable to the use of transistors as drivers is that the ULN2003 has an internal diode to take care of back EMF.

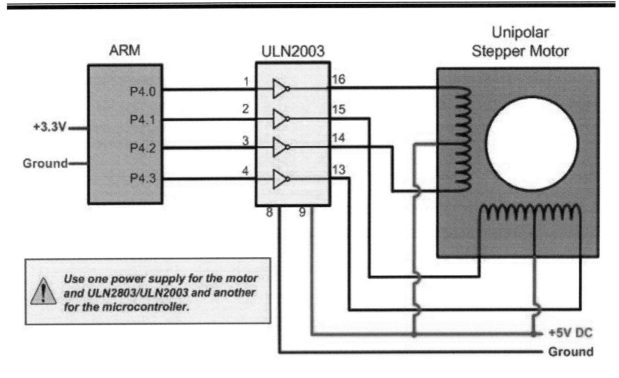

Figure 10-9: ARM Connection to Stepper Motor

Steps per second and RPM relation

The relation between RPM (revolutions per minute), steps per revolution, and steps per second is as follows.

$$Step\ per\ second = \frac{RPM \times Steps\ per\ revolution}{60}$$

280

The 4-step sequence and number of teeth on rotor

The switching sequence shown earlier in Table 10-3 is called the 4-step switching sequence because after four steps the same two windings will be "ON". How much movement is associated with these four steps? Therefore, in a stepper motor with 200 steps per revolution, the rotor has 50 teeth because 4 × 50 = 200 steps are needed to complete one revolution. This leads to the conclusion that the minimum step angle is always a function of the number of teeth on the rotor. In other words, the smaller the step angle, the more teeth the rotor has. See Example 10-2.

Example 10-2

Give the number of times the four-step sequence in Table 10-3 must be applied to a stepper motor to make an 80-degree move if the motor has a 2-degree step angle.

Solution:

A motor with a 2-degree step angle has the following characteristics:

Step angle: 2 degrees

Steps per revolution: 180

Number of rotor teeth: 45

Movement per 4-step sequence: 8 degrees

To move the rotor 80 degrees, we need to send 10 consecutive 4-step sequences, because 10 × 4 steps × 2 degrees = 80 degrees.

Looking at Example 10-2, one might wonder what happens if we want to move 45 degrees, because the steps are 2 degrees each. To provide finer resolutions, all stepper motors allow what is called an 8-step switching sequence. The 8-step sequence is also called half-stepping, because in the 8-step sequence each step is half of the normal step angle. For example, a motor with a 2-degree step angle can be used as a 1-degree step angle if the sequence of Table 10-5 is applied.

	Step #	Winding A	Winding B	Winding C	Winding D	
Clockwise	1	1	0	0	1	Counter Clockwise
	2	1	0	0	0	
	3	1	1	0	0	
	4	0	1	0	0	
	5	0	1	1	0	
	6	0	0	1	0	
	7	0	0	1	1	
	8	0	0	0	1	

Table 10-5: Half-Step 8-Step Sequence

Motor speed

The motor speed, measured in steps per second (steps/s), is a function of the switching rate. Notice in Example 10-1 that by changing the length of the time delay loop, we can achieve various rotation speeds.

Holding torque

The following is a definition of holding torque: "With the motor shaft at standstill or zero rpm condition, the amount of torque, from an external source, required to break away the shaft from its holding position. This is measured with rated voltage and current applied to the motor." The unit of torque is ounce-inch (or kg-cm).

Wave drive 4-step sequence

In addition to the 8-step and the 4-step sequences discussed earlier, there is another sequence called the *wave drive 4-step sequence*. It is shown in Table 10-6.

	Step #	Winding A	Winding B	Winding C	Winding D	
Clockwise	1	1	0	0	0	Counter Clockwise
	2	0	1	0	0	
	3	0	0	1	0	
	4	0	0	0	1	

Table 10-6: Wave Drive 4-Step Sequence

Notice that the 8-step sequence of Table 10-5 is simply the combination of the wave drive 4-step and normal 4-step normal sequences shown in Tables 10-6 and 10-3, respectively. Experimenting with the wave drive 4-step sequence is left to the reader.

Unipolar versus bipolar stepper motor interface

There are three common types of stepper motor interfacing: universal, unipolar, and bipolar. They can be identified by the number of connections to the motor. A universal stepper motor has eight, while the unipolar has six and the bipolar has four. The universal stepper motor can be configured for all three modes, while the unipolar can be either unipolar or bipolar. Obviously the bipolar cannot be configured for universal nor unipolar mode. Table 10-7 shows selected stepper motor characteristics.

Part No.	Step Angle	Drive System	Volts	Phase Resistance	Current
151861CP	7.5	unipolar	5 V	9 ohms	550 mA
171601CP	3.6	unipolar	7 V	20 ohms	350 mA
164056CP	7.5	bipolar	5 V	6 ohms	800 mA

Table 10-7: Selected Stepper Motor Characteristics (www.Jameco.com)

Figure 10-10 shows the basic internal connections of all three types of configurations.

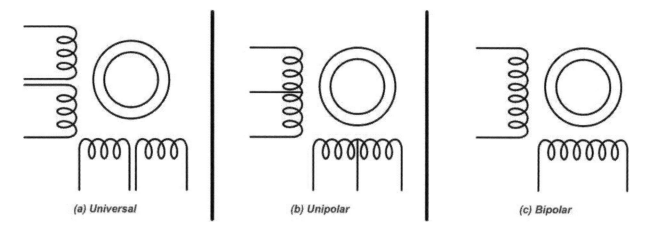

(a) Universal   (b) Unipolar   (c) Bipolar

Figure 10-10: Common Stepper Motor Types

Unipolar stepper motors can be controlled using the basic interfacing shown in Figure 10-11, whereas the bipolar stepper requires H-Bridge circuitry. Bipolar stepper motors require a higher operational current than the unipolar; the advantage of this is a higher holding torque.

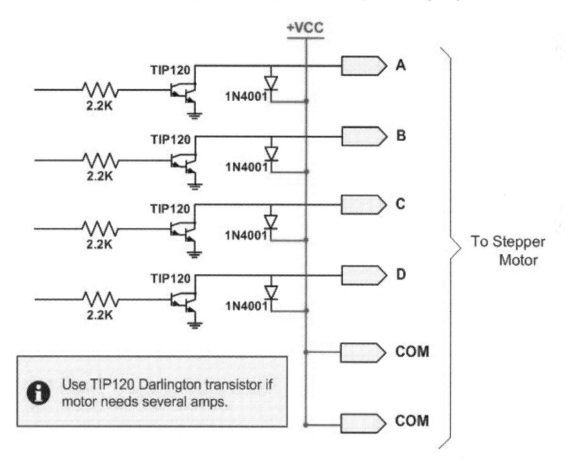

Figure 10-11: Using Transistors for Stepper Motor Driver

Using transistors as drivers

Figure 10-11 shows an interface to a unipolar stepper motor using transistors. Diodes are used to reduce the back EMF spike created when the coils are energized and de-energized, similar to the electromechanical relays discussed earlier. TIP transistors can be used to supply higher current to the motor. Table 10-8 lists the common industrial Darlington transistors. These transistors can accommodate higher voltages and currents.

NPN	PNP	V_{CEO} (volts)	I_C (amps)	hfe (common)
TIP110	TIP115	60	2	1000
TIP111	TIP116	80	2	1000
TIP112	TIP117	100	2	1000
TIP120	TIP125	60	5	1000
TIP121	TIP126	80	5	1000
TIP122	TIP127	100	5	1000
TIP140	TIP145	60	10	1000
TIP141	TIP146	80	10	1000
TIP142	TIP147	100	10	1000

Table 10-8: Darlington Transistor Listing

Controlling stepper motor via optoisolator

In the first section of this chapter we examined the optoisolator and its use. Optoisolators are widely used to isolate the stepper motor's EMF voltage and keep it from damaging the digital/microcontroller system. This is shown in Figure 10-12.

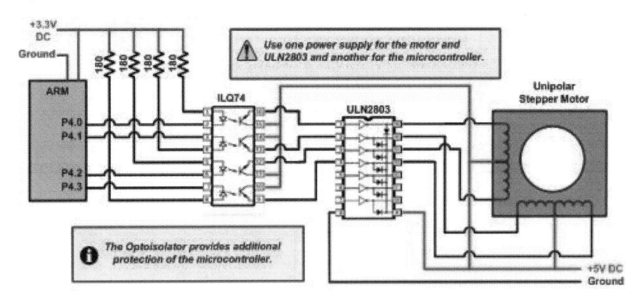

Figure 10-12: Controlling Stepper Motor via Optoisolator

See Program 10-2.

Program 10-2: Controlling a stepper motor

```
/* p10_2.c: Stepper motor control
 *
 * This program controls a unipolar stepper motor
 * using P4.3, P4.2, P4.1, P4.0.
 *
```

```
 * Tested with Keil 5.20 and MSP432 Device Family Pack V2.2.0.
 */

#include "msp.h"

void delayMs(int n);

int delay = 10;
int direction = 0;

int main(void) {
    const char steps[ ] = {0x9, 0x3, 0x6, 0xC};
    int i = 0;

    P4->SEL1 &= ~0xF;               /* configure P4.0 as simple I/O */
    P4->SEL0 &= ~0xF;
    P4->DIR |= 0xF;                 /* P4.0 set as output pin */

    while (1) {
        if (direction)
            P4->OUT = (steps[i++ & 3]);
        else
            P4->OUT = (steps[i-- & 3]);
        delayMs(delay);
    }
}

/* delay milliseconds when system clock is at 3 MHz */
void delayMs(int n) {
    int i, j;

    for (j = 0; j < n; j++)
        for (i = 250; i > 0; i--);      /* delay 1 ms */
}
```

Review Questions

1. Give the 4-step sequence of a stepper motor if we start with 0110.
2. A stepper motor with a step angle of 5 degrees has _____ steps per revolution.
3. Why do we put a driver between the microcontroller and the stepper motor?

Answers to Review Questions

Section 10.1

1. With a relay we can use a 5 V digital system to control 12 V–120 V devices such as horns and appliances.
2. Because microcontroller/digital outputs lack sufficient current to energize the relay, we need a driver.
3. When the coil is not energized, the contact is closed.
4. When current flows through the coil, a magnetic field is created around the coil, which causes the armature to be attracted to the coil.

5. It is faster and needs less current to get energized.
6. It is smaller and can be connected to the microcontroller directly without a driver.

Section 10.2

1. 1100, 0110, 0011, 1001 for clockwise; and 1001, 0011, 0110, 1100 for counterclockwise
2. 72
3. The microcontroller pins do not provide sufficient current to drive the stepper motor.

Chapter 11: PWM and DC Motor Control

This chapter discusses the topic of PWM (pulse width modulation) and shows ARM interfacing with DC motors. The characteristics of DC motors are discussed along with their interfacing to the ARM. We use C programming examples to create PWM pulses.

Section 11.1: DC Motor Interfacing and PWM

This section begins with an overview of the basic operation of the DC motors. Then we describe how to interface a DC motor to the ARM. Finally, we use C language programs to demonstrate the concept of pulse width modulation (PWM) and show how to control the speed and direction of a DC motor.

DC motors

A direct current (DC) motor is a widely used device that translates electrical current into mechanical movement. In the DC motor we have only + and − leads. Connecting them to a DC voltage source moves the motor in one direction. By reversing the polarity, the DC motor will rotate in the opposite direction. One can easily experiment with the DC motor. While a stepper motor moves in discrete steps of 1 to 15 degrees, the DC motor moves continuously. In a stepper motor, if we know the starting position we can easily count the number of steps the motor has moved and calculate the final position of the motor. This is not possible in a DC motor. The maximum speed of a DC motor is indicated in RPM and is given in the data sheet. The DC motor has two types of RPM: no-load and loaded. The manufacturer's data sheet gives the no-load RPM. The no-load RPM can be from a few thousand to tens of thousands. The RPM is reduced when moving a load and it decreases as the load is increased. For example, a drill turning a screw has a much lower RPM speed than when it is in the no-load situation. DC motors also have voltage and current ratings. The nominal voltage is the voltage for that motor under normal conditions, and can be from 1 to 150 V, depending on the motor. As we increase the voltage, the RPM goes up. The current rating is the current consumption when the nominal voltage is applied with no load, and can be from 25 mA to a few amps. As the load increases, the RPM is decreased, unless the current or voltage provided to the motor is increased, which in turn increases the torque. With a fixed voltage, as the load increases, the current (power) consumption of a DC motor is increased. If we overload the motor it will stall, and that can damage the motor due to the heat generated by high current consumption.

Unidirectional control

Figure 11-1 shows the DC motor clockwise (CW) and counterclockwise (CCW) rotations.

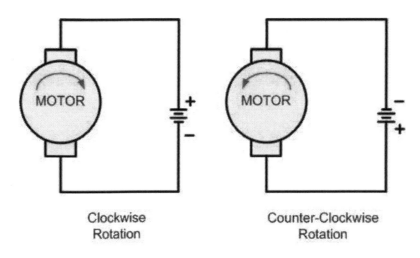

Clockwise
Rotation

Counter-Clockwise
Rotation

Figure 11-1: DC Motor Rotation (Permanent Magnet Field)

See Table 11-1 for selected DC motors.

Part No.	Nominal Volts	Volt Range	Current	RPM	Torque
154915CP	3 V	1.5–3 V	0.070 A	5,200	4.0 g-cm
154923CP	3 V	1.5–3 V	0.240 A	16,000	8.3 g-cm
177498CP	4.5 V	3–14 V	0.150 A	10,300	33.3 g-cm
181411CP	5 V	3–14 V	0.470 A	10,000	18.8 g-cm

Table 11-1: Selected DC Motor Characteristics (http://www.Jameco.com)

Bidirectional control

With the help of relays, transistor circuit or some specially designed chips we can change the direction of the DC motor rotation. Figures 11-2 through 11-4 show the basic concepts of the H-Bridge control of DC motors.

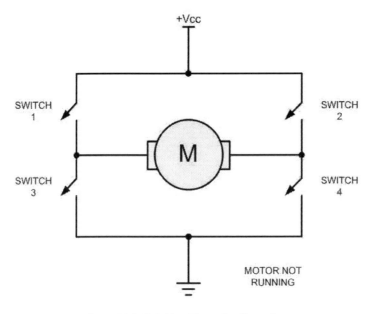

Figure 11-2: H-Bridge Motor Configuration

Figure 11-2 shows the connection of an H-Bridge using simple switches. All the switches are open, which does not allow the motor to turn.

Figure 11-3 shows the switch configuration for turning the motor in one direction. When switches 1 and 4 are closed, current is allowed to pass through the motor.

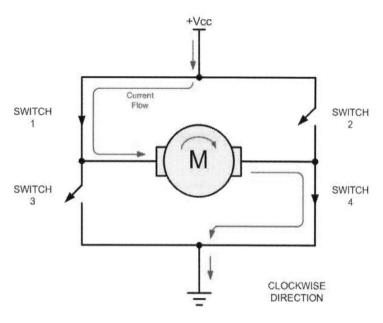

Figure 11-3: H-Bridge Motor Clockwise Configuration

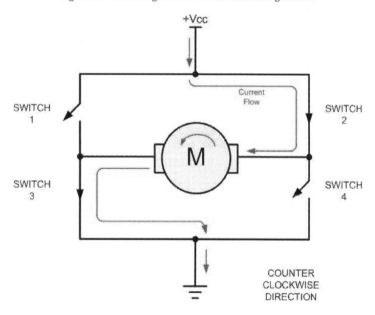

Figure 11-4: H-Bridge Motor Counterclockwise Configuration

Figure 11-4 shows the switch configuration for turning the motor in the opposite direction from the configuration of Figure 11-3. When switches 2 and 3 are closed, current is allowed to pass through the motor.

Figure 11-5 shows an invalid configuration. Current flows directly to ground, creating a short circuit. The same effect occurs when switches 1 and 3 are closed or switches 2 and 4 are closed.

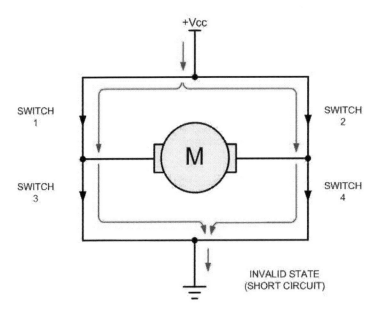

Figure 11-5: H-Bridge in an Invalid Configuration

Table 11-2 shows some of the logic configurations for the H-Bridge design.

Motor Operation	SW1	SW2	SW3	SW4
Off	Open	Open	Open	Open
Clockwise	Closed	Open	Open	Closed
Counterclockwise	Open	Closed	Closed	Open
Invalid	Closed	Closed	Closed	Closed

Table 11-2: Some H-Bridge Logic Configurations for Figure 11-2

H-Bridge control can be created using relays, transistors, or a single IC solution such as the L298. When using relays and transistors, you must ensure that invalid configurations do not occur.

Example 11-1 shows a simple program to operate a basic H-Bridge.

Example 11-1

A switch is connected to input pin P6.1. Using relay H-Bridge in Table 11-2 and write the proper program to control the motor direction by the switch:

(a) If P6.1 = 0, the DC motor moves clockwise.

(b) If P6.1 = 1, the DC motor moves counterclockwise.

Solution 1 (Using SPST Relays):

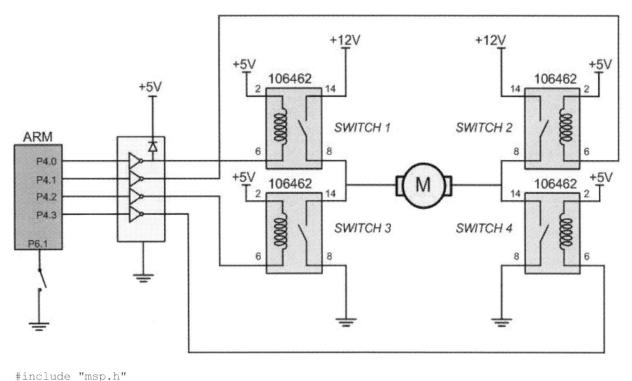

```
#include "msp.h"

int main(void) {
    void delayMs(int n);
    P4->SEL1 &= ~0x0F;          /* configure P4.3-P4.0 as simple I/O output */
    P4->SEL0 &= ~0x0F;
    P4->DIR |= 0x0F;
    P6->SEL1 &= ~0x02;          /* configure P6.1 as simple I/O input */
    P6->SEL0 &= ~0x02;
    P6->DIR &= ~0x02;
    P6->REN |= 0x02;            /* P6.1 pull-up resistor enabled */
    P6->OUT |= 0x02;

    while (1) {
        if((P6->IN & 0x02) == 0) {  /* P6.1 == 0 */
            P4->OUT &= ~0x0F;           /* open all switches */
            delayMs(100);               /* wait 0.1 second */
            P4->OUT |= 0x09;            /* close SW1 & SW4 */
            while((P6->IN & 0x02) == 0);    /* wait till switch change */
        } else {                    /* P6.1 == 1 */
            P4->OUT &= ~0x0F;           /* open all switches */
            delayMs(100);               /* wait 0.1 second */
            P4->OUT |= 0x06;            /* close SW1 & SW4 */
            while((P6->IN & 0x02) != 0);    /* wait till switch change */
        }
    }
}
```

Solution 2 (Using SPDT Relays):

The H-bridge can also be made using two SPDT relays as shown in the following figure.

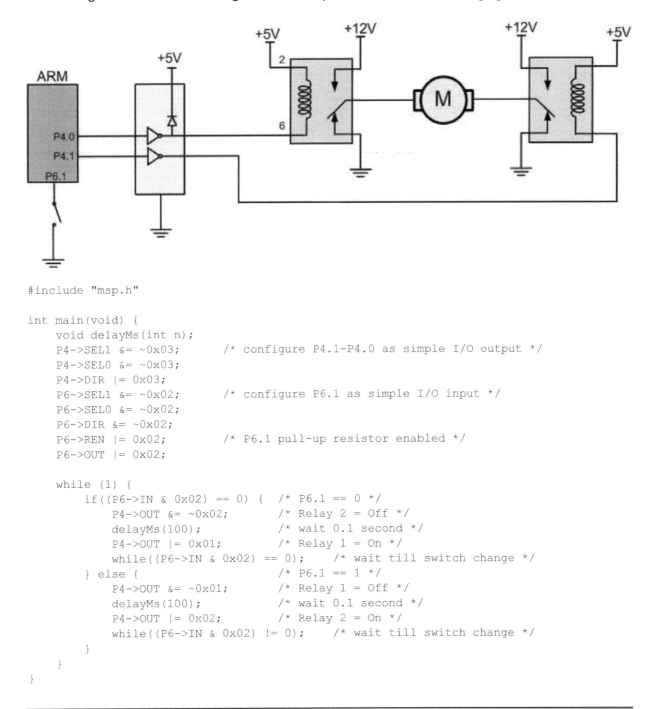

```
#include "msp.h"

int main(void) {
    void delayMs(int n);
    P4->SEL1 &= ~0x03;          /* configure P4.1-P4.0 as simple I/O output */
    P4->SEL0 &= ~0x03;
    P4->DIR |= 0x03;
    P6->SEL1 &= ~0x02;          /* configure P6.1 as simple I/O input */
    P6->SEL0 &= ~0x02;
    P6->DIR &= ~0x02;
    P6->REN |= 0x02;            /* P6.1 pull-up resistor enabled */
    P6->OUT |= 0x02;

    while (1) {
        if((P6->IN & 0x02) == 0) {  /* P6.1 == 0 */
            P4->OUT &= ~0x02;       /* Relay 2 = Off */
            delayMs(100);           /* wait 0.1 second */
            P4->OUT |= 0x01;        /* Relay 1 = On */
            while((P6->IN & 0x02) == 0);    /* wait till switch change */
        } else {                    /* P6.1 == 1 */
            P4->OUT &= ~0x01;       /* Relay 1 = Off */
            delayMs(100);           /* wait 0.1 second */
            P4->OUT |= 0x02;        /* Relay 2 = On */
            while((P6->IN & 0x02) != 0);    /* wait till switch change */
        }
    }
}
```

Figure 11-6 shows the connection of the L298N to the microcontroller. Be aware that the L298N will generate heat during operation. For sustained operation of the motor, use a heat sink.

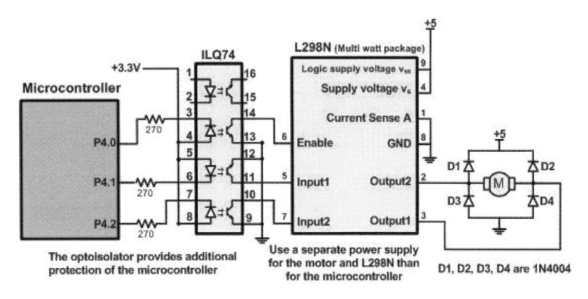

Figure 11-6: Bidirectional Motor Control Using an L298 Chip

Pulse width modulation (PWM)

The speed of the motor depends on three factors: (a) load, (b) voltage, and (c) current. For a given fixed load we can maintain a steady speed by using a method called pulse width modulation (PWM). By changing (modulating) the width of the pulse applied to the DC motor we can increase or decrease the amount of power provided to the motor, thereby increasing or decreasing the motor speed. Notice that, although the voltage has a fixed amplitude, it has a variable duty cycle. That means the wider the pulse, the higher the speed. PWM is so widely used in DC motor control that many microcontrollers come with an on-chip PWM circuitry. In such microcontrollers all we have to do is load the proper registers with the values of the high and low portions of the desired pulse, and the rest is taken care of by the microcontroller. This allows the microcontroller to do other things. For microcontrollers without on-chip PWM circuitry, we must create the various duty cycle pulses using software, which prevents the microcontroller from doing other things. The ability to control the speed of the DC motor using PWM is one reason that DC motors are preferable over AC motors. AC motor speed is dictated by the AC frequency of the voltage applied to the motor and the frequency is generally fixed. As a result, we cannot control the speed of the AC motor when the load is increased. As will be shown later, we can also change the DC motor's direction and torque. See Figure 11-7 for PWM comparisons.

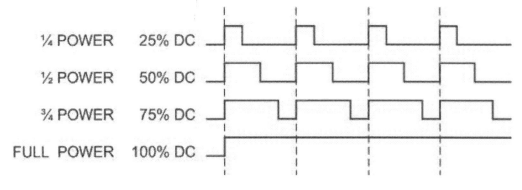

Figure 11-7: Pulse Width Modulation Comparison

DC motor control with optoisolator

The optoisolator is indispensable in many motor control applications. Figures 11-8 and 11-9 show the connections to a simple DC motor using a bipolar and a MOSFET transistor. Notice that the microcontroller is protected from EMI created by motor brushes by using an optoisolator and a separate power supply.

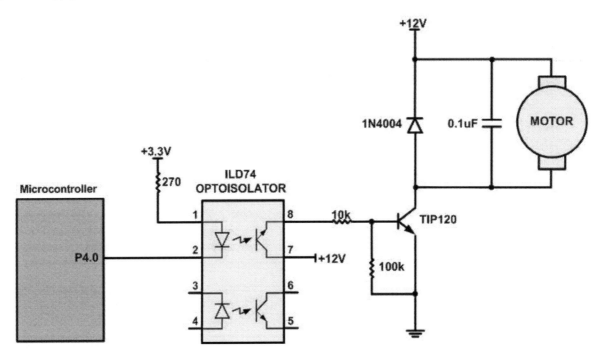

Figure 11-8: DC Motor Connection Using a Darlington Transistor

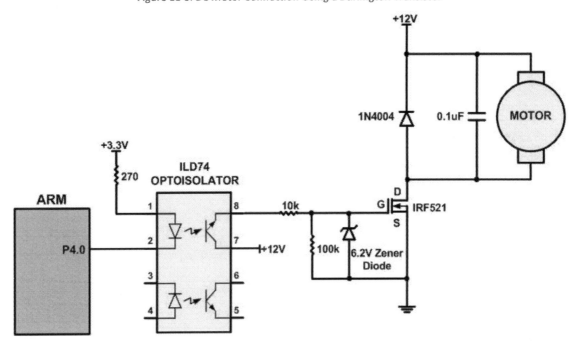

Figure 11-9: DC Motor Connection Using a MOSFET Transistor

Figures 11-8 and 11-9 show optoisolators for single directional motor control, and the same principle should be used for most motor applications. Separating the power supplies of the motor and logic will reduce the possibility of damage to the control circuit. Figure 11-8 shows the connection of a bipolar transistor to a motor. Protection of the control circuit is provided by the optoisolator. The motor and the microcontroller use separate power supplies. The separation of power supplies also allows the use of high-voltage motors. Notice that we use a decoupling capacitor across the motor; this helps reduce the EMI created by the motor. The motor is switched on by clearing bit PTD0.

Figure 11-9 shows the connection of a MOSFET transistor. The optoisolator protects the microcontroller from EMI. The Zener diode is required for the transistor to reduce gate voltage below the rated maximum value.

Review Questions

1. True or false. The permanent magnet field DC motor has only two leads for + and – voltages.
2. True or false. As with a stepper motor, one can control the exact angle of a DC motor's move.
3. Why do we put a driver between the microcontroller and the DC motor?
4. How do we change a DC motor's rotation direction?
5. What is stall in a DC motor?
6. The RPM rating given for the DC motor is for _____ (no-load, loaded).

Section 11.2: Programming PWM in MSP432

In MSP432, the PWM (Pulse Width Modulation) is incorporated into the Timer. As we saw in Chapter 5, MSP432P401R has four Timer_A modules. To program the PWM features of the chip, we must understand the Timer_A topics covered in Chapter 5 since PWM is a subset of the timer functions. In this section, we examine the PWM features and show how to program them.

MC bits and the TAxR counting

As discussed in Chapter 5, the TAxCTL register has control on the counting of the timer. See Figure 11-10 and Table 11-3.

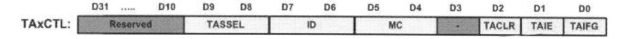

Figure 11-10: TAxCTL (Timer_A Control Register)

bit	Name	Description
0	TAIFG	Timer-A Interrupt Flag 0: Timer did not overflow 1: Timer overflowed
1	TAIE	Timer_A Interrupt Enable (0: Disabled, 1: Enabled)
2	TACLR	Timer_A Clear
4-5	MC	Mode Control: *00: Stop mode:* timer is halted *01: Up mode:* Timer counts up to TAxCCR0 *10: Continuous mode:* Timer counts up to 0xFFFF

		11: Up/down mode: Timer counts up to TAxCCR0 then down to 0.
6-7	ID	Input divider: These bits select the divider for the input clock: **00:** divide by 1 **01:** divide by 2 **10:** divide by 4 **11:** divide by 8
8-9	TASSEL	Timer_A clock Source Select: These bits select the Timer_A clock source: **00:** TAxCLK (external clock): The timer uses external clock which is fed to the PM_TAxCLK pin. 01: ACLK (internal clock) **10:** SMCLK (internal clock) **11:** INCLK

Table 11-3: TAxCTL (Timer_A Control Register)

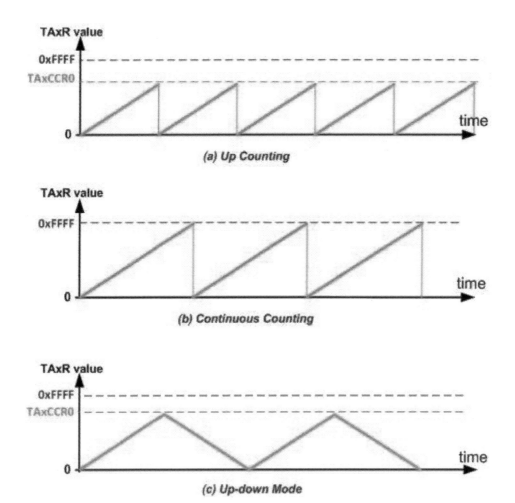

Figure 11-11: Up/Down-Counter and Up-Counter

The MC bits can be set as up-counter, continuous counter, or up-down counter. The counter has three modes:

1) **Count Up:** The TAxR counts up from 0 until it reaches the value of TAxCCR0 register. Upon matching the TAxCCR0, the TAxR is cleared to zero and count-up starts again.

2) **Continuous:** The TAxR counts up from 0 until it reaches the maximal value, 0xFFFF. Then it rolls over to 0 and starts counting up again.

Count Up-Down: counts up from 0 until it reaches the TAxCCR0 value. After reaching the TAxCCR0 value, it turns around and counts down to 0. And upon reaching 0, it repeats the process. See Figure 11-11.

In MSP432P401R, each Timer_A has five TAxCCRn registers and five Compare/Capture blocks. Figure 11-13 shows the simplified structure of a Timer_A together with the compare blocks. For simplicity, the capture parts of the blocks are omitted.

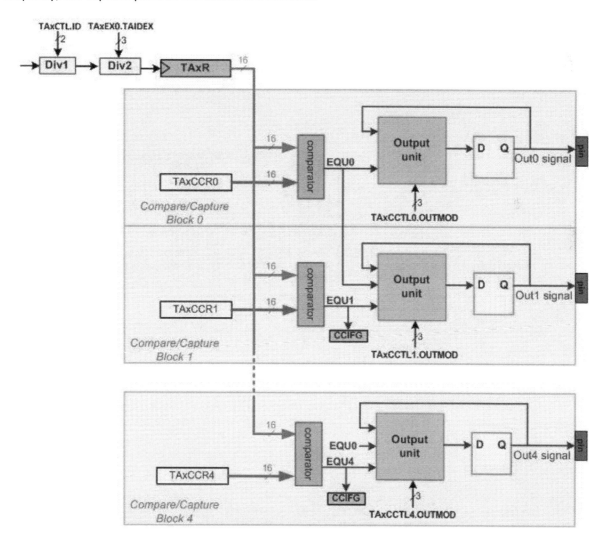

Figure 11-12: The Wave Generators of a Timer_A

In Chapter 5, we used TAxCCTLn (Timer_A Capture/Compare Control n) registers to program the Input Capture feature of the Timer. We use the same register to control the output waveform generation. See Figure 11-13 and Table 11-4. For PWM, we can use the options of Center-aligned (up-down counting) or Edge-aligned (up counting). Each is discussed next.

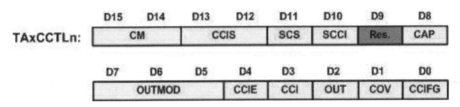

Figure 11-13: TAxCCTLn Register

bit	Name	Description
15-14	CM	Capture mode 00: No capture 01: Capture on rising edge 10: Capture on falling edge 11: Capture on both rising and falling edges
13-12	CCIS	Capture/compare input select. These bits select the TAxCCR0 input signal: 00: CCIxA 01: CCIxB 10: GND 11: VCC
11	SCS	Synchronize capture source. This bit is used to synchronize the capture input signal with the timer clock. 0: Asynchronous capture 1: Synchronous capture
10	SCCI	Synchronized capture/compare input. The selected CCI input signal is latched with the EQUx signal and can be read via this bit.
8	CAP	Capture mode 0: Compare mode 1: Capture mode
7-5	OUTMOD	Output mode. Modes 2, 3, 6, and 7 are not useful for TAxCCR0 because EQUx = EQU0 000: OUT bit value 001: Set 010: Toggle/reset 011: Set/reset 100: Toggle 101: Reset 110: Toggle/set 111: Reset/set
4	CCIE	Capture/compare interrupt enable. This bit enables the interrupt request of the corresponding CCIFG flag. 0: Interrupt disabled 1: Interrupt enabled

3	CCI	Capture/compare input. The selected input signal can be read by this bit.
2	OUT	Output. For output mode 0, this bit directly controls the state of the output. 0: Output low 1: Output high
1	COV	Capture overflow. This bit indicates a capture overflow occurred. COV must be reset with software. 0: No capture overflow occurred 1: Capture overflow occurred
0	CCIFG	Capture/compare interrupt flag 0: No interrupt pending 1: interrupt pending

Table 11-4: TAxCCTLn Register

CAP bit

Each TAxCCTLn register has a CAP bit. The CAP bit must be 0 to generate output waveforms.

OUTMODE

See Figure 11-14. In each compare block there is an output unit which generates waveforms. The output unit has 3 input signals:

- Outn signal: it is the current output of the waveform generator.
- EQU0: it is the current result of comparing TAxR and TAxCCR0. The signal is high when TAxR and TAxCCR0 are equal.
- EQUn: The signal becomes high when TAxR and TAxCCRn are equal.

The Output unit has different reactions to the input signals depending on the values of OUTMOD.

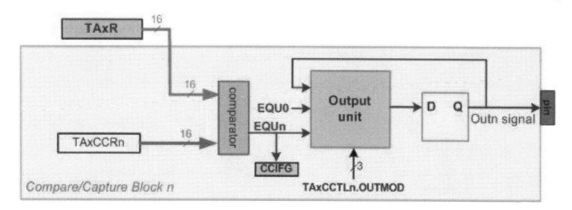

Figure 11-14: A Compare Block

When OUTMODE=000, the OUT bit of the TAxCCTLn is sent out to the pin. In other cases, the Output unit changes the pin depending on the input signals. Next, we discuss generating waves in different counting modes.

299

Up counting and continuous counting modes

In up and continuous counting modes the output is changed as shown in Table 11-5 and Figure 11-16.

OUTMODE	output mode	when EQUn rises (TAxR = TAxCCRn)	when EQU0 rises (TAxR = TAxCCR0)
001	Set	sets the output	does nothing
010	Toggle/Reset	toggles the output	resets the output
011	Set/Reset	sets the output	clears the output
100	Toggle	toggles the output	does nothing
101	Reset	clears the output	does nothing
110	Toggle/Set	toggles the output	sets the output
111	Reset/Set	clears the output	sets the output

Table 11-5: Output Changes in Up and Continuous Modes

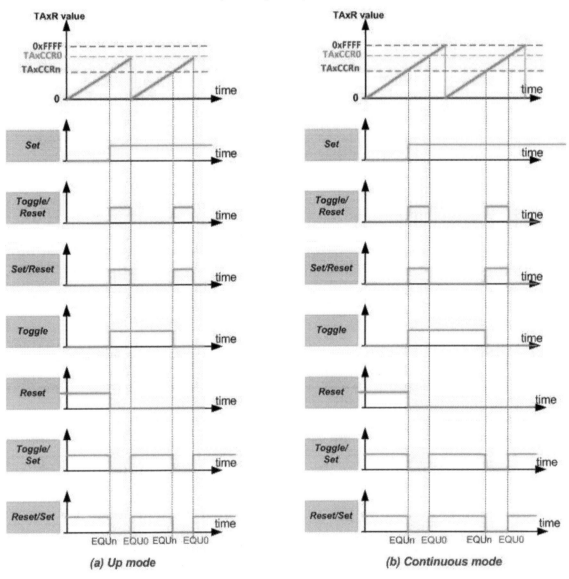

(a) Up mode   (b) Continuous mode

Figure 11-15: Output Modes in Up-Counting and Continuous-Counting

Set mode

In the Set mode, the output is set HIGH when the TAxR value is equal to TAxCCRn and remains high until the timer is reset or the output mode is changed to another mode and changes the output. For example, to turn on 5 devices with different delays, you can set the TAxCCTLn registers of the comparators 5 to Set mode, and initialize TAxCCRn registers with proper values. See the following figure.

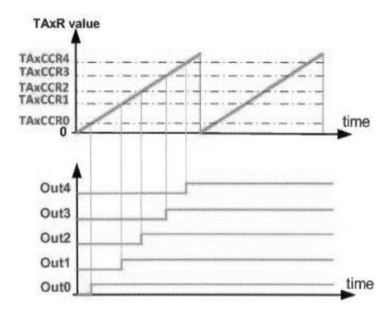

Figure 11-16: Setting 5 Outputs using 5 Comparators

Notice that we need not necessarily set the output modes of every comparator to the same. Each comparator can be configured independently of each other except some modes are working in conjunction with comparator 0.

Reset Mode

Similar to Set mode, in the Reset mode, the output is cleared when the TAxR value is equal to TAxCCRn and remains LOW until the output mode is changed to another mode and changes the output.

Toggle Mode

In Toggle Mode, the output is toggled when TAxR and TAxCCRn are equal. This mode can be used to generate square waves.

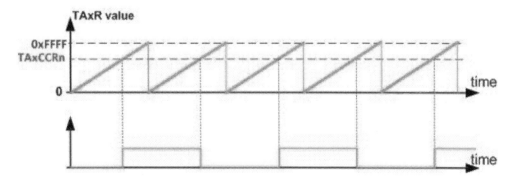

Figure 11-17: Generating Square Waves using Toggle Mode

If we use this mode together with up-counting mode, we can change the frequency of generated wave by changing the TAxCCR0. When the TAxCCR0 value is lower, the cycle repeats faster and the generated wave has higher frequency. See the following figure.

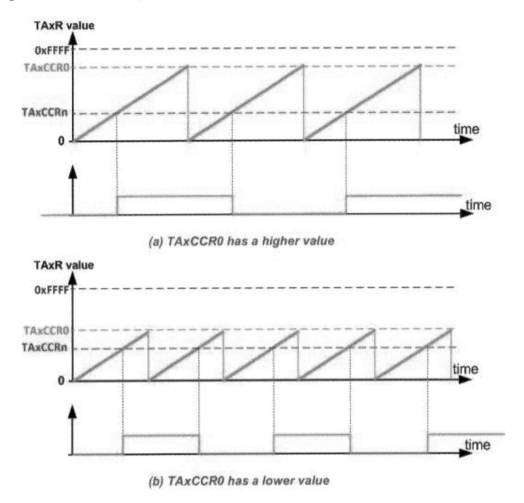

(a) TAxCCR0 has a higher value

(b) TAxCCR0 has a lower value

Figure 11-18: Changing the Frequency using TAxCCR0

Generating edge-aligned PWM waves using Up mode

Up-counting mode, together with Set/Reset or Reset/Set modes are good choices to generate PWM. In these modes, the leading edge of the pulse starts at the beginning of the period. See Figure 11-19.

The pulse period is set by the TAxCCR0 register value (actually TAxCCR0+1) and the pulse width value is set by the TAxCCRn register. In Reset/Set mode, the output is high at the beginning of the pulse when the counter is reloaded and it goes low when the TAxR value matches TAxCCRn register. In Set/Reset mode, the output is low at the beginning of the pulse when the counter is reloaded and it goes high when the counter value matches TAxCCRn register.

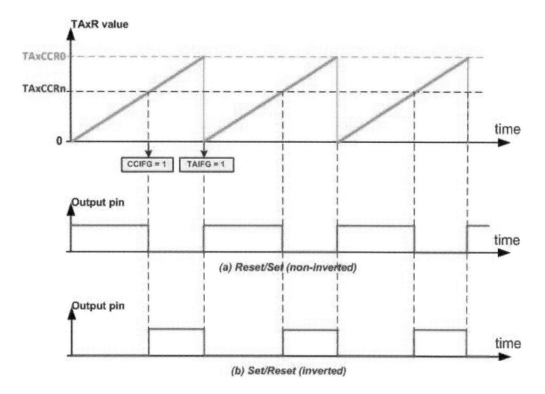

Figure 11-19: Edge-Aligned PWM

The PWM output duty cycle and frequency

The pulse period is programmed by the TAxCCR0 register value. Using the TAxCCRn register we program the pulse width (duty cycle). Now, if TAxCCRn = 0, then Channel output has 0% duty cycle. The same way, if TAxCCRn greater than or equal to TAxCCR0, the duty cycle is 100% since there is never a match.

Figure 11-16 shows the output waveform when Reset/Set (non-inverted), TAxCCR0 = 8, and TAxCCRn = 5. The output is set on counter overflow (reload) and it is cleared on compare match. The TAxR is reloaded with 0 after TAxCCR0 + 1 clocks and the output is set to HIGH for TAxCCRn clocks. So, the duty cycle can be calculated using the following formula:

$$Duty\ Cycle = \frac{TAxCCRn}{TAxCCR0 + 1} \times 100\%$$

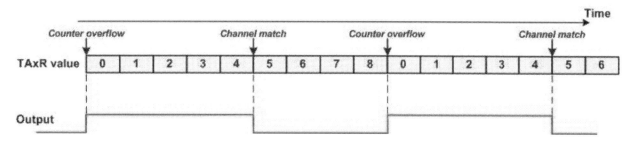

Figure 11-20: The PWM output for TAxCCR0 = 8, TAxCCRn = 5, Output Mode = Set/Reset (non-inverted)

In Set/Reset, the output is inverted and the duty cycle is:

303

$$Duty\ Cycle = 100\% - \left(\frac{TAxCCRn}{TAxCCR0 + 1} \times 100\%\right)$$

In up mode, the timer counts from 0 to TAxCCR0 and then rolls over. So, the frequency of the output is 1/(TAxCCR0+1) of the frequency of timer clock. The frequency of the timer clock can be selected using the prescalers. So, the frequency of the output can be calculated as follows:

$$F_{output} = \frac{F_{timer\ clock}/prescalers}{TAxCCR0 + 1}$$

See Examples 11-2 through 11-5.

Example 11-2

Find the period (T), frequency (F) and pulse width (DC, duty cycle) of a PWM if TAxCCR0=999 and TAxCCRn=250. Assume Reset/Set, no prescaler, and SMCLK frequency of 3MHz.

Solution:

1/3MHz = 333.3ns. Now T= (TAxCCR0+1) × 333.3ns = (999+1) x 333.3ns = 333.3ms.
Frequency=1/333.3ms=3000Hz.
The Duty Cycle is [TAxCCRn/(TAxCCR0+1)] × 100% = (250/1000) × 100% = 25%.

Example 11-3

Assume the SMCLK clock frequency is 3MHz. Find the value of the TAxCCR0 register if we want the PWM output Frequency of (a) 5KHz, (b) 10KHz, and (c) 25KHz.

Solution:

The clock period for timer module is 1/3MHz=0.333μs (micro second).
(a) The PWM output period is 1/5KHz = 200μs. Now, TAxCCR0 = (200μs/0.333μs) − 1 = 600 − 1 = 599.
(b) The PWM output period is 1/10KHz = 100μs. Now, TAxCCR0 = (100μs/0.333μs) − 1 = 300 − 1 = 299.
(c) The PWM output period is 1/25KHz = 40μs. TAxCCR0 = (40μs/0.125μs) − 1 = 120 − 1 = 119.

Example 11-4

In a given PWM application, we need the PWM output frequency of 60Hz with 33.3% duty cycle. Using the SMCLK frequency of 3 MHz, find out the values of the TAxCCR0 and TAxCCRn register.

Solution:

TAxCCR0 = (3MHz / 60Hz) − 1 = 50,000 − 1 = 49,999.
Assume using reset/set mode (non-inverting), TAxCCRn = 50,000 / 3 = 16,666.

Example 11-5

Assume the clock frequency after prescaler is 16MHz and Reset/Set (non-inverting). Find the value of the TAxCCR0 and TAxCCRn registers for the following PWM output frequencies and duty cycles:
(a) 1KHz with 25%, (b) 5KHz with 60%, (c) 20KHz with 80%, and (d) 2KHz of 50%.

Solution:

The System Clock period for PWM0 Module is 1/16MHz = 62.5ns (nano second).
(a) The PWM output period is 1 / 1KHz = 1msec. Now, TAxCCR0 = (1ms / 62.5ns) − 1 = 16,000 − 1 = 15,999
TAxCCRn = (TAxCCR0 + 1) × Duty Cycle = 16000 × 25%= 4,000

(b) The PWM output period is 1 / 5KHz = 0.2msec. Now, TAxCCR0 = (0.2ms / 62.5ns) − 1 = 3,200 − 1 = 3,199
TAxCCRn = 3,200 × 60% = 1920

(c) The PWM output period is 1 / 20KHz = 0.05msec. Now, TAxCCR0 = (0.05ms / 62.5ns) − 1 = 800 − 1 = 799
TAxCCRn = 800 × 80% = 640

(d) The PWM output period is 1 / 2KHz = 0.5msec. Now, TAxCCR0 = (0.5ms / 62.5ns) − 1 = 8000 − 1 = 7,999
TAxCCRn = 8000 × 50% / 100 = 4000

Configuring GPIO pin for PWM

In using PWM, we must configure the I/O pins for timer output. In this regard, it is same as all other peripherals. The steps are as follow:

1. Set PxSEL0 to 1 and PxSEL1 to 0 to associate the pin with Timer_A (Section 6.10 MSP432 reference manual).
2. Set PxDIR to 1 to make it timer output.

Configuring PWM generator to create pulses

After the I/O configuration, we need to take the following steps to configure the PWM:

1. Load the value into TAxCCR0 register to set the desired output frequency.
2. Load the value into TAxCCRn register to set the desired duty cycle.
3. Set the OUTMOD bits (7-5) of TAxCCTLn register to 111 binary for reset/set mode
4. Configure TAxCTL register to select timer clock source, timer clock prescaler, count up mode

See the next few programming examples. Program 11-1 uses Timer_A0.4 to generate 60 Hz and 33.3% duty cycle output. You do need an oscilloscope on P2.7 pin of the MSP432 LaunchPad board to observe the waveform. The register values of Program 11-1 are from Example 11-4.

Program 11-1: Using Timer_A0.4 to create 60Hz with 33% duty cycle on P2.7 pin

```
/* p11_1.c Toggling P2.7 at 60 Hz using Timer_A0.4 PWM
 *
 * This program uses Timer_A0.4 to generate PWM output at 60 Hz
 * and 33.3% duty cycle.
 * Subsystem Master Clock (SMCLK) running at 3 MHz is used.
 * Timer_A0 is configured to count up from 0 to 50,000-1, which
 * is loaded in TIMER_A0->CCR[0].
 * The timer counter roll over interval is:
 * 3,000,000 / 50,000 = 60 Hz.
 * TIMER_A0->CCR[4] is loaded with 50000/3 and CCR4 is configured
 * as reset/set mode. The output is set to 1 at the beginning
 * of the counting cycle when the counter is 0. When the counter
 * counts up to 50000/3, the output is reset to 0 and stays 0 until
 * the next counting cycle. So the output stays at 1 for 1/3=33.3% of the time.
 *
 * Tested with Keil 5.20 and MSP432 Device Family Pack V2.2.0.
 */

#include "msp.h"

void delayMs(int n);

int main(void) {
    /* Configure P2.7 as Timer A0.4 output */
    P2->SEL0 |= 0x80;
    P2->SEL1 &= ~0x80;
    P2->DIR |= 0x80;

    /* configure TimerA0.4 as PWM */
    TIMER_A0->CCR[0] = 50000-1;     /* PWM Period */
    TIMER_A0->CCR[4] = 50000/3;     /* CCR4 PWM duty cycle */
    TIMER_A0->CCTL[4] = 0xE0;       /* CCR4 reset/set mode */
    TIMER_A0->CTL = 0x0214;         /* use SMCLK, count up, clear TA0R register */

    while (1) {
    }
}
```

Program 11-2 is based on Program 11-1 but in the infinite loop, the value of CCR4 is incremented by 5% every 50 ms. The increasing CCR4 value lengthens the duty cycle and increases the LED light intensity when the output is mapped to the green LED on the LaunchPad.

Program 11-2: Use PWM to control LED intensity

```c
/* p11_2.c Variable duty cycle PWM to control LED intensity
 *
 * This program uses Timer_A0.4 to generate PWM output at 60 Hz
 * and variable duty cycle.
 * The program is based on p11_1.c with two changes.
 * 1. In the infinite loop, the duty cycle is increased by 5%
 *      every 50ms. When it reaches 100%, it wraps around.
 * 2. The timer output is available on P2.7 and is also mapped to
 *      P2.1 (Green LED).
 *
 * Tested with Keil 5.20 and MSP432 Device Family Pack V2.2.0.
 */

#include "msp.h"

void delayMs(int n);
void portRemap(void);

int main(void) {
    /* Configure P2.7 as Timer A0.4 output */
    P2->SEL0 |= 0x80;
    P2->SEL1 &= ~0x80;
    P2->DIR  |= 0x80;

    portRemap();                    /* remap output to P2.1 green LED */

    /* configure TimerA0.4 as PWM */
    TIMER_A0->CCR[0] = 50000-1;     /* PWM Period */
    TIMER_A0->CCR[4] = 500;         /* begin from 1% */
    TIMER_A0->CCTL[4] = 0xE0;       /* CCR4 reset/set mode */
    TIMER_A0->CTL = 0x0214;         /* use SMCLK, count up, clear TA0R register */

    while (1) {
        /* increase duty cycle by 5% */
        TIMER_A0->CCR[4] += 2500;
        if (TIMER_A0->CCR[4] > 50000)   /* wrap around when reaches 100% */
            TIMER_A0->CCR[4] = 500;     /* begin from 1% */
        delayMs(50);
    }
}

void portRemap(void) {
    PMAP->KEYID = 0x2D52;               /* unlock PMAP */

    P2MAP->PMAP_REGISTER1 = 23;         /* remap P2.1 to 23 (TPM0.4) */
    P2->DIR  |= 2;
    P2->SEL0 |= 2;
    P2->SEL1 &= ~2;
```

```
        PMAP->CTL = 1;                      /* lock PMAP */
        PMAP->KEYID = 0;
}

/* delay milliseconds when system clock is at 3 MHz */
void delayMs(int n) {
    int i, j;

    for (j = 0; j < n; j++)
        for (i = 250; i > 0; i--);          /* Delay */
}
```

Program 11-3 uses the slow 32kHz clock for timer counter clock. This is slow enough that the duty cycle changes can be observed with naked eyes.

Program 11-3: Based on Program 11-2 but slow down the PWM frequency so that the duty cycle change can be observed with naked eyes

```
/* p11_3.c Visible duty cycle change PWM by Timer_A0.4
 *
 * This program uses Timer_A0.4 to generate PWM output at
 * 1 Hz and variable duty cycle.
 * This program is based on P11_2.c but using a slow clock
 * so that the change of duty cycle is visible by naked eyes
 * without the aid of an oscilloscope.
 * ACLK (32 KHz) is used for timer clock
 *
 * The duty cycle of generated waves are:
 * 1%, 11%, 21%, 31%, 41%, 51%, 61%, 71%, 81%, and 91%
 *
 * Tested with Keil 5.20 and MSP432 Device Family Pack V2.2.0.
 *
 */

#include "msp.h"

void delayMs(int n);
void portRemap(void);

int main(void) {
    /* Configure P2.7 as Timer A0.4 output */
    P2->SEL0 |= 0x80;
    P2->SEL1 &= ~0x80;
    P2->DIR  |= 0x80;

    portRemap();                            /* remap pins */

    /* configure TimerA0.4 as PWM */
    TIMER_A0->CCR[0] = 50000-1;             /* PWM Period */
    TIMER_A0->CCR[4] = 500;                 /* begin from 1% */
    TIMER_A0->CCTL[4] = 0xE0;               /* CCR4 reset/set mode */
    TIMER_A0->CTL = 0x0114;                 /* use ACLK, count up, clear TA0R register */
```

```
    while (1) {
        /* increase duty cycle by 10% */
        TIMER_A0->CCR[4] += 5000;
        if (TIMER_A0->CCR[4] > 50000)    /* wrap around when reaches 100% */
            TIMER_A0->CCR[4] = 500;                 /* begin from 1% */

            /* wait a cycle */
            while((TIMER_A0->CCTL[0]& 1) == 0); /*wait until the CCIFG of CCR0 is set*/
            TIMER_A0->CCTL[0]&= ~1;              /* clear the CCIFG flag */
    }
}

void portRemap(void) {
    PMAP->KEYID = 0x2D52;                /* unlock PMAP */

    P2MAP->PMAP_REGISTER1 = 23;          /* remap P2.1 to 23 (TPM0.4) */
    P2->DIR  |= 2;
    P2->SEL0 |= 2;
    P2->SEL1 &= ~2;

    PMAP->CTL = 1;                       /* lock PMAP */
    PMAP->KEYID = 0;
}
```

Generating waves using Up-Down Counting mode

In up and continuous counting modes the output is changed as shown in Table 11-6 and Figure 11-21. In this section, we will demonstrate using up-down counting mode to generate PWM output.

OUTMODE	mode	when TAxR = TAxCCRn	when TAxR = TAxCCR0
001	Set	sets the output	does nothing
010	Toggle/Reset	clears the output if the timer is increasing; otherwise, toggles.	does nothing
011	Set/Reset	sets the output if the timer is decreasing	clears the output
100	Toggle	toggles the output in all matches	does nothing
101	Reset	clears the output	does nothing
110	Toggle/Set	sets the output if the timer is increasing; otherwise, toggles.	does nothing
111	Reset/Set	clears the output if the timer is decreasing	sets the output

Table 11-6: Output Changes in Up-Down Mode

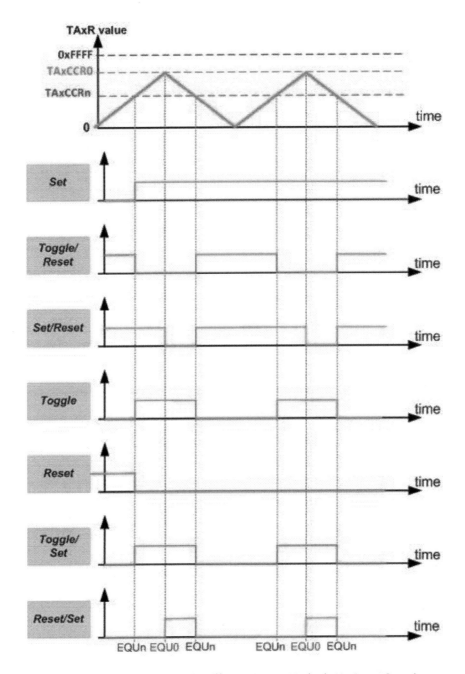

Figure 11-21: Generated Waves in Different Output Modes in Up-Down Counting

Generating Center-Aligned PWM waves using Up-Down Counting mode

If we use Up-Down Counting mode, then the output is Center-Aligned PWM. The counter will count up from 0 to the value in TAxCCR0 register then turn around and count down to 0. That means, the period of the pulse is 2 × TAxCCR0. In the same way, the pulse width = 2 × TAxCCRn. Whenever the TAxCCRn=TAxCCR0, the output pin is forced High or Low depending on the selected output mode. See Figure 11-21 and Figure 11-22.

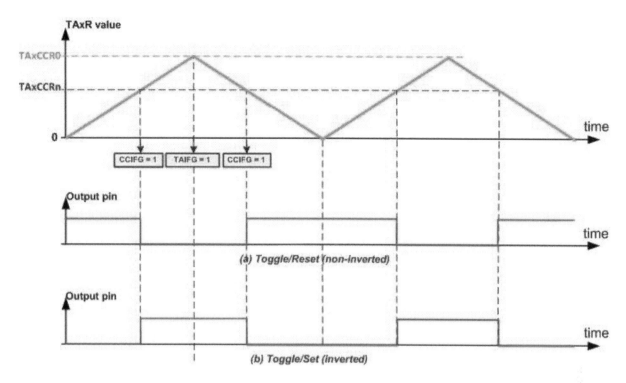

Figure 11-22: Center-Aligned PWM using Up-Down Mode

The PWM output duty cycle and frequency

Figure 11-23 shows the output when TAxCCR0 = 7 and TAxCCRn = 4. The output is set on compare match when counting down, and is cleared on compare match when counting up. The output is HIGH for TAxCCRn×2 clocks and each cycle takes TAxCCR0 × 2 clocks. As a result, the duty cycle is:

$$Duty\ Cycle = \frac{TAxCCRn \times 2}{TAxCCR0 \times 2} \times 100\% = \frac{TAxCCRn}{TAxCCR0} \times 100\%$$

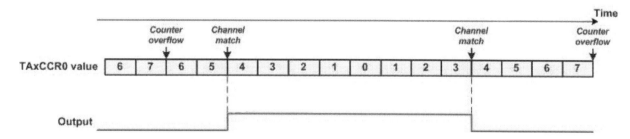

Figure 11-23: The PWM output for TAxCCR0 = 7, TAxCCRn = 4, Toggle/Reset (non-inverted)

In Toggle/Set mode, the output is inverted and the duty cycle is:

$$Duty\ Cycle = 100\% - \left(\frac{TAxCCRn}{TAxCCR0} \times 100\%\right)$$

The frequency of the generated wave is:

$$F_{output} = \frac{F_{timer\ clock}/prescaler}{TAxCCR0 \times 2}$$

311

Example 11-6

Find the period (T), frequency (F) and pulse width (DC, duty cycle) of a PWM if TAxCCR0=400 and TAxCCRn=250. Assume Toggle/Reset mode (non-inverted), no prescaler, and timer clock frequencies of (a) 8MHz, (b) 3MHz, and (c) 1MHz.

Solution:

(a) 1/8MHz = 125ns. Now T = TAxCCR0 × 2 × 125ns = 400 × 2 × 125ns = 100μs.

Frequency = 1 / 100μs = 10 kHz.

The Duty Cycle is (TAxCCRn / TAxCCR0) × 100% = (250 / 400) × 100% = 62.5%.

(b) 1/3MHz= 333ns. Now T=400 × 2 × 333.3ns = 266.6μs.

Frequency = 1 / 266.6μs = 3.75 kHz.

The Duty Cycle is (TAxCCRn / TAxCCR0) × 100% = (250/400) × 100% = 62.5%.

(c) 1/1MHz = 1μs. Now T = 400 × 2 × 1μs = 800μs.

Frequency = 1 / 800μs = 1.25 kHz.

The Duty Cycle is (TAxCCRn / TAxCCR0) × 100% = (250/400) × 100% = 62.5%.

Program 11-4 generates a waveform of 30Hz with duty cycle of 33.3% using center aligned PWM mode.

Program 11-4: Generate 30Hz 33.3% center-aligned PWM

```
/* p11_4.c Toggling P2.7 at 30 Hz using Timer_A0.4 PWM
 *
 * This program uses Timer_A0.4 to generate PWM output at 30 Hz
 * and 33.3% duty cycle.
 * Subsystem Master Clock (SMCLK) running at 3 MHz is used.
 * Timer_A0 is configured to up/down mode from 0 to 50,000-1, which
 * is loaded in TIMER_A0->CCR[0].
 * The timer counter roll over interval is:
 * 3,000,000 / 50,000 / 2 = 30 Hz.
 * TIMER_A0->CCR[4] is loaded with 50000/3 and CCR4 is configured
 * as toggle/reset mode. The output is clear to 0 when the TAxR
 * counter reaches TAxCCR4 on the up count and toggled to 1 when
 * the TAxR counter reaches TAxCCR4 on the down count. So the output
 * is 1 when TAxR is below the value of TAxCCR4.
 *
 * Tested with Keil 5.20 and MSP432 Device Family Pack V2.2.0.
 *
 */

#include "msp.h"

void delayMs(int n);

int main(void) {
```

```
/* Configure P2.7 as Timer A0.4 output */
  P2->SEL0 |= 0x80;
  P2->SEL1 &= ~0x80;
  P2->DIR  |= 0x80;

  /* configure TimerA0.4 as PWM */
  TIMER_A0->CCR[0]  = 50000-1;        /* PWM Period */
  TIMER_A0->CCR[4]  = 50000/3;        /* CCR4 PWM duty cycle */
  TIMER_A0->CCTL[4] = 0x40;           /* CCR4 toggle/reset mode */
  TIMER_A0->CTL     = 0x0234;         /* use SMCLK, up/down mode, clear TA0R register */

  while (1) {
  }
}
```

Edge-aligned vs. center-aligned mode

See Figure 11-24. In both figures the bold vertical blue lines are repeated periodically. In the edge-aligned mode, the left edge of the pulse is always on the bold blue line while in center-aligned mode, the center of the pulse is always fixed on the bold line. In other words, in edge-aligned mode, the phase of the wave is different for different duty cycles, while it remains unchanged in the center-aligned mode. For driving motors, it is preferable to use center-aligned rather than edge-aligned.

In edge-aligned mode, the frequency of the generated wave is twice that of the center-aligned mode. Thus, edge-aligned mode is preferable when we need to generate waves with higher frequencies.

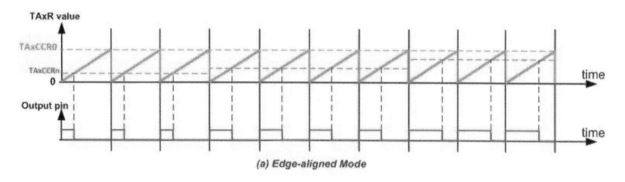

(a) Edge-aligned Mode

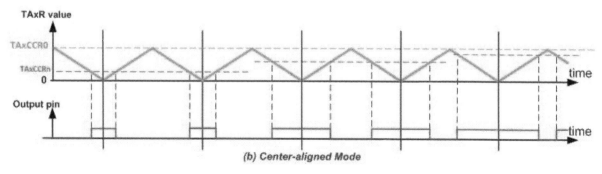

(b) Center-aligned Mode

Figure 11-24: Edge-aligned vs. Center-aligned Mode

Dead-band generation (Case Study)

One application of center-aligned PWM is to generate outputs with deadband. Review Example 11-1, when we switched the direction of the H-bridge circuit, we opened all switches and delayed for a period of time. That is deadband, a period of time when all switches are open to avoid the possibility of overlapping time when both switches on the same leg of the H-bridge are on which may cause a short circuit. The same problem exists with transistor circuits because transistors are faster to turn on and slower to turn off. If we turn one on and the other off, there will be a short period of time that both transistors are on.

To generate dead band, we use two center-aligned channels on the PWM module. One of the channels has positive pulse and the other negative pulse. Assuming the circuit is active high, now we have one channel centered at the time when the timer counter reaches the value in TAxCCR0 register and the other channel centered at the time when the timer counter reaches 0 so they will be 180 degrees out of phase. For each channel we program them to have less than 50% duty cycle therefore dead bands are created between the two channels. See Figure 11-25.

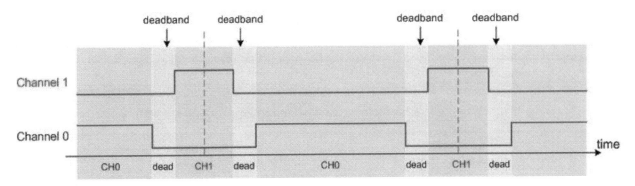

Figure 11-25: Dead band

Program 11-5 generates two 40% duty cycle outputs with 10% dead bands between them using center aligned PWM mode.

Program 11-5: Dead band generation

```
/* p11_5.c Deadband creation using Center-aligned PWM
 *
 * The Timer_A0 is configured for center-aligned PWM.
 * channel 3 is configured for 40% duty cycle pulse high.
 * channel 4 is configured for 60% duty cycle pulse low.
 * This creates a 10% deadband between channel 3 high and
 * channel 4 high.
 *
 * Tested with Keil 5.20 and MSP432 Device Family Pack V2.2.0.
 *
 */

#include "msp.h"

void delayMs(int n);
```

314

```
int main(void) {
  /* Configure P2.7 and P2.6 as Timer A0.4 output */
  P2->SEL0 |= 0xC0;
  P2->SEL1 &= ~0xC0;
  P2->DIR |= 0xC0;

  /* configure TimerA0.3 and TimerA0.4 as PWM */
  TIMER_A0->CCR[0] = 50000-1;          /* PWM Period */
  TIMER_A0->CCR[3] = 50000*40/100;     /* CCR3 PWM duty cycle 40% */
  TIMER_A0->CCTL[3] = 0x40;            /* CCR3 toggle/reset mode */
  TIMER_A0->CCR[4] = 50000*60/100;     /* CCR4 PWM duty cycle 60% inverted */
  TIMER_A0->CCTL[4] = 0xC0;            /* CCR4 toggle/set mode */
  TIMER_A0->CTL = 0x0234;          /* use SMCLK, up/down mode, clear TA0R register */

  while (1) {
  }
}
```

Review Questions

1. We use _____ register to set the PWM output Period/Frequency.
2. We use _____ register to set the PWM output pulse width.
3. True or false. Reset mode is a good choice to generate PWM waves.
4. True or false. Center-Aligned PWM can be generated using Up-Down mode.

Answers to Review Questions

Section 11.1

1. True
2. False
3. Because microcontroller/digital outputs lack sufficient current to drive the DC motor.
4. By reversing the polarity of voltages connected to the motor leads
5. The DC motor is stalled if the load is beyond what it can handle.
6. No-load

Section 11.2

1. TAxCCR0
2. TAxCCRn
3. False
4. True

Chapter 12: Programming Graphic LCD

Chapter 3 used the character LCD. In this chapter, we examine the graphic LCDs and show some programming examples, although an entire book can be dedicated to graphic LCD and its programming. Section 12.1 covers some basic concepts of graphic LCDs. In Section 12.2, we give some programming examples of graphic LCD.

Section 12.1: Graphic LCDs

The screen of graphic LCDs is made of pixels. The pictures and the texts are created using pixels and the programmers have control over each and every individual pixel. See Figures 12-1 and 12-2.

Figure 12-1: A picture on a Mono-color LCD

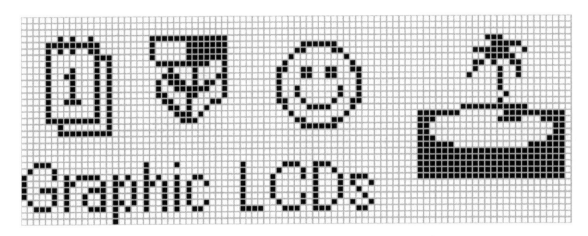

Figure 12-2: A Zoomed Picture on a Mono-color LCD

The graphic LCDs can be mono-colored (monochorme) or colored. In mono-colored LCDs each pixel can be on or off or different shades of gray; in contrast in colored LCDs each pixel can have different colors. In fact, the colored pixels can display red, green, and blue; using the 3 primary color lights they make different colors.

Some LCD Characteristics

Resolution

The total number of pixels (dots) per screen is a major factor in assessing an LCD and is shown below:

$$\text{Resolution} = \text{Pixels per line} \times \text{number of lines}$$

For example, when the resolution of an LCD is 720 × 350, there are 720 pixels per line and 350 lines per screen, giving a total of 252,000 pixels. The total number of pixels per screen is determined by the size of the pixel and how far apart the pixels are spaced. For this reason, one must look at what is called the *dot pitch* in LCD specifications.

Dot pitch

Dot pitch is the distance between adjacent pixels (dots) and is given in millimeters. For example, a dot pitch of 0.31 means that the distance between pixels is 0.31 mm. Consequently, the smaller the size of the pixel itself and the smaller the space between them, the higher the total number of pixels and the better the resolution. Dot pitch varies from 0.6 inch in some low-resolution LCDs to 0.2 inch in higher-resolution LCDs. Figure 12-3 shows Dot Pitch and Dot Size parameters.

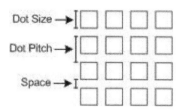

Figure 12-3: Dot Pitch and Dot Size

The specifications of a sample mono-colored LCD are shown in Figure 12-4.

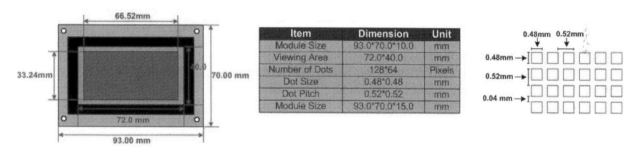

Item	Dimension	Unit
Module Size	93.0*70.0*10.0	mm
Viewing Area	72.0*40.0	mm
Number of Dots	128*64	Pixels
Dot Size	0.48*0.48	mm
Dot Pitch	0.52*0.52	mm
Module Size	93.0*70.0*15.0	mm

Figure 12-4: Mechanical specifications of a GDM12864 128x64 LCD

In some LCD specifications, it is given in terms of the number of dots per square inch, which is the same way it is given for laser printers, for example, 300 DPI (dots per inch).

Dot pitch and LCD size

LCDs, like televisions, are advertised according to their diagonal size. For example, a 14-inch monitor means that its diagonal measurement is 14 inches. There is a relation between the number of horizontal and vertical pixels, the dot pitch, and the diagonal size of the image on the screen. The diagonal size of the image must always be less than the LCD's diagonal size. The following simple equation can be used to relate these three factors to the diagonal measurement. It is derived from the Pythagorean Theorem:

$$(\text{image diagonal size})^2 = (\text{number of horizontal pixels} \times \text{dot pitch})^2$$

$$+ (\text{number of vertical pixels} \times \text{dot pitch})^2$$

Since the dot pitch is in millimeters, the size given by the equation above would be in mm, so it must be multiplied by 0.039 to get the size of the monitor in inches. See Example 12-1.

Example 12-1

A manufacturer has advertised a 14-inch monitor of 1024 × 768 resolution with a dot pitch of 0.28. Calculate the diagonal size of the image on the screen. It must be less than 14 inches.

Solution:

The calculation is as follows:

(image diagonal size)^2 = (number of horizontal pixels × dot pitch)^2 + (number of vertical pixels × dot pitch)^2

(diagonal size)^2 = (1024 × 0.28 mm)^2 + (768 × 0.28 mm)^2 = 358.4 mm
diagonal size (inches) = 358.4 mm × 0.039 inch per mm = 13.98 inches

In the LCD the diagonal size of the image area is 13.98 inches while the diagonal size of the viewing area is 14 inches.

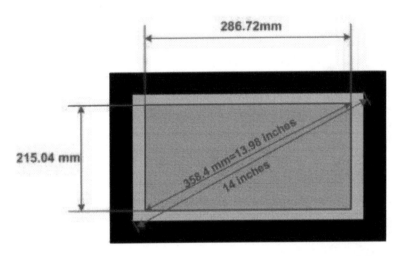

Displaying on the graphic LCDs

To display a picture on the screen, a distinct color must be shown on each pixel of the LCD. To do so, there is a display memory (frame buffer) that retrieves the attributes (colors) of the entire pixels of the screen and there is an LCD controller which displays the contents of the frame buffer memory on the LCD. See Figure 12-5.

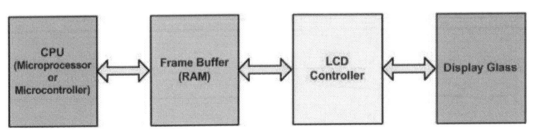

Figure 12-5: The Relationship between CPU and LCD

Graphic LCDs might come with or without frame buffer and the LCD controller. In cases that the LCD does not have frame buffer memory or controller they must be provided externally. Some new microcontrollers have the LCD controllers internally which can directly drive the LCDs. To display a picture on the screen the microcontroller writes it to the frame buffer memory.

Since the attributes (colors) of the entire pixels are stored in the frame buffer memory, the higher the number of pixels and colors options, the larger the amount of memory is needed to store them. In other words, the memory requirement goes up as the resolution and the number of supported colors go up. The number of colors displayed at one time is always 2^n where n is the number of bits set aside for the color. For example, when 4 bits are assigned for the color of the pixel, this allows 16 combinations of colors to be displayed at one time because $2^4 = 16$. The number of bits used for a pixel color is called color depth or bits per pixel (BPP). See Table 12-1.

BPP	Colors
1	on or off (monochrome)
2	4
4	16
8	256
16	65,536
24	16,777,216

Table 12-1: BPP (bit per pixel) vs. color

In Table 12-1, notice that in a monochrome LCD a single bit is assigned for the color of the pixel and it is for "on" or "off".

Mixing RGB (Red, Green, Blue) colors

We can get other colors by mixing the three primary colors of Red, Green, and Blue. The intensity (proportion) of the colors mixed can also affect the color we get. In many high-end graphics systems, an 8-bit value is used to represent the intensity. Its value can be between 0 and 255 (0 to 0xFF) representing high intensity (255) and zero intensity. See Table 12-2. Using three primary colors and intensity, we can make many colors we want. See Figure 12-6.

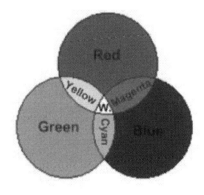

Figure 12-6: Making New Light Colors by Mixing the 3 Primary Light Colors

I	R	G	B	Color
0	0	0	0	Black
0	0	0	1	Blue
0	0	1	0	Green
0	0	1	1	Cyan
0	1	0	0	Red
0	1	0	1	Magenta
0	1	1	0	Brown
0	1	1	1	Light Gray
1	0	0	0	Dark Gray
1	0	0	1	Light blue
1	0	1	0	Light green
1	0	1	1	Light cyan
1	1	0	0	Light red
1	1	0	1	Light Magenta
1	1	1	0	Yellow
1	1	1	1	White

Table 12-2: The 16 Possible Colors

Example 12-2

In a certain graphic LCD, a maximum of 256 colors can be displayed at one time. How many bits are set aside for the color of the pixels?

Solution:

To display 256 colors at once, we must have 8 bits set for color since $2^8 = 256$.

LCD Buffer memory size and color

In discussing the graphics, we need to clarify the relationship between pixel resolution, the number of colors supported, and the amount of frame buffer RAM needed to store them. There are two facts associated with every pixel on the screen:

1. The location of the pixel
2. Its attributes: color and intensity

These two facts must be stored in the frame buffer RAM. The higher the number of pixels and colors options, the larger the amount of memory that is needed to store them. In other words, the memory requirement goes up as the resolution and the number of colors supported goes up. As we just mentioned, the number of colors displayed at one time is always 2^n where n is the number of bits set aside for the color. For example, when 4 bits are assigned for the color of the pixel, this allows 16 combinations of colors to be displayed at one time because $2^4 = 16$. The commonly used graphics resolutions are 176 x 144 (QCIF), 352x288 (CIF), 320x240 (QVGA), 480x272 (WQVGA), 640x480 (VGA) and 800x480 (WVGA). You may find the definitions of these abbreviations on the Internet.

We use the following formula to calculate the minimum frame buffer memory requirement for a graphic LCD:

$$Buffer\ memory\ size\ (in\ byte) = \frac{Horizontal\ Pixels\ \times Vertical\ Pixels\ \times color\ BPP}{8}$$

Example 12-3 shows how to calculate the memory need for various resolutions and color depth.

Example 12-3

Find the frame buffer RAM needed for (a) 176x144 with 4 BPP and (b) 640x480 resolution with 256 colors.

Solution:

(a) For this resolution, there are a total of 25,344 pixels (176 columns × 144 rows = 25,344). With 4 bits for the color of each pixel, we need total of (25,344 × 4)/8= 16,672 bytes of frame buffer RAM. These 4 bits give rise to 16 colors.

(b) For this resolution, there are a total of 640 × 480=307200 pixels. With 256 colors, we need 8 bits for color of each pixel. Now, total of (640 × 480 × 8) / 8 = 307200 bytes of frame buffer RAM needed.

In VGA, 640 x 480 resolution with support for 256 colors displayed at one time requires a minimum of 640 × 480 × 8 = 2,457,600 bits =307,200 bytes of memory, but due to the memory organization used, the amount of memory used is higher.

Storing pixels in the memory of mono-color LCDs

In mono-colored LCDs each pixel can be on or off. Therefore, 1 bit can preserve the state of 1 pixel and a byte preserves 8 adjacent pixels. In some LCDs, e.g. GDM12864A and PCD8544, pixels are stored vertically in the bytes, as shown in Figure 12-7, while in some other LCDs, e.g. T6963, the pixels are stored horizontally.

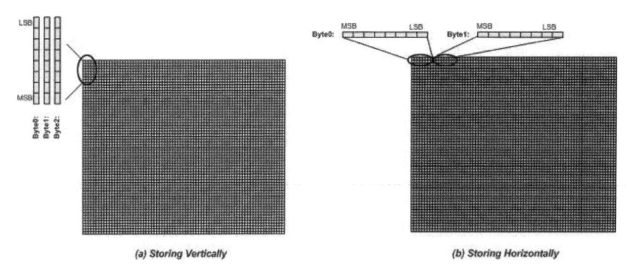

(a) Storing Vertically   (b) Storing Horizontally

Figure 12-7: Storing Data in the LCD Memory of Mono-colored LCDs

Review Questions

1. As the number of pixels goes up, the size of display memory _____ (increases, decreases).
2. If a total of 24 bits is set aside for color, how many colors are available?
3. Calculate the total video memory needed for 1024 × 768 resolution with 16 colors displayed at the same time.
4. With BPP of 16, we get _____ colors.

Section 12.2: Displaying Texts on Graphic LCDs

As shown in Figure 12-8 each character can be made by putting pixels next to each other.

Hex	Binary
7E	01111110
81	10000001
A5	10100101
81	10000001
BD	10111101
99	10011001
81	10000001
7E	01111110

Hex	Binary
30	00110000
78	01111000
CC	11001100
CC	11001100
FC	11111100
CC	11001100
CC	11001100
00	00000000

```
unsigned char font8x8 [ ][8]={
0x7E,0x81,0xA5,0x81,0xBD,0x99,0x81,0x7E, //smile
0x30,0x78,0xCC,0xCC,0xFC,0xCC,0xCC,0x00  //A
};
```

Figure 12-8: Pixel Patterns of Characters Happy Face and Letter A

To display characters on the screen, we must have the pixel patterns of the entire characters. Whenever we want to display a character on the screen we copy its pixel pattern into the display memory. See Figure 12-9.

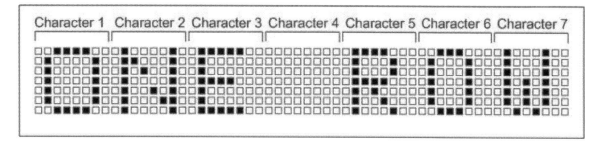

Figure 12-9: A Sample Text

The pixel patterns are stored in an array in the same way that they should be stored in the LCD memory. This means that for horizontal LCDs the bits are stored horizontally and for vertical LCDs the pixels are stored vertically. Figure 12-8 shows the way patterns are stored for horizontal LCDs. In Figure 12-10 the same patterns are stored for vertical LCDs.

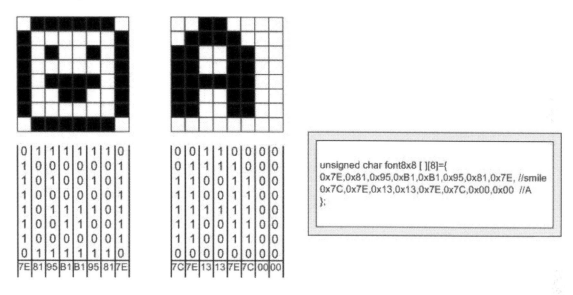

```
unsigned char font8x8 [ ][8]={
0x7E,0x81,0x95,0xB1,0xB1,0x95,0x81,0x7E, //smile
0x7C,0x7E,0x13,0x13,0x7E,0x7C,0x00,0x00  //A
};
```

Figure 12-10: Pixel Patterns of Happy Face and Character A and its Font for Vertical LCD

To get better-looking characters, the font resolution must be increased, which translates to more pixels horizontally and vertically. See Figure 12-11.

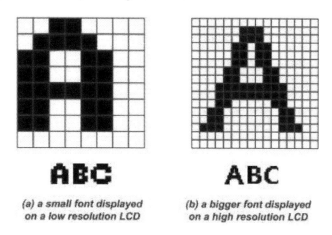

(a) a small font displayed
on a low resolution LCD

(b) a bigger font displayed
on a high resolution LCD

Figure 12-11: A Bigger Font vs. a Smaller Font

See Program 12-1. A lookup table of the pixel patterns of the characters is made using an array. The GLCD_putchar function accesses the lookup array to display characters on the LCD. The connection between the PCD8544 LCD and the microcontroller is shown in Figure 12-12. For more information about the PCD8544 see its datasheet on the Web.

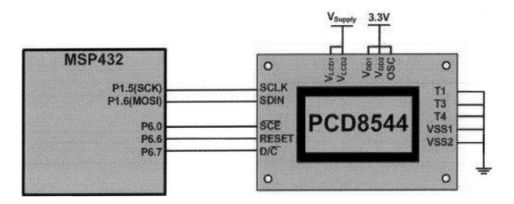

Figure 12-12: The PCD8544 LCD connection to the MSP432 LaunchPad

Program 12-1: Displaying a text on the PCD8544 GLCD

```
* P12_1.c: PCD8544 (Nokia5110) GLCD via SPI with MSP432 LaunchPad
 *
 * Interface uses UCB0 of MSP432 LaunchPad.
 * P1.5 SCLK
 * P1.6 MOSI
 * P6.0 chip select (CE)
 * P6.6 reset
 * P6.7 register select (DC)
 *
 * Tested with Keil 5.20 and MSP432 Device Family Pack V2.2.0.
 */

#include "msp.h"

#define CE     0x01     /* P6.0 chip select */
#define RESET 0x40      /* P6.6 reset */
#define DC     0x80     /* P6.7 register select */

/* define the pixel size of display */
#define GLCD_WIDTH  84
#define GLCD_HEIGHT 48

void GLCD_setCursor(unsigned char x, unsigned char y);
void GLCD_clear(void);
void GLCD_init(void);
void GLCD_data_write(unsigned char data);
void GLCD_command_write(unsigned char data);
void GLCD_putchar(int c);
void SPI_init(void);
void SPI_write(unsigned char data);

/* sample font table */
const char font_table[][6] = {
```

```c
    {0x7e, 0x11, 0x11, 0x11, 0x7e, 0},   /* A */
    {0x7f, 0x49, 0x49, 0x49, 0x36, 0},   /* B */
    {0x3e, 0x41, 0x41, 0x41, 0x22, 0}};  /* C */

int main(void) {
    GLCD_init();            /* initialize the GLCD controller */
    GLCD_clear();           /* clear display and home the cursor */

    GLCD_putchar(0);    /* display letter A */
    GLCD_putchar(1);    /* display letter B */
    GLCD_putchar(2);    /* display letter C */

    while(1) { }
}

void GLCD_putchar(int c) {
    int i;
    for (i = 0; i < 6; i++)
        GLCD_data_write(font_table[c][i]);
}

void GLCD_setCursor(unsigned char x, unsigned char y) {
    GLCD_command_write(0x80 | x);  /* column */
    GLCD_command_write(0x40 | y);  /* bank (8 rows per bank) */
}

/* clears the GLCD by writing zeros to the entire screen */
void GLCD_clear(void) {
    int32_t index;
    for (index = 0 ; index < (GLCD_WIDTH * GLCD_HEIGHT / 8) ; index++)
        GLCD_data_write(0x00);

    GLCD_setCursor(0, 0); /* return to the home position */
}

/* send the initialization commands to PCD8544 GLCD controller */
void GLCD_init(void) {
    SPI_init();

    /* hardware reset of GLCD controller */
    P6->OUT |= RESET;               /* deassert reset */

    GLCD_command_write(0x21);           /* set extended command mode */
    GLCD_command_write(0xB8);           /* set LCD Vop for contrast */
    GLCD_command_write(0x04);           /* set temp coefficient */
    GLCD_command_write(0x14);           /* set LCD bias mode 1:48 */
    GLCD_command_write(0x20);           /* set normal command mode */
    GLCD_command_write(0x0C);           /* set display normal mode */
}

/* write to GLCD controller data register */
void GLCD_data_write(unsigned char data) {
    P6->OUT |= DC;                  /* select data register */
    SPI_write(data);                /* send data via SPI */
}

/* write to GLCD controller command register */
```

```
void GLCD_command_write(unsigned char data) {
    P6->OUT &= ~DC;                        /* select command register */
    SPI_write(data);                       /* send data via SPI */
}

void SPI_init(void) {
    EUSCI_B0->CTLW0 = 0x0001;              /* put UCB0 in reset mode */
    EUSCI_B0->CTLW0 = 0x69C1;              /* PH=0, PL=1, MSB first, Master, SPI, SMCLK */
    EUSCI_B0->BRW = 3;                     /* 3 MHz / 3 = 1 MHz */
    EUSCI_B0->CTLW0 &= ~0x0001;            /* enable UCB0 after config */

    P1->SEL0 |= 0x60;                      /* P1.5, P1.6 for UCB0 */
    P1->SEL1 &= ~0x60;

    P6->DIR |= CE | RESET | DC;            /* P6.7, P6.6, P6.0 set as output */
    P6->OUT |= CE;                         /* CE idle high */
    P6->OUT &= ~RESET;                     /* assert reset */
}

void SPI_write(unsigned char data) {
    P6->OUT &= ~CE;                        /* assert /CE */
    EUSCI_B0->TXBUF = data;                /* write data */
    while(EUSCI_B0->STATW & 0x01) ;        /* wait for transmit done */
    P6->OUT |= CE;                         /* deasssert /CE */
}
```

Review Questions

1. True or false. The same font table can be used for vertical and horizontal LCDs.
2. True or false. To display a character on the LCD, its pixel pattern should be copied onto the LCD display memory.

Answers to Review Questions

Section 12-1:

1. increases
2. 2^{24} = 16.7 million
3. $1024 \times 768 \times 4$ = 3,145,728 bits = 384K bytes, but it uses 512 KB due to bit planes.
4. 2^{16} = 65,536

Section 12-2:

1. False
2. True

Made in the USA
Monee, IL
08 January 2020